Economic and Social Rights and the Maintenance of International Peace and Security

This text comprises cutting-edge research on one of the greatest global challenges: the failure to address systematic economic and social exclusion, and attendant violations of economic and social rights (ESR), as a driver of conflict. The text explores what the UN's obligation to maintain international peace and security can mean when it is informed by the requirement to protect and promote ESR, rights that play a crucial role in maintaining international peace and security but which are often overlooked. The book considers the extent to which Security Council mandated peace operations have been informed by human rights and efforts to promote economic and social development. The approach is to analyse the extent to which the Security Council has interacted with the General Assembly, the Economic and Social Council as well as other Charter-based mechanisms such as the Human Rights Council, and its predecessor, with particular reference to the role of the Special Procedure Mechanisms. The role of the UN High Commissioner for Human Rights is also considered. In this way, the text shows that the connection between peace and security and human rights is well recognised by these organs. In addition, the text considers States' ESR obligations stemming from the extraterritorial application of such rights in the context of peace operations. Given that States' obligations stemming from ESR have often been neglected, the book examines how such provision could be improved using ESR-grounded plans reflecting the rights to health, food, water, education, work and life. The text concludes with a call to reimagine what international peace and security can look like when it is informed by the need to recognise the emergence of post-conflict legal obligations based on broader concepts of international peace and security that draw from ESR. This text will appeal to legal scholars, policy advisors, members of the military, those working in the area of development, NGOs and final-year undergraduate and/or postgraduate students working in the areas of international law, political science and international relations, and associated fields of research.

Claire Breen is Associate Professor in Law at Te Piringa – Faculty of Law, University of Waikato in New Zealand. She holds a BCL from University College, Cork. She also holds an LLM (International Law) and a PhD from the University of Nottingham. Dr Breen has previously been awarded a significant New Zealand Law Foundation Grant to undertake research on a project entitled 'The National and International Legal Obligations and Consequences for New Zealand Arising from its Peace Support Operations'. Her interest in the legal obligations stemming from New Zealand's peace-support missions is a reflection of her interest in the confluence between human rights law and peace operations. She has numerous publications in the area of human rights and peace operations and has also published extensively in the area of children's rights.

'Why do we go to war? A question soldiers, scholars and politicians have pondered throughout the ages. Understanding the reasons for conflict, we hope, may help us avoid its scourge. Dr Claire Breen takes an exciting new look at the imperative to maintain international peace and security. She lays bare the gap between aspiration and reality in that "other" field of rights – the economic and social ones. This dislocation, she demonstrates, has massive potential to generate conflict and instability. [As a former peacekeeper, a lawyer and as an academic I believe that] this is scholarship which will be of great interest and value to all people concerned with peace and security – both from a practical and theoretical perspective.' Kevin Riordan, ONZM, Judge Advocate General of the New Zealand Armed Forces.

Economic and Social Rights and the Maintenance of International Peace and Security

Claire Breen

Routledge
Taylor & Francis Group
LONDON AND NEW YORK

First published 2017
by Routledge

2 Park Square, Milton Park, Abingdon, Oxfordshire OX14 4RN
52 Vanderbilt Avenue, New York, NY 10017

Routledge is an imprint of the Taylor & Francis Group, an informa business

First issued in paperback 2019

British Library Cataloguing-in-Publication Data
A catalogue record for this book is available from the British Library

Library of Congress Cataloging-in-Publication Data
Names: Breen, Claire, author.
Title: Economic and social rights and the maintenance of international peace and security / Claire Breen.
Description: New York, NY : Routledge, 2017. | Includes bibliographical references and index.
Identifiers: LCCN 2016052365 | ISBN 9781472465788 (hardback) | ISBN 9781317146292 (adobe reader) | ISBN 9781317146285 (epub) | ISBN 9781317146278 (mobipocket)
Subjects: LCSH: Human rights—Economic aspects. | Human rights—Social aspects. | Social rights. | Peace. | Security, International.
Classification: LCC K3240 .B73 2017 | DDC 323—dc23
LC record available at https://lccn.loc.gov/2016052365

ISBN: 978-1-4724-6578-8 (hbk)
ISBN: 978-0-367-26644-8 (pbk)

Typeset in Galliard
by Apex CoVantage, LLC

For Conor

Contents

Preface

As a child growing up in Ireland, I was fascinated by the idea of Irish peacekeepers going to Lebanon in the late 1970s. Comfortable in the security of my family and my local community, I wondered at their bravery for leaving their own families and communities for a foreign and dangerous land. I remember the sadness that we felt as a family on hearing of deaths of Irish soldiers there. Those memories have always stayed with me.

As a University student studying law, I developed an interest in economic and social rights. That interest ignited a broader interest in human rights, which in turn evolved into an interest in children's rights. I became interested in the question of what giving effective realisation to the economic and social rights of children meant for the promotion and protection of human rights more generally. (New) beginnings are important.

A little over a decade ago my early childhood interest in peacekeeping was reignited as the peacekeepers of my new home, New Zealand, were being deployed to Timor-Leste and Afghanistan, amongst other places. With the support of a research grant from the New Zealand Law Foundation, I was able to pursue this research. Ensuing journal articles and conference papers led me to focus on the often-neglected influence of economic and social rights upon international peace and security. This neglect is extremely curious, as it has long been recognised that efforts to maintain peace and security are much strengthened when they are combined with efforts to improve economic and social conditions for all. The Charter of the United Nations enshrines this relationship, as it seeks to save succeeding generations from 'the scourge of war' and 'to promote social progress and better standards of life in larger freedom'. As noted above, new beginnings are important.

Unfortunately, for millions of people affected by conflict over the last 70 years, the Charter has not been able to live up to its promise. This failure in part has been driven by the changing nature of conflict; many of the legal tools that were developed during that period are now not quite fit for purpose, and the development of other more useful tools were neglected. Having said that, law is dynamic and can respond to changing circumstances. The need to respond is a complex, but not insurmountable, challenge. The interpretation of the content of economic and social rights and the attendant obligations for States spell out what must be done, and to the extent that it is being done, how such efforts can be improved.

The aim of this work is not to add to the complexity of peacebuilding and peacekeeping. Rather, it is a call to return to what we already know and what has already been enshrined in international law; that is, sustainable peace can only be achieved when it is supported by improved social and economic conditions for everyone. This most fundamental of ideas must underpin the efforts of those charged with building and keeping the peace.

Acknowledgements

Many people have supported me to reach this point in my research. I would like to thank the New Zealand Law Foundation for its support. I would also like to thank Professor Paul Hunt and Kevin Riordan for their support, particularly in the publication of this research. I would like to thank Professor Margaret Bedggood who has been an invaluable listener and advisor. I would also like to thank my husband and my children for their patient support, particularly over the last few months. My brother has also supplied important practical support and I would like to thank him. Final thanks must go to my parents. Their sense of social justice has had a strong influence on me and I thank them for their support, which has brought me to where I am today.

Claire Breen

Introduction

Although they span millennia and appear in different guises, the causes of violence and conflict remain uncomfortably familiar; these are the struggle over land and resources that support human existence.[1] Although the world has been spared the type of global devastation that accompanied both World Wars, the United Nations (UN or the Organisation) has, nonetheless, failed to spare ensuing generations from the scourge of war. Freedom from fear and want remain elusive for many as the UN continues to search for effective responses to rising levels of conflict that are characterised by local struggles for resources and control of government, often in some of the world's poorest countries.

In many instances, the UN is engaged in efforts to prevent a relapse into conflict, and, in this regard, the Security Council has increasingly been engaged in a peacebuilding role, a role which is often intertwined with the deployment of peacekeeping operations, which themselves have become increasingly complex. Both endeavours have been underpinned by the recognition of the relationship between economic and social inequality and conflict. The Security Council has attempted to address this relationship by incorporating economic and social reconstruction into its peacebuilding mandates and, as relevant, into related peacekeeping operations. The Security Council has also recognised the importance of human rights. It has recognised that gross human rights violations can act as an early warning system of impending armed conflict. It has also recognised that the promotion and effective realisation of human rights can strengthen conflict prevention efforts. According to a former UN Secretary-General:

> The proximate cause of conflict may be an outbreak of public disorder or a protest over a particular incident, but the root cause may be, for example, socio-economic inequities and inequalities, systematic ethnic discrimination, denial of human rights, disputes over political participation or long-standing grievances over land and other resource allocation.[2]

1 See generally, Alexander Gillespie, *A History of the Laws of War* (Hart, Oxford 2011).

2 UNGA, 'Report of the Secretary General 2001/574' (2001) UN Doc A/55/985-S/2001/574, para 7. See further, Lisa J Laplante, 'Transitional Justice and Peace Building: Diagnosing and Addressing the Socioeconomic Roots of Violence through a Human Rights Framework' (2008) 2(3) *International Journal of Transitional Justice* 331.

Similarly, the World Bank has noted that vicious cycles of conflict commence when political and economic stresses and pressures on justice and security meet weak institutions.[3] It has also recognised that poor citizens think that the lack of well-being relates to the psychological experience of lacking voice, power and independence more than to the anxiety of meeting their basic material needs.[4] This view resonates with other findings that indicate that it is not the level of absolute disparity that is of concern to conflict prevention but the degree to which the disparities are based on, or perceived to be due to, discriminatory exclusions and therefore injustice. Such inequality can arise from failures in basic service delivery such as education, health services, water, and transport and energy infrastructure, which can be indicative of human rights violations.[5]

Even if conflict was not driven by socio-economic inequality and corrupt governments, as there is still some debate about whether poverty constitutes a direct cause of political violence,[6] societies emerging from armed conflict will still face varying degrees of challenges to their physical, economic, social and political infrastructures stemming from high levels of death, trauma (both physical and mental) and displacement amongst civilians who must cope, in many instances, without roads, power, water and sanitation, schools and hospitals, which can often undermine any efforts to achieve peace. These overall concerns between exclusion and insecurity have also been identified in the context of foreign intervention on the basis that although it might be possible to promote both security and development by ensuring the equal distribution of the benefits of development, the fragmentation of society that results from foreign military intervention, like the fragmentation that results from domestic wars, makes it difficult if not impossible to address the inequalities that lead to conflict and violent

3 World Bank, *World Development Report 2011: Conflict, Security, and Development* (World Bank, Washington DC 2011) 6.

4 Deepa Narayan and others, 'Can Anyone Hear Us? Voices from 47 Countries' (Voices of the Poor, Volume 1, Poverty Group, PREM World Bank, December 1999) 26 <http://siteresources.worldbank.org/INTPOVERTY/Resources/335642-1124115102975/1555199-1124115187705/vol1.pdf> accessed 31 January 2017. See also, Deepa Narayan (ed), *Empowerment and Poverty Reduction: A Sourcebook* (World Bank, Washington DC 2002) 14, which calls for 'the expansion of assets and capabilities of poor people to participate in, negotiate with, influence, control, and hold accountable institutions that affect their lives'.

5 Derek Evans, 'Human Rights and State Fragility: Conceptual Foundations and Strategic Foundations for State-Building' (2009) 1(2) *Journal of Human Rights Practice* 181, 196 citing Frances Stewart and Graham Brown, *Fragile States* (CRISE, Oxford 2006) 25. See also, Frances Stewart, 'Policies towards Horizontal Inequalities in Post-conflict Reconstruction' (2005) CRISE Working Paper No. 7, 15–17 <http://www3.qeh.ox.ac.uk/pdf/crisewps/workingpaper7.pdf> accessed 27 September 2016; Oskar N T Thoms and James Ron, 'Do Human Rights Violations Cause Internal Conflict?' (2007) 29(3) *Human Rights Quarterly* 674; and Louise Arbour, 'Economic and Social Justice for Societies in Transition' (2007) 40(1) *Journal of International Law and Politics* 1, 8.

6 Lars Waldorf, 'Anticipating the Past: Transitional Justice and Socio-Economic Wrongs' (2012) 21(2) *Social and Legal Studies* 171, 175.

extremism.[7] More particularly, it has also been observed that when UN peacekeepers side with one party to a conflict, such actions substantially affect conflict and political dynamics at a particular time.[8]

Many UN policy frameworks and statements now make reference to international legal instruments as the source of human rights in security and in development or as an overall guiding framework for international cooperation.[9] The UN, and the Security Council in particular, has had to respond to the changing nature of the threats to international peace and security, a change that is evident in its recognition of the economic and social causes of conflict, the need to address these issues so as to create a sustainable peace and the underpinning role of human rights in such endeavours. The significance of such an approach was explained in *In Larger Freedom*,[10] wherein the Secretary-General, in returning to the enunciation of the UN's determination 'to promote social progress and better standards of life in larger freedom',[11] explained that larger freedom means that men and women everywhere, 'must also be free from want – so that the death sentences of extreme poverty and infectious disease are lifted from their lives – and free from fear – so that their lives and livelihoods are not ripped apart by violence and war'.[12] Many other related UN documents encapsulate themes such as peacebuilding, peacekeeping and conflict prevention, and many of them make reference to the central role of economic and social reconstruction and human rights in the post-conflict environment.[13]

7 Graham Mayeda, 'Legal Aspects of the Security-Development Nexus: International Administrative Law as a Check on the Use of Development Assistance in the War on Terror' (2012) 13(1) *Chicago Journal of International Law* 71, 74–75 and 87. See also, Marianne Dahl and Bjørn Høyland, 'Peace on Quicksand? Challenging the Conventional Wisdom about Economic Growth and Post-conflict Risks' (2012) 49(3) *Journal of Peace Research* 423, OECD, *Principles for Good Engagement in Fragile States* (OECD, Paris 2007); and OECD, *Evaluating Peacebuilding Activities in Settings of Conflict and Fragility: Improving Learning for Results* (OECD, Paris 2012).

8 Mateja Peter, 'Between Doctrine and Practice: The UN Peacekeeping Dilemma' (2015) 21(3) *Global Governance: A Review of Multilateralism and International Organizations* 351, 364. See also, Han Dorussen and Theodora-Ismene Gizelis, 'Into the Lion's Den: Local Responses to UN Peacekeeping' (2013) 50(6) *Journal of Peace Research* 691.

9 Compare UNGA, 'Report of the Secretary-General 59/2005' (2005) UN Doc A/59/2005, which underscores the interrelationship of security, development and human rights, and UNDP, *Human Development Report 9* (UNDP, New York 2000), which identifies the need for a more integrated approach between human rights and development and the creation of robust methodologies for evaluating the human rights position of individuals and groups, and the compliance of States with their international human rights obligations. See, generally, Polly Vizard, Sakiko Fukuda-Parr and Diane Elson, 'Introduction: The Capability Approach and Human Rights' (2011) 12(1) *Journal of Human Development and Capabilities* 1.

10 UNGA, 'Report of the Secretary-General 59/2005' (2005) UN Doc A/59/2005 'In Larger Freedom: Towards Development, Security and Human Rights for All'.

11 Charter of the United Nations (24 October 1945) 1 UNTS XVI, preambular paragraph 1.

12 UNGA (n 9), para 15.

13 See Chapter 3, Section 2.

However, there is a gap in the Security Council's approach, stemming from the marginalisation of economic and social rights in efforts to advance economic and social progress, development and cooperation, as the Council attempts to combat economic and social inequality, as enshrined in the UN Charter itself. In short, economic and social rights still struggle to be recognised as part of the solution to conflict. A number of reasons for this situation have been identified, such as the failure to include economic and social rights explicitly in peace agreements, which, when they do include human rights, tend to favour civil and political rights. Legislative and judicial machinery, whether it is the pre-existing national machinery or that negotiated or imposed in the immediate aftermath of conflict, may not be able to cater to violations of economic and social rights. Furthermore, there is a tendency to view economic and social rights not as a legislative or judicial matter but rather as a matter for development where the latter is regarded as being a subsidiary to political stability.[14] In the context of development, it has been asserted that part of this difficulty stems from the:

> intrinsic difficulty in identifying the contents of policies and action that meet state obligations because there is no indisputable consensus on the causal impact of policy on human well being. There are always controversies about data, methodology, and analysis over policy choices. . . . Moreover, there are multiple factors and actors behind any given outcome, making attributing responsibility for human rights violations extremely difficult.[15]

However, such difficulties and controversies do not relieve a State of its obligations to comply with its positive obligations in fulfilling economic and social rights because, 'as a matter of public international law, human rights treaty obligations are legally binding [on] States parties, and under custom bind all [S]tates other than persistent objectors: as such they should be respected in all contexts . . .' (original emphasis).[16]

The importance of the role of economic and social rights as a means to respond to inequality and exclusion has been recognised in the utilisation of other

14 Christine Chinkin, *The Protection of Economic, Social and Cultural Rights Post Conflict* (Paper series commissioned by OHCHR, 2008) 8–9 <www2.ohchr.org/english/issues/women/docs/Paper_Protection_ESCR.pdf> accessed 5 August 2016.

15 Sakiko Fukuda-Parr, 'Millennium Development Goal 8: Indicators for International Human Rights Obligations?' (2006) 28(4) *Human Rights Quarterly* 966, 978.

16 Siobhán McInerney-Lankford, 'Human Rights and Development: A Comment on Challenges and Opportunities from a Legal Perspective' (2009) 1(1) *Journal of Human Rights Practice* 51, 52. It is increasingly recognised that human rights obligations are no longer confined to State actors. According to the International Court of Justice, 'the United Nations Organisation is not a party to international human rights treaties, and whether it has the legal capacity to adhere to them is questionable. Nevertheless, important non-treaty sources of international law are binding upon the United Nations.' *Reparation for Injuries Suffered in the Service of the United Nations* (Advisory Opinion) [1949] ICJ Rep 174. See further, Frédéric Mégret and Florian Hoffmann, 'The UN as a Human Rights Violator?: Some Reflections on the United Nations Changing Human Rights Responsibilities' (2003) 25(2) *Human Rights Quarterly* 314. See further, Chapter 5, footnotes 91–113 and accompanying text.

measures to assist States emerging from conflict. Transitional justice measures, in particular, have increasingly recognised the consequences of massive violations of economic and social rights and have incorporated these rights as a tool in the transition towards peace.[17] In Guatemala, for example, it was recognised that the violations of economic and social rights and the corresponding lack of social justice had represented a source of conflict and instability, and respect for those rights became a precondition for development and peace.[18] According to the Truth Commission in Timor-Leste,[19] 'the impact of the conditions in which [the people of East Timor] lived, while often less remarked on, was equally damaging and possibly more long-lasting' than violations of civil and political rights.[20] It identified violations of economic and social rights stemming from the discriminatory fashion of failing to 'meet the basic needs of the population for food, shelter and essential medicines'.[21] At a more general level,[22] the UN is increasingly responding to economic and social rights as an aspect of transitional justice, and a Special Rapporteur on the promotion of truth, justice, reparation and guarantees of non-recurrence was established by the Human Rights Council in September 2012.[23] The Special Rapporteur has drawn attention to the socio-economic dimensions of conflict and peace, although the framework of economic and social rights is yet to inform the execution of the mandate.[24] An in-depth analysis

17 See, for example, Frank Haldemann and Rachelle Kouassi, 'Transitional Justice Without Economic, Social, and Cultural Rights?' in Eibe Riedel, Gilles Giacca and Christophe Golay (eds), *Economic, Social, and Cultural Rights in International Law: Contemporary Issues and Challenges* (Oxford University Press, Oxford 2014); and Evelyne Schmid and Aoife Nolan, '"Do No Harm"? Exploring the Scope of Economic and Social Rights in Transitional Justice' (2014) 8(3) *International Journal of Transitional Justice* 362.

18 The Commission for Historical Clarification in Guatemala (CEH) noted that 'political violence was . . . a direct expression of structural violence' in Inter-American Commission on Human Rights 'Fifth Report on the Situation of Human Rights in Guatemala' (6 April 2001) OEA/Ser.L/V/II.111 doc. 21 rev., Chapter III, para 3(5). See also, International Council on Human Rights Policy, *Negotiating Justice?: Human Rights and Peace Agreements* (International Council on Human Rights Policy, Versoix 2006) 101.

19 UNTAEF, 'Regulation 2001/10 on the Establishment of a Commission for Reception, Truth and Reconciliation in East Timor' (2001) UN Doc UNTAET/REG/2001/10, sec 2.1.

20 Timor-Leste Commission for Reception, Truth and Reconciliation, 'Chega! The Report of the Commission for Reception, Truth and Reconciliation' (CAVR, 2005) Chapter 7.9, para 1. The Report further noted, at 3, that violations of economic and social rights stemmed from the forced displacement and the resettlement of entire villages in areas that had previously been avoided on the basis of health risks including poor soil and malarial conditions. Coffee farmers' right to an adequate standard of living was violated by the manipulation of coffee prices to fund military operations.

21 Ibid, Chapter 7.9, para 131.

22 OHCHR, *Transitional Justice and Economic, Social and Cultural Rights* (HR/PUB/13/5, United Nations, New York and Geneva 2014).

23 UNGA, 'Resolution Adopted by the Human Rights Council: Special Rapporteur on the Promotion of Truth, Justice, Reparation and Guarantees of Non-Recurrence 18/7' (2011) UN Doc A/HRC/RES/18/7.

24 See, for example, UNGA, 'Report of the Special Rapporteur on the Promotion of Truth, Justice, Reparation and Guarantees of Non-Recurrence, Pablo de Greiff 30/42' (2015)

of transitional justice falls outside the scope of this work, but the relevance of transitional justice arises from the fact that, in spite of early tensions stemming from the prioritisation of peace over justice, transitional justice is regarded by peacebuilders as the path to building long-term peace,[25] despite concerns having been raised regarding the narrow interpretation of justice and peace alike.[26]

The recasting of socio-economic concerns in terms of economic and social rights provides a legal framework by which socio-economic inequality can be addressed. The focus on economic and social rights is not to deny the importance of cultural rights, because the effective application and implementation of economic and social rights requires that such rights be culturally mediated.[27] The effective realisation of economic and social rights means that socio-economic inequality must be addressed as a matter of law, not merely as a matter of charity, development and/or international aid. Nonetheless, using economic and social rights law as an analytical framework poses a number of challenges. Economic and social rights themselves were marginalised within international human rights law for a number of decades and, although there is now much greater understanding of the nature and content of these rights within that discipline, the contribution of economic and social rights to other realms of international law suffers from the same problem. So, whilst there is increasing recognition of the relationship between peace and security and human rights, the failure to accord due recognition to economic and social rights means that the full potential of human rights, as an aspect of this relationship, remains untapped.

A further challenge to the incorporation of economic and social rights into the Security Council's endeavours to maintain international peace and security is the lack of legal symmetry between the rights and obligations of the UN, as an International Organisation, and the State-centric nature of the obligations stemming from international human rights law. This lack of symmetry is particularly evident in the context of post-conflict peacebuilding. The UN as an International Organisation must operate within the confines of its founding document, whilst international human rights law – whose origins can be traced to the same legal

---

UN Doc A/HRC/30/42, paras 34–36; and UNGA, 'Report of the Special Rapporteur on the Promotion of Truth, Justice, Reparation and Guarantees of Non-Recurrence, Pablo de Greiff 21/46' (2012) UN Doc A/HRC/21/46, paras 50–53.

25 UNSC, 'Report of the Secretary-General 2004/616' (2004) UN Doc S/2004/616, para 2; See further, Rama Mani, *Beyond Retribution: Seeking Justice in the Shadows of War* (Polity Press, Cambridge 2002); Dustin N Sharp, 'Beyond the Post-conflict Checklist: Linking Peacebuilding and Transitional Justice Through the Lens of Critique' (2013) 14(1) *Chicago Journal of International Law* 165; Paul van Zyl, 'Promoting Transitional Justice in Post-conflict Societies' in Alan Bryden and Heiner Hanggi (eds), *Security Governance in Post-conflict Peacebuilding* (Centre for the Democratic Control of Armed Forces, Geneva 2005); and Chandra Lekha Sriram, Olga Martin-Ortega and Johanna Herman, 'Beyond Justice Versus Peace: Transitional Justice and Peacebuilding Strategies' in Karin Aggestam and Annika Bjorkdahl (eds), *Rethinking Peacebuilding: The Quest for Just Peace in the Middle East and the Western Balkans* (Routledge, New York 2012).

26 See Chapter 3, Section 5.

27 Chinkin (n 14) 5.

document – is State-centric in nature. So, although the Security Council's deliberations may be underpinned by the Charter's own references to human rights, the UN, and thus the Security Council, is not a party to human rights treaties and it is not bound by the obligations that ensue from such treaties. This situation brings us back to the need to reconsider the role of the Security Council, especially since the UN (via Security Council action) is now an indispensable actor in many post-conflict environments.

This lack of symmetry manifests itself in a number of other ways. It is apparent in the disjointed relationship between the Security Council, the General Assembly and the Economic and Social Council (the ECOSOC), despite the Charter's provisions for inter-organ dialogue to underpin its recognition of the relationship between peace and security, international economic and social cooperation, and human rights. There is increasing symmetry between peacebuilding and peacekeeping, where the latter is a mechanism progressively being charged with implementing the peacebuilding policy of the UN as manifested in the work of the Security Council. Peacebuilding and peacekeeping endeavours are creatures of the UN; however, peacekeepers are also bound by the international legal obligations of their contributing States. Finally, these complex relationships suffer from an overarching imbalance which is the nature of the peace that is being built and kept, which has been criticised for being a narrow liberal peace based on minimal government, free markets and a focus on civil and political rights, which continues to marginalise potential socio-economic causes for conflict and which excludes the potential for economic and social rights to contribute to a more lasting peace.

So, how to redress these imbalances? Chapter 1 proceeds on the view that it is important to remember that the relationship between improved socio-economic conditions and a more stable social order is evident not only in the domestic law and policy of a number of States in the 19th and 20th centuries, it is also evident in a number of international legal developments from that time. The pinnacle of such recognition is to be found in the provisions of the UN Charter. The recording of the relationship between peace, security, international social and economic progress, development and cooperation and the realisation of human rights in the Charter brings us to consider the evolution of international human rights law after WWII and the difficult birth of economic and social rights law. Chapter 1 also shows that the difficult early decades for economic and social rights, during which their status as real human rights was challenged due to the view that they were merely aspirational, non-justiciable and costly, has been largely overcome with detailed and careful elaboration of the normative content and attendant State obligations of these rights. Although much of the scepticism around economic and social rights has been eliminated, the marginalisation of economic and social rights in the maintenance of international peace and security continues.

Chapter 2 proceeds on the view that it is appropriate to examine the provisions of the Charter that allow for a more holistic approach to the maintenance of international peace and security, an approach that can draw from the Charter's commitment to economic and social progress and human rights. Thus,

Chapter 2 considers how the Security Council, the General Assembly and the ECOSOC can work together to achieve not only their own individual goals but also the collective goals of the UN. Much of the content of Chapter 2 draws from briefings to the Security Council by representatives of the General Assembly, the ECOSOC and the Office of the High Commissioner for Human Rights (OHCHR), which, as meeting records show, facilitated debate amongst Council members also. On occasion, these statements have been imbued with considerations of economic and social factors as well as human rights considerations. These records also signal States' own awareness of the importance of both sets of considerations to maintaining peace and security so that, although the Council as a body may not be bound by such considerations, States are sensitive to them. Chapter 2 also shows that many of these statements have gone on to be encapsulated in presidential statements and Security Council resolutions, which are more significant indicators of the evolving relationship between the organs and the impact of this relationship upon international peace and security. This approach goes some way to rebalancing the critiques that current peace initiatives, with their emphasis on a liberal peace, cannot incorporate the more ambiguous or aspirational standards entailed in the economic and social dimensions of peace, in particular to the extent that such dimensions are captured by economic and social rights law.

Chapter 3's consideration of peacebuilding and peacekeeping brings us further along the line of giving practical effect to the provisions of the Charter regarding peace and security, economic and social development and human rights for all. UN peacebuilding policy clearly recognises this relationship, and so too do many of the thematic mandates of the Security Council. Recognition of this relationship is also evident both in UN peacekeeping policy and in Security Council peacekeeping resolutions, both thematic and country-specific, which also reflect an expanding role for peacekeepers as early peacebuilders. However, these two aspects of Chapter 3 bring us back to the need to consider economic and social rights for two reasons. One, the critique of peacebuilding for advancing a narrow liberal peace which is disassociated from the socio-economic drivers of conflict has tended to mean that such drivers are excluded from conflict prevention strategies. Two, the dual nature of peacekeeping operations means that they are subsidiary organs of the Security Council, but it also means that they are also bound by their contributing States' international legal obligations, including those stemming from economic and social rights.

The dual nature of peacekeeping operations provides a mechanism by which economic and social rights can inform peacekeeping mandates and begin the process of overcoming the marginalisation of these rights in the context of international peace and security. This connection brings us to Chapter 4's elaboration of the application of economic and social rights and ensuing State obligations in the extraterritorial context, a context which to date has been dominated by civil and political rights. The aim of Chapter 4 is to build on the elaboration of economic and social rights contained in Chapter 1 and to demonstrate that such rights apply extraterritorially. Chapter 4 shows not only how economic and social rights apply extraterritorially but also that they can do so in a measurable fashion. Given that a core theme of this work is the identification of economic and social rights as a tool to address socio-economic inequality, Chapter 4 shows that a proper understanding of economic and social rights can overcome such marginalisation by advancing a framework of best practices, to which end contributing States and the international community can consider what has been done and what must be done within the parameters of the extraterritorial application of economic and social rights, as is also necessary. Chapter 4 provides one such framework by suggesting how indicators measuring economic and social rights can help to determine to what extent contributing States are meeting their extraterritorial obligation. Such an understanding can inform the activities of contributing States in target States, but such understanding can also help inform human rights elements of peacebuilding and peacekeeping mandates more generally.

Chapter 5 brings together the preceding analysis by considering four questions: is there a legal obligation to build peace; what should that peace look like; is the Security Council under any legal obligation to build (any kind of) peace; and finally, what role must economic and social rights be allowed to play in efforts to reimagine international peace and security? To answer these questions, Chapter 5 explores *jus post bellum* theory, which calls for post-conflict endeavours to be framed in terms of State obligations. Of particular interest is the question of the extent of such obligations; do they extend to restoring the *status quo* that existed before the conflict, or should they go beyond that in an attempt to avoid a repeat of the egregious behaviour of the State that might have precipitated the original conflict? If, in spite of concerns around State sovereignty, the latter approach to post-conflict endeavours is to be favoured, then the door is opened for a recalibration of international peace and security. In that regard, Chapter 5 explores the contribution of positive peace and human security, which seek not only to end armed conflict but also to end structural and cultural violence so that the security of the individual is protected from severe and pervasive threats and s/he is empowered to act on his/her own behalf. In this way, the concepts of positive peace and human security echo aspects of *jus post bellum* theory that call for steps to be taken to mitigate risks to States emerging from conflict, risks such as those identified in Chapter 1. Calls to move beyond the *status quo ante*, as advocated by some interpretations of *jus post bellum*, resonate with the UN's recognition of the need to build a more sustainable peace, as indicated in Chapters 2 and 3. Chapter 5 concludes with consideration of the potential impact of these concepts upon the workings of the Security Council because the Council and its resolutions are, for the most part, the genesis of peacebuilding mandates and peacekeeping operations. It explores the question of the legal accountability of the UN for breaches of international law, a question that raises the issue of UN immunity from civil suit in domestic courts. This type of insulation from the legal consequences of what could otherwise be regarded as a breach of international law entailing the requirement to provide reparation puts the focus back on the accountability of States, a matter that is addressed in terms of State Responsibility and the complaints mechanism of the International Covenant on Economic,

Social and Cultural Rights (ICESCR). The lack of symmetry identified earlier in this Introduction manifests itself in the breadth of matters dealt with in Chapter 5. Nonetheless, the chapter concludes with the call for the Security Council to adopt a more nuanced approach to international peace and security, an approach that reflects the permeation of the UN Charter, as the UN's founding legal document, by the obligation to advance economic and social progress, development and cooperation, as well as the requirement to protect and promote human rights.

This work draws from a number of key concepts that have been identified by scholars and practitioners. These concepts are informed by a variety of scholarly disciplines such as international relations, economics and development, history, philosophy and theology. For the purposes of this work, these disciplines, which contribute to the creation and legitimation of a diverse array of post-conflict policies and practices, come together around a consideration of international human rights law. This body of international law serves to reaffirm the position of human rights in the face of international law and policy regarding international peace and security. However, the focus on the international law of human rights can be further concentrated with a focus on the legal framework underpinning economic and social rights. Somewhat paradoxically, this further focus has the effect of actually expanding our understanding of the role of law in post-conflict peacebuilding to support the building of a version of peace and security that might, more successfully, save succeeding generations from the scourge of war.

1 The significance of economic and social rights to peace and security

1 Introduction

Evidence of concern for the poor and the oppressed is to be found in various political, philosophical and religious systems spanning millennia, but the social and economic exploitation that was endemic in Western Europe and North America, particularly from the early 19th century, led to an array of philosophical, social and legal responses. Such responses were not always altruistic and reveal broader concern with maintaining a stable and secure society. Nonetheless, such responses did serve to improve the economic and social – and ultimately political – situation of those whose marginalisation at the social and economic level precluded their full participation in society. In due course, philosophical, and then political, responses found expression in legal change. Initially, such changes came at the domestic level as States moved to secure improved socio-economic conditions and then, at the international level, as States began to recognise the benefits of international cooperation. Whilst many of the developments were driven by advances in technology and communications from the mid-19th century, the cost of regional and then global conflict had a strong influence.

It is against this background that this chapter traces various philosophical and legal responses to secure improved economic and social conditions at the domestic and the international level. What emerges is a recognition of the interrelated nature of economic and social conditions and stability and security in the national and international arenas. Such recognition informed the founding documents of the League of Nations[1] and the United Nations (UN or the Organisation).[2] Both organisations were premised upon notions of economic and social progress and cooperation. However, the latter took a step further as it expressed its determination to 'save succeeding generations from the scourge of war', to reaffirm 'faith in fundamental human rights, in the dignity and worth of the human person' and 'to promote social progress and better standards of life in larger

1 Covenant of the League of Nations (adopted 28 April 1919, entered into force 10 January 1920) 225 CTS 195.

2 Charter of the United Nations (adopted 26 June 1945, entered into force 24 October 1945) 1 UNTS XVI (UN Charter).

freedom'.[3] With the taking of this first step, international legal standards elaborating the content of economic and social rights, and concomitant State obligations, began to emerge, albeit with some challenges. This chapter demonstrates that today there is a clear legal framework underpinning economic and social rights, which rests on a detailed elaboration of what these rights entail and what States must do to meet their obligations stemming from those rights. This chapter serves as a reminder of the centrality of just economic and social conditions to stable societies and international law's endeavours to capture and advance that centrality. It also demonstrates what steps can be taken to eliminate the social and economic marginalisation that often drives conflict.

2 The relationship between economic and social conditions and a stable domestic and international order

The origins of the modern concept of economic and social rights (as well as civil and political rights) can be found in various political, philosophical and religious systems that made provision for the oppressed and the poor, though such systems also were based on a need to maintain an orderly society. The Magna Carta (1215) was premised on the assumption that inequality creates conflict and should be mitigated by governmental or other intervention. The demise of the feudal system and the emergence of the Age of Enlightenment, and the accompanying political philosophy of the 17th and 18th centuries, allowed traditional authority and beliefs, including the proper relationship between the State and the market, to be challenged. This development also facilitated challenges to the endemic exploitation of the poor and their marginalisation at the social, economic and political levels.[4] The adoption of the British Bill of Rights (1690–1691), the American Declaration of Independence 1776 (and the ensuing Bill of

3 Ibid, Preamble, paras 1, 2 and 4, respectively.

4 The idea of social justice based on a social contract was mentioned in Plato's *Republic*, while Aristotle sought to establish a framework for 'social justice' to be the proper, or proportionate distribution of common assets: see Richard McKeon, 'Philosophy and History in the Development of Human Rights' in Howard Kiefer and Milton Karl Munitz (eds), *Ethics and Social Justice* (State University of New York Press, Albany 1968) 316–317. The social contract, as a concept, remerges in C B Macpherson (ed), *John Locke: 1632–1704: Second Treatise of Government 1690* (Hackett Publishing, Indiana 1980); and George Douglas and Howard Cole (trs), *The Social Contract: And, Discourses* (Dent Publishing, New York 1973) authored by Jean Jacques Rousseau. See, more generally, Samuel Moyn, *The Last Utopia* (The Belknap Press of Harvard University Press, Cambridge 2010); Paul G Lauren, *The Evolution of International Human Rights: Visions Seen* (3rd edn, University of Pennsylvania Press, Philadelphia 2011); Micheline R Ishay, *The History of Human Rights: From Ancient Times to the Globalisation Era* (University of California Press, Berkeley 2008); Lynn Hunt, *Inventing Human Rights: A History* (W W Norton, New York 2007); Louis Henkin, 'Rights: American and Human' (1979) 79(3) *Columbia Law Review* 405; Stephen P Marks, 'From the "Single Confused Page" to the "Decalogue for Five Billion Persons": The Roots of the Universal Declaration of Human Rights in the French Revolution' (1998) 20(3) *Human Rights Quarterly* 459; and Lynn

Rights of the Constitution of the newly emergent United States) as well as the French Declaration of the Rights of Man and Citizen 1789 are best known for their advancement of what we now regard as civil and political rights. However, their calls for democracy and equality set in motion the recognition of economic and social rights as an aspect of developing democratic ideals. For example, the impact of the French Declaration can be seen in the provisions of the French Constitution mandating public relief for the poor and free public education, which subsequently influenced many other European and Latin American civil codes. Although these Declarations were underpinned by the rights to equality, the inclusion of the principles of brotherhood reveals that the rights that they contained extended to only a limited portion of society, predominately free, land-owning men. In spite of the adoption of the *Declaration of the Rights of Woman and Citizen*[5] and *A Vindication of the Rights of Woman*[6] and the abolition of the Trans-Atlantic slave trade, the impact of efforts to achieve equality remained uneven in the face of on-going discrimination against women and minorities.

The extension of property rights to include the right to public assistance was advocated by Thomas Paine in the late 18th century. He contended that society owed a debt to individuals that they had a right to collect in the form of education and public assistance.[7] Paine expanded his views in *Agrarian Justice* wherein he called for a basic income scheme for young families, the elderly and the disabled. Such payments were to be derived from a national fund, which would be financed by tax on inherited property to be paid by landowners for the needs of those who had no land. Most notably, such payments were to be a matter of right, rather than charity.[8] In 1797, Thomas Spence went further by calling for the abolishment of the aristocracy and for the equal distribution of rents to be given to parishes to administer and to make land available for use by all inhabitants as a source of basic, unconditional income, which would be used to support families.[9]

The contribution of the philosophical, legal and political movements underpinning the developing ideals around democracy and economic rights as property rights were further advanced in response to the negative effects of the unrestricted expansion of capitalism during the Industrial Revolution and the economic and social inequities that stemmed from the exploitation of an ever-expanding

Hunt (ed), *The French Revolution and Human Rights: A Brief Documentary History* (Bedford Books of St Martin's Press, Boston 1996).

5 Olympe de Gouges, *Declaration of the Rights of Woman* (Printed for the Author, Paris 1791).

6 Mary Wollstonecraft, *A Vindication of the Rights of Woman* (J Johnson, London 1792).

7 See generally, Thomas Allen Horne, *Property Rights and Poverty: Political Argument in Britain, 1605–1834* (University of North Carolina Press, Chapel Hill 1990) 206–209.

8 Thomas Paine, 'Agrarian Justice' in Bruce Kuklick (ed), *Paine: Political Writings Revised Student Edition* (Cambridge University Press, Cambridge 2000).

9 Thomas Spence, *The Rights of Infants, Or, the Imprescriptable Right of Mothers to Such a Share of the Elements As Is Sufficient to Enable Them to Suckle and Bring Up Their Young: In a Dialogue between the Aristocracy and a Mother of Children: To Which Are Added, by Way of Preface and Appendix, Strictures on Paine's Agrarian Justice* (Printed for the Author, London 1797).

class of marginalised poor, mainly in Europe and North America. In addition to the exploitation of workers, widespread poverty, starvation, epidemics and crime comprised a further combination of factors that prompted social and legal reform. Natural law principles of equality, mutuality and justice informed such social legislation. In terms of workers' rights, the right to possess property had already been identified as an economic right,[10] but the expansion of welfare legislation in the late 19th and early 20th centuries was a means to deal with the new social problems that had been caused by the Industrial Revolution. The extension of the right to vote (at least amongst male voters) and the introduction of compulsory education facilitated political participation and the resultant social legislation for better working conditions, the introduction of systems of public health and overall improved standards of living. In the 19th century, (Western) industrialised States began to see that concern with the health and welfare of their citizens was a way to look after a key resource of State power – the working population – and by the late 19th and early 20th centuries, medicine had come to provide much of the focus on the discourse on social issues, both nationally and internationally.

Socio-economic legislation relating to work and trade unions, social security, education, health and an adequate standard of living (encompassing rights to food and water, clothing and housing) was enacted in a number of countries by the end of the 19th century. National campaigns sought to ensure that every house had access to clean water and an on-site toilet. Water supply was regarded as the material expression of political inclusion and so that citizenship was cast not only in terms of political representation but also in terms of services provision. Access to water was important not only because it prevented disease but also because it was regarded as being critical for a 'minimum level of dignity to which all citizens have a right'.[11] Further initiatives included Britain's Education Act 1870, which made education compulsory for all children under the age of 13 years and extended access to education to working-class children. In Germany, Chancellor Bismarck introduced social insurance schemes in the 1880s. In the context of the introduction of social legislation in New Zealand in the early to mid-1880s, it has been observed that this initiative reflected 'the fledgling notion that all citizens should be able to achieve a level of participation in New Zealand society.'[12] Elsewhere, the dangers of ignoring dire socio-economic conditions was highlighted by a number of revolutions, which led to new constitutional protections.[13]

10 Macpherson (n 4).

11 Karen Bakker, *Privatizing Water: Governance Failure and the World's Urban Water Crisis* (Cornell University Press, Ithaca 2010) 55, 165–169.

12 Mamari Stephens, 'The Right to Social Security' in Margaret Bedggood and Kris Gledhill (eds), *Law into Action: Economic, Social and Cultural Rights in Aotearoa New Zealand* (Thomson Reuters, Wellington 2011) 134.

13 See, for example, the Russian Declaration of the Rights of the Working and Exploited Working People of 1918, which formed part of the 1918 Constitution of the Russian Soviet Federated Socialist Republic, established the duty to work (Article 18) and the right to

Developments such as these at the national level were facilitated by some specific international developments in the late 19th and early 20th centuries, including the increasing internationalisation of trade, communication and the recognition of the value of transnational conversations amongst philanthropists, experts, scholars and, ultimately, policy- and law-makers. Between 1840 and WWI, increasingly frequent international congresses were held to discuss charity, sponsorship, assistance or penal reform. These networks and congresses disseminated information, helped develop national models for social welfare and were behind the adoption of many national policies on education, welfare and sanitation.[14] From the latter part of the 19th century, States increasingly began to understand that many domestic provisions could be strengthened through international legal cooperation, leading to the advent of modern treaty law. For example, cooperation on public health can be traced back to national and then international efforts to develop conventions to prevent the spread of communicable diseases, in particular the adoption of sanitary conventions on cholera and the plague. A number of these conventions were adopted into a single text in 1903,[15] and, in 1907, the Office International d'Hygiene Publique was established. Early international cooperation regarding the right to education was more limited and included the establishment of the International Bureau of Education in 1924, which was a private organisation. Particular efforts to minimise the increasing burden of suffering imposed by war on the civilian population began to underpin international treaties such as the Hague Conventions of 1899 and 1907,[16] which ushered in a new era in international law where the plight of the individual could no longer be ignored.[17] The (domestic) recognition of rights from civil and political rights in the 18th century to the recognition of (domestic) social rights particularly in the 19th century is a reflection of the realisation that 'political rights had little meaning if it remained economically impossible for people to live a life of dignity.'[18]

---

education (Article 17). The Mexican Constitution of 1917 includes the right to education (Article 3), as did the Constitution of the German Reich of 1919, usually known as the Weimar Constitution (Article 120). Bunreacht na h'Eireann Constitution of Ireland of 1937 also enshrined the right to education (Article 42) as well as aspects of the advancement of social and economic justice and equality (Article 45).

14 Zoe Moody, 'The United Nations Declaration of the Rights of the Child (1959): Genesis, Transformation and Dissemination of a Treaty (re)constituting a Transnational Cause' (2015) 45 *Prospects*, 15, 16–17.

15 International Sanitary Convention (signed 3 December 1903, entered into force 6 April 1907) (1903) 35 Stat. 1770.

16 Convention with Respect to the Laws and Customs of War on Land and its annex: Regulations Respecting the Laws and Customs of War on Land (Hague – II) (signed 29 July 1899, entered into force 4 September 1900) 32 Stat. 1803; Convention Respecting the Laws and Customs of War on Land (Hague – IV) (signed 18 October 1907, entered into force 26 January 1910) (1907) 36 Stat. 2277.

17 See Gerd Oberleitner, 'Humanitarian Law as a Source of Human Rights Law' in Dinah Shelton (ed), *The Oxford Handbook of International Human Rights Law* (Oxford University Press, Oxford 2013) 275–294.

18 Eugeen Verhellen, *The Convention on the Rights of the Child: Background, Motivation, Strategies, Main Themes* (3rd edn, Garant, Leuven 2000) 58.

The mitigation of poor socio-economic conditions, driven in part from the need to deal with the power of labourers and the potential dangers stemming from the return of soldiers, underpinned national and international efforts to secure social order and international peace after WWI. Such efforts continued to favour the social welfare model that had emerged towards the end of the 19th century, and many of the earlier international cooperative initiatives were brought together under the Covenant of the League of Nations.[19] The aims of the League were to stop wars and to encourage disarmament, but WWI had also succeeded in elevating the position of labour in society, resulting in a closer relationship between workers' and employers' associations and governments. The Bolshevik Revolution in Russia had also influenced the working classes in other countries, which motivated a number of labour organisations to seek a solution to industrial problems at the Paris Peace Conference in 1919. Consequently, there was keen appreciation of the threat posed to peace by socio-economic exploitation given the background of exploitation of workers in the industrialising nations of that time. To that end, under Article 23(a) of the Covenant, League Members endeavoured 'to secure and maintain fair and humane conditions of labour for men, women, and children', through the establishment of the necessary International Organisations, which facilitated the founding of the International Labour Organisation (ILO). The establishment of the ILO was further driven by security, humanitarian, political and economic considerations, which were reflected in the Preamble to the Constitution of the ILO that stated:

> Whereas universal and lasting peace can be established only if it is based upon social justice.
>
> And whereas conditions of labour exist involving such injustice, hardship and privation to large numbers of people as to produce unrest so great that the peace and harmony of the world are imperilled; and an improvement of those conditions is urgently required; . . .[20]

Thus, the ILO's advocacy for social justice is regarded as being 'especially relevant to the incipient UN system for the implementation of economic and social rights'.[21]

The Covenant of the League of Nations also sought to respond to other social concerns. As noted above, a series of international treaties on public health had been concluded at the end of the 19th century and in the early years of the 20th century, in addition to the establishment of the Office International d'Hygiene

19 Covenant of the League of Nations (n 1).

20 Constitution of the International Labour Organisation (adopted 1 April 1919, entered into force 28 June 1919) 15 UNTS 40, preambular paras 1 and 2.

21 Virginia Leary, 'Lessons from the Experience of the International Labour Organisation' in Philip Alston (ed), *The United Nations and Human Rights: A Critical Appraisal* (Clarendon Press, Oxford 1992) 580. See also, C W Jenks, 'Human Rights, Social Justice and Peace: The Broader Significance of the ILO Experience' in Asbjørn Eide and August Shou (eds), *International Protection of Human Rights: Proceedings* (Interscience Publishers, New York 1968) 227.

Publique. These steps were advanced by the Covenant, as Article 23(f) placed League Members under an obligation to 'endeavour to take steps in matters of international concern for the prevention and control of disease'.[22] This provision formed the basis for the establishment of the Health Organisation of the League. Additional international legal protection was also afforded to individuals by a series of 'Minorities Treaties',[23] which were an outcome of the Paris Peace Conference that redrew the borders of Europe and created large numbers of new minorities in new States. According to these treaties, the rights of minorities, 'so far as they affect persons belonging to racial, religious, or linguistic minorities, constitute obligations of international concern and shall be placed under the guarantee of the League of Nations',[24] a provision that allowed members of such groups to claim discrimination in the provision of education during the inter-war years.[25] Provisions such as these were the culmination of early 20th-century efforts to put social reforms into practice at the level of international law.

In spite of the work of the League of Nations, and its affiliated organisations, in advancing the recognition of the rights to work and health, against a background of maintaining peace, there were increasing calls for the State to play a greater role in improving socio-economic conditions, calls that were highlighted by the Great Depression of the 1930s. In 1937, the American President, Franklin D Roosevelt, stated, 'The test of our progress is not whether we add more to the abundance of those who have much; it is whether we provide enough for those who have too little.'[26] In Britain, in 1938, Harold Macmillan published *The Middle Way* in which he called for social reconstruction and the elimination of poverty.[27] In the midst of WWII, States were already considering how best to rebuild shattered societies and re-establish global peace. In his 1941 State of the Union Address, President Roosevelt spoke of a world with four major freedoms: freedom of speech, freedom of religion, freedom from want and freedom from fear. According to the President, freedom from want meant 'economic understandings which will secure to every nation a healthy peacetime life for its inhabitants everywhere in the world'.[28] The 'Four Freedoms Address' responded to a time when many countries were engaged in a struggle against the effects of laissez-faire economics, which had ushered in the Great Depression and fuelled

22 Covenant of the League of Nations (n 1).

23 See, for example, Minorities Treaty Between the Principal Allied and Associated Powers (The British Empire, France, Italy, Japan, and the United States) and Poland (signed 28 June 1919) 225 CTS 412. Further treaties were drawn up between the Allies and Albania, Austria, Bulgaria, Czechoslovakia, Estonia, Greece, Hungary, Iraq, Latvia, Lithuania, Poland, Romania, Turkey, and Yugoslavia.

24 Minorities Treaty (Poland), ibid, article 12.

25 *Rights of Minorities in Upper Silesia (Minority Schools)* (1928) PCIJ Rep Series A no 15; and *Minority Schools in Albania* (Advisory Opinion) PCIJ Rep Series A/B No. 64.

26 Franklin D Roosevelt, 'Second Inaugural Address' (Inaugural Address on Wednesday 20 January 1937) <http://www.bartleby.com/124/pres50.html> accessed 1 October 2016.

27 Harold Macmillan, *The Middle Way* (Macmillan & Co, London 1938).

28 Franklin D Roosevelt, 'Annual Message to Congress on the State of the Union' (Speech to the Congress on 6 January 1941) <http://www.presidency.ucsb.edu/ws/?pid=16092> accessed 26 September 2016.

the emergence and appeal of authoritarianism, extremist nationalism and totalitarianism, to devastating effect.[29] Widespread unemployment and poverty had facilitated the rise of these regimes, leading to a genuine interest in securing economic and social rights, not only for their own sake but also for the preservation of individual freedom and democracy so that, even in periods of recession, basic economic and social rights should be enjoyed by all.[30]

In 1942, in Britain, Lord Beveridge called for the establishment of a welfare state with social security, a national health service, free education, council housing and full employment to overcome obstacles to reconstruction. In his 1944 State of the Union Address, President Roosevelt continued his earlier themes, stating that:

> an equally basic essential to peace is a decent standard of living for all individual men and women and children in all Nations. Freedom from fear is eternally linked with freedom from want . . .
>
> We have come to a clear realisation of the fact that true individual freedom cannot exist without economic security and independence. "Necessitous men are not free men". People who are hungry and out of a job are the stuff of which dictatorships are made.[31]

He went on to advance a Second Bill of Rights, including rights to a useful and remunerative job; to earn enough to provide adequate food and clothing and recreation; of every family to a decent home; to adequate medical care and the opportunity to achieve and enjoy good health; adequate protection from the economic fears of old age, sickness, accident, and unemployment; and to a good education. According to the President, 'All of these rights spell security. And after this war is won we must be prepared to move forward, in the implementation of these rights, to new goals of human happiness and well-being.'[32] Similarly, when he established the Office of Foreign Relief and Rehabilitation Operations, President Roosevelt was of the view that the role of this new office ought to be more than the shipping of supplies and that it should plan and rebuild the shattered economies of liberated territories.[33]

At the international level, recognition of the link between economic and social conditions and international peace and security also re-emerged during the course of WWII. The Common Programme of Purposes and Principles (the

29 Asbjørn Eide, 'Economic, Social and Cultural Rights as Human Rights' in Asbjørn Eide, Catarina Krause and Allan Rosas (eds), Economic, Social and Cultural Rights: A Textbook (2nd edn, Martinus Nijhoff, Dordrecht and London 2001) 15.

30 Ibid, 16.

31 Franklin D Roosevelt, 'State of the Union Message to Congress' (Speech to the Congress on 11 January 1944) <http://www.presidency.ucsb.edu/ws/?pid=16518> accessed on 2 October 2016.

32 Ibid.

33 James A Gillespie, 'International Organizations and the Problem of Child Health, 1945–1960' (2003) 23 *Dynamis* 115, 122–123.

Atlantic Charter), issued on 14 August 1941, was a key policy statement that sought to define the Allied goals for the post-war world. It was adopted by President Roosevelt and British Prime Minister Churchill who deemed 'it right to make known certain common principles in the national policies of their respective countries on which they base their hopes for a better future for the world'.[34] The Charter listed eight principles, including:

> the object of securing, for all, improved labor standards, economic advancement and social security; . . . [the establishment of] a peace which will afford to all nations the means of dwelling in safety within their own boundaries, and which will afford assurance that all the men in all lands may live out their lives in freedom from fear and want.[35]

The ILO also continued to play a significant role with its adoption of the Declaration of Philadelphia 1944, which was subsequently incorporated into the Constitution of that organisation. According to Article II of the Declaration, 'lasting peace can be established only if it is based on social justice'. Delegates at the Bretton Woods Conference, in 1944, noted, with respect to the creation of the International Bank for Reconstruction and Development, that '[p]rograms of reconstruction and development will aid economic progress everywhere, will speed political stability and foster peace'.[36] Thus, after WWII, attempts to reconstruct Germany and Japan, and other States, which had been devastated by the war were again driven by the need to maintain social order and international peace, and many European States moved towards social democracy as a more inclusive form of democracy.

Accordingly, the recognition of the link between democracy, participation in social movements generating social reform and the introduction of health and education reforms in the 18th and 19th centuries continued to find expression in the middle of the 20th century, at the national level, as both individual States and the international community responded to the events of WWII. In Britain, links between political inequality and economic and social inequality were also recognised, most notably by Thomas H Marshall in 1950. Marshall is credited with the formulation of the concept of social citizenship in the context of post-WWII Britain. Social citizenship, according to Marshall, is 'a status bestowed on those who are full members of a community. All who possess the status are equal with respect to the rights and duties with which the status is endowed.'[37] He was

34 The Atlantic Charter (signed 14 August 1941) reprinted in *United States President (1933–1945: Roosevelt)* and Great Britain Prime Minister, *The Atlantic Charter: The Full Text of the Declaration* (Whitcombe & Tombs, Christchurch 1942), Principle 1.

35 The Atlantic Charter, Principles 5 and 6.

36 AIS, *Pamphlet No. 4, Pillars of Peace – Documents Pertaining to American Interest in Establishing a Lasting World Peace: January 1941–February 1946* (Book Department, Army Information School, Carlisle Barracks PA 1946).

37 Thomas H Marshall and T B Bottomore (eds), *Citizenship and Social Class* (Pluto Press, London 1992) 18.

concerned with the contradiction between formal political equality and individual freedom and significant social and economic inequality. Marshall was of the view that 20th century social rights (such as widespread access to education, health care and social insurance when faced with unemployment, sickness, old age and other kinds of hardship) were citizenship rights which would enable people to exercise their civil and political rights, rights that he identified as having emerged in the 18th and 19th centuries, respectively. Social rights would also give individuals a sense of security, which, in turn, would foster a sense of a collective identity between the State and its citizens. Even though citizenship – social or otherwise – remains a contested concept, as there is no one single definition, and it is a contextualised concept whose 'meanings vary according to social, political and cultural context and reflect different historical legacies',[38] Marshall's underlying concern with economic and social exclusion remains legitimate.

In a similar vein, the period from 1950–1975 is considered the Golden Age of Social Welfare. State responsibility for social welfare was widely accepted. It marked a period of rapid and sustained economic growth both in developing and developed countries. In Western countries in particular, the high rates of economic growth allowed States to expand their social welfare expenditures.[39] In very broad terms, this period:

> represented an effort to bring about economic, moral and political reconstruction. Economically, it departed from the orthodoxies of the pure market nexus and required the extension of income and employment security as a right of citizenship. Morally, it sought to defend the ideas of social justice, solidarity and universalism. Politically, the welfare state formed part of a project of nation building, affirming liberal democracy against the twin perils of fascism and bolshevism. Many countries became self-proclaimed welfare states, not so much to give a label to their social policies as to foster national social integration.[40]

Therefore, by the middle of the 20th century, the relationship between poverty-induced exclusion and conflict led to the recognition of the need to develop universal standards in the economic and social field. However, as Chapter 3 demonstrates, peacebuilding efforts, since the end of the Cold War, have moved away from building social democracies that had been favoured by the Bretton Woods system.

38 Ruth Lister, 'Unpacking Children's Citizenship' in Jane Williams and Antonella Invernizzi (eds), *Children and Citizenship* (Sage Publications, London 2008) 9.

39 James Midgley, *Social Welfare in Global Context* (Sage Publications, Thousand Oaks CA 1997) 36.

40 Gøsta Esping-Andersen, 'After the Golden Age: The Future of the Welfare State in the New Global Order' (1994) United Nations Research Institute for Social Development Occasional Paper No. 7, World Summit for Social Development, at 1, <http://www.unrisd.org/80256B3C005BCCF9/(httpAuxPages)/D93F019CFA85A04280256B650041F3F5/$file/OPWSSD7.pdf> accessed 2 October 2016.

Instead, any threat posed to the social order and international peace by inequality has come to be regarded as being dealt with by a neoliberalist view which regards inequality as being necessary to achieve the benefits of capitalism's free markets.

3 Economic and social progress: Introducing a role for human rights

After WWII, the idea of human rights became more important internationally and international law began to reinforce human rights both in content and in status with the adoption of declarations and, increasingly, treaties to give binding power to such obligations. (International) law increasingly served a protective function, rather than an instrumental function, so that (human) rights were no longer merely to be respected, they also had to be protected.[41]

However, during the drafting of the UN Charter, the promotion of respect for human rights and fundamental freedoms had initially been relegated to being 'merely an incidental aspiration'[42] of the UN, which would have resulted in nothing more than 'a passing reference'[43] to human rights within the Charter. Originally, there was the rather equivocal statement that 'the Organization should facilitate solutions of international economic, social and other humanitarian problems and promote respect for human rights and fundamental freedoms'.[44] However, much stronger language on human rights was included in the draft Charter at the San Francisco Conference. Latin American States and 42 United States' nongovernmental organisations have been credited with successful efforts to include the promotion of respect for human rights as being one of the purposes of the UN.[45] In 1945, in his address at the closing session of the San Francisco Conference, the American President, Harold Truman, underlined the necessity of human rights to peace and security, stating:

> The Charter is dedicated to the achievement and observance of human rights and fundamental freedoms. Unless we can attain those objectives for all men and women everywhere – without regard to race, language or religion – we cannot have permanent peace and security in the world.[46]

41 Verhellen (n 18), 57–58.

42 Geoffrey Robertson, *Crimes against Humanity: The Struggle for Global Justice* (Penguin Books, London 2000) 24.

43 William Korey, *NGOs and the Universal Declaration of Human Rights: "A Curious Grapevine"* (Palgrave, New York 2001) 28.

44 Dumbarton Oaks 'Washington Conversations on International Peace and Security Organisation, October 7, 1944 Proposals' (1945) 39 (Supplement) *American Journal of International Law* 42.

45 Jan Herman Burgers, 'The Road to San Francisco: The Revival of the Human Rights Idea in the Twentieth Century' (1992) 14(4) *Human Rights Quarterly* 447.

46 *Closing Plenary Session. The United Nations Conference on International Organization. San Francisco, June 26, 1945* (Washington DC, 1946) 683.

The Charter itself reflects international determination to save succeeding generations from the scourge of war, reaffirms 'faith in fundamental human rights'[47] and promotes 'the economic and social advancement of all peoples'.[48] The essence of the mission of the UN is to be found in Article 1, which is to maintain international peace and security[49] and to achieve international cooperation in promoting and encouraging respect for human rights and fundamental freedoms for all without distinction as to race, sex, language or religion.[50]

The commitment of the UN and its Member States to respect for human rights is supported by the mandatory wording of Article 13 regarding the initiation of studies and the making of recommendations by the General Assembly. According to Article 13(1)(b), such work would include 'assisting in the realisation of human rights and fundamental freedoms for all without distinction as to race, sex, language, or religion'. Article 13(2) signals the more in-depth role to be undertaken by the UN with its reference to the further responsibilities, functions and powers of the General Assembly with respect to human rights matters that are set out in Chapters IX and X of the Charter. The overlap between economic and social progress and human rights is apparent from the contents of Chapter IX. According to Article 55(c):

> With a view to the creation of conditions of stability and well-being which are necessary for peaceful and friendly relations among nations based on respect for the principle of equal rights and self-determination of peoples, the UN shall promote: . . . universal respect for, and observance of, human rights and fundamental freedoms for all without distinction as to race, sex, language, or religion.

In addition to setting out the obligations for the UN, the Article also identifies the interdependent nature of both aims of the Organisation. The effect of these aims upon UN Member States is elaborated upon by the provisions of Article 56, whereby Member States pledge to take 'joint and separate action in co-operation with the Organization for the achievement of the purposes set forth in Article 55'.

Article 60 provides that responsibility for the discharge of the economic and social functions contained in Chapter IX, including those functions aimed at human rights promotion and protection, are vested in the General Assembly and, under the authority of the General Assembly, in the ECOSOC. Although the wording of Article 60 indicates that the ECOSOC is an organ subsidiary to the General Assembly, the principal organ of the UN in terms of coordinating the promotion and protection of human rights is, arguably, the ECOSOC.[51]

47 UN Charter (n 2), preambular para 2.
48 Ibid, preambular para 8.
49 Article 1(1).
50 Article 1(3).
51 For further discussion on the overlap between the General Assembly and the ECOSOC in terms of the UN's human rights functions, see Werner Meng, 'Article 60' and Volker Roben,

The Council's powers in this regard are set out in Chapter 10 of the Charter. In particular, Article 62(2) outlines the powers and functions of the ECOSOC, which includes the making of 'recommendations for the purpose of promoting respect for, and observance of, human rights and fundamental freedoms for all'. The power vested in the ECOSOC, by Article 68, to set up commissions led to the establishment of the Commission on Human Rights (the Commission) in 1946. The Commission became the body responsible for the drafting of an International Bill of Rights, which led to the creation of States' human rights obligations, including those expressed as economic, social (and cultural) rights.

Although the Charter is a treaty that is legally binding upon those States that have ratified it, the legal character of the human rights provisions of the Charter were drafted to be weak and vague because major world powers involved in the drafting would not agree to strong international commitments on human rights as they all had serious human rights problems of their own.[52] The Charter did not establish any immediate obligation to guarantee or to observe human rights, nor does it contain any actual definition of human rights, and it fails to identify any specific follow-up action stemming from the provisions of Articles 55(c) and 56. The dual lack of international commitment to, and definition of, human rights standards downplayed the significance attached to the achievement of these standards, especially compared with the highest of priorities that was the maintenance of international peace and security. That said, the human rights bodies and protection mechanisms that have emanated from a number of the Charter's provisions have elaborated significantly the rights and obligations stemming from UN membership. It is against this background that the emergence of economic and social rights, within the framework of UN international human rights law, will be considered, bearing in mind the Organisation's determination 'to establish conditions under which justice and respect for the obligations arising from treaties and other sources of international law can be maintained'.[53]

4 Economic and social rights in international law

The elaboration of economic and social rights in international human rights law provides a further legal basis for the Charter's concern with social and economic progress. The first step in elaborating the normative content of economic and social rights is the Universal Declaration of Human Rights (the UDHR or the Declaration),[54]

'Article 62' in Bruno Simma and others (eds), *The Charter of the United Nations: A Commentary. Volume III* (3rd edn, Oxford University Press, Oxford 2012) 1658 and 1678, respectively.

52 Ruth Russell, *A History of the United Nations Charter: The Role of the United States 1940–1945* (Brookings Institution, Washington 1958) 786; and Thomas Buergenthal, 'The Normative and Institutional Evolution of International Human Rights' (1997) 19(4) *Human Rights Quarterly* 703, 706–707.

53 UN Charter, (n 2) preambular para 3.

54 Universal Declaration of Human Rights (adopted 10 December 1948) UNGA Res 217 A(III) (UDHR).

which seeks to provide a 'common understanding' as to the human rights and fundamental freedoms provided for in the Charter.[55] It enshrines civil, political, economic, social and cultural rights, noting:

> the peoples of the United Nations have in the Charter reaffirmed their faith in fundamental human rights, in the dignity and worth of the human person and in the equal rights of men and women and have determined to promote social progress and better standards of life in larger freedom.[56]

The Declaration's inclusion of economic rights, such as the rights to social security (Article 22) and work (Article 23), and social rights, such as the right an adequate standard of living (Article 25) and education (Article 26), is a recognition by States that the political upheavals and the emergence of totalitarian regimes during WWI and WWII had been facilitated by widespread poverty and unemployment. Their inclusion led to the recognition that economic and social rights should be secured not only for their own sake but also for the preservation of individual freedom and democracy. This view is based on the conviction that, even in periods of recession, it is necessary to ensure that everyone enjoys basic economic and social rights.[57] The inclusion of economic and social rights was also a response to the systematic discrimination, coercive measures and indoctrination in the areas of work, living, health, education, or cultural participation, from which many millions of people had suffered under the Nazi regime.[58]

It is against this background that particular features of the Declaration must be considered. The Declaration has been described as the constitution of the entire human rights movement.[59] Its provisions on economic and social rights drew heavily from the provisions of national constitutions of Latin American States, as well as Communist States,[60] and since its adoption, the Declaration's principles have been embodied in many constitutions. It has also been observed that many of the provisions of the Declaration are now considered to form part of customary international law.[61] The Declaration was also to be a precursor to one treaty

55 Ibid, preambular para 7.

56 Ibid, preambular para 5.

57 Asbjørn Eide, 'Economic and Social Rights' in Januz Symonides, *Human Rights: Concepts and Standards* (UNESCO Publishing and Ashgate Publishing, Burlington 2000) 118.

58 Ulrike Davy, 'Social Citizenship Going International: Changes in the Reading of UN-Sponsored Economic and Social Rights' 22(S1) *International Journal of Social Welfare* S15. See also, Asbjørn Eide and others (eds), *The Universal Declaration of Human Rights: A Commentary* (Scandinavian University Press, Oslo 1993); and Johannes Morsink, *The Universal Declaration of Human Rights: Origins, Drafting and Intent* (University of Pennsylvania Press, Pennsylvania 1999).

59 Henry J Steiner, Philip Alston and Ryan Goodman, *International Human Rights in Context: Law, Politics, Morals: Text and Materials* (3rd edn Oxford University Press, Oxford 2008) 136.

60 Nehemiah Robinson, *The Universal Declaration of Human Rights: Its Origin, Significance, Application and Interpretation* (Institute of Jewish Affairs and World Jewish Congress, New York 1958); Eide (n 58); and Morsink (n 58).

61 Bruno Simma and Philip Alston, 'The Sources of Human Rights Law: Custom, Jus Cogens, and General Principles' (1988–1989) 12 *Australian Year Book of International Law* 82, 84,

that would be an International Bill of Rights, but the drafting process of the latter was captured by the Cold War battle of political ideology. Whilst the West emphasised civil and political rights, Eastern European and Soviet States focused on economic and social rights and 'expressed reluctance and often outright animosity' towards proposals regarding international monitoring devices.[62] The outcome of this ideological struggle was that the intended single treaty was divided into two separate treaties,[63] ultimately becoming the International Covenant on Economic, Social and Cultural Rights (ICESCR)[64] and the International Covenant on Civil and Political Rights (ICCPR).[65] This outcome 'prevented objective consideration of the key issues raised by the concept of economic and social rights'[66] and its legacy pervaded for many years.

90–96; and Steiner (n 59), 137. It may now reflect customary international law, if not in its entirety then in relation to some of its provisions. See Ian Brownlie and G S Goodwin-Gill (eds), *Basic Documents on Human Rights* (5th edn, Oxford University Press, Oxford and New York 2006) 23.

62 Allan Rosas and Jan E Helgesen, 'Introduction' in Allan Rosas and Jan E Helgesen with the Collaboration of Donna Gomien (eds), *Human Rights in a Changing East-West Perspective* (Pinter Publishers, New York 1990) 1; and Matthew C R Craven, *The International Covenant on Economic, Social, and Cultural Rights: A Perspective on Its Development* (Clarendon Press, Oxford 1995) 352.

63 UNGA Res 2200A (XXI) (16 December 1966) UN Doc A/RES/21/2200.

64 International Covenant on Economic, Social and Cultural Rights (adopted 16 December 1966, entered into force 3 January 1976) 993 UNTS 3 (ICESCR). The ICESCR is the primary UN treaty on economic and social rights. However, these rights are also protected in a number of other core UN treaties, including the following: International Convention on the Elimination of All Forms of Racial Discrimination (adopted 7 March 1966, entered into force 4 January 1969) 660 UNTS 195 (ICERD); Convention on the Elimination of All Forms of Discrimination Against Women (adopted 18 December 1979, entered into force 3 September 1981) 1249 UNTS 13 (CEDAW); Convention on the Rights of the Child (adopted 20 November 1989, entered into force 2 September 1990) 1577 UNTS 3 (CRC); International Convention on the Protection of the Rights of All Migrant Workers and Members of their Families (adopted 18 December 1990, entered into force 1 July 2003) 2220 UNTS 3 (Migrant Workers Convention); and Convention on the Rights of Persons with Disabilities (adopted by UNGA Res 61/106 (24 January 2007) UN Doc A/RES/61/106, Annex 1, entered into force 3 May 2008) (CRPD). Economic and Social Rights have also been elaborated in a number of regional human rights treaties, such as the following: African Charter on Human and Peoples' Rights (adopted 27 June 1981, entered into force 21 October 1986) 2206 UNTS 230; Arab Charter on Human Rights (adopted 15 September 1994) reprinted in (1997) 18 *Human Rights Law Journal* 151; Additional Protocol to the American Convention on Human Rights in the Area of Economic, Social and Cultural Rights (entered into force 16 November 1999) OAS Treaty Series No. 69 (Protocol of San Salvador); European Social Charter (Revised) (adopted 3 May 1996, entered into force 1 July 1999) 2151 UNTS 277; and Association of Southeast Asian Nations, Human Rights Declaration (adopted 18 November 2012) <http://aichr.org/documents> accessed 3 October 2016.

65 International Covenant on Civil and Political Rights (adopted 16 December 1966, entered into force 23 March 1976) 999 UNTS 171 (ICCPR).

66 Philip Alston, 'Economic and Social Rights' in Louis Henkin and John Lawrence Hargrove (eds), *Human Rights: An Agenda for the Next Century* (American Society for International Law, Washington DC 1994) 137, 152.

In terms of economic and social rights in international law, the Preamble to the ICESCR spells out its relationship with the Declaration and the UN Charter. Notably, the Preamble recalls the provisions of Article 1(3) of the Charter which identifies one of the purposes of the UN as being 'To achieve international cooperation . . . in promoting and encouraging respect for human rights and for fundamental freedoms for all'.[67] The Preamble also references Article 55 of the Charter. The Covenant recognises and protects economic rights such as the right to work and to favourable conditions of work (Articles 6 and 7, respectively), the right to organise and take collective labour actions (Article 8) and the right to social security (Article 9). In terms of social rights, it recognises the right to an adequate standard of living including adequate food, clothing, and housing (Article 11), the right to enjoyment of the highest attainable standard of health (Article 12) and the right to education (Article 13).

4.1 *The content of economic and social rights: Some recurring themes*

Despite its initial history – indeed, perhaps it is because of this history – extensive work has been undertaken to elaborate the content of economic and social rights and the extent of the ensuing obligations upon ratifying States. The Committee on Economic, Social and Cultural Rights (the CESCR or the Committee) has contributed significantly to the textual clarity of the rights, particularly through the use of General Comments which, despite their non-binding nature, are an important and authoritative source of interpretation. A number of recurring themes are apparent. The first is that the rights are essential to the realisation of human dignity.[68] Thus, the CESCR regards the right to food as being 'inseparable from social justice'.[69] The right to adequate water means adequate water for human dignity, life and health, where adequacy of water should also be treated as a social and cultural good, and not primarily as an economic good.[70] The right to education means the right to an education that is directed to the full development of the human personality and the sense of its dignity and which strengthens respect for human rights and fundamental freedoms. In a similar vein, the right

67 ICESCR (note 64), preambular paragraph 3.
68 See for example, CESCR, 'General Comment 12, Right to Adequate Food' in 'Compilation of General Comments and General Recommendations Adopted by Human Rights Treaty Bodies' (2003) UN Doc HRI/GEN/1/Rev.6, 62, para 4; CESCR, 'General Comment 13, Right to Education' in 'Compilation of General Comments and General Recommendations Adopted by Human Rights Treaty Bodies' (1999) UN Doc E/C.12/1999/10, para 4; CESCR, 'General Comment 15, The Right to Water' in 'Compilation of General Comments and General Recommendations Adopted by Human Rights Treaty Bodies' (2003) UN Doc HRI/GEN/1/Rev.6, para 1; and CESCR, 'General Comment 18, Article 6: The Equal Right of Men and Women to the Enjoyment of All Economic, Social and Cultural Rights' (2006) UN Doc E/C.12/GC/18, para 1.
69 CESCR, 'General Comment 12', ibid, para 4.
70 CESCR, 'General Comment 15' (n 68), para 11.

to work has been described as contributing simultaneously to the survival of the individual and his/her family, and to his/her development. This right also contributes to the individual's recognition within the community, where such work is freely accepted.[71]

The second theme is the role of economic and social rights in achieving social and economic equality, an achievement that has been assisted by an expansive interpretation of the content of these rights. Realisation of the right to food, for example, means the right, either individually or communally, to have physical and economic access at all times to adequate food or means for its procurement.[72] The right to water includes access to a system of water supply and management that provides equality of opportunity for people to enjoy the right to water.[73] In relation to the right to health, the Committee has interpreted that right as embracing a wide range of socio-economic factors that promote conditions in which people can lead a healthy life. This interpretation extends to the underlying determinants of health, such as food and nutrition, housing, access to safe and potable water and adequate sanitation, safe and healthy working conditions, and a healthy environment.[74] The right to work includes the right to decent work, that is, work that respects the fundamental rights of the human person, such as the right to safe working conditions and remuneration that allows workers to support themselves and their families.[75] According to the CESCR, the right to education is the primary vehicle by which economically and socially marginalised adults and children can lift themselves out of poverty and obtain the means to participate fully in their communities.[76] The right to education is also a right that enables all persons to participate effectively in a free society, promote understanding, tolerance and friendship amongst all nations and all racial, ethnic or religious groups, and further the activities of the UN for the maintenance of peace.[77]

A further feature of the elaboration of the content of economic and social rights is that they provide concrete examples of the interrelated nature of rights. The universal, indivisible, interdependent and interrelated nature of human rights was first recorded in the Universal Declaration with its inclusion of economic, social, cultural, civil and political rights. The interrelationship has been stressed in the Preambles to the ICESCR and the ICCPR, which recognises:

> that in accordance with the Universal Declaration of Human Rights, the ideal of free human beings enjoying freedom from fear and want can only be achieved if conditions are created whereby everyone may enjoy

71 CESCR, 'General Comment 18' (n 68), para 1.
72 CESCR, 'General Comment 12' (n 68), para 6. Also see para 8.
73 CESCR 'General Comment 15' (n 68), para 10.
74 ICESCR, 'General Comment 14, The Right to the Highest Attainable Standard of Health' in 'Compilation of General Comments and General Recommendations Adopted by Human Rights Treaty Bodies' (2003) UN Doc HRI/GEN/1/Rev.6, para 4.
75 CESCR, 'General Comment 18' (n 68), paras 6 and 7.
76 CESCR, 'General Comment 13' (n 68), para 1.
77 ICESCR (n 64), Article 13(1).

> his economic, social and cultural rights, as well as his civil and political rights.[78]

The Vienna Declaration was more specific with its statement that 'All human rights are universal, indivisible and interdependent and interrelated. The international community must treat human rights globally in a fair and equal manner, on the same footing, and with the same emphasis.'[79] The CESCR has reaffirmed these characteristics in its interpretive documents,[80] as have various 'soft law' principles elaborating on the meaning of the provisions of the Covenant.[81] All States are, therefore, obliged to observe and to protect all human rights and fundamental freedoms for all people in accordance with the UN Charter, other instruments relating to human rights, and international law. Not only that, the Human Rights Committee has stated that the right to life renders it desirable for States Parties to take all possible measures to reduce infant mortality and to

78 ICESCR, ibid, preambular para 3; Compare, ICCPR (n 65), preambular para 3. See also, International Conference on Human Rights, 'Proclamation of Teheran, Final Act of the International Conference on Human Rights Teheran 22 April–13 May 1968' (1968) UN Doc A/CONF.32/41 (Proclamation of Teheran), Article 13 states, 'Since human rights and fundamental freedoms are indivisible, the full realization of civil and political rights without the enjoyment of economic, social and cultural rights, is impossible.' In addition, the 'Alternative Approaches and Ways and Means within the United Nations System for Improving the Effective Enjoyment of Human Rights and Fundamental Freedoms' provides, 'All human rights and fundamental freedoms are indivisible and interdependent; equal attention and urgent consideration should be given to the implementation, promotion and protection of both civil and political, and economic, social and cultural rights'; UNGA Res 32/130 (16 December 1977) UN Doc A/RES/32/130 para 1(a).

79 World Conference on Human Rights 'Vienna Declaration and Programme of Action' (1993) UN Doc A/CONF.157/23, Article 5.

80 CESCR 'General Comment 10, The Role of National Human Rights Institutions in the Protection of Economic, Social and Cultural Rights' in 'Compilation of General Comments and General Recommendations Adopted by Human Rights Treaty Bodies' (2003) UN Doc HRI/GEN/1/Rev.6'; and CESCR 'General Comment 5, Persons with Disabilities' in 'Compilation of General Comments and General Recommendations Adopted by Human Rights Treaty Bodies' (2003) UN Doc HRI/GEN/1/Rev.6. See also, CEDAW 'General Recommendation 18, Disabled Women' in 'Compilation of General Comments and General Recommendations Adopted by Human Rights Treaty Bodies' (2003) UN Doc HRI/GEN/1/Rev.6; and UNCRC 'General Comment 5, General Measures of Implementation of the Convention on the Rights of the Child (arts. 4, 42 and 44, para. 6)' (2003) UN Doc CRC/GC/2003/5, paras 6 and 25.

81 See also, UNCHR, 'Note Verbale dated 86/12/05 from the Permanent Mission of the Netherlands to the United Nations Office at Geneva Addressed to the Centre for Human Rights' (8 January 1987) UN Doc E/CN.4/1987/17, Annex (the Limburg Principles) reprinted in (1987) 9(2) *Human Rights Quarterly* 122, Principle 3; and the Maastricht Guidelines on Violations of Economic, Social and Cultural Rights, Maastricht, 22–26 January 1997 (the Maastricht Guidelines) reprinted in (1998) 20(3) *Human Rights Quarterly* 691, Guideline 4; Victor Dankwa, Cees Flinterman and Scott Leckie, 'Commentary to the Maastricht Guidelines on Violations of Economic, Social and Cultural Rights' (1998) 20(3) *Human Rights Quarterly* 705, 711; Vienna Declaration and Programme of Action (n 79), Article 5; and Proclamation of Teheran (n 78), Article 13.

increase life expectancy.[82] More recently, the Special Rapporteur on the Right to Adequate Housing has called on the Human Rights Committee, as it drafts the new General Comment 36 on the right to life, to adopt an approach to the right to life that emphasises indivisibility and interdependence rather than seeking to distinguish the right to life from socio-economic rights such as the right to adequate housing.[83] Similarly, the European Court of Human Rights, as the arbiter of civil and political rights that make up the European Convention on Human Rights (the ECHR),[84] has not been prevented from decision-making that very obviously strays into the area of economic and social rights, as the following pronouncement from the Court indicates:

> Whilst the ECHR sets forth what are essentially civil and political rights, many of them have implications of a social or economic nature . . . The mere fact that an interpretation of the Convention may extend into the sphere of social and economic rights should not be a decisive factor against such an interpretation; there is no water-tight division.[85]

Views such as these affirm the interrelated and indivisible nature of human rights.

It is apparent therefore that the denial of economic and social rights can lead to the denial of civil and political rights. In a manner resonant of historical struggles to overcome the economic and social marginalisation of the poor, it has been observed that for the poor, ill-educated members of a society, the exercise of their civil and political rights may be displaced equally by the struggle to survive, as well as political decisions (both international and domestic) to curb the exercise of such rights.[86] The interdependent nature of civil, political, economic, social and cultural rights signals that effective promotion and protection of human rights is to be a broad-spectrum endeavour.

82 HRC, 'General Comment 6, Article 6' in 'Compilation of General Comments and General Recommendations Adopted by Human Rights Treaty Bodies' (1994) UN Doc HRI/GEN/1/Rev.1 regarding the right to life, para 5. See also, HRC, 'General Comment 31, Nature of the General Legal Obligation on States Parties to the Covenant' (2004) UN Doc CCPR/C/21/Rev.1/Add.13, para 8.

83 OHCHR, 'The Right to Life and the Right to Housing, Presentation to the Human Rights Committee, Special Rapporteur on Adequate Housing as a component of the Right to an Adequate Standard of Living and on the Right to Non-Discrimination in this regard, Ms Leilani Farha' (Geneva, 11 July 2016) 7 <http://www.ohchr.org/Documents/Issues/Housing/11072016_SR_Housing_Presentation-HR_Committee.pdf> accessed 3 October 2016.

84 Convention for the Protection of Human Rights and Fundamental Freedoms (adopted 4 November 1950, entered into force 3 September 1953) 213 UNTS 222 (ECHR).

85 *Airey v Ireland* (App no. 6289/73) (1979) 2 EHRR 305, para 26. See further, for example, Claire Breen, 'The Policy of Direct Provision in Ireland: A Violation of Asylum-seekers' Right to an Adequate Standard of Housing' (2008) 20(4) *International Journal of Refugee Law* 611, 618–623.

86 Ida Elisabeth Koch, 'The Justiciability of Indivisible Rights' (2003) 72(1) *Nordic Journal of International Law* 3.

4.2 Frameworks for effective realisation

The CESCR has provided further explanation of what economic and social rights entail by adopting a framework underpinned by the concepts of Accessibility, Acceptability, Availability and Quality (the AAAQ framework) – or variations thereof – to give practical effect to economic and social rights.

Accessibility as an aspect of the right to food, for example, means economic and physical accessibility. Economic accessibility means that the cost of acquiring food for an adequate diet should not mean that the attainment and satisfaction of other basic needs are threatened or compromised. Physical accessibility implies that adequate food must be accessible to everyone, including physically vulnerable individuals, as well as the mentally ill.[87] The rights to equality and non-discrimination are often considered as an aspect of the requirement of accessibility,[88] but these rights also exist independently, a point that will be discussed below.[89] Acceptability as an aspect of the right to health means that all health facilities, goods and services must be respectful of medical ethics and culturally appropriate, sensitive to gender and life-cycle requirements.[90] With regards to the right to education, availability means that there must be enough functioning educational institutions and programmes within the jurisdiction of the State Party. Functioning includes matters such as buildings or other protection from the elements, sanitation facilities for both sexes, safe drinking water, trained teachers receiving domestically competitive salaries, and teaching materials, with the attainment of such elements being dependent on a number of factors, including the developmental context.[91] Quality, as an aspect of the right to water, means water, that is for personal or domestic use, that must be safe and free from microorganisms, chemical substances and radiological hazards that constitute a threat to a person's health. It should also be of an acceptable colour, odour and taste.[92]

This brief summary highlights what the realisation of economic and social rights looks like. The next question is what States must do to realise these rights.

4.3 The nature of States' obligations

4.3.1 Challenges to the existence of States' obligations: Questions of enforceability and cost

Ratification of the ICESCR places States under an international legal obligation:

> to take steps, individually and through international assistance and co-operation, especially economic and technical, to the maximum of its available resources,

87 CESCR, 'General Comment 12' (n 68), para 13.

88 See, for example, CESCR, 'General Comment 15' (n 68), para 12(c)(iii); and CESCR, 'General Comment 13' (n 68), para 6(b)(i).

89 See Section 5 below.

90 CESCR, 'General Comment 14' (n 73), para 12(c).

91 CESCR, 'General Comment 13' (n 68), para 6(a).

92 CESCR, 'General Comment 15' (n 68), para 12(b).

> with a view to achieving progressively the full realization of the rights recognized in the present Covenant by all appropriate means, including particularly the adoption of legislative measures.[93]

The nature of this obligation has been the subject of much debate, which focused on the programmatic nature of economic and social rights, as well as their overlap with economic development and social policy. This focus led to the assertion that the implementation of such rights could not be a matter for the law and that compliance could not be adequately measured by the courts. Consequently, economic and social rights were regarded as not legally enforceable and, therefore, they were non-justiciable.[94] Consequently, economic and social rights came to be regarded as not being true human rights. However, such assertions have been countered on an increasing basis in the literature and in the courts.[95] The adoption of a complaints mechanism whereby the CESCR can hear complaints of alleged violations of the Covenant's rights is an important step in this regard.[96] A further challenge advanced against economic and social rights has been the financial investment – or cost – that is involved, whereas civil and political rights are regarded as being cost-free.[97] However, post-conflict situations that include retraining of the military and the police, the (re-)establishment of an independent judiciary, the need to provide vehicles and to train personnel to drive those vehicles, to (re)build police stations, courthouses and prisons and to raise the money

93 ICESCR (n 64), Article 2(1). See Fons Coomans, 'The Extraterritorial Scope of the International Covenant on Economic, Social and Cultural Rights in the Work of the United Nations Committee on Economic, Social and Cultural Rights' (2011) 11(1) *Human Rights Law Review* 1, 16 and 35 where the negotiating history of the ICESCR and the Optional Protocol is discussed.

94 See, generally, Paul Hunt, *Reclaiming Economic, Social and Cultural Rights: International and Comparative Perspectives* (Dartmouth Publishing Company Ltd, Aldershot 1996).

95 See, for example, Malcolm Langford (ed), *Social Rights Jurisprudence Emerging Trends in International and Comparative Law* (Cambridge University Press, Cambridge 2009); Mashood A Baderin and Robert McCorquodale (eds), *Economic, Social and Cultural Rights in Action* (Oxford University Press, Oxford, Toronto 2007); Aoife Nolan, Bruce Porter and Malcolm Langford, 'The Justiciability of Social and Economic Rights: An Updated Appraisal' (2009) CHRGJ Working Paper No. 15 <http://socialrightscura.ca/documents/publications/BP-justiciability-belfast.pdf> accessed 12 August 2016; International Commission of Jurists, *Courts and the Legal Enforcement of Economic, Social and Cultural Rights: Comparative Experiences of Justiciability* (International Commission of Jurists, Geneva 2008); and Egbert W Vierdag, 'The Legal Nature of the Rights Granted by the International Covenant on Economic, Social and Cultural Rights' (1978) 9 *Netherlands Yearbook of International Law* 69. See also, *The Government of the Republic of South Africa v Grootboom* (2000) 11 BCLR 1169 (CC), paras 28 and 38–44; and *Minister of Health v Treatment Action Campaign* (2002) 10 BCLR 1033, paras 68 and 100.

96 Arne Vandenbogaerde and Wouter Vandenhole, 'The Optional Protocol to the International Covenant on Economic, Social and Cultural Rights: An *Ex Ante* Assessment of its Effectiveness in Light of the Drafting Process' (2010) 10 *Human Rights Law Review* 207, 223–226.

97 Philip Alston and Gerard Quinn, 'The Nature and Scope of States Parties' Obligations under the International Covenant on Economic, Social and Cultural Rights' (1987) 9(2) *Human Rights Quarterly* 156, 172 and 184.

to pay for the personnel – who should be adequately educated in human rights norms – somewhat belies this 'cost-free' concept of civil and political rights. According to Alston and Quinn:

> The reality is that the full realization of civil and political rights is heavily dependent both on the availability of resources and the development of the necessary societal structures. The suggestion that realization of civil and political rights requires only abstention on the part of the State and can be achieved without significant expenditure is patently at odds with reality.[98]

The CESCR has elaborated the nature of States' obligations stemming from Article 2(1). It regards the obligation to 'take steps' as being an obligation of immediate effect.[99] This means that States must show that, within a reasonably short period of time, steps are being taken to achieve that goal and that the steps in question are 'deliberate, concrete and targeted as clearly as possible towards meeting the obligations recognized in the Covenant'.[100] Whilst the requirement to take steps creates an immediate obligation, the obligation to realise progressively relates to States' obligation to realise the Covenant's rights *in full*. In this way, the obligation can act as both a measurement tool as well as a planning tool. However, it is recognised that this obligation is highly dependent on a State having adequate resources and that the availability of such resources may vary from one State to another depending on its level of economic development.[101] However, it must still be read in conjunction with the obligations to take steps with the effect that 'the State cannot use the "progressive realisation" provisions in Article 2 of the Covenant as a pretext for non-compliance.'[102]

The progressive realisation of the ICESCR's rights in full must also be balanced with the obligation upon States to meet a minimum core obligation to ensure the satisfaction of minimum essential levels of each of the Covenant's

98 Ibid, 172.

99 CESCR, 'General Comment 3, The Nature of States Parties' Obligations' in 'Compilation of General Comments and General Recommendations Adopted by Human Rights Treaty Bodies' (2003) UN Doc HRI/GEN/1/Rev.6, paras 1 and 2.

100 Ibid, para 2; CESCR, 'General Comment 1, Reporting by States Parties' in 'Compilation of General Comments and General Recommendations Adopted by Human Rights Treaty Bodies' (2003) UN Doc HRI/GEN/1/Rev.6; CESCR, 'General Comment 2, International Technical Assistance Measures' in 'Compilation of General Comments and General Recommendations Adopted by Human Rights Treaty Bodies' (2003) UN Doc HRI/GEN/1/Rev.6; CESCR, 'General Comment 3', ibid; UNESC, 'Revised General Guidelines Regarding The Form and Contents of Reports to be Submitted by States Parties under Articles 16 and 17 of the International Covenant on Economic, Social and Cultural Rights 1991/1' (1991) UN Doc E/C.12/1991/1; and CESCR, 'General Comment 9, The Domestic Application of the Covenant' in 'Compilation of General Comments and General Recommendations Adopted by Human Rights Treaty Bodies' (2003) UN Doc HRI/GEN/1/Rev.6.

101 CESCR, 'General Comment 3' (n 99), para 9.

102 Maastricht Guidelines (n 81), para 8.

rights.[103] A State must demonstrate that every effort has been made to use all resources that are at its disposal in an effort to satisfy, as a matter of priority, those minimum obligations.[104] Thus, for example, a State in which any significant number of individuals, including children, is deprived of essential foodstuffs, of essential primary health care, of basic shelter and housing or of the most basic forms of education is, *prima facie*, failing to discharge its obligations under the Covenant. In this regard, it is noted that the drafters of the Covenant intended Article 2(1)'s provision regarding 'maximum available resources' to span both the resources existing within a State and those available from the international community through international cooperation and assistance,[105] a point that will be revisited below.

The obligations in Article 2(1) must also be read in light of the limitations clause in Article 4 of the ICESCR, which allows States to impose limitations in the enjoyment of the rights contained in the Covenant, though the imposition of such limitations is itself subject to restrictions. To that end, Article 4 provides that limitations can only be imposed in conformity with the law and 'for the purpose of protecting the general welfare in a democratic society',[106] where 'general welfare' primarily refers to the economic and social well-being of individuals and the community, and excludes notions of 'public morals', 'public order', and 'national security'.[107] Any deliberately retrogressive act requires the most careful consideration and full justification by reference to the totality of the rights provided for in the Covenant and in the context of the full use of the maximum available resources.[108] When they are read together, Article 2(1) and Article 4 give States, especially those that may be struggling with the political instability and its attendant economic difficulties that may flow from the post-conflict environment, some flexibility to deal with the negative impact of armed conflict. However, the ICESCR makes no provision allowing States to derogate from their Covenant obligations in times of public emergency.[109] Derogation from 'survival rights' such as the rights to water, food and health are not necessary to restore

103 Ibid, para 9.

104 Ibid, para 10.

105 Compare, the Limburg Principles (n 81) and the Maastricht Guidelines (n 81). See also, Judith Bueno de Mesquita, Paul Hunt and Rajat Khosla, 'The Human Rights Responsibility of International Assistance and Cooperation in Health' in Mark Gibney and Sigrun Skogly (eds), *Universal Human Rights and Extraterritorial Obligations* (University of Pennsylvania Press, Philadelphia 2010); but see also, CESCR, 'General Comment 14' (n 74), para 45 where the Committee emphasises that it is incumbent on States in a position to do so, to provide assistance and cooperation.

106 See further, Alston and Quinn (n 97), 198, 205–206.

107 Ibid, 201–02; and Amrei Muller, 'Limitations to and Derogations from Economic, Social and Cultural Rights' (2009) 9(4) *Human Rights Law Review* 557, 570–575.

108 CESCR, 'General Comment 3' (n 99), para 9. See generally Muller, ibid, 569.

109 Amrei Muller, 'The Right To Health and International Humanitarian Law: Parallel Application for Building Peaceful Societies and the Prevention of Armed Conflict' (2014) 32(3) *Wisconsin International Law Journal* (2014) 415, 422–424.

public order,[110] but the CESCR and the ILO have accepted derogations from labour rights in times of armed conflict and other emergencies that 'threaten the life of the nation'.[111]

Obligations stemming from the ratification of the ICESCR should also be read in light of Article 8 of the Universal Declaration which sets out the right to an effective remedy by competent national tribunals for acts in violation of fundamental rights. In this regard, the CESCR is itself very clear on the nature of States' obligations:

> It is sometimes suggested that matters involving the allocation of resources should be left to the political authorities rather than the courts. While the respective competences of the various branches of government must be respected, it is appropriate to acknowledge that courts are generally already involved in a considerable range of matters which have important resource implications. The adoption of a rigid classification of economic, social and cultural rights which puts them, by definition, beyond the reach of the courts would thus be arbitrary and incompatible with the principle that the two sets of human rights are indivisible and interdependent. It would also drastically curtail the capacity of the courts to protect the rights of the most vulnerable and disadvantaged groups in society.[112]

Debates on the justiciable nature of economic and social rights stemming from their cost must also be viewed in light of this assessment.

4.3.2 Affirming and explaining the nature of States' obligations: The obligations to respect, protect and fulfil

Further substantial clarification of States' obligations has been achieved with the adoption of a tripartite framework comprising the obligations to respect, to protect and to fulfil.[113] The obligation to respect requires States to refrain from interfering with the enjoyment of economic and social rights. The obligation to protect requires States to prevent violations of such rights by third parties. The obligation to fulfil requires States to take appropriate legislative, administrative, budgetary, judicial and other measures towards the full realisation of such rights. Failure to perform any one of these three obligations constitutes a violation of such rights.[114] This tripartite approach has been elaborated subsequently by analysing the nature

110 Ibid, 599; Allan Rosas and Monika Sandvik-Nylund, 'Armed Conflicts' in Eide (n 29); and Alston and Quinn (n 97), 217.

111 Muller (n 107), 594–597.

112 CESCR, 'General Comment 9' (n 100), para 10. See also, UNCRC, 'General Comment 5' (n 80), paras 6 and 25.

113 Henry Shue, *Basic Rights: Subsistence, Affluence and U.S. Foreign Policy* (2nd edn, Princeton University Press, Princeton 1996) 52.

114 Ibid.

of States' obligations with regards to particular rights. For example, the obligation to respect, as an aspect of the right to water, means that States must refrain from engaging in any practice or activity that denies or limits equal access to adequate water, arbitrarily interferes with customary or traditional arrangements for water allocation, unlawfully diminishes or pollutes water, or limits access to, or destroys, water services and infrastructure as a punitive measure.[115] Violations of this obligation would arise from actions such as arbitrary or unjustified disconnection or exclusion from water services or facilities, discriminatory or unaffordable increases in the price of water, and the pollution and diminution of water resources affecting human health.[116] Availability is regarded as being an essential feature of the right to education and, thus, the obligation to respect entails respecting the availability of education by not closing private schools.[117]

Obligations to protect the right to adequate health include the duties of States to adopt legislation or to take other measures ensuring equal access to health care and health-related services provided by third parties and to ensure that medical practitioners and other health professionals meet appropriate standards of education, skill and ethical codes of conduct. States should also ensure that third parties do not limit people's access to health-related information and services.[118] Violations of the obligation to protect the right to adequate health follow from the failure of a State to take all necessary measures to safeguard persons within their jurisdiction from infringements of the right to health by third parties, such as the failure to protect women against violence or the failure to enact or enforce laws to prevent the pollution of water, air and soil by extractive and manufacturing industries.[119] The obligation to protect has also been linked to accessibility as a core feature of the right to education so that the obligation to protect the accessibility of education means, for example, that States must ensure that third parties, including parents and employers, do not stop girls from going to school.[120]

The obligation to fulfil (facilitate) the right to adequate food, for example, means the State must proactively engage in activities intended to strengthen people's access to and utilisation of resources and means to ensure their livelihood, including food security. It can also mean that States have the obligation to fulfil (provide) that right directly in situations where an individual or group is unable, for reasons beyond their control, to enjoy the right to adequate food by means at their disposal. This obligation also applies for persons who are victims of natural or other disasters.[121] The obligation to fulfil the right to health requires States to

115 CESCR, 'General Comment 15' (n 68), para 21. The obligation to respect also means that during armed conflicts, emergency situations and natural disasters, the right to water embraces those obligations by which States Parties are bound under international humanitarian law: para 22.

116 Ibid, para 44(a).

117 CESCR, 'General Comment 13' (n 68), para 50.

118 CESCR, 'General Comment 14' (n 74), para 35.

119 Ibid, para 51.

120 CESCR, 'General Comment 13' (n 68), para 50.

121 CESCR, 'General Comment 12' (n 68), para 15.

ensure the provision of health care, including immunisation programmes against major infectious diseases, and to ensure equal access for all to the underlying determinants of health, such as nutritiously safe food and potable drinking water, basic sanitation and adequate housing and living conditions.[122] Violations of this obligation occur when States, for example, fail to adopt or implement a national health policy designed to ensure the right to health for everyone; to monitor the realisation of the right to health at the national level, for example by identifying right to health indicators and benchmarks; take measures to reduce the inequitable distribution of health facilities, goods and services; to adopt a gender-sensitive approach to health; or, to reduce infant and maternal mortality rates.[123] A further example of the obligation to fulfil can be seen with the right to work which places States under an obligation to adopt appropriate legislative, administrative, budgetary, judicial and other measures to ensure the full realisation of this right.[124] A violation of this right would occur where a State failed to adopt or implement a national employment policy designed to ensure the right to work for everyone or took actions such as the provision of insufficient expenditure or the misallocation of public funds resulting in the non-enjoyment of the right to work by individuals or groups, particularly the disadvantaged and marginalised.[125]

A number of key points emerge from the above paragraphs. Economic and social rights are true human rights; the contents of these rights have been elaborated in some detail, as have the nature of States' obligations. The evolution of economic and social rights is significant because it elaborates a legal basis for the establishment of a minimum core set of social and economic conditions, as well as a legal basis for the continued advancement of these conditions. The obligations for States that flow from the establishment of these core and progressive rights provide a clear framework for State action and any violative conduct that States are to avoid. Whilst earlier State action may have been driven by a degree of self-interest in maintaining a secure order, either domestic or international, it, nonetheless, facilitated a more rounded notion of citizenship. The current framework of economic and social rights gives a legal basis to both such endeavours but with an important difference which is the recognition of the individual as a rights holder rather than the disempowered recipient of charity or welfare. This latter development underpins the conceptualisation of economic and social progress and human rights in the ensuing chapters.

5 The rights to equality and non-discrimination: Fundamental principles for economic and social rights

In the context of this work, the greatest problem with systemic social exclusion and its attendant inequalities is the degree to which the disparities are based on,

122 CESCR, 'General Comment 14' (n 74), para 36.
123 Ibid, para 52.
124 CESCR, 'General Comment 18' (n 68), para 22.
125 Ibid, para 36.

or perceived to be due to, discriminatory exclusions and therefore injustice so that failures in basic service delivery, such as education, health services, water, and transport and energy infrastructure, can lead to conflict.[126] The CESCR has also noted that 'Economic growth has not, in itself, led to sustainable development, and individuals and groups of individuals continue to face socio-economic inequality, often because of entrenched historical and contemporary forms of discrimination.'[127] Thus, efforts to improve socio-economic conditions can only benefit from adopting an approach that spells out the content of the rights to equality and non-discrimination rights as they apply to economic and social rights.

As noted above, the inclusion of economic and social rights in the UDHR was prompted by the suffering endured by millions of people during WWII. Many of these millions were specifically targeted because they were members of minority groups. In order to prevent a recurrence of such targeted suffering, the UN Charter reaffirms the equal rights of men and women,[128] whilst Article 1(3) encourages 'respect for human rights and for fundamental freedoms for all without distinction as to race, sex, language, or religion'. All but one of the six other references to human rights within the Charter are followed by the phrase 'without discrimination on the basis of race, sex, language or religion'. The principle of equality is also reaffirmed in the Universal Declaration which proclaims that the 'equal and inalienable rights of all members of the human family is the foundation of freedom, justice and peace in the world',[129] whilst Article 1 states, 'All human beings are born free and equal in dignity and rights.' Article 2 reiterates that 'Everyone is entitled to all the rights and freedoms set forth in this Declaration, without distinction of any kind, such as race, colour, sex, language, religion, political or other opinion, national or social origin, property, birth or other status.' Article 7 brings both rights together with its statement that 'All are equal before the law and are entitled without any discrimination to equal protection of the law.'

The Preamble to the ICESCR recognises the inherent dignity and the equal and inalienable rights of all members of the human family, whilst Article 2(2) states that the Covenant's rights 'will be exercised without discrimination of any kind as to race, colour, sex, language, religion, political or other opinion, national or social origin, property, birth or other status'. The CESCR regards the rights to equality and non-discrimination as being 'an immediate and cross-cutting obligation in the Covenant'.[130] Thus, States must show that they are taking steps to realise these rights quite quickly after ratification. According to the Committee,

126 Frances Stewart, 'Policies towards Horizontal Inequalities in Post-conflict Reconstruction' (2005) CRISE Working Paper No. 7 <http://www3.qeh.ox.ac.uk/pdf/crisewps/workingpaper7.pdf> accessed 15 August 2016.

127 CESCR, 'General Comment 20, Non-Discrimination in Economic, Social and Cultural Rights (art. 2, para. 2)' (2009) UN Doc E/C.12/GC/20, para 1.

128 UN Charter (n 2), preambular paragraph 2.

129 UDHR (n 54), preambular paragraph 1.

130 CESCR, 'General Comment 20' (n 127), para 7.

such steps can include the adoption of legislation and/or the adoption of policies, plans and strategies to eliminate formal and/or substantive inequality.[131] In terms of the nature and extent of States' obligations under Article 2(1) of the ICESCR, the Committee has also stated that:

> A failure to remove differential treatment on the basis of lack of available resources is not an objective and reasonable justification unless every effort has been made to use all resources that are at a State Party's disposition in an effort to address and eliminate the discrimination, as a matter of priority.[132]

All human beings have the right to equality, a right that is enumerated in treaty and customary law, irrespective of the individual's status or his/her membership of any particular group. The right to non-discrimination is a separate right, which has evolved to deal with the consequences of the failure to secure the right to equality. It affirms the right of everyone 'without distinction' to enjoy all human rights and fundamental freedoms.

The rights to equality and non-discrimination encompass formal and substantive elements. Formal equality (de jure equality) focuses on consistency of treatment rather than the outcome of such treatment. This version of equality reflects the view that no one group should be given preferential treatment and that individuals should be treated solely on their individual merit, regardless of whether they belong to a group. Substantive equality includes calls for equality of opportunity which requires the removal of barriers to the advancement of vulnerable or disadvantaged groups with the aim to redress past inequalities of treatment. Although States are required to ensure that their constitutions, laws and policy documents do not discriminate on prohibited grounds (formal discrimination), ratification of the ICESCR immediately requires States to adopt the necessary measures to prevent, diminish and eliminate the conditions and attitudes that cause or perpetuate substantive or de facto discrimination. For example, non-discrimination is an underpinning feature of accessibility and the rights to water,[133] food,[134] and health.[135] This feature means that States must ensure that all individuals have equal access to adequate housing, water and sanitation that, for example, will help to overcome discrimination against women and girl children and persons living in informal settlements and rural areas.[136]

Discrimination for the purposes of the ICESCR means both direct and indirect discrimination. Thus, the Covenant prohibits the less favourable treatment of an individual when compared to another in a similar situation for a reason related to a

131 CESCR, 'General Comment 20' (n 127), paras 37 and 38.
132 Ibid, para 13.
133 CESCR, 'General Comment 15' (n 68), para 12(c)(iii) and more generally, paras 13–16.
134 CESCR, 'General Comment 12' (n 68), para 18.
135 CESCR, 'General Comment 14' (n 74), para 12(b)(i).
136 CESCR 'General Comment 20' (n 127), para 8.

prohibited ground (direct discrimination). However, the Covenant's prohibition on discrimination also covers situations of indirect discrimination that allows an individual to challenge conduct, policies or practices which appear neutral but have a disproportionate impact on the exercise of the Covenant rights as distinguished by prohibited grounds of discrimination.[137] The right to non-discrimination also covers laws or policies that specifically disadvantage members of certain groups where there is a failure to take into account the impact of such conduct on the specific situation of members of certain groups (unintentional discrimination). For example, in relation to the right to water, the CESCR has stated that investments in water should not disproportionately favour expensive water supply services and facilities that are often accessible only to a small, privileged fraction of the population.[138]

International human rights law and its interpretive bodies also recognise that differential treatment having a negative impact may not comprise discrimination. The CESCR has stated:

> Differential treatment based on prohibited grounds will be viewed as discriminatory unless the justification for differentiation is reasonable and objective. This will include an assessment as to whether the aim and effects of the measures or omissions are legitimate, compatible with the nature of the Covenant rights and solely for the purpose of promoting the general welfare in a democratic society. In addition, there must be a clear and reasonable relationship of proportionality between the aim sought to be realised and the measures or omissions and their effects.[139]

This view of the right to non-discrimination reflects one whereby the right is regarded as entailing the positive obligation to eliminate the social and institutional structures that perpetuate disadvantage to, and exclusion of, members of vulnerable groups. Such preferential treatment is permitted on the basis that the prioritisation of the achievement of substantive equality over the requirement of consistent treatment is legitimate or even required. Similarly, the right to equality 'does not mean identical treatment in every instance',[140] and the principle of equality sometimes requires States Parties to take affirmative action in order to correct discrimination, in which case it is a case of legitimate differentiation.[141] In terms of the right to health, for example, the CESCR has identified women, children and young people, persons with disabilities and

137 Ibid, para 10(b).
138 CESCR, 'General Comment 15' (n 68), para 14.
139 CESCR, 'General Comment 20' (n 127), para 13.
140 HRC, 'General Comment 18, Non-Discrimination' in 'Compilation of General Comments and General Recommendations Adopted by Human Rights Treaty Bodies' (1994) UN Doc HRI/GEN/1/Rev 1, para 8.
141 CESCR, 'General Comment 20' (n 127), para 13.

indigenous peoples as groups potentially in need of targeted measures to overcome unequal access to the goods and services that underpin the right to adequate health.[142]

Other UN and regional treaties that contain economic and social rights are also underpinned by the rights to equality and non-discrimination.[143] Most notable amongst these provisions is Article 26 of the ICCPR, which contains an autonomous right to equality, which extends the right to equality beyond those rights contained in the Covenant.[144] The right to non-discrimination on the grounds of race and gender (as well as religion) has also become part of customary international law.[145]

The elaboration of the rights to equality and non-discrimination[146] is especially significant given that acts or omissions that can be cast as violations of the rights to equality and non-discrimination within the context of economic and social rights have been drivers for claims of violations of economic and social rights.

6 Monitoring economic and social rights: The nature and role of indicators

Ratification of the ICESCR requires States to report on the manner and extent to which they have realised the rights contained in the Covenant;[147] this requirement is a core obligation and is effective immediately. Monitoring of economic and social rights can include monitoring legislation, policies and budgets, as well

142 CESCR, 'General Comment 14' (n 74), paras 21–27.

143 ICERD (n 64); CEDAW (n 64); Convention Relating to the Status of Refugees (adopted 28 July 1951, entered into force 22 April 1954) 189 UNTS 137; the Convention Relating to the Status of Stateless Persons (adopted 28 September 1954, entered into force 6 June 1960) 360 UNTS 117; CRC (n 64); Migrant Workers Convention (n 64); and CRPD (n 64). Other instruments protecting economic and social specifically prohibit discrimination such as the ILO No. 111 Convention Concerning Discrimination in Employment and Occupation (adopted 25 June 1958, entered into force 15 June 1960) 362 UNTS 31; UNESCO Convention Against Discrimination in Education (adopted 14 December 1960, entered into force 22 May 1962) 1960 UNTS 429; and Organization of American States, Inter-American Convention on the Elimination of All Forms of Discrimination against Persons with Disabilities (adopted 7 June 1999, entered into force 4 September 2001) OAS AG/Res 1608.

144 See also, CESCR, 'General Comment 20' (n 127), para 5. See also, *S W M Broeks v The Netherlands* (Communication No. 172/1984) (1990) UN Doc CCPR/C/OP/2, para 12.3.

145 Regarding race, see *Barcelona Traction (Second Phases)* [1970] ICJ Rep 3, para 34. In the *Legal Consequences for States of the Continued Presence of South Africa in Namibia (South-West Africa) Notwithstanding Security Council Resolution* 276 (1970) (Advisory Opinion) [1971] ICJ Rep 16 *(Namibia Advisory Opinion)*, at para 131, the ICJ also held that South Africa's denial of human rights on the basis of race constituted 'flagrant violation of the purposes and principles of the Charter'.

146 See, in particular, Ben Saul, David Kinley and Jaqueline Mowbray, *The International Covenant on Economic, Social and Cultural Rights: Commentary, Cases, and Materials* (Oxford University Press, Oxford 2014), Chapters 4 and 6.

147 ICESCR (n 64), Article 16.

as judicial and quasi-judicial responses to such rights. Such monitoring can take place generally or in relation to specific events.

Monitoring the efforts of States has been facilitated by the development of human rights indicators and benchmarks.[148] The rationale for using indicators was recognised as far back as 1990 on the basis that:

> without the availability of a measurement device based on some form of statistical data, there is little chance of obtaining an overall picture which shows the extent which these rights are realised . . . Additionally, indicators can help to reveal some of the difficulties associated with fulfilling these rights.[149]

Human rights indicators are the translation of human rights standards into measurable units with a view to determining the extent to which States abide by international human rights law. Measurable units means information that, at a minimum, is quantitative (units that can be counted). Quantitative information can be complemented by qualitative information (such as subjective statements or personal stories), which can provide some context for the quantitative data (a point which will be considered again below). The framework for identifying what States must do as a consequence of ratification of human rights treaties, such as the ICESCR, has led to the creation of a number of frameworks of indicators and benchmarks that may provide a reference tool to measure the effectiveness of peace operations in realising human rights, and economic and social rights in particular. The OHCHR has also developed a guide on human rights indicators, the aim of which:

> is to highlight the human rights norms and principles, spell out the essential attributes of the rights enshrined in international instruments and translate this narrative into contextually relevant indicators and benchmarks for implementing and measuring human rights at country level.[150]

148 Audrey R Chapman, 'A "Violations Approach" for Monitoring the International Covenant on Economic, Social and Cultural Rights' (1996) 18(1) *Human Rights Quarterly* 24; Gauthier de Beco, 'Human Rights Indicators for Assessing State Compliance with International Human Rights' (2008) 77(1–2) *Nordic Journal of International Law* 23; Maria Green, 'What We Talk About When We Talk About Indicators: Current Approaches to Human Rights Measurement' (2001) 23(4) *Human Rights Quarterly* 1065; Shareen Hertel and Lanse Minkler, 'Economic and Social Rights: The Terrain' in Shareen Hertel and Lanse Minkler (eds), *Economic Rights: Conceptual Measurement and Policy Issues* (Cambridge University Press, Cambridge 2007), 1; Todd Landman, 'Measuring Human Rights: Principles, Practice, Policy' (2004) 26(4) *Human Rights Quarterly* 906; Todd Landman and Edzia Carvalho, *Measuring Human Rights* (Routledge, Oxon 2010); and Sakiko Fukuda-Parr, 'Millennium Development Goal 8: Indicators for International Human Rights Obligations?' (2006) 28(4) *Human Rights Quarterly* 966.

149 UNCHR (Sub-Commission), 'Report by Special Rapporteur Danilo Turk 1990/19' (1990) UN Doc E/CN.4/Sub.2/1990/19, para 7.

150 OHCHR, 'Human Rights Indicators: A Guide to Measurement and Implementation' (HR/PUB/12/5, United Nations 2012) iii <http://www.ohchr.org/Documents/Publications/Human_rights_indicators_en.pdf> accessed 25 August 2016.

Given the increasing interaction between the Security Council and the OHCHR, this chapter will focus on the OHCHR's Guide, which has defined a human rights indicator as:

> specific information on the state or condition of an object, event, activity or outcome that can be related to human rights norms and standards; that addresses and reflects human rights principles and concerns; and that can be used to assess and monitor the promotion and implementation of human rights.[151]

Indicators help to identify the type of information that needs to be gathered, which can assist, for example, UN country teams to report to the CESCR. Indicators may be useful when monitoring the specific situation of a given province/region or a particular sector of the population and they can facilitate the identification of human rights priorities to be measured against objective parameters. Human rights indicators also contribute to the human rights endeavour by setting objective benchmarks by which to monitor human rights.

One approach to the identification of indicators has been to establish a framework of structural, process and outcome indicators (and benchmarks) that allows States to understand and organise their efforts to meet their economic and social rights obligations. The process of tailoring is further facilitated by the AAAQ framework,[152] which will be considered below. The effect is to tease out the different obligations of States that are dependent on the level of control that States have over the achievement of the difference types of indicators and the setting of benchmarks.[153] The context in which indicators are identified and utilised is important, particularly given the spectrum of obligations stemming from Article 2(1) of the ICESCR. The selection and utilisation of indicators must be tailored to account for the impact of particular situations such as armed conflict, natural disasters or States transitioning from conflict during the evaluation process,[154] an issue that is of particular importance when measuring extraterritorial obligations.

151 Ibid, 16. See also, Green (n 148); Hertel (n 148); Landman (n 148); and Landman and Carvalho (n 148).

152 Gauthier de Beco, 'Human Rights Indicators: From Theoretical Debate to Practical Application' (2013) 5(2) *Journal of Human Rights Practice* 380, 384.

153 OHCHR, 'Report on Indicators for Promoting and Monitoring the Implementation of International Human Rights Instruments 2008/3' (2008) UN Doc HRI/MC/2008/3, para 17; the Limburg Principles (n 81), para 71; IACHR, 'Guidelines for Preparation of Progress Indicators in the Area of Economic, Social and Cultural Rights' (5 October 2007) OEA/Ser/ L/V/II. 129, Doc. 5, paras 31–32; the Maastricht Guidelines (n 81), paras 14–15; and Sital Kalantry, Jocelyn Getgen Kestenbaum and Stephen Arrigg Koh, 'Enhancing Enforcement of Economic, Social, and Cultural Rights Using Indicators: A Focus on the Right to Education in the ICESCR' (2010) 32(2) *Human Rights Quarterly* 253, 295–296.

154 de Beco (n 152), 386–387.

Structural indicators help to assess the acceptance, intent and commitment of States to undertake measures in keeping with their human rights obligations.[155] Process indicators help in assessing States' efforts, through their implementation of policy measures and programmes of action, to transform their human rights commitments into the desired results.[156] These are sensitive to changes and are better at capturing the progressive realisation of a right or State efforts to protect rights.[157] Therefore, whilst structural indicators focus on the existence of domestic laws that comply with international treaty obligations, process indicators answer the question of what mechanisms the State has put in place to implement its existing laws towards the realisation of the right. Outcome indicators measure the extent to which human rights are effectively enjoyed in a given context,[158] with States being held responsible for outcomes even if the result could not be directly linked to their policies or practices.[159] Thus, process indicators measure the quality and extent of government strategies, whereas outcome indicators measure the actual impact of those strategies.[160] States tend to have a higher level of control over the obligations that structural and process indicators measure than they do over the obligations that outcome indicators measure. As a result, violations are more clearly attributable to State failures when looking at structure and process indicators. On the other hand, States have a lower level of control over the obligations that outcome indicators measure. In assessing violations, taking into account the level of State control is important because it adds legitimacy, reasonableness and fairness to the evaluation process.[161]

Related to this process is the setting of benchmarks which, in the context of assessing the compliance of State Parties, strengthen States' accountability by making them commit to a certain performance standard on the issue under assessment[162] that is contingent on the nature of the rights and the resources of

155 OHCHR (n 150), 34, Box 5. See also, OHCHR (n 153), para 18; the Limburg Principles (n 81), para 79; and the Maastricht Guidelines (n 81), para 15(f). See Claire Breen, 'Progressing Towards Peace? States' Extraterritorial Obligations in Peace Operations and the Added Value of Human Rights Indicators' (2015) 9 (2) *Human Rights and International Legal Discourse* 123.

156 OHCHR (n 150) 36. IACHR (n 153), para 31 states that process indicators 'measure the quality and extent of state efforts to implement rights by measuring the scope, coverage, and content of strategies, plans, programs, or policies, or other specific activities and interventions designed to accomplish the goals necessary for the realisation of [the right]'.

157 OHCHR (n 153), para 19.

158 OHCHR (n 150), 37.

159 See Sigrun I Skogly, 'Causality and Extraterritorial Human Rights Obligations' in Malcolm Langford and others (eds), *Global Justice, State Duties: The Extraterritorial Scope of Economic, Social and Cultural Rights in International Law* (Cambridge University Press, New York 2013) 233.

160 IACHR (n 153), paras 31–32.

161 Breen (n 155), 141.

162 OHCHR (n 150), 20. See also, CESCR, 'General Comment 12' (n 68), para 29; CESCR, 'General Comment 13' (n 68) para 52; CESCR, 'General Comment 14' (n 74) paras 57–58; and CESCR, 'General Comment 15' (n 68), paras 53–54.

the State. Deviations from benchmarks can be considered violations.[163] Structural benchmarks are mostly resource independent and thus harder to avoid. Deviations from process benchmarks may be more excusable as they are often based on resource-intensive benchmarks. As regards outcome benchmarks, it may be very difficult for the Committee to criticise these outcomes if a State has met its structural and process benchmarks and where there are factors that the State cannot control, or can influence but only with great difficulty.[164] Similar to the issue of indicators, the issue of State control is particularly significant in the context of the extraterritorial application of economic and social rights in peacekeeping operations.

There are three broad sources of human rights indicators. The first, events-based, qualitative or quantitative data, is primarily useful for measuring economic and social rights that must be realised immediately, such as the rights to non-discrimination and equality. The second, socio-economic (or statistical) data, comprises aggregated data sets upon which there is strong consensus, providing quantitative or qualitative information on the living conditions of the citizens of a State.[165] They often measure standards of living, literacy levels, infant mortality and other facets of life that also relate to economic and social rights. Socio-economic data that are linked to human rights treaty standards, and disaggregated, are most relevant for measuring trends in the extent to which economic and social rights are being progressively realised in a State. Such data may explain the reasons behind certain socio-economic statistics by completing, confirming or questioning other kinds of data. As such, socio-economic indicators can be used as a human rights indicator.[166] Finally, as a preliminary indicator of the human rights situation in a State, data based on expert judgements comprise the evaluation of the performance of States, using cardinal or ordinal scales and sets of relevant criteria or 'checklists'.[167]

Indicators help to make policy and human rights planning and monitoring more efficient and transparent. Advances have been made in the creation of measurement tools that capture quantitative and qualitative data. The ESRF Index seeks to overcome challenges that economic and social rights are vague in nature

163 See Eibe Riedel, 'The IBSA Procedure as a Tool of Human Rights Monitoring' (2009) 74 <http://riedel.uni-mannheim.de/inhalt/unterdokumente/downloads/ibsa/ibsa2/2_the_ibsa_procedure_as_a_tool_of_human_rights_monitoring_1_1.pdf> accessed 3 October 2016.

164 Ibid.

165 Breen (n 155), 142. See further, Fukuda-Parr (n 148), 978; and Polly Vizard, Sakiko Fukuda-Parr and Diane Elson, 'Introduction: The Capability Approach and Human Rights' (2011) 12(1) *Journal of Human Development and Capabilities* 1, 8. However, the utilisation of such indicators has not been without debate: Ann Janette Rosga and Margaret L Satterthwaite, 'The Trust in Indicators: Measuring Human Rights' (2009) 27(2) *Berkeley Journal of International Law* 253, 279–287.

166 OHCHR (n 153), para 13.

167 Kalantry (n 153), 287.

by using available survey-based objective data that focus on State obligations and capture the progressive realisation of human rights so as to increase the rigour of human rights measurement.[168] The OPERA framework combines a range of methodologies and tools to address the multidimensional factors affecting the assessment of economic and social rights by identifying how poor human rights outcomes may be linked to deficiencies in social and economic policies and programmes.[169] The CESCR has identified discrimination against vulnerable groups, in particular as a cross cutting theme which means that data that inform human rights indicators must be disaggregated by gender, race, ethnicity and age, minority and the other grounds of discrimination prohibited by the ICESCR and other human rights treaties. More significantly, however, is that the obligation to eliminate discrimination is an obligation of immediate effect, and so although these obligations must take into account a post-conflict situation, that situation does not allow a State contributing to peacekeeping to sidestep its obligations in this regard.

Substantive data is useful in taking account of information about a country's socio-economic situation, poverty levels or demographics. However, such information alone is not sufficient to monitor State compliance with obligations stemming from economic and social rights, as the absence of disaggregated information may fail to show a specific violation, or to provide the nuances needed to understand a specific event. It is because of this potential for masking outcomes that the disaggregation of information is critical to monitoring discrimination and inequality, especially in the context of the link between armed violence and socio-economic exclusion, despite the challenges of cost and determining with certainty who is a member of a vulnerable group. Disaggregated information can reveal the de facto discriminatory nature of some policies and laws that would otherwise appear neutral, such as the impact on an ethnic minority of closing down a school in a particular neighbourhood.

Whichever form of data is utilised, the problem of collection, compilation and disaggregation is one that may be exacerbated in fragile or post-conflict societies where there may be difficulty in accessing historical data and/or where there is a complete lack of up-to-date data of the necessary quality.[170] Such difficulties should not stand in the way of selecting and contextualising indicators at the State level and ensuring that they measure the participation of the populace in decisions affecting both institutional design and policy priorities in the field of human rights. Field presences can urge national authorities to collect data

168 Sakiko Fukuda-Parr, Terra Lawson-Remer and Susan Randolph, 'An Index of Economic and Social Rights Fulfillment: Concept and Methodology' (2009) 8(3) *Journal of Human Rights* 195, 198.

169 Allison Corkery and Sally-Anne Way, 'Integrating Quantitative and Qualitative Tools to Monitor the Obligation to Fulfil Economic, Social and Cultural Rights: The OPERA Framework' (2012) 8(3) *Nordic Journal of Human Rights* 324. See also, Riedel (n 163).

170 Rosga (n 165), 282.

effectively and systematically, to disaggregate them based on various criteria and to make them available for public use. In other words, one way to improve the adequacy and pertinence of social policies and services and, therefore, the progressive realisation of economic and social rights is to guarantee a say in the design and implementation of government strategies for civil society organisations, NGOs with technical resources and expertise, and groups that represent the sectors targeted by the policies and services, as well as establishing forums for social participation in the evaluation, oversight and responsibility mechanisms, which increases transparency and accountability.[171] The OHCHR has also dealt with the issue of participation by identifying it as a cross-cutting issue that should be addressed through the choice of indicators designed to capture the extent to which the process to implement and realise human rights is, for instance, participatory, inclusionary, empowering, non-discriminatory, accountable or, where required, supported by international cooperation.[172]

Indicators frameworks allow economic and social rights indicators to be recast into more quantifiable and tangible measures of assessment that are capable of greater alignment with data measuring the promotion and protection of economic and social rights by contributing States during peace operations. Implicit in the nature and sources of indicators is a degree of flexibility that spans a spectrum of obligations from baseline obligations that make no allowances for violations through to those that are often highly context dependent and subject to the level of control that a State can exercise.

7 Conclusion

Early efforts to address socio-economic inequality were driven, on the one hand, by the potential, and sometimes real, conflict resulting from the disenfranchisement of the poor leading States to adopt measures to maintain social order at the national level and then to maintain peace at the international level. Such efforts culminated in the inclusion in the UN Charter of the recognition of social progress, international cooperation and human rights as tools to save succeeding generations from the scourge of war. This was a first important step in the establishment of what has become a well-developed international legal framework for the realisation of economic and social rights since the middle of the 20th century. This framework reflects the significance of the contribution that is made by just economic and social conditions to peace and security, at the State level as well as the regional and global levels. This chapter signals just some of the detailed elaboration of the content of economic and social rights and the concomitant obligations imposed upon ratifying States. This detail will be further elaborated upon in the context of peacekeeping operations in Chapter 4. For now, however, this

171 IACHR (n 153), para 82. Rosga, ibid, 312–313. In the context of peacebuilding, see Chapter 3, footnotes 15–19 and accompanying text.

172 OHCHR Report on Indicators for Monitoring Compliance with International Human Rights Instruments UN Doc HRI/MC/2006/7, para 21.

chapter serves to highlight the broad scope of human rights that underpins the interrelated nature of the work of the three main organs of the United Nations – the Security Council, the General Assembly and the ECOSOC – as they seek to give effect to that Organisation's efforts to maintain international peace and security, promote economic and social progress, and realise human rights.

2 Peace and security, socio-economic progress, and human rights

The inseparable roles of the Security Council, the General Assembly and the ECOSOC

1 Introduction

As indicated in the previous chapter, by the middle of the 20th century, the twin goals of improving socio-economic conditions and protecting and promoting human rights underpinned efforts to maintain international peace and security. The ensuing elaboration of economic and social rights contributes to the understanding of what States must do to realise effectively those rights that facilitate economic and social progress, which is a necessary component of peace and security. For much of the early history of the UN, however, the detrimental impact of economic and social marginalisation, and related violations of economic and social rights, upon the maintenance of international peace and security was largely overlooked. This compartmentalised approach persisted in spite of the fact that the Charter facilitates, if not demands, dialogue between those organs with responsibility for the twin goals of the UN, namely, the Security Council, the General Assembly and the ECOSOC.

By the early 1990s, however, it was becoming evident that the Security Council was engaging more broadly with the General Assembly and the ECOSOC, particularly as regards the relationship between economic and social progress, human rights and international peace and security. Representatives of the General Assembly, the ECOSOC, the OHCHR and the Special Procedures Mechanisms of the Human Rights Council (the Special Procedures Mechanism or the Special Rapporteur) have been invited to address Security Council meetings[1] with increased frequency. They have provided factual information on human rights abuses that raised concerns for the Council's work in maintaining international peace and security. The clearest manifestation of such recognition by the Council, as well as the General Assembly and the ECOSOC, can be seen in the establishment of the Peacebuilding Commission in 2006 by resolutions of the Security Council and the General Assembly.

1 Rule 39 of the Council's Rules of Procedure provides, 'The Security Council may invite members of the Secretariat or other persons, whom it considers competent for the purpose, to supply it with information or to give other assistance in examining matters within its competence.' See UNSC Provisional Rules of Procedure of the Security Council, S/96/Rev.7 (1982).

This chapter will explore the legal bases and the evolving relationship between the Security Council, the General Assembly and the ECOSOC, the OHCHR, the Human Rights Council and its Special Procedures Mechanism, in order to reveal the extent to which human rights and economic and social development have impacted upon in the Security Council's efforts to maintain international peace and security. The role of the Peacebuilding Commission, as a sub-organ of the Security Council and the General Assembly, will also be explored. This chapter shows that increased dialogue facilitates the broad approach to peace and security provided for in the Charter, which itself was a response to the mass civilian suffering of WWII.

2 Security Council relations with the General Assembly and the ECOSOC

2.1 The General Assembly

The General Assembly is the main deliberative, policymaking and representative organ of the UN. Every Member State of the UN is a member of the General Assembly so that all States, large and small, can debate and discuss any question that falls within the scope of the UN Charter, leading the Assembly to be described as the open conscience of the world.[2] As noted in Chapter 1, its powers extend to the formulation of international law, the realisation of human rights and the promotion of economic and social cooperation. The General Assembly also has some powers in relation to maintaining international peace and security, such as those contained in Article 14 of the Charter. The Assembly has also taken some further initiatives in relation to this role. Most notable, is UNGA Res 377 A(V) (3 November 1950) which allows the Assembly to take action to maintain international peace and security when the Security Council has failed to act owing to the negative vote of a permanent member. In such instances, the Assembly may consider the matter immediately and recommend to its members collective measures to maintain or restore international peace and security. Early peacekeeping operations stemmed from the General Assembly such as the establishment and deployment of the United Nations Emergency Force (UNEF I) by UNGA Resolution 1001. The Emergency Force was established in response to the Suez Canal crisis in 1956 in the face of Security Council inaction when France and the United Kingdom vetoed a Security Council response.

In terms of the General Assembly's role as a deliberative body, concern with international peace and security is a recurring theme in the General Assembly's own resolutions. For example, early resolutions on the causes of conflict in Africa illustrate the Assembly's holistic approach to the maintenance of peace and

2 Leland Matthew Goodrich, and Edvard Isak Hambro 'Charter of the United Nations' (Boston, World Peace Foundation, 1949), at 151.

security and conflict prevention on that continent, an approach that, according to the Assembly, should be undertaken within the Organisation itself.[3] Such a holistic approach includes an enhanced relationship with regional organisations, including training in international human rights for national standby contingents and assistance with national capacities of governance, including the launch of income-generation activities, particularly for youth and women, and the delivery of basic public services.[4] The Assembly has also noted that achieving peace, stability and sustainable development in Africa has been hampered by the increased prevalence of infectious disease, such as HIV/AIDS, extremely high rates of youth unemployment, human trafficking, massive displacements of people, and the illegal exploitation of natural resources, and the Assembly has encouraged the UN to assist African countries to effectively address these challenges.[5]

The General Assembly also has a recommendatory role when it comes to the maintenance of international peace and security. According to Article 10 of the UN Charter, the Assembly can make an assessment of a particular situation and make non-binding recommendations to the UN or the Security Council in that regard.[6] In this way, the Charter allows the General Assembly to complement and facilitate the Security Council, where the latter is the main body charged with the maintenance of international peace and security. Article 11 of the Charter makes further provision for a relationship between the General Assembly and the Security Council. Article 11(1) provides that the General Assembly may consider the general principles of cooperation in the maintenance of international peace and security and identifies the Assembly's recommendation-making powers to the Security Council in that regard. Article 11(2) provides that the Assembly may request action from the Council with regard to questions stemming from international peace and security, whilst Article 11(3) makes provision for the role of the General Assembly in drawing the attention of the Security Council to any situations likely to endanger international peace and security. In addition to the powers and functions of the General Assembly to communicate with the Security Council, certain subsidiary organs established by the General Assembly play a part in the work of the Security Council. A second basis stems from the Security Council making use of the services of the subsidiary bodies or, as indicated above, the Council can invite the officers of these bodies to participate in its meetings. Notable in this regard are the Peacebuilding Commission and the Human Rights Council. One basis for such a contribution may stem from the placing of the

3 See, for example, UNGA Res 55/217 (21 December 2000) UN Doc A/RES/55/217.

4 UNGA Res 62/275 (11 September 2008) UN Doc A/RES/62/275, para 24.

5 UNGA Res 62/275, (ibid.). See also, UNGA Res 63/304 (23 July 2009) UN Doc A/RES/63/304.

6 Charter of the United Nations (adopted 26 June 1945, entered into force 24 October 1945) 1 UNTS XVI (UN Charter). Article 10 states, 'The General Assembly may discuss any questions or any matters within the scope of the present Charter or relating to the powers and functions of any organs provided for in the present Charter, and, except as provided in Article 12, may make recommendations to the Members of the United Nations or to the Security Council or to both on any such questions or matters.'

subsidiary bodies in a special relationship to the Security Council by a resolution of the General Assembly.

The General Assembly utilises its Article 11 powers to make recommendations, both general and specific, on matters relating to the Security Council's powers and functions or with regard to the general principles of cooperation in the maintenance of international peace and security. For example, the Assembly has encouraged the Security Council to give prompt consideration to early warning or prevention cases brought to its attention by other UN organs, Member States or the Secretary-General[7] or International Organisations.[8] As regards peacekeeping, the Assembly has called for clear objectives and realistic mandates that reflected the obligations of deploying States. The Assembly has called for periodic reviews of operations by the Security Council and greater consultation between Security Council, the Secretariat and contributing States from the inception to the conclusion of peacekeeping operations.[9] The Assembly has recommended that the Security Council include, as appropriate, peacebuilding elements in peacekeeping operations to generate conditions that would help to avoid the recurrence of armed conflict, as an aspect of the prevention of armed conflict.[10] The Assembly also encouraged the Security Council and the ECOSOC to strengthen their mutual cooperation and coordination, in accordance with their respective mandates, for the prevention of armed conflict.[11] The President of the General Assembly described the relationship between the two organs, when he addressed the Security Council as the latter debated its working methods (Implementation of the note by the President of the Security Council (S/2010/507)), as being, or at least it could be, both mutually reinforcing and complementary. He also noted that there were several areas where the actions of both the Council and the Assembly were closely linked and interdependent, including certain peace and security issues.[12] For its part, the Council has also acknowledged the role of the General Assembly. As regards the varying debates on conflict in Africa,

7 In UNGA Res 57/337 (3 July 2003) UN Doc A/RES/57/337, Annex, para 21; UNGA Res 53/71 (4 December 1998) UN Doc A/RES/53/71; and UNGA Res 51/55 (10 December 1996) UN Doc A/RES/51/55.

8 UNGA Res 53/71 and UNGA Res 51/55, ibid.

9 UNGA Res 48/42 (10 December 1993) UN Doc A/RES/48/42, paras 24, 44 and 76(b). See also, UNGA Res 67/301 (16 September 2013) UN Doc A/RES/67/301; UNGA Res 66/297 (17 September 2012) UN Doc A/RES/66/297; UNGA Res 65/310 (19 July 2011) UN Doc A/RES/65/310; UNGA Res 65/290 (30 June 2011) UN Doc A/RES/65/290 on 'Strengthening the Capacity of the United Nations to Manage and Sustain Peacekeeping Operations'; UNGA Res 47/71 (14 December 1992) UN Doc A/RES/47/71; and UNGA Res 47/72 (14 December 1992) UN Doc A/RES/47/72 on the 'Protection of Peacekeeping Personnel'.

10 UNGA Res 57/337 (n 7) on the 'Prevention of Armed Conflict.' See also, UNGA Res 67/293 (24 July 2013) UN Doc A/RES/67/293 on the 'Implementation of the Recommendations contained in the Report of the Secretary-General on the Causes of Conflict and the Promotion of Durable Peace and Sustainable Development in Africa', paras 13–16.

11 UNGA Res 57/337, ibid.

12 UNSC Verbatim Record (20 October 2015) UN Doc S/PV.7539, 3–4.

it was stated that the economic and social aspects of conflict impacted on peace and security and that the General Assembly should coordinate the work of both Councils.[13] Similarly, the Council has been reminded of the 2005 World Summit during which the Heads of State had stressed the need for the Security Council, the General Assembly, the ECOSOC and the Secretary-General to coordinate their activities within their respective Charter mandates.[14] The Council has continued to stress, on numerous occasions, the importance of strengthening its partnership with the General Assembly in connection with the maintenance of international peace and security.[15]

Thus, the Security Council has strengthened its relationship with the General Assembly as it seeks to discharge its responsibilities to maintain international peace and security. However, as regards the impact of economic and social progress as expressed through human rights, subsidiary bodies of the Assembly have had a greater impact. Most notable amongst such subsidiary organs is the ECOSOC.[16]

2.2 The ECOSOC

The ECOSOC is the principal organ of the UN in terms of coordination, policy review, policy dialogue and recommendations on economic, social, cultural, educational, health and related matters, as well as for implementation of internationally agreed development goals,[17] not to mention the information that the ECOSOC receives from NGOs.[18] As a result, the ECOSOC has an unparalleled

13 UNSC Verbatim Record (22 May 2002) UN Doc S/PV.4538, 31–32 (India).

14 UNSC Verbatim Record (28 August 2007) UN Doc S/PV.5735 on the 'Maintenance of International Peace and Security Role of the Security Council in Conflict Prevention and Resolution, in particular in Africa,' 4 (Haiti).

15 UNSC Presidential Statement UN Doc 2 (2010) S/PRST/2010/2, 2; UNSC Presidential Statement UN Doc 15 (2010) S/PRST/2010/15, 1; UNSC Presidential Statement UN Doc 18 (2010) S/PRST/2010/18, 2 and 3; UNSC Presidential Statement UN Doc 4 (2011) S/PRST/2011/4; UNSC Presidential Statement UN Doc 17 (2011) S/PRST/2011/17, para 11; UNSC Presidential Statement UN Doc 18 (2011) S/PRST/2011/18, 2, as well as UNSC Res 1983 (7 June 2011) UN Doc S/RES/1983, preambular para 7.

16 UN Charter (n 6), Article 60 of which sets out the powers of the ECOSOC with its statement that 'Responsibility for the discharge of the functions of the Organization set forth in this Chapter shall be vested in the General Assembly and, under the authority of the General Assembly, in the Economic and Social Council.' For further discussion on the overlap between the General Assembly and the ECOSOC in terms of the UN's human rights functions, see Werner Meng, 'Article 60' and Volker Roben, 'Article 62', in Bruno Simma and others (eds), *The Charter of the United Nations: A Commentary. Volume III* (3rd edn, Oxford University Press, Oxford 2012) 1658 and 1678, respectively.

17 UN Charter (n 6), Article 62(1).

18 In terms of NGO input to UN human rights bodies, see Claire Breen, 'Rationalising the Work of UN Human Rights Bodies or Reducing the Input on NGOs? The Changing Role of Human Rights NGOs at the United Nations' (2005) 5(2) *Non-State Actors and International Law* 101; and Claire Breen, 'The Role of NGOs in the Formulation of and Compliance with the Optional Protocol to the Convention on the Rights of the Child on Involvement of Children in Armed Conflict' (2003) 25(2) *Human Rights Quarterly* 453.

body of information with regard to international economic and social development, as well as human rights. This information comes from the ECOSOC's Charter-mandated functions, including the coordination of information flowing from UN Specialised Agencies (Article 63), as well as from functional commissions set up by the ECOSOC itself, such as the Commission on Human Rights and its successor, the Human Rights Council, which will be considered in further detail below. It is because of this role that the relationship between the Security Council and the ECOSOC is of particular significance.[19]

The phase of increased collaboration between the Security Council and the ECOSOC can be traced to an invitation by the Security Council to the ECOSOC asking the latter to contribute to designing a long-term programme of support for Haiti, in 1998, and a subsequent request for the involvement of the ECOSOC in discussions on the impact of HIV/AIDS on peace and security in Africa, in 2000.[20] Further early recognition of the benefits of a more collaborative relationship have been captured in the work of the Security Council in relation to specific situations such as those in Africa,[21] Guinea-Bissau,[22] and Haiti[23] as Council members increasingly recognised the deepening relationship between both Councils.

Similar evidence of the close relationship appears in thematic matters. During Council discussions on civilians in armed conflict,[24] the parameters of the relationship were noted when it was observed that the critical issue of funding for humanitarian missions was beyond the Security Council's purview[25] and, as conflict prevention and post-conflict settlement had to be informed by fundamental

19 See generally, Claire Breen, 'The Necessity of a Role for the ECOSOC in the Maintenance of International Peace and Security' (2007) 12(2) *Journal of Conflict and Security Law* 261.

20 See UNGA, 'Report of the Secretary General 2001/574' (2001) UN Doc S/2001/574, paras 40–44.

21 UNSC Res 1170 (28 May 1998) UN Doc S/RES/1170; UNSC Presidential Statement UN Doc 29 (1998) S/PRST/1998/29, 2–3. See also, UNSC Verbatim Record (15 December 1999) UN Doc S/PV.4081, 6 (China), 11 (Argentina), 14 (Bahrain) and 17–18 (Russian Federation); UNSC Res 1576 (29 November 2004) UN Doc S/RES/1576, preambular paras 3–4; and UNSC Verbatim Record (12 January 2005) UN Doc S/PV.5110, 9 (Brazil). Support had been given previously: UNSC Verbatim Record (12 January 2005) UN Doc S/PV.5110, 21 (Romania), 27 (Philippines) and 22 (Greece). UNSC Verbatim Record (22 May 2002) UN Doc S/PV.4538, 15 (Egypt), 16 (Algeria), 17–18 (Korea), 21 (Bangladesh), 26 (Bahrain) and 42 (Costa Rica); and UNSC Verbatim Record (15 April 2004) UN Doc S/PV.4943, 9–10 (President of the ESOCOC).

22 UNSC Presidential Statement UN Doc 20 (2004) S/PRST/2004/20 and UNSC Presidential Statement UN Doc 39 (2005) S/PRST/2005/39.

23 UNSC Verbatim Record (25 November 1998) UN Doc S/PV.3949, 5 (Brazil). See also, UNSC Verbatim Record (12 January 2005) UN Doc S/PV.5110 (Resumption 1), 6 (Benin), 9 (Luxembourg), 10 (Guatemala), 20 (Uruguay) and 23 (El Salvador). UNSC Verbatim Record (13 May 2005) UN Doc S/PV.5178, 11–12 (Canada), 13 (Luxembourg, speaking on behalf of the European Union), 13–15 (Chile), 15 (Guatemala), 17 (Peru), 20–21 (Spain) and 23–24 (Haiti).

24 UNSC Verbatim Record (14 December 2004) UN Doc S/PV.5100.

25 UNSC Verbatim Record (14 June 2004) UN Doc S/PV.4990, 21 (Brazil) and 27 (Philippines); UNSC Verbatim Record (14 June 2004) UN Doc S/PV.4990 (Resumption 1), 5 (Ukraine) and 10–11 (Japan).

humanitarian principles, there was an ever-growing role for the ECOSOC.[26] Although the ECOSOC is not specifically identified, the Security Council has '*underline[d]* the importance of a coherent, comprehensive and coordinated approach by the principal organs of the United Nations, cooperating with one another and within their respective mandates' (original emphasis).[27] During the debate on civilian aspects of conflict management and peacebuilding, it was recalled that the ECOSOC, not the Security Council, was the Charter organ with responsibility for matters relating to social development. It was stated that it was part of the work of the Security Council to promote the work of the ECOSOC in fulfilling its tasks.[28] Calls for closer coordination more generally have also been made in relation to the issue of children in armed conflict,[29] whilst in relation to the matter of women and peace and security, the Security Council expressed its readiness to promote further the implementation of Resolution 1325 (2000), in particular through active cooperation with the ECOSOC and the General Assembly.[30]

During Council debates on the maintenance of international peace and security, it was noted that Resolution 1625 (2005) was aimed at strengthening the effectiveness of the role of the Security Council in the prevention of armed conflicts, and a coordination of this wide range of actions with those of the Secretariat and the ECOSOC was key to the Resolution's operationalisation.[31] The

26 UNSC Verbatim Record (21 June 2005) UN Doc S/PV.5209, 14; UNSC Verbatim Record (27 May 2008) UN Doc S/PV.5898, 9 (China); and UNSC Verbatim Record (27 May 2008) UN Doc S/PV.5898 (Resumption 1), 17 (United Arab Emirates). For further discussion on the nature of the Organ's roles, see Section 2.3 below.

27 UNSC Res 1894 (11 November 2009) UN Doc S/RES/1894, para 28; see also UNSC Res 1674 (28 April 2006) UN Doc S/Res/1674, para 2.

28 UNSC Verbatim Record (22 September 2004) UN Doc S/PV.5041, 17 (Brazil). The need for an increased role for the ECOSOC was reiterated by Angola at 19 and Algeria at 28. The Security Council addressed the issue of the protection of civilians in armed conflict in December 2004; UNSC Verbatim Record (14 December 2004) UN Doc S/PV.5100; and UNSC Verbatim Record (12 February 2013) UN Doc S/PV.6917 wherein sustainable development, poverty and human rights were seen as tools for conflict prevention in context of protection of civilians.

29 UNSC Verbatim Record (12 February 2008) UN Doc S/PV.5834 (Resumption 1), 8; and UNSC Verbatim Record (17 July 2008) UN Doc S/PV.5936, 23–24 (Russian Federation). See also, UNSC Verbatim Record (17 July 2008) UN Doc S/PV.5936 (Resumption 1), 16–17 (Egypt) and 18–19 (Malawi). See further, UNSC Verbatim Record (29 April 2009) UN Doc S/PV.6114, 17 (China); and UNSC Verbatim Record (29 April 2009) UN Doc S/PV.6114 (Resumption 1), 42 (Thailand).

30 UNSC Presidential Statement UN Doc 40 (2004) S/PRST/2004/40, 3. Council members have expressed similar views: UNSC Verbatim Record (19 June 2008) UN Doc S/PV.5916, 19–20 (China); UNSC Verbatim Record (29 October 2008) UN Doc S/PV.6005, 26 (China); UNSC Verbatim Record (5 October 2009) UN Doc S/PV.6196 (Resumption 1), 7 (Luxembourg); UNSC Verbatim Record (17 April 2013) UN Doc S/PV.6948, 12 (China); UNSC Verbatim Record (26 October 2010) UN Doc S/PV.6411, 9–10; and UNSC Verbatim Record (28 October 2011) UN Doc S/PV.6642, 5–6.

31 UNSC Verbatim Record (28 August 2007) UN Doc S/PV.5735, 32 (Argentina); UNSC Verbatim Record (21 April 2009) UN Doc S/PV.6108 (Resumption 1), 16 (Senegal);

Security Council has also stated its intention to continue to strengthen its partnerships with all other relevant players, in particular the General Assembly and the ECOSOC (and the Peacebuilding Commission).[32] The Security Council's recognition of the need for further coordination can be seen in the President's statement on post-conflict peacebuilding:

> The Security Council underlines that for countries emerging from conflict significant international assistance for economic and social rehabilitation and reconstruction is indispensable. In this regard the Security Council acknowledges the role that ECOSOC plays, including in sustainable development, and reiterates its willingness to improve co-operation with United Nations bodies and organs directly concerned with peacebuilding.[33]

As the preceding paragraphs show, the Security Council has recognised the need for inter-Council dialogue at a general level. However, the Charter contains a particular provision for a relationship between the Security Council and the ECOSOC. According to Article 65, 'the Economic and Social Council may furnish information to the Security Council and shall assist the Security Council upon its request',[34] which enables the ECOSOC to contribute to the work of the Security Council.

UNSC Verbatim Record (23 September 2010) UN Doc S/PV.6389, 2 (President), 8 (Nigeria) and 16 (Brazil); UNSC Verbatim Record (7 June 2011) UN Doc S/PV.6547, 13 (Russian Federation), 16 (Brazil) and 18 (Bosnia and Herzegovina); UNSC Verbatim Record (11 February 2011) UN Doc S/PV.6479, 3 (Secretary-General), 10 (Colombia), 17 (South Africa), 20 (Nigeria), 21–22 (Russian Federation) and 27 (Brazil); and UNSC Verbatim Record (11 February 2011) UN Doc S/PV.6479 (Resumption 1), 2 (Thailand), 5 (Pakistan), 15 (Luxembourg), 25 (Chile), 32 (Senegal), 38 (Malaysia), 42 (El Salvador) and 42 (Nicaragua).

32 UNSC Presidential Statement UN Doc 18 (2011) S/PRST/2011/18, 2. Similar views had been expressed in UNSC Presidential Statement UN Doc 18 (2010) S/PRST/2010/18, 2 and 3; and UNSC Presidential Statement UN Doc 4 (2011) S/PRST/2011/4, 3.

33 UNSC Presidential Statement UN Doc 20 (2005) S/PRST/2005/20, 2. See also, UNSC Presidential Statement UN Doc 5 (2001) S/PRST/2001/5, 3. In connection with post-conflict peacebuilding, see UNSC Verbatim Record (16 April 2010) UN Doc S/PV.6299, 18 (Russian Federation) and 33 (China); and UNSC Verbatim Record (16 April 2010) UN Doc S/PV.6299 (Resumption 1), 6–7 (Egypt), 10 (Pakistan), 27 (Rwanda), 30 (Botswana) and 32 (Bangladesh); UNSC Verbatim Record (16 December 1998) UN Doc S/PV.3954 on the 'Maintenance of Peace and Security and Post-conflict Peace-building,' 14–16.

34 The question of an actual working relationship between the ECOSOC and the Security Council was identified and discussed in the early days of the Organisation, culminating in the view within the ECOSOC that the ECOSOC should confine itself to affirming its readiness to assist the Security Council upon request. In relation to the ECOSOC, some of the few examples include the following: ECOSOC, 'Consultation with the World Jewish Congress' Res 214B (VIII) (16 Feb 1949); UNSC Res 329 (10 March 1973) UN Doc S/Res/329; UNSC Res 402 (22 December 1976) UN Doc S/Res/402; UNSC Res 386 (17 March 1976) UN Doc S/Res/386; UNSC Res 406 (25 May 1977) UN Doc S/Res/406; UNSC Res 1212 (25 November 1998) UN Doc S/Res/1212; ECOSOC, 'Letter Dated 16

The potential relevance of Article 65, as part of an early warning system, was indicated in *An Agenda for Peace*.[35] Security Council members themselves also began to suggest that the Security Council make far greater use of Article 65 to address the root causes of conflict, including the high level of poverty and under-development and the inequalities in opportunity amongst different groups.[36] The Security Council recalled the role of Article 65 in stating that economic rehabilitation and reconstruction often constituted the major tasks facing societies emerging from conflict.[37] Likewise, during debates on post-conflict national reconciliation and the role of the UN, it was observed by Council members that the Security Council could do a lot to achieve objectives such as development, democratisation and the strengthening of the rule of law by using Article 65, as well as greater collaboration with the ECOSOC.[38] These underlying causes of conflict are also identified in relation to the Security Council's debates on conflict prevention, and the Council has highlighted the importance of strengthening

---

February 1999 from the President of the Economic and Social Council to the President of the Security Council' (18 February 1999) UN Doc E/1999/7-S/1999/170; and UNSC, 'Letter Dated 7 April 1999 from the President of the Security Council to the President of the Economic and Social Council' (9 April 1999) UN Doc E/1999/12-S/1999/403. Compare, Report of the Secretary General, 'Collective Economic Security' (1974) UN Doc E/5529. See United Nations, Repertory of Practice of United Nations Organs, *Extracts Relating to Article 65 of the Charter of the United Nations: Repertory of Practice (1945–1954)*, vol 3, paras 21–22. See, in general, Philip Kunig and Christian Tietje, 'Article 65' in Bruno Simma and others (eds), *The Charter of the United Nations: A Commentary. Volume III* (3rd edn, Oxford University Press, Oxford 2012) 1718–1722.

35 UNGA, 'Report of the Secretary-General 24111' (1995) UN Doc S/24111, para 26. Security Council deliberations on subsequent reports of the Secretary-General reveal support between the Councils to help better identify and address economic and social tensions before the outbreak of conflict or after its conclusion. See also, UNGA, 'Report of the Secretary General 1995/1' (1995) UN Doc S/1995/1 as discussed in UNSC Verbatim Record (18 January 1995) UN Doc S/PV.3492, 24 (United States); UNSC Verbatim Record (18 January 1995) UN Doc S/PV.3492 (Resumption 1), 32 (Canada); and UNSC Verbatim Record (19 January 1995) UN Doc S/PV.3492 (Resumption 2), 18 (Ireland). In a follow-up report entitled 'Implementation of the Recommendations Contained in an "Agenda for Peace"', the Secretary General recalled his earlier recommendation and expressed the hope that discussion would continue on ways to put it into practice: UNGA, 'Report of the Secretary General 25944' (1993) UN Doc S/25944, para 42.

36 UNSC Verbatim Record (15 December 1999) UN Doc S/PV.4081 (Resumption 1) and Corr.1, 14 (New Zealand) and 29 (Italy).

37 UNSC Presidential Statement UN Doc 38 (1998) S/PRST/1998/38, 2.

38 UNSC Verbatim Record (26 January 2004) UN Doc S/PV.4903, 18 (Brazil). Similar views can be found at 21 (Pakistan) and 27 (Angola). See also, UNSC Verbatim Record (28 May 2004) UN Doc S/PV.4980, 24 (United Kingdom), 26 (Germany) and 28 (Romania); and UNSC Verbatim Record (14 June 2004) UN Doc S/PV.4990 relating to the issue of civilians in armed conflict when it was noted, by the representative of Pakistan at 14, that most of the contemporary conflicts were complex in nature, requiring a comprehensive, coherent and multidimensional response. This observation was reiterated by Brazil at 21, by the Philippines at 27, by Syria at 28 and during UNSC Verbatim Record (14 June 2004) UN Doc S/PV. 4990 (Resumption 1), by Ukraine at 5, by Japan at 10, by Malaysia at 19 and by Nepal at 21.

its cooperation with the ECOSOC, in accordance with Article 65, including in addressing the economic, social, cultural and humanitarian problems that are often the root causes of conflicts.[39] The Council has affirmed its determination to strengthen the UN's conflict prevention capacities by requesting, as necessary and appropriate, information and assistance from the ECOSOC in accordance with Article 65 of the Charter.[40] In relation to the maintenance of international peace and security, it was noted that the international community must be more focused on the structural dysfunctions within States, which have a real impact on international peace and security. In that regard it was noted that 'this problem could be the subject of information-exchange between the Security Council and the Economic and Social Council under Article 65 of the Charter of the United Nations'.[41] Subsequently, the President of the Council underlined the importance of close cooperation in accordance with Article 65.[42]

During its open debates on improving the Security Council's working methods, many speakers,[43] including the President of the ECOSOC,[44] have underlined the need for strengthened cooperation and coordination between the Security Council and other UN bodies, especially the General Assembly and the ECOSOC (as well as the Peacebuilding Commission). Such statements have called for an improved information flow[45] and the establishment of regular and substantive dialogue with the ECOSOC, thereby reinforcing the communication

39 UNSC Presidential Statement UN Doc 25 (2000) S/PRST/2000/25, 3.

40 UNSC Res 1625 (14 September 2005) UN Doc S/RES/1625, para 2(e).

41 UNSC Verbatim Record (19 January 2015) UN Doc S/PV.7361, 86 (Benin).

42 UNSC Presidential Statement UN Doc 3 (2015) S/PRST/2015/3, 4; and UNSC Presidential Statement UN Doc 4 (2011) S/PRST/2011/4, 3.

43 UNSC Verbatim Record (27 August 2008) UN Doc S/PV.5968, 6 (China), 12 (Viet Nam), 16 (Russian Federation), 27 (Mexico), 28 (Iceland), 29 (New Zealand) and 34 (Cuba, on behalf of members of the Non-Aligned Movement). UNSC Verbatim Record (27 August 2008) UN Doc S/PV.5968, (Resumption 1), 15 (Argentina), 24 (Pakistan) and 25 (Guatemala). See also, UNSC Verbatim Record (22 April 2010) UN Doc S/PV.6300, 3 (Turkey), 10 (Lebanon), 14 (Bosnia and Herzegovina) and 29 (Slovakia); UNSC Verbatim Record (22 April 2010) UN Doc S/PV. 6300 (Resumption 1), 8 (Argentina), 10 (India), 18 (Colombia), 19 (Kenya), 21–22 (Czech Republic) and 27 (Pakistan); UNSC Verbatim Record (23 September 2010) UN Doc S/PV.6389, 16 (Brazil); UNSC Verbatim Record (30 November 2011) UN Doc S/PV.6672, 4 (Russian Federation), 8 (Nigeria), 11 (Lebanon) and 14 (China); UNSC Verbatim Record (30 November 2011) UN Doc S/PV.6672 (Resumption 1), 7 (Luxembourg) and 11–12 (Sudan); and UNSC Verbatim Record (29 October 2013) UN Doc S/PV.7052, 12 (Republic of Korea), 14 (Russian Federation), 17 (Togo) and 24 (Brazil).

44 UNSC Verbatim Record (20 October 2015) UN Doc S/PV.7539.

45 UNSC Verbatim Record (27 August 2008) UN Doc S/PV.5968, 6 (China) and 28 (Iceland); UNSC Verbatim Record UN Doc S/PV.5968 (Resumption 1), 5 (Belarus) and 24 (Pakistan); and UNSC Verbatim Record (30 November 2011) UN Doc S/PV.6672, 4 (Russian Federation), 8 (Nigeria), 14 (China) and 25 (Egypt speaking on behalf of the Non-Aligned Movement (NAM)).

procedure provided for by Article 65, as well as with the Human Rights Council and the Peacebuilding Commission.[46]

2.3 Staking out the relationship between the Security Council, the General Assembly and the ECOSOC

The Security Council's practice of encouraging the involvement of the General Assembly and the ECOSOC is evident. Nonetheless, there has been some resistance to this enhanced relationship. In the context of the maintenance of peace and security, and post-conflict peacebuilding, early concerns were expressed that UN organs, such as the Assembly and the ECOSOC, were being marginalised and that the increasing consideration of social issues by the Council would impair its efficiency.[47] It was noted that the ECOSOC, and not the Security Council, was the Charter organ with responsibility for matters relating to social development and efforts to build lasting peace and that reconstruction was a matter of social and economic development. In that regard, it was stated that the Security Council ought to promote the work of the ECOSOC in fulfilling its tasks.[48] During deliberations on strengthening international law and the rule of law, and maintenance of international peace and security, there were calls for any encroachment by the Council on the competence of the General Assembly or the ECOSOC to cease.[49] It was also asserted, during the discussion on the maintenance of international peace and security focusing on the role of the Security Council in supporting security sector reform, that the debate on security sector reform had fallen into a grey area, which the Council attempted to exploit in order to strengthen its control of an issue that fell primarily within the prerogatives of the General Assembly and the ECOSOC.[50] In the context of the maintenance of international peace and security and conflict prevention and natural resources, it was observed that issues pertaining to sustainable development, transparency and the fight against corruption were matters that fell within the purview of the General Assembly, the ECOSOC and other agencies and bodies of the UN.[51] More recently, it has been stated that a concerted push has been made to include several normative issues on to the Council's agenda under the pretext that they affect international peace and security and that such a move should be avoided. To that end, the view was expressed that all UN bodies, including the

46 UNSC Verbatim Record (22 April 2010) UN Doc S/PV.6300 (Resumption 1), 8 (Argentina), 10 (India), 15 (Singapore), 18 (Colombia), 19 (Kenya) and 21 (Czech Republic).

47 UNSC Verbatim Record (16 December 1998) UN Doc S/PV.3954, 3 (China).

48 UNSC Verbatim Record (22 September 2004) UN Doc S/PV.5041, 17 (Brazil).

49 UNSC Verbatim Record (22 June 2006) UN Doc S/PV.5474 (Resumption 1), 4 (Egypt).

50 UNSC Verbatim Record (20 February 2007) UN Doc S/PV.5632 (Resumption 1), 13–14 (Egypt).

51 UNSC Verbatim Record (19 June 2013) UN Doc S/PV.6982 (Resumption 1), 6–7 (Plurinational State of Bolivia). Similar views had been expressed previously. See UNSC Verbatim Record (25 June 2007) UN Doc S/PV.5705, 9–10 (Qatar), 18 (China) and 19–20 (Italy); and UNSC Verbatim Record (25 June 2007) UN Doc S/PV.5705 (Resumption 1), 2 (Brazil).

Security Council, had to respect the division of roles and responsibilities between the General Assembly, the Security Council and the ECOSOC, as provided for in the UN Charter.[52]

Security Council debates on its own working methods have also revealed a divergence of opinion with some members stating that efforts at coordination and complementarity were not to undermine the mandates and prerogatives of the Security Council, the General Assembly and the ECOSOC.[53] In relation to the latter, it was stated that:

> many of the open meetings held by the Security Council correspond precisely to topics that fall outside its jurisdiction, but which, regrettably, it continues to seek to cast, in a forced way, as threats to international peace and security in order to interfere with the mandates of the General Assembly and the Economic and Social Council.[54]

Concerns have been expressed that increased cooperation might lead to encroachment by the Security Council on the work of other, more appropriate, UN bodies.[55] Other Council members have been more explicit and have stated that Article 24 of the Charter does not necessarily provide the Security Council with the competence to address issues that fall within the functions and powers of the General Assembly and the ECOSOC. They have called on the Presidents of the General Assembly, the ECOSOC and the Security Council to conduct regular discussions and coordination amongst themselves regarding the agenda and programme of work of the respective principal organs.[56] More recently, it was stated that such efforts should be respectful of one another's mandates and with a view to generating mutual understanding amongst all three bodies.[57] These debates have allowed the Council to describe the relationship between the three organs as one where it:

> underscores the importance of increased coordination, cooperation and interaction among the principal organs of the United Nations, in particular the Security Council, the General Assembly, the Economic and Social

52 UNSC Verbatim Record (19 June 2013) UN Doc S/PV.6982 (Resumption 1), 15 (India).

53 UNSC Verbatim Record (22 April 2010) UN Doc S/PV.6300, 21 (Egypt speaking on behalf of NAM); and UNSC Verbatim Record (30 November 2011) UN Doc S/PV.6672 (Resumption 1), 11–12 (Sudan), 14–15 (Islamic Republic of Iran) and 21–22 (Bolivarian Republic of Venezuela).

54 UNSC Verbatim Record (22 April 2010) UN Doc S/PV.6300 (Resumption 1), 24 (Ecuador).

55 UNSC Verbatim Record (26 November 2012) UN Doc S/PV.6870, 5–6 (Russian Federation).

56 UNSC Verbatim Record (26 November 2012) UN Doc S/PV.6870, 31 (Islamic Republic of Iran speaking on behalf of NAM). Similar views had been expressed previously: UNSC Verbatim Record (22 June 2006) UN Doc S/PV.5474 (Resumption 1), 16 (Bolivarian Republic of Venezuela).

57 UNSC Verbatim Record (29 October 2013) UN Doc S/PV.7052 (Resumption 1), 13 (Islamic Republic of Iran speaking on behalf of NAM).

> Council . . . and reaffirms that the relationship between the principal organs of the United Nations is mutually reinforcing and complementary, in accordance with and with full respect for their respective functions, authority, powers and competencies as enshrined in the Charter.[58]

As the preceding paragraphs show, the Security Council is willing to take a broader approach to maintaining international peace and security, including the adoption of more proactive measures to advance economic and social development, not only as ends in themselves, but also as a means to avoid conflict. In this regard, the Council has recognised the need for the assistance of other UN bodies in carrying out its mandate to maintain international peace and security. The contributions of the General Assembly and the ECOSOC, in this regard, have been largely welcomed.

3 Human rights mechanisms: Cementing the nexus between the Security Council, the General Assembly and the ECOSOC

The Human Rights Council and its predecessor, the Commission on Human Rights, have generated a vast body of international human rights law as they discharged their functions to develop treaty standards. They have also gathered further human rights information through the establishment of a Special Procedures Mechanism, fact-finding commissions and, latterly, the Universal Periodic Review.[59] In this way, both bodies have facilitated the articulation of human rights – as social and legal standards – to be achieved and maintained.

The Security Council has drawn upon such standards on an increasing basis since the early 1990s. In the face of gross human rights violations, the Council has set aside Member States' rights to sovereign equality and territorial integrity, as provided for in Article 2(4) of the Charter, to deploy peace enforcement operations.[60] The view of one Secretary-General was to insist that in local conflicts,

58 UNSC Presidential Statement UN Doc 19 (2015) S/PRST/2015/19, 1.

59 See UNSC Res 2282 (27 April 2016) UN Doc S/RES/2282, para 11, where the Council encouraged Member States participating in the Universal Periodic Review to consider the human rights dimensions of peacebuilding.

60 The most notable recent example in the Council's adoption of UNSC Res 1973 (17 March 2011) UN Doc S/RES/1973, in which the Council authorised UN Member States to take all necessary measures, to protect civilians and civilian populated areas under threat of attack in the Libyan Arab Jamahiriya. However, the adoption of such resolutions is not without precedent. In UNSC Res 713 (25 September 1991) UN Doc S/RES/713, the Security Council determined that the situation in former Yugoslavia which was characterised by 'fighting causing heavy loss of human life and material damage, and by the consequences for the countries in the region, in particular in the border areas of neighbouring countries', preambular para 3. Similarly, in UNSC Res 688 (5 April 1991) UN Doc S/RES/688, the Security Council had determined that the consequences of the Iraqi repossession of its civilian population in different parts of the country, including areas populated by Kurds, involving considerable refugee flows over the borders with Turkey

'when all semblance of state authority vanishes, as in Somalia, and when whole populations are singled out for genocide as in Rwanda', then the Security Council was acting under the Charter to maintain international peace and security and was not intervening in internal affairs.[61] In 2004, the Secretary-General's High-level Panel on Threats, Challenges and Change also reported that:

> the Council and the wider international community have come to accept that, under Chapter VII . . . it can always authorize military action to redress catastrophic internal wrongs if it is prepared to declare that the situation is a "threat to international peace and security", not especially difficult when breaches of international law are involved.[62]

The concept of peace enforcement for the protection of populations is reflected in the Outcome Document of the 2005 World Summit,[63] the adoption of UNSC Resolution 1674 and the evolution of Security Council practice around the protection of civilians and, in particular, the need to protect children and women in armed conflict. However, what is also clear is that States themselves have the primary responsibility for the protection of their populations and that the UN will intervene only when the threat to the civilian population is regarded as being a threat to international peace and security.

Much of the Security Council's efforts in this regard have drawn from its improved relationship with the UN's human rights bodies. The Security Council has used Rule 39 of its Rules of Procedures to engage with the Special Procedures Mechanism established by the Human Rights Council, as well as to engage with the High Commissioner for Human Rights (the High Commissioner), a subsidiary and functional Commission of the ECOSOC. Similarly to the extension of

---

and Iran threatened international peace and security. UNSC Res 733 (23 January 1992) UN Doc S/RES/733 held that the situation in Somalia amounted to a threat, and in UNSC Res 794 (3 December 1992) UN Doc S/RES/794 the Council underlined that 'the magnitude of the human tragedy caused by the conflict in Somalia, further exacerbated by the obstacles being created to the distribution of humanitarian assistance, constitutes a threat to international peace and security', preambular para 3. In UNSC Res 788 (19 November 1992) UN Doc S/RES/788, the Council decided that the deteriorating civil war situation in Liberia constituted a threat to international peace. In UNSC Res 955 (8 November 1994) UN Doc S/RES/955, the genocide in Rwanda constituted a threat to international peace and security. The situation in Haiti was a significant development, as in UNSC Res 841 (16 June 1993) UN Doc S/RES/841, the Council identified 'incidences of humanitarian crises, including mass displacements of population, becoming or aggravating threats to international peace and security' and the 'climate of fear of persecution and economic dislocation which could increase the number of Haitians seeking refuge in neighbouring Member States' as comprising threats to the peace, paras 9 and 10 respectively.

61 Boutros Boutros-Ghali, 'Beleaguered Are the Peacekeepers' *New York Times* (New York 30 October 1994) <http://www.nytimes.com/1994/10/30/opinion/beleaguered-are-the-peacekeepers.html> accessed 8 July 2016.

62 UN Secretary-General, *A More Secure World: Our Shared Responsibility: Report of the High level Panel on Threats, Challenges and Change* (United Nations 2004), para 202.

63 UNGA Res 60/1 (24 October 2005) UN Doc A/RES/60/1.

invitations to the Presidents of the General Assembly and the ECOSOC, the extension of these invitations resulted in some discussion within the Council regarding the respective competencies of the Security Council and the General Assembly.[64]

3.1 *The Human Rights Council's Special Procedures Mechanism at the Security Council*

The Human Rights Council is a subsidiary body of the General Assembly.[65] It replaced the Commission on Human Rights, which was a subsidiary body of the ECOSOC. The Human Rights Council is the principal UN intergovernmental body charged with promoting and protecting human rights. The Council has a number of mechanisms by which it discharges its role, and these mechanisms have also contributed to the work of the Security Council.

The most well-established mechanism is the Special Procedures Mechanism, which was established by the Commission on Human Rights.[66] Special procedures are mechanisms established to monitor the implementation of human rights. The mandates of the Special Procedures are established and defined by resolution passed the Human Rights Council.[67] Some Special Procedures may be arranged by theme with the mandate of investigating the extent to which specific human rights are promoted and protected globally. Alternatively, the Special Procedures Mechanism can be country specific and thus devoted to examining the extent to which human rights are promoted and protection within a particular State. Current mandates include torture, violence against women, issues of health and housing, and specific country situations, such as Myanmar, Sudan and North Korea. Mandate-holders are required to monitor, analyse, advise and, as necessary, rapidly respond to reported human rights violations anywhere in the world. They carry out their tasks through country visits, carrying out studies, intervening on behalf of individuals, and reporting back with recommendations for action. The precise approach adopted may vary from one mandate to another,[68]

64 For the relevant statements, see UNSC Verbatim Record (11 August 1992) UN Doc S/PV.3105, 6–12 (India, Zimbabwe and China); UNSC Verbatim Record (13 November 1992) UN Doc S/PV.3134, 9–11 (China and Zimbabwe); and UNSC Verbatim Record (23 November 1992) UN Doc S/PV.3139, 3–5 (China and Zimbabwe) and 6–12 (Ecuador). On the question of participation under rule 39 of the Council's provisional rules of procedure, see UNSC (n 1).

65 UNGA Res 60/251 (15 March 2006) UN Doc A/RES/60/251, para 1.

66 See generally, Claire Breen, 'Revitalising the United Nations Human Rights Special Procedures Mechanisms as a Means of Achieving and Maintaining International Peace and Security' (2008) 12 *Max Planck Yearbook of United Nations Law* 177.

67 The mechanism may designate either an individual (who may be accorded one of a number of titles such as 'Special Rapporteur') or a group of individuals, a Working Group, with the responsibility of operating the Special Procedure.

68 Examples of well-developed follow-up arrangements can be found, for example, in the work of the Working Group on enforced and involuntary disappearances, the Special Rapporteur on the question of torture and other cruel, inhuman or degrading treatment or punishment, and the Special Rapporteur on extrajudicial, summary or arbitrary executions.

but it will include the adoption of a full range of 'measures taken to encourage, facilitate and monitor the implementation of recommendations by any of the [S]pecial [P]rocedures'.[69] Although their titles vary, each mandate-holder is considered to be an 'expert on mission' within the meaning of the 1946 Convention on Privileges and Immunities of the United Nations.[70] Mandate-holders are not employees of the UN, and they serve in their personal capacity and as independent experts. Such independence is crucial to the requirement that they act impartially.[71] This impartiality and independence has allowed mandate-holders to operate more freely than other UN positions, such as Special Representatives of the Secretary-General, and it has allowed mandate-holders to be critical of UN organs, including the Security Council, when necessary.[72] One of the key functions of the Special Procedures system is to act as an early warning mechanism in relation to situations involving serious violations of human rights.[73] Where such situations amount to a threat to or breach of the peace, more effective engagement with the Security Council has been recommended,[74] 'whether on the basis of the Arria [sic.] formula or some other basis'.[75] On occasion, such warnings have been ignored with disastrous consequences.[76]

See OHCHR, 'Manual of Operations of the Special Procedures of the Human Rights Council' (August 2008) <http://www.ohchr.org/Documents/HRBodies/SP/Manual_August_2008.doc> accessed 8 July 2016.

69 ECOSOC, 'Note by the High Commissioner for Human Rights Transmitting to the Commission the Report of the Twelfth Meeting of Special Rapporteurs/Representatives, Independent Experts and Chairpersons of Working Groups of the Special Procedures of the CHR' (2005) UN Doc E/CN.4/2006/4, para 85.

70 Convention on Privileges and Immunities of the United Nations (adopted 13 February 1946, entered into force 17 September 1946) 1 UNTS 15; and *Applicability of Article VI, Section 22, of the Convention on the Privileges and Immunities of the United Nations* (Advisory Opinion) [1989] ICJ Rep 177.

71 OHCHR, 'Human Rights Fact Sheet N.27: Seventeen Frequently Asked Questions about United Nations Special Rapporteurs' <http://www.ohchr.org/Documents/Publications/FactSheet27en.pdf> accessed 8 July 2016.

72 Joanna Naples-Mitchell, 'Perspectives of UN Special Rapporteurs on Their Role: Inherent Tensions and Unique Contributions to Human Rights' (2011) 15(2) *International Journal of Human Rights* 232, 236.

73 See, for example, UNSC, 'Report of the Independent Inquiry into the Actions of the United Nations during the 1994 Genocide in Rwanda 1999/1257' (1999) UN Doc S/1999/1257.

74 OHCHR, 'Enhancing and Strengthening the Effectiveness of the Special Procedures of the Commission on Human Rights: An Open-Ended Seminar in Consultation with the Expanded Bureau of the Commission, as Part of the Effort to Enhance and Strengthen the Effectiveness of the Special Procedures' (Background Paper) HCR December 2005/113, 9.

75 See OHCHR, Report of the United Nations High Commissioner for Human Rights and Follow-Up to the World Conference on Human Rights, Effective Functioning of Human Rights Mechanisms, E/CN.4/2006/4 (2005), para 76.

76 See, Micah Zenko and Rebecca R Friedman, 'UN Early Warning for Preventing Conflict' (2011) 18(1) *International Peacekeeping* 21; Jeroen Gutter, 'Special Procedures and the Human Rights Council: Achievements and Challenges Ahead' (2007) 7(1) *Human Rights Law Review* 93; and Ralph Mamiya and Haidi Willmot, 'Early Warning, the Protection of Civilians and United Nations Peacekeeping Operations' (2013) 22(2) *African Security Review* 68.

In the early 1990s, the Council began to rely upon the Special Rapporteurs that had been appointed by the Commission on Human Rights in response to situations of grave human rights abuses and violations of international humanitarian law in Iraq, former Yugoslavia, Rwanda and Burundi. During their review of the situation in Iraq,[77] in March 1992, several Council members[78] referred to the findings contained in the report of the Special Rapporteur on the human rights situation in Iraq (UN Doc S/23685/Add.1). The President of the Council made specific mention of the fact that the Special Rapporteur had, in his report, linked the continued repression of the Iraqi population with the on-going threat to international peace and security in the region as identified in Resolution 688 (1991).[79] The Special Rapporteur also addressed the Council, during which he reported on the Iraqi government's continued policy of repression against the Kurdish population in the north and the Shiites in the southern marshes, in violation of Resolution 688 (1991).[80] The Special Rapporteur attended a subsequent Council meeting,[81] and the ensuing Council statement referred to the Special Rapporteur's reports and his participation in that meeting.[82]

In response to the situation in former Yugoslavia, the Council demanded that the Special Rapporteur on the situation in former Yugoslavia, amongst others, be given immediate and unrestricted access by the Bosnian Serb party to investigate atrocities.[83] The reports of the Special Rapporteur formed part of the proceedings of the Security Council, and the Security Council also invited the Special Rapporteur to participate in its meeting.[84] Amongst the Special Rapporteur's recommendations was that a commission should be created to assess and further investigate specific cases in which prosecution might be warranted. The Council requested the Secretary-General to establish a Commission of Experts. Several Council members were of the view that the Special Rapporteur's report should

77 The Security Council had condemned human rights violations in Iraq and expressed its hope that the human and political rights of all Iraqi citizens would be respected: UNSC Res 688 (5 April 1991) UN Doc S/RES/688, paras 1 and 2.

78 UNSC Verbatim Record (11 March 1992) UN Doc S/PV.3059, 22 (Austria), 30 (United Kingdom), 45–46 (United States), 51–52 (Russian Federation) and 67 (Belgium).

79 UNSC, 'Statement by the President of the Security Council Concerning General and Specific Obligations of Iraq under Various Security Council Resolutions Relating to the Situation between Iraq and Kuwait' (11 March 1992) UN Doc S/23699.

80 UNSC Verbatim Record (11 August 1992) UN Doc S/PV.3105, 17. The Special Rapporteur had noted the high levels of dysentery and cholera and related deaths, and that food insecurity and extreme poverty had meant that the Kurdish population were resorting to extreme measures to stay alive: UNSC Verbatim Record (11 August 1992) UN Doc S/PV.3105, 14–17.

81 UNSC Verbatim Record (23 November 1992) UN Doc S/PV.3139.

82 UNSC, 'Note by the President of the Security Council 24836' (1992) UN Doc S/24836.

83 UNSC Res 1034 (21 December 1995) UN Doc S/RES/1034, para 8. See also, UNSC Res 787 (16 November 1992) UN Doc S/RES/787, paras 7 and 8.

84 UNSC Verbatim Record (6 October 1992) UN Doc S/PV.3119.

be taken into account by this Commission.[85] Following its consideration of two reports of the Special Rapporteur (UN Docs S/24516 and S/24766) and the participation of the Special Rapporteur,[86] the Council:

> not[ed] with grave concern the report of the Special Rapporteur . . . which ma[de] clear that massive and systematic violations of human rights and grave violations of international humanitarian law continue[d] in the Republic of Bosnia and Herzegovina.[87]

The role of the Special Rapporteur on the situation in Rwanda was also considered by the Council. It requested the Secretary-General to ensure that the United Nations Assistance Mission for Rwanda (UNAMIR) extended close cooperation with the Special Rapporteur.[88] The Council further requested that the information submitted to the Special Rapporteur be made available to the Commission of Experts to investigate grave violations of international humanitarian law, and it called for adequate coordination and cooperation between the work of the Commission of Experts and the Special Rapporteur in the performance of their respective tasks.[89] The representative of New Zealand welcomed 'the recognition given in [the] resolution to the importance of close cooperation between UNAMIR and the activities of the . . . recently appointed United Nations Special Rapporteur for Rwanda'.[90] A role for the mandate-holders was also implicit in S/RES/1012 (1995) by which the Council called upon States and relevant UN bodies, and appropriate international humanitarian organisations, to collate substantiated information in their possession and to make such information available as soon as possible and to provide appropriate assistance to the Commission of Inquiry on the situation in Burundi to be established by the Secretary-General. More recently, in relation to the situation in the Democratic People's Republic of Korea, Council members called upon that State to allow the Special Rapporteur to visit the country.[91]

As with the participation of representatives of the General Assembly and the ECOSOC, there were differing views about the participation of the Special Rapporteurs in Security Council meetings, as well as the competency of the Council to deal with human rights issues on the basis that matters relating to human rights

85 See UNSC Verbatim Record (6 October 1992) UN Doc S/PV.3119, 8 (Venezuela), 12 (United States), 13 (Hungary) and 16–17 (France).
86 UNSC Verbatim Record (13 November 1992) UN Doc S/PV.3134, 9–11.
87 UNSC Res 787 (16 November 1992) UN Doc S/RES/787, preambular para 9.
88 UNSC Res 925 (8 June 1994) UN Doc S/RES/925, para 10.
89 UNSC Res 935 (1 July 1994) UN Doc S/RES/935, para 4.
90 UNSC Verbatim Record (8 June 1994) UN Doc S/PV.3388, 10 and also see 3–4; and UNSC Verbatim Record (1 July 1994) UN Doc S/PV.3400, 3–4 (United States), 7 (China) and 5 (France).
91 UNSC Verbatim Record (10 December 2015) UN Doc S/PV.7575, 10 (Jordan) and 14 (Chile).

did not fall within the competence of the Security Council.[92] In relation to the situation in Rwanda, reservations were expressed at Resolution 934's elements relating to the Special Rapporteur.[93] The Charter's explicit provisions on the mandates of the Security Council, the General Assembly and other UN organs were also recalled, and it was stressed that the Security Council should 'refrain from involvement in activities that [went] beyond its mandate'.[94] The matter of the participation of the Special Rapporteurs was resolved by the Council noting that the Special Rapporteurs were to be invited in their personal capacity and not in any representative capacity.[95]

This initial period of formal dialogue between the Special Rapporteurs and the Security Council was short-lived and seems to have ended in the mid 1990s, despite a further brief re-emergence in the first three years of the 21st century. The apparent decrease in direct and formal dialogue between the OHCHR and the Security Council also came at a time of the increased use of Arria Formula meetings.[96] The Council seems to have revived its recognition of the work of the Special Rapporteurs more recently. As regards the situation concerning Western Sahara, the Council welcomed Morocco's on-going interaction with the Special Procedures Mechanism.[97] In establishing the human rights mandate of the United Nations Operation in Côte d'Ivoire (UNOCI), the Council decided that UNOCI would support efforts to promote and protect human rights in close coordination with the independent expert of the Human Rights Council.[98] In relation to the situation in the Central African Republic (CAR), the Council has noted, with appreciation, the decision to appoint a UN independent expert to monitor the situation of human rights in the CAR and to make recommendations concerning technical assistance and capacity-building in the field of human rights.[99] The report of the Special Rapporteur on the human rights situation in the Democratic People's Republic of Korea was identified as a further source of information by Council members.[100]

92 UNSC Verbatim Record (11 August 1992) UN Doc S/PV.3105, on the situation in Iraq, 6–7 (India), 7–10 (Ecuador), 11–12 (Zimbabwe) and 12 (China); and UNSC Verbatim Record (13 November 1992) UN Doc S/PV.3134, on the situation in former Yugoslavia, 9–11. See also, UNSC Verbatim Record (23 November 1992) UN Doc S/PV.3139.

93 UNSC Verbatim Record (8 June 1994) UN Doc S/PV.3388, 12 (China).

94 Ibid.

95 See, for example, UNSC Verbatim Record (23 November 1992) UN Doc S/PV.3105, 3.

96 Loraine Sievers and Sam Daws, *The Procedure of the UN Security Council* (4th edn, Oxford University Press, Oxford 2014) 76. For a complete list of Arria-Formula meetings between 1992 and 2016, see Security Council Report, Arria-Formula Meetings (19 August 2016) <http://www.securitycouncilreport.org/un-security-council-working-methods/arria-formula-meetings.php> accessed 28 September 2016.

97 UNSC Res 2099 (25 April 2013) UN Doc S/RES/2099, preambular para 14. See also, UNSC Res 1979 (27 April 2011) UN Doc S/RES/1979, preambular para 12.

98 UNSC Res 2000 (27 July 2011) UN Doc S/RES/2000, para 7(g) and UNSC Res 2112 (30 July 2013) UN Doc S/RES/2112, para 6(f).

99 UNSC Res 2121 (10 October 2013) UN Doc S/RES/2121, preambular para 6.

100 UNSC Verbatim Record (10 December 2015) UN Doc S/PV.7575, 6 (United Kingdom) and 8 (New Zealand).

The impartial and independent nature of the Special Procedures Mechanism makes the information that they gather, often at the grassroots level, a useful tool for the Security Council to draw upon as it seeks to respond to human rights violations that threaten its efforts to maintain international peace and security. Given that human rights violations have been a driver for Security Council action and given that they increasingly appear in peace operation mandates, calls by the Council for greater cooperation between Special Procedures Mechanisms and peacekeeping operations such as UNAMIR and UNOCI are notable.

3.2 The United Nations High Commissioner for Human Rights

The post of the High Commissioner was established in 1993.[101] The High Commissioner leads the OHCHR, which is a subsidiary of the UN Secretariat. The OHCHR provides substantive and Secretariat support to Charter-based and treaty-based human rights bodies. As the principal human rights official of the UN, the High Commissioner can play a key role linking the Security Council, the OHCHR and the Human Rights Council. The Security Council has drawn upon the expertise of the OHCHR and the High Commissioner, particularly since the late 1990s, and the High Commissioner has addressed the Council on numerous occasions in the intervening years. The input of the High Commissioner has, on the whole, been welcomed particularly in the thematic debates. However, strong resistance to the input of the High Commissioner is notable during certain country-specific debates, with much of such resistance being cast in terms of the appropriate role of the Security Council and UN human rights bodies under the terms of the Charter.

Some of the closest and positive relations between the High Commissioner and the Security Council have emerged in relation to the Council's consideration of the issue of civilians in armed conflict, debates that reveal the particular relevance of the relationship between human rights and peace and security. The High Commissioner first addressed the Council during its debate on the protection of civilians in armed conflict in 2001, and welcomed the increased usage of the Commission's special mechanisms and expressed hope that the Council could draw on the work of the OHCHR.[102] This theme re-emerged in 2007 when it was stated that regular briefings by the OHCHR (and the Special Procedures Mechanisms) could greatly contribute to the capacity of the Security Council both to provide effective prevention against abuses of civilian populations and to monitor the implementation of the relevant provisions of resolutions that the

101 UNGA Res 48/141 (20 December 1993) UN Doc A/RES/48/141.

102 UNSC Verbatim Record (23 April 2001) UN Doc S/PV.4312, 4–5 and 20. Further support for a closer relationship between the OHCHR and the Security Council was expressed at 10 (Ukraine), 12 (Tunisia), 17 (China), 18 (United States), 21 (Russian Federation) and 26 (Mali).

Council had adopted.[103] The importance of human rights has been highlighted subsequently with the statement that the resolution of conflict and the maintenance of peace and security would be neither achieved nor sustained without due attention being paid to redressing grievances, ending impunity and protecting the human rights of civilians. More particularly, in the context of this work, it was stated that international law should afford such protection and that the authority of international law could not be replaced by more amorphous notions of protection, or by less obligatory notions of charitable action.[104] These comments were received favourably.[105] The broader relevance of the role of the OHCHR and UN human rights mechanisms, including Special Rapporteurs, to the Security Council continues to be identified, as the High Commissioner has stated that the monitoring of human rights conditions by these bodies could serve to sound an alarm when situations are at risk of degenerating into violence.[106] In response, Council members have observed that the High Commissioner had very clearly shown the link between human rights and protection concerns[107] and that the voice of the High Commissioner was particularly relevant in the debate.[108] The High Commissioner, or a representative of the OHCHR, has continued to participate in Security Council debates on civilians in armed conflict in more recent years. Council members have continued to identify the role of the OHCHR in providing information on human rights violations not only as violations in their own right but also as violations that may impact on international peace and security.[109] Such views culminated in Resolution 2171 (2014), when the Security Council stated that it continues to recognise:

> the important role that the Office of the United Nations High Commissioner for Human Rights, inter alia, can play in conflict prevention and also

103 UNSC Verbatim Record (22 June 2007) UN Doc S/PV.5703, 26 (Japan) and 31 (Germany). See also, the comments of the President, speaking in his capacity as the UK representative, in UNSC Verbatim Record (9 December 2005) UN Doc S/PV.5319 (Resumption 1), 9; UNSC Verbatim Record (4 December 2006) UN Doc S/PV.5577 (2006), 15 (Greece); and UNSC Verbatim Record (4 December 2006) UN Doc S/PV.5577 (Resumption 1), 11 (Finland, speaking on behalf of the EU).

104 UNSC Verbatim Record (11 November 2009) UN Doc S/PV.6216, 8 (Deputy High Commissioner of Human Rights).

105 UNSC Verbatim Record (11 November 2009) UN Doc S/PV.6216; and UNSC Verbatim Record (11 November 2009) UN Doc S/PV.6216 (Resumption 1), 8.

106 UNSC Verbatim Record (7 July 2010) UN Doc S/PV.6354, 8.

107 UNSC Verbatim Record (7 July 2010) UN Doc S/PV.6354, 11 (Austria).

108 UNSC Verbatim Record (7 July 2010) UN Doc S/PV.6354, 31 (Germany). The High Commissioner also addressed the Council on the matter of civilians in armed conflict in November 2010: UNSC Verbatim Record (22 November 2010) UN Doc S/PV.6427; and UNSC Verbatim Record (22 November 2010) UN Doc S/PV.6427 (Resumption 1).

109 See also, for example, UNSC Verbatim Record (10 May 2011) UN Doc S/PV.6531, 16 (Colombia); UNSC Verbatim Record (10 May 2011) UN Doc S/PV.6531 (Resumption 1), 15–16 (Croatia), 17 (Austria) and 27 (Bangladesh); UNSC Verbatim Record (9 November 2011) UN Doc S/PV.6650; UNSC Verbatim Record (9 November 2011) UN Doc S/PV.6650 (Resumption 1), 17 (Japan); UNSC Verbatim Record (25 June 2012)

recognizes the role that their briefings on human rights violations and hate speech play in contributing to early awareness of potential conflict (original emphasis).[110]

Other thematic debates have facilitated calls for enhanced cooperation and dialogue between the Security Council and the High Commissioner.[111] In relation to the Council's working methods, representatives of a large number of States have called for more frequent meetings with the High Commissioner,[112] particularly given that human rights violations can be a harbinger of more serious trouble.[113] More specifically, during the Council's discussion on conflict prevention, the High Commissioner observed that human rights grievances can build up over years and even decades, making specific mention of the denial of economic and social rights in that regard. According to the High Commissioner, early detection systems, such as the Special Procedures experts, and systematic scrutiny by treaty bodies had provided repeated alerts to those shortfalls. The High Commissioner noted that, in spite of the Council's increased interest in human rights, there had not always been a firm and principled decision by members of the Council to put an end to crises.[114]

Some of the earliest indications of a closer interrelationship between the High Commissioner and the Security Council have stemmed from country-specific

UN Doc S/PV.6790; UNSC Verbatim Record (25 June 2012) UN Doc S/PV.6790 (Resumption 1); UNSC Verbatim Record (12 February 2013) UN Doc S/PV.6917; UNSC Verbatim Record (12 February 2013) UN Doc S/PV.6917 (Resumption 1); UNSC Verbatim Record (19 August 2013) UN Doc S/PV.7019; UNSC Verbatim Record (17 July 2013) UN Doc S/PV.7003; UNSC Verbatim Record (17 July 2013) UN Doc S/PV.7003 (Resumption 1); and UNSC Verbatim Record (12 February 2014) UN Doc S/PV.7109, 2.

110 UNSC Res 2171 (21 August 2014) UN Doc S/RES/2171 on 'Maintenance of International Peace and Security', para 17.

111 In connection with maintenance of international peace and security, see UNSC Verbatim Record (16 July 2010) UN Doc S/PV.6360 (Resumption 1), 10 (Senegal). In connection with women and peace and security, see UNSC Verbatim Record (26 October 2010) UN Doc S/PV.6411, 28 (Russian Federation) and 30 (China). In connection with protection of civilians in armed conflict, see UNSC Verbatim Record (10 May 2011) UN Doc S/PV.6531, 16 (Colombia); and UNSC Verbatim Record (9 November 2011) UN Doc S/PV.6650 (Resumption 1), 17 (Japan).

112 See, for example, UNSC Verbatim Record (22 April 2010) UN Doc S/PV.6300 (Resumption 1), 8 (Argentina); UNSC Verbatim Record (30 November 2011) UN Doc S/PV.6672, 10 (Germany); UNSC Verbatim Record (28 August 2014) UN Doc S/PV.7254; UNSC Verbatim Record (20 October 2015) UN Doc S/PV.7539, 19 (France); UNSC Verbatim Record (20 October 2015) UN Doc S/PV.7539 (Resumption 1), 33 (Spain); UNSC Verbatim Record (23 October 2014) UN Doc S/PV.7285, 7 (Australia); UNSC Verbatim Record (22 December 2014) UN Doc S/PV.7352, 7 (Luxembourg); and UNSC Verbatim Record (26 November 2012) UN Doc S/PV.6870, 15 (France).

113 UNSC Verbatim Record (20 October 2015) UN Doc S/PV.7539, 12 (Lithuania); UNSC Verbatim Record (20 October 2015) UN Doc S/PV.7539 (Resumption 1), 3 (Italy); UNSC Verbatim Record (28 August 2014) UN Doc S/PV.7254, 10 (Luxembourg); and UNSC Verbatim Record (23 October 2014) UN Doc S/PV.7285, 8 (Jordan).

114 UNSC Verbatim Record (21 August 2014) UN Doc S/PV.7247, 4.

situations. The Council identified the High Commissioner as being one entity having a role in expediting the establishment of the Truth and Reconciliation Commission and the Special Court for Sierra Leone.[115] The High Commissioner has addressed the Security Council on the extensive and gross human rights abuses occurring in the Democratic Republic of the Congo (the DRC).[116] The High Commissioner presented the findings of the International Commission of Inquiry on the conflict in Darfur (S/2005/60) to the Council, stating that a referral to the International Criminal Court was the only credible way to bring the perpetrators of the crimes to justice. On the situation in the Middle East, the Council has noted the concerns expressed by the High Commissioner.[117] The High Commissioner has gone on to participate in Council debates on the situation in the Middle East,[118] with the presence of the High Commissioner being welcomed by Council members.[119] The High Commissioner has briefed the Council on the situation in Libya and has reiterated the OHCHR's willingness to work with the UN Support Mission in Libya (UNSMIL), its readiness to respond to requests for technical assistance, to help in consultation processes, to build institutional capacity and to monitor and report on human rights developments.[120] The High Commissioner's efforts and those of the OHCHR were subsequently welcomed by Security Council members.[121] During debates on the situation in the Ukraine, the work of the OHCHR was referred to positively as a source of information by a number of Council members,[122] although the Russian representative did describe the reports of the OHCHR as 'baseless fabrications'.[123] The High Commissioner, along with the Special Advisor to the Secretary-General on the Prevention of Genocide, also reported to the Council on their visit to South Sudan,[124] reports which were received favourably.[125]

115 UNSC Res 1346 (30 March 2001) UN Doc S/RES/1346, para 14.
116 UNSC Verbatim Record (13 February 2003) UN Doc S/PV.4705, 4–7; and UNSC Verbatim Record (7 July 2003) UN Doc S/PV.4784, 4–9 (Deputy High Commissioner for Human Rights).
117 UNSC Res 2014 (21 October 2011) UN Doc S/RES/2014, preambular para 7.
118 UNSC Verbatim Record (22 December 2015) UN Doc S/PV.7596, 2.
119 See, for example, UNSC Verbatim Record (22 December 2015) UN Doc S/PV.7596, 7 (United Kingdom), 12 (China), 15 (Russian Federation) and 16 (New Zealand).
120 UNSC Verbatim Record (25 January 2012) UN Doc S/PV.6707, 8–9.
121 UNSC Verbatim Record (16 May 2012) UN Doc S/PV.6772, 6 (Russian Federation), 7 (Portugal) and 13 (Togo).
122 See, for example, UNSC Verbatim Record (6 March 2015) UN Doc S/PV.7400, 6–7 (Lithuania), 12 (United Kingdom) and 14 (Jordan); and UNSC Verbatim Record (16 April 2014) UN Doc S/PV.7157, 7 (United Kingdom), 9 (United States of America) and 18 (Nigeria).
123 UNSC Verbatim Record (16 April 2014) UN Doc S/PV.7157, 7.
124 UNSC Verbatim Record (2 May 2014) UN Doc S/PV.7168, 2.
125 See for example, UNSC Verbatim Record (2 May 2014) UN Doc S/PV.7168, 6 (United States of America), 7 (Australia), 9 (China) and 10 (Russian Federation).

Although the High Commissioner did not initially address the Council on the situation in the Democratic People's Republic of Korea, the work of the OHCHR was subject to much discussion during the first of recent debates.[126] The High Commissioner has addressed the Council on the situation, speaking about the independent International Commission of Inquiry established by the Human Rights Council. The High Commissioner noted that the Commission of Inquiry had concluded that '[t]he gravity, scale and nature of [the human rights] violations reveal a State that does not have any parallel in the contemporary world' (A/HRC/25/63, para 80) before outlining further allegations which had emerged from OHCHR's recent monitoring and documentation efforts.[127] The High Commissioner also stated that the General Assembly's call to the Security Council to take action by referring the situation to the International Criminal Court was essential, given the scale and extreme gravity of the allegations.[128]

In relation to the situation in Burundi, the High Commissioner has called upon the Security Council to act, stating:

> it is the responsibility of the Security Council to address a situation of profound concern, well known for many months, and which could lead to even greater carnage. . . . The Council may also wish to consider involving Chapter VII of the Charter of the United Nations to stop the ongoing violence and prevent a regional conflict.[129]

Subsequently, the Council, after '[R]ecognizing the role and efforts of the High Commissioner for Human Rights to assess and report on the situation of human rights in Burundi', called 'upon the Government of Burundi to respect, protect and guarantee all human rights and fundamental freedoms for all, . . . and to cooperate fully with the Office of the High Commissioner in the fulfilment of its mandate . . .'.[130]

Although the High Commissioner's briefings have been largely welcomed over the years,[131] the situation in North Korea has provided some of the strongest pushback on the roles of the Security Council and the Human Rights Council. According to the representative of China, 'China is always opposed to the Security Council's intervention in issues that concern a country's human rights. The Security Council is not the place to address human rights issues. More important,

126 UNSC Verbatim Record (22 December 2014) UN Doc S/PV.7353.
127 UNSC Verbatim Record (10 December 2015) UN Doc S/PV.7575, 5.
128 Ibid, 6.
129 UNSC Verbatim Record (9 November 2015) UN Doc S/PV.7553, 5.
130 UNSC Res 2248 (12 November 2015) UN Doc S/RES/2248, preambular para 10 and para 2, respectively.
131 See, for example, UNSC Verbatim Record (10 December 2015) UN Doc S/PV.7575, 6 (United Kingdom) and 12 (Lithuania).

human rights issues should not be politicized.'[132] Similarly, the representative of Russia stated that:

> We believe that the issue of the human rights situation in any given country does not fall within the mandate of the Security Council and should be taken up in the specialized bodies, above all in the Human Rights Council . . . Burdening the agenda of the Security Council with matters that do not fall within its purview will only lead to duplication of effort, thereby dissipating the Council's focus and energy and consequently reducing the effectiveness of its work.[133]

In a similar vein, the representative of the Bolivarian Republic of Venezuela rejected trends by the Council to deal with topics outside its specific mandate, which it identified as being the maintenance of international peace and security. Such trends were regarded as being a de facto attempt to alter the founding principles of the Charter and to employ a double standard to redefine what does and does not constitute a threat to international peace and security and the meaning of the principle of sovereignty.[134]

The previous paragraphs show that the High Commissioner has drawn the Council's attention to significant human rights violations for a number of years. The reception of such information has been mixed, on occasion. However, the relationship between human rights, armed conflict and conflict prevention has been highlighted by the High Commissioner and has been acknowledged by the Council, as demonstrated by the degree to which human rights now permeate the discussions, statements and resolutions of the Council.

4 The Peacebuilding Commission: Supporting the nexus between the Security Council, the General Assembly and the ECOSOC

The Peacebuilding Commission was established in response to recognition of the fact that although there was increasing clarity as to the meaning and significance to be attached to the concept of peacebuilding, a problem remained, and that was that there was 'a gaping hole in the United Nations institutional machinery: no part of the United Nations system effectively addresse[d] the challenge of helping countries with the transition from war to lasting peace'.[135] To achieve this

132 UNSC Verbatim Record (10 December 2015) UN Doc S/PV.7575, 7 (China). See also, 8 (Angola) and 9 (Chad).

133 UNSC Verbatim Record (10 December 2015) UN Doc S/PV.7575, 14 (Russian Federation).

134 UNSC Verbatim Record (10 December 2015) UN Doc S/PV.7575, 10 (Bolivia).

135 UNGA, 'Report of the Secretary-General 59/2005' (2005) UN Doc A/59/2005 'In Larger Freedom: Towards Development, Security and Human Rights for All', para 114.

end, the Secretary-General recommended the establishment of the Peacebuilding Architecture (comprising the Peacebuilding Commission and a Peacebuilding Support Office).[136] The Peacebuilding Commission was established in 2005,[137] as a subsidiary body of the Security Council and the General Assembly.[138] Its main aim is to bring together all relevant actors to marshal resources and to advise on and propose integrated strategies for post-conflict peacebuilding and recovery[139] in relation to agreed country-specific situations.[140] The Commission provides advice to the Security Council on the planning and commencement of peacebuilding activities[141] and it can work with the ECOSOC, bearing in mind the latter's role as a principal body for issues of economic and social cooperation and development.[142] The Commission has a standing Organizational Committee, which is responsible for developing its own rules of procedure and working methods. One of the most significant features of the Commission, from the perspective of inter-organ relationships, is that 21 of the 31 members of the Organisational Committee are drawn evenly from the Security Council, the General Assembly and the ECOSOC.[143] The equality in membership numbers suggests that the UN recognises the value of economic and social cooperation, and the promotion and protection of human rights within that framework, as necessary elements of conflict prevention.

The Security Council has specifically referred to the role of the Peacebuilding Commission during its thematic debates, including those on strengthening international law: rule of law and maintenance of international peace and security,[144]

136 Ibid. The Secretary-General went on to elaborate the concept of peacebuilding in his position paper 'Supplement to An Agenda for Peace', in which he noted that 'Demilitarization, the control of small arms, institutional reform, improved police and judicial systems, the monitoring of human rights, electoral reform and social and economic development can be as valuable in preventing conflict as in healing the wounds after conflict has occurred.' See UNGA, 'Report of the Secretary General 1995/1' (1995) UN Doc A/50/60-S/1995/1, para 47.

137 UN Charter (n 6), Articles 7, 22 and 29.

138 UNSC Res 1645 (20 December 2005) UN Doc S/RES/1645; and UNGA Res 60/80 (30 December 2005) UN Doc A/RES/60/180, respectively. Although these resolutions brought the new bodies into operation, the origins of the Peacebuilding Commission can be traced to the decision to found the Commission, which was taken at the actual founding decision was taken at the World Summit in September 2005. However, the origins of peacebuilding within the UN go back 1995 when the Secretary-General defined and discussed peacebuilding in 'An Agenda for Peace', which informed the UN reports *A More Secure World* (n 62) and 'In Larger Freedom' (n 135).

139 UNSC Res 1645 (20 December 2005) UN Doc S/RES/1645, para 2(a).

140 Ibid, para 7.

141 Ibid, para 16.

142 Ibid, para 17.

143 UNSC Res 1645 (20 December 2005) UN Doc S/RES/1645, para 4.

144 The Council attached vital importance to promoting justice and the rule of law, including respect for human rights, as an indispensable element for lasting peace. In that regard, the Council considered enhancement of the rule of law activities as crucial in the peacebuilding strategies in post-conflict societies and emphasised the role of the

threats to international peace and security,[145] maintenance of international peace and security,[146] women and peace and security,[147] and children and armed conflict.[148] The role of the Commission has been welcomed at the country-specific level.[149] The Security Council's broader approach to the maintenance of international peace and security and its emphasis on laying the foundation for sustainable peace and development to assist countries emerging from conflict through post-conflict peacebuilding can be seen as its readiness to make continued, if not greater, use of the advisory role of Peacebuilding Commission. The Council has emphasised the need for further harnessing the Commission's advisory, advocacy and resource mobilisation roles in advancing and supporting an integrated and coherent approach with respect to multidimensional peacekeeping mandates in countries on its agenda.[150]

Although it was hoped that the Commission would build bridges between the three pillars of peace and security, economic and social development and human rights and that it would bridge the traditional divide between the Security Council, the General Assembly and the ECOSOC, in recent years, the Commission seems to have been condemned to occupy a sort of no man's land within the fragmented landscape to which it now belongs.[151]

Peacebuilding Commission: UNSC Presidential Statement UN Doc 28 (2006) S/PRST/2006/28, 1.

145 UNSC Presidential Statement UN Doc 1 (2007) S/PRST/2007/1, 1.

146 UNSC Presidential Statement UN Doc 3 (2007) S/PRST/2007/3, 2; and UNSC Presidential Statement UN Doc 22 (2007) S/PRST/2007/22, 2.

147 UNSC Presidential Statement UN Doc 42 (2006) S/PRST/2006/42.

148 UNSC Res 1998 (12 July 2011) UN Doc S/RES/1998, para 19; and UNSC Presidential Statement UN Doc 8 (2013) S/PRST/2013/8, 4.

149 For the situation in the Central African Republic, see UNSC Presidential Statement UN Doc 26 (2010) S/PRST/2010/26, 2; and UNSC Res 2217 (28 April 2015) UN Doc S/RES/2217, para 5. For the situation in Burundi, see UNSC Res 1902 (17 December 2009) UN Doc S/RES/1902, preambular para 8 and para 14; UNSC Res 1959 (16 December 2010) UN Doc S/RES/1959, preambular para 8; UNSC Res 2137 (13 February 2014) UN Doc S/RES/2137, preambular para 14; UNSC Presidential Statement UN Doc 16 (2007) S/PRST/2007/16, 2; UNSC Res 1791 (19 December 2007) UN Doc S/RES/1791, preambular para 6; UNSC Res 2090 (13 February 2013) UN Doc S/RES/2090, preambular para 14; and UNSC Res 2137 (13 February 2014) UN Doc S/RES/2137, paras 3 and 19. For Guinea-Bissau, see UNSC Presidential Statement UN Doc 15 (2010) S/PRST/2010/15, 2; UNSC Res 1949 (23 November 2010) UN Doc S/RES/1949, preambular para 13; UNSC Res 2030 (21 December 2011) UN Doc S/RES/2030, preambular para 14; UNSC Res 2267 (26 February 2016) UN Doc S/RES/2267, preambular para 24; and UNSC Res 2203 (18 February 2015) UN Doc S/RES/2203, preambular para 21. For the situation in Sierra Leone, see UNSC Res 2065 (12 September 2012) UN Doc S/RES/2065, preambular para 14; UNSC Res 2097 (26 March 2013) UN Doc S/RES/2097, preambular para 11; and UNSC Presidential Statement UN Doc 6 (2014) S/PRST/2014/6, 2.

150 UNSC Res 2086 (21 January 2013) UN Doc S/RES/2086 relating to United Nations peacekeeping operations, para 19.

151 United Nations, 'The Challenge of Sustaining Peace. Report of the Advisory Group of Experts for the 2015 Review of the United Nations Peacebuilding Architecture'

5 Conclusion

This chapter has identified the legal basis for collaboration between the Security Council, the General Assembly and the ECOSOC, and it has provided evidence of the extent to which such collaboration has taken place. The chapter has also noted the concern and resistance expressed by some members of the Security Council in response to such collaboration. Such concerns stem from the differing perceptions of which situations meet the criterion of threats to international peace and security, as well as from the fact that many members of the General Assembly regard as encroachment any consideration by the Security Council of topics such as the security dimensions of development and environmental issues. Similarly, the Security Council (or some of its members, at least) has expressed unease at what it perceives as attempts by the General Assembly to encroach on matters relating to the maintenance of international peace through the so-called back door of peacebuilding.[152] Similar concerns have been expressed at the input of the ECOSOC, and discussions of human rights situations have been regarded by some States (but not always in a consistent manner) as falling outside the mandate of the Security Council. Such concerns are reflected in the observation that:

> From the UN's perspective, the triangular relationship between peace, development and human rights demands that the Organization's three respective pillars work closely together. But this continues to prove enormously challenging, a painful reflection of the fragmentation of the United Nations, born in the distribution of responsibilities contemplated in the Charter between the Security Council and the General Assembly, with the Economic and Social Council occupying an intermediate and somewhat ambiguous space in-between.[153]

For its part, the Security Council has emphasised that sustaining peace requires coherence, sustained engagement, and coordination between the General Assembly, the Security Council and the ECOSOC, consistent with their mandates as set out in the Charter.[154] Although the Security Council has not always been understood as a key peacebuilding actor,[155] the UN Charter provides the legal basis for the Security Council to adopt a broad approach in discharging its responsibility to maintain international peace and security, which allows the Council to draw from the expertise of other UN bodies charged with realising the Organisation's aim to promote economic and social progress and to

(29 June 2015), para 96 <http://www.un.org/en/peacebuilding/pdf/150630%20Report%20of%20the%20AGE%20on%20the%202015%20Peacebuilding%20Review%20FINAL.pdf> accessed 15 July 2016.

152 Ibid, para 62.

153 Ibid, para 40.

154 UNSC Res 2282 (27 April 2016) UN Doc S/RES/2282, para 2.

155 United Nations (n 151), para 67.

give effective realisation to human rights. These three goals underpin the aim of the Organisation to save succeeding generations from the scourges of war. Increased and more effective usage of such mechanisms can only be to the advantage of the Security Council and the mechanisms themselves. It is against this understanding that the role of the Council in peacebuilding and peacekeeping can be examined.

3 Peacebuilding and peace operations

The nexus of peace, economic and social progress and human rights

1 Introduction

The Security Council, the General Assembly and the ECOSOC individually – and through their combined efforts in the Peacebuilding Commission – recognise the link between peace and security, on the one hand, and economic and social progress on the other. The role for the High Commissioner of Human Rights, and the Special Procedures Mechanism of the Human Rights Council, as subsidiary bodies, reaffirms the contribution of human rights to such debates. Drawing from Chapter 2's analysis, this chapter will explore the extent to which the Security Council has incorporated the creation of just economic and social conditions, as well as human rights, into its own efforts to maintain international peace and security by focusing upon two of the Council's tools – namely, peacebuilding and peacekeeping operations.[1]

The chapter will open with an exploration of the economic and social dimensions of peace, as captured in UN policy on peacebuilding, as well as the Security Council's engagement with peacebuilding at a general level. Following from this examination, Chapter 3 will consider the role of peacekeeping as a means to give practical effect to the Council's, and the UN's, peacebuilding policy. The role of peacekeeping operations in this regard is also considered in light of the progressively complex nature of peacekeeping operations that are being deployed into a greater number of increasingly hostile environments, where the need for post-conflict reconstruction is increasingly emphasised. Chapter 3 also explores the integration of human rights standards into peacekeeping operations, both in thematic terms as well as in relation to country-specific operations, on the basis that it is one example of the Security Council's increasing recognition of the importance of human rights to the maintenance of international peace

1 In this regard, the Security Council is empowered to establish subsidiary organs as set out under Article 29 of the Charter of the United Nations (adopted 26 June 1945, entered into force 24 October 1945) 1 UNTS XVI (UN Charter), and as reflected in rule 28 of UNSC Provisional Rules of Procedure of the Security Council, S/96/Rev.7 (1982). These include peacekeeping operations, political missions, peacebuilding offices, sanctions and other committees overseeing international tribunals and working groups.

and security. Recognition of the integration of human rights into peacekeeping and peacebuilding in this way is one means to view the extent to which socio-economic considerations inform the Security Council's decision-making. Consideration of the economic and social dimensions of peace through the lens of human rights leads to a final consideration of this chapter, which is the concern that has been raised around the narrow nature of the peace that is being built, which does not adequately recognise socio-economic marginalisation as a driver of conflict, and which perpetuates the sidelining of economic and social rights as a solution to conflict.

2 Peacebuilding within the Security Council: The economic and social dimensions of international peace and security

From the early 1990s, post-conflict peacebuilding, comprising missions to strengthen and solidify peace, became the UN's principal peace and security activity. The Secretary-General's Report, *Agenda for Peace*, defined peacebuilding as an 'action to identify and support structures which will tend to strengthen and solidify peace in order to avoid a relapse into conflict'.[2] The Report suggested that peacebuilding would include functions such as:

> disarming the previously warring parties and the restoration of order, the custody and possible destruction of weapons, repatriating refugees, advisory and training support for security personnel, monitoring elections, advancing efforts to promote human rights, reforming or strengthening governmental institutions and promoting formal and informal processes of political participation.[3]

Modern peacebuilding would mean tackling 'root causes' of violence in order to 'build a lasting peace'.[4] The central goal of post-conflict peacebuilding was described as 'the consolidation of peace'.[5] In 2004, it was observed, in the 'Report of the High-level Panel on Threats, Challenges and Change', that:

> Along with establishing security, the core task of peacebuilding is to build effective public institutions that, through negotiations with civil society, can establish a consensual framework for governing within the rule of law. Relatively cheap investments in civilian security through police, judicial and

2 UNGA, 'Report of the Secretary General 24111' (1992) UN Doc A/47/277-S/24111, para 21.

3 Ibid, para 55. See also, UNGA, 'Report of the Secretary General 1995/1' (1995) UN Doc A/50/60-S/1995/1.

4 UNSG, 'Secretary-General Outlines Key Lessons for Building Peace in War-Torn Societies, in Lecture at University of Ulster' (18 October 2004) Press Release UN Doc SG/SM/9549. <http://www.un.org/press/en/2004/sgsm9549.doc.htm> accessed 21 July 2016.

5 UNGA, 'Report of the Secretary General 1998/318' (1998) UN Doc A/52/871-S/1998/318, para 63.

> rule-of-law reform, local capacity-building for human rights and reconciliation, and local capacity-building for public sector service delivery can greatly benefit long-term peacebuilding.[6]

In 2009, the UN non-paper, *New Horizons*, described peacebuilding in the immediate aftermath of conflict as requiring, amongst other things, support to basic safety and security, and for the provision of basic services such as water and sanitation, health and primary education, economic revitalisation (including employment generation), and livelihoods. Support to basic infrastructure, remuneration for national armed forces and police, and investment in emergency employment initiatives were regarded as being particularly critical for early peacebuilding.[7] More recently, the 2015 Review of the Peacebuilding Architecture adopted the term 'sustaining peace', which is a broader approach than peacebuilding. The Advisory Group of Experts on the 2015 Review of the United Nations Peacebuilding Architecture (the Advisory Group) regarded this term as being liberated from the strict limitation of post-conflict contexts that had been favoured by the Security Council.[8] Collectively, these reports constitute a rethinking of international policy on the maintenance of international peace and conflict prevention.

These broad institutional views have been reflected within the Security Council, as it has stated that it considered post-conflict peacebuilding to be closely linked to its primary responsibilities.[9] The importance of economic stability and development has manifested itself in the Security Council's vision of collective security in fragile and post-conflict States. From its earliest statements on peacebuilding, the Council has stressed the importance of promoting good governance, the rule

6 United Nations, 'A More Secure World: Our Shared Responsibility, Report of the Secretary-General's High-level Panel on Threats, Challenges and Change' (2004), para 229. <http://www.un.org/en/peacebuilding/pdf/historical/hlp_more_secure_world.pdf> accessed 15 July 2016. Outside of the UN, this view was echoed by the International Commission on Intervention and State Sovereignty (ICISS), which stated that:

> True and lasting reconciliation occurs with sustained daily efforts at repairing infrastructure, at rebuilding housing, at planting and harvesting, and cooperating in other productive activities. External support for reconciliation efforts must be conscious of the need to encourage this cooperation, and dynamically linked to joint development efforts between former adversaries.

ICISS, 'The Responsibility to Protect: Report of the International Commission on Intervention and State Sovereignty' (International Development Research Centre, Ottawa 2001), para 5.4.

7 Department of Peacekeeping Operations and Department of Field Support, 'A New Partnership Agenda Charting a New Horizon for UN Peacekeeping' (A Non-Paper, 2009) 23 <http://www.un.org/en/peacekeeping/documents/newhorizon.pdf> accessed 21 July 2016 (New Horizons).

8 United Nations, 'The Challenge of Sustaining Peace. Report of the Advisory Group of Experts for the 2015 Review of the United Nations Peacebuilding Architecture' (29 June 2015), para 26. <http://www.un.org/en/peacebuilding/pdf/150630%20Report%20of%20the%20AGE%20on%20the%202015%20Peacebuilding%20Review%20FINAL.pdf> accessed 15 July 2016.

9 See UNSC Presidential Statement UN Doc 20 (2005) S/PRST/2005/20, 1.

of law and sustainable development as essential factors in the prevention of conflicts.[10] In relation to conflict in Africa, the Council observed that it:

> recognizes the close linkage between the promotion of economic and social development and the prevention of conflict. It stresses that the quest for peace in Africa requires a comprehensive, concerted and determined approach, encompassing the eradication of poverty, the promotion of democracy, sustainable development and respect for human rights, as well as conflict prevention and resolution, including peacekeeping, and humanitarian assistance.[11]

In the context of the maintenance of peace and security and post-conflict peacebuilding, the Council underlined that economic rehabilitation and reconstruction often constitute the major tasks facing societies emerging from conflict and that significant international assistance becomes indispensable to promote sustainable development in such cases.[12] The Security Council has noted that conflict (in Africa) causes massive human displacement, suffering and poverty, perpetuates instability and diverts scarce resources from long-term development.[13] The Council has returned to this theme recently, as it welcomed initiatives by post-conflict countries to reduce poverty, deter conflict and provide better conditions to their populations.[14] More significantly, the Council has emphasised 'the importance of inclusivity in advancing national peacebuilding processes and objectives in order to ensure that the needs of all segments of society are taken into account'.[15]

The Council has recognised the broad nature of efforts required and the impact of short-term and long-term timescales. In recognising the preventive nature of peacebuilding, the Council stated that peacebuilding encompassed 'a wide range of political, development, humanitarian and human rights programmes and mechanisms', which required short-term and long-term actions tailored to address the particular needs of societies sliding into conflict or emerging from it.[16] In Resolution 2086 (2013), the Council reiterated its commitment to enhance the effectiveness of the UN in addressing conflict at all stages, from

10 UNSC Res 1170 (28 May 1998) UN Doc S/RES/1170, preambular para 13. See also, UNSC Res 1230 (26 February 1999) UN Doc S/RES/1230, para 16; and UNSC Presidential Statement UN Doc 34 (1999) S/PRST/1999/34, 3.

11 UNSC Presidential Statement UN Doc 29 (1998) S/PRST/1998/29, 1. See also, UNSC Presidential Statement UN Doc 46 (1997) S/PRST/1997/46, 2.

12 UNSC Presidential Statement UN Doc 38 (1998) S/PRST/1998/38, 2. In this regard the Security Council acknowledged the role that ECOSOC played, including in sustainable development, and reiterated its willingness to improve cooperation with UN bodies and organs directly concerned with peacebuilding. See UNSC Presidential Statement UN Doc 20 (2005) S/PRST/2005/20, 2.

13 UNSC Res 1170 (28 May 1998) UN Doc S/RES/1170, preambular para 9.

14 UNSC Presidential Statement UN Doc 29 (2012) S/PRST/2012/29, 1.

15 Ibid.

16 UNSC Presidential Statement UN Doc 5 (2001) S/PRST/2001/5, 1.

prevention to settlement to post-conflict peacebuilding.[17] The Council has also stated that the relationship between security and development is complex, multifaceted and case specific.[18] It has gone on to reiterate that:

> in order to support a country to emerge sustainably from conflict, there is a need for a comprehensive and integrated approach that incorporates and strengthens coherence between political, security, development, human rights and rule of law activities, and addresses the root causes of each conflict, including through strengthening the rule of law at national and international levels, promoting sustainable economic growth and development, poverty eradication, political, religious and cultural tolerance, freedom of opinion and expression, social cohesion and inclusiveness, national reconciliation, good governance, democracy, gender equality, respect for, and protection of, human rights, and facilitating reintegration and rehabilitation.[19]

At a general level, therefore, the Council has demonstrated its understanding of the importance of a broad approach to peacebuilding that reflects the promotion and protection of human rights and the need for an inclusive society to the maintenance of international peace and security. However, recognition of these elements of conflict prevention by itself only brings the Council so far, which raises the question of the extent to which the Council has given practical effect to its emphasis on peacebuilding.

3 Peacekeeping operations as a peacebuilding tool

Peacekeeping[20] is a high-profile tool by which the Council can discharge its responsibility to maintain international peace and security. The legal basis for this

17 UNSC Res 2086 (21 January 2013) UN Doc S/RES/2086, 1.

18 UNSC Presidential Statement UN Doc 3 (2015) S/PRST/2015/3, 1.

19 Ibid, See also, UNSC Presidential Statement UN Doc 2 (2015) S/PRST/2015/2, 1; and UNSC Presidential Statement UN Doc 1 (2007) S/PRST/2007/1, 2.

20 Although this work generally refers to peacekeeping operations, the use of this term should be understood to include the broader range of activities that is encompassed in the term 'United Nations peace operations' identified in UNGA, 'Report of the High-level Independent Panel on Peace Operations on Uniting Our Strengths for Peace: Politics, Partnership and People 2015/446' (2015) UN Doc A/70/95-S/2015/446 (the HIPPO Report). According to the HIPPO Report, at paragraph 18, the term 'United Nations peace operations' embraces a broad suite of tools ranging from special envoys and mediators; political missions, including peacebuilding missions; regional preventive diplomacy offices; observation missions, including both ceasefire and electoral missions; to small, technical-specialist missions such as electoral support missions; multidisciplinary operations both large and small drawing on civilian, military and police personnel to support peace process implementation, and that have included even transitional authorities with governance functions; as well as advance missions for planning. All of those missions draw upon expertise mobilised by the Secretariat, including mediation and electoral specialists, and human rights, rule of law, gender, police and military experts.

tool lies in Chapter VI (pacific settlement of disputes)[21] and Chapter VII (peace enforcement) of the UN Charter.[22] Peacekeeping operations are also subsidiary organs of the Council,[23] which means that they are subject to international law to the same extent that the UN itself is.[24] The implementation of peacekeeping operations is guided by three mutually reinforcing core principles: (i) consent of the parties to the conflict; (ii) impartiality, which means that all parties to a conflict are held to the same standards; and (iii) non-use of force, meaning that peacekeepers will use force only in self-defence, defence of the mandate or where they have been mandated by the Security Council to use force to protect the civilian population from imminent threat of physical violence.[25] It is on this basis that the incorporation of peacebuilding elements into peace operations must be viewed.

The significance of the relationship between peacebuilding and peacekeeping has been commented upon both within and outside of the Council. In terms of the former, the Brahimi Report provides one of the most cogent rationales for such a relationship with its statement that:

> History has taught that peacekeepers and peacebuilders are inseparable partners in complex operations: while the peacebuilders may not be able to

21 In particular, Article 36(1) of the UN Charter states, 'The Security Council may, at any stage of a dispute of the nature referred to in Article 33 or of a situation of like nature, recommend appropriate procedures or methods of adjustment.' Charter of the United Nations (adopted 26 June 1945, entered into force 24 October 1945) 1 UNTS XVI (UN Charter).

22 Article 42 of the Charter, ibid, permits peace enforcement operations to use coercive actions if the Council has previously determined, under the terms of Article 39, that a specific situation amounts to a threat to the peace, a breach of the peace or an act of aggression.

23 However, it is the UN Secretary-General who is responsible for the organisation and implementation of the peacekeeping operations. Member States also play a critical role in the support and maintenance of peacekeeping missions through the General Assembly. The Special Committee on Peacekeeping Operations, which reports to the General Assembly through the Fourth Committee (Special Political and Decolonisation), meets annually in New York to negotiate a report that provides a context for the work of UN peacekeeping and sets broad policy parameters for it. Mandates are usually negotiated by the Council in response to analysis and recommendations provided in reports of the Secretary-General about the situation in the country: United Nations, 'Secretariat' <http://www.un.org/en/sections/about-un/secretariat/> accessed 30 September 2016.

24 See Chapter 5, footnotes 91–113 and accompanying text.

25 Department of Peacekeeping Operations and Department of Field Support, 'The United Nations Peacekeeping Operations: Principles and Guidelines' (2008) (Capstone Doctrine) 3.1. <http://www.un.org/en/peacekeeping/documents/capstone_eng.pdf> accessed 21 July 2016. The Security Council Working Group on Peacekeeping Operations was established by UNSC Presidential Statement UN Doc 3 (2001) S/PRST/2001/3, 1. This operation of this mechanism consists of joint meetings between the Security Council Working Group on Peacekeeping Operations and relevant troop-contributing countries. However, recent peacekeeping practice, in its attempts to respond to the challenges of peacekeeping in the early 21st century, has been criticised for not being aligned with the Capstone Doctrine. See Mateja Peter, 'Between Doctrine and Practice: The UN Peacekeeping Dilemma' (2015) 21(3) *Global Governance: A Review of Multilateralism and International Organizations* 351, 358–362.

> function without the peacekeepers' support, the peacekeepers have no exit without the peacebuilders' work.[26]

This theme was revisited in *An Agenda for Peace*, where the Secretary-General stated that in order for peacemaking and peacekeeping operations to be truly successful, they had to include efforts both to identify and to support structures that would consolidate peace and advance a sense of confidence and well-being.[27]

The Security Council, for its part, has expressed its determination to consult, at various stages of any peacekeeping operations that include peacebuilding elements, with the State and with relevant actors who are primarily responsible for coordinating and implementing aspects of peacebuilding activities[28], including the General Assembly and the ECOSOC. The Council has also stressed the importance of it being kept regularly informed of the progress achieved, as well as of difficulties encountered.[29] It has emphasised:

> that effective peacebuilding requires an integrated and comprehensive approach based on coherence among political, security, development, human rights, humanitarian and rule of law objectives and that peacebuilding perspectives need to be considered starting from the first stages of planning and implementation of peacekeeping operations.[30]

It has noted that the successful implementation of many peacekeeping tasks – such as security sector reform, disarmament, demobilisation and reintegration, rule of law, transitional justice, and human rights – requires an ability to act with a perspective that takes into account the close links between security and development. In this context, the Council has noted, with appreciation, the contribution that peacekeepers and peacekeeping missions make to early peacebuilding, including through the creation of a conducive environment that enables economic recovery and the provision of basic services. It has acknowledged that such contributions can help to establish and build confidence in a mission.[31] The

26 UNGA, 'Report of the Panel on United Nations Peace Operations 2000/809' (2000) UN Doc A/55/305-S/2000/809 (the Brahimi Report), para 28. See also, UNGA, 'Report of the Secretary General on Global Field Support Strategy 64/633' (2010) UN Doc A/64/633, para 9.

27 UNGA, 'Report of the Secretary General 24111' (n 2), para 55.

28 UNSC Presidential Statement UN Doc 5 (2001) S/PRST/2001/5, para 4. Views such as these find further expression in the establishment of the Peacebuilding Commission, as the Security Council and the General Assembly also identified the interlinking nature of peacebuilding and peacekeeping with its recognition of the role of Member States in supporting UN peacekeeping and peacebuilding efforts. See UNSC Res 1645 (20 December 2005) UN Doc S/RES/1645, preambular paras 13 and 16.

29 UNSC Presidential Statement UN Doc 5 (2001) S/PRST/2001/5, 3.

30 UNSC Presidential Statement UN Doc 18 (2010) S/PRST/2010/18, 3; UNSC Presidential Statement UN Doc 34 (1999) S/PRST/1999/34, 1; and UNSC Presidential Statement UN Doc 25 (2000) S/PRST/2000/25, 3.

31 UNSC Presidential Statement UN Doc 4 (2011) S/PRST/2011/4, 2; and UNSC Presidential Statement UN Doc 3 (2015) S/PRST/2015/3, 3.

Council has also underlined that reconstruction, economic revitalisation and capacity-building constitute crucial elements for the long-term development of post-conflict societies and the generation of sustainable peace. In this regard, the Council has attached special importance to national ownership and has stressed the significance of international assistance,[32] and to that end, the manner in which peacekeeping operations can best support national authorities to articulate peacebuilding priorities.[33] In particular, the Council has noted the importance of conflict analysis and contextual information on, inter alia, social and economic issues, when such issues are drivers of conflict and represent a challenge to the implementation of Council mandates or endanger the process of consolidation of peace.[34] It is against this background that the current nature of peacekeeping operations must be considered.

During the Cold War, peacekeeping typically involved the deployment of lightly armed military forces to monitor ceasefires or to patrol neutral buffer zones between former belligerents.[35] Peacekeepers stayed out of the domestic politics of States, and the Security Council's peace enforcement powers were rarely used. The end of the Cold War signalled a change to that role, as operations were increasingly required to respond to intra-State conflict, rather than to inter-State conflict.[36] Many of today's armed conflicts have been described as being more intractable and less conducive to political resolution, in addition to which there is a blurring between inter-State and intra-State conflict with no linear path to peace.[37] 'Robust' peacekeeping is increasingly being required to provide protection to civilians.[38] Such conflicts can be caused by bad governance and a failure to establish inclusive political arrangements, a fair sharing of resources and just accommodation of ethnic and religious diversity. More

32 UNSC Presidential Statement UN Doc 4 (2011) S/PRST/2011/4, 2; and UNSC Presidential Statement UN Doc 3 (2015) S/PRST/2015/3, 3.

33 UNSC Presidential Statement UN Doc 4 (2011) S/PRST/2011/4, 2.

34 UNSC Presidential Statement UN Doc 3 (2015) S/PRST/2015/3, 3.

35 See, for example, the establishment of the UN Emergency Force (UNEF) by UNGA Res 997 (2 November 1956) UN Doc 997; UNGA Res 998 (4 November 1956) UN Doc 998; and UNGA Res 1000 (5 November 1956) UN Doc 1000. In relation to the crisis in the Congo in 1960, see UNSC Res 143 (14 July 1960) UN Doc S/4426; UNSC Res 145 (22 July 1960) UN Doc S/4405; and UNSC Res 146 (9 August 1960) UN Doc S/4426. The latter called on member states to carry out the decisions of the Security Council. More recently, see UNSC Res 1312 (31 July 2000) UN Doc S/RES/1312; UNSC Res 1320 (15 September 2000) UN Doc S/RES/1320; UNSC Res 1640 (23 November 2005) UN Doc S/RES/1640; and UNSC Res 1798 (30 January 2008) UN Doc S/RES/1798, which established peace operations to oversee peace between Ethiopia and Eritrea.

36 Paul F Diehl and Alexandru Balas, *Peace Operations* (2nd edn, Polity Press, Cambridge 2014) 28–80.

37 The HIPPO Report (n 20), para 10.

38 For the economic and social impacts on the civilian population see, for example, UNSC Verbatim Record (7 July 2010) UN Doc S/PV.6354 and UNSC Verbatim Record (7 July 2010) UN Doc S/PV.6354 (Resumption 1). More generally, see Frédéric Mégret, 'Between R2P and the ICC: "Robust Peacekeeping" and the Quest for Civilian Protection' (2015) 26(1) *Criminal Law* Forum 101.

often than not, root causes and conflict drivers are not effectively addressed.[39] Peacekeeping operations have been increasingly deployed into more complex political environments in which peace agreements are faltering or completely lacking.[40] The typical field environment into which operations are deployed today has been described as 'remote, austere and, increasingly, dangerous, and sometimes openly hostile to a UN presence'.[41] The rule of law can, at best, be tenuous, and local markets are limited or non-existent. Such difficulties are compounded by basic economic and social difficulties. For example, potable water can be scarce and in high demand, fresh food can be difficult to procure in quantity, housing stock is frequently in short supply, and reliable communications infrastructure is lacking.[42] Challenges such as these are multiplied in large, infrastructure-poor countries, where it becomes much harder for UN missions to make their presence felt. Logistical supply lines in vast, landlocked, and often insecure, operating environments are often stretched thin and left vulnerable to disruption.[43]

Peacekeeping operation mandates themselves have become increasingly complex. The influence of peacebuilding can be seen in the fact that peacekeepers are now often mandated to perform or to support complex civilian and military functions that are regarded as being essential to maintaining peace and to begin reconstruction and institution-building in societies devastated by war.[44] Peacekeepers may provide critical support to basic infrastructure, remuneration for national armed forces and police, and investment in emergency employment initiatives for early peacebuilding.[45] At their most complex, (transitional civil) peace operations are tasked with setting and enforcing the law, establishing customs services and regulations, setting and collecting business and personal taxes, attracting foreign investment, and adjudicating property disputes and liabilities for war damage. They may be charged with reconstructing and operating all public utilities, creating a banking system, running schools and paying teachers. They may even have to collect the garbage. In addition to such tasks, these missions must also try to rebuild civil society and promote respect for human rights, in places where grievance is widespread and grudges run deep.[46]

39 The HIPPO Report (n 20), paras 13–14.
40 Ibid, para 23.
41 UNGA, 'Report of the Secretary General on Global Field Support Strategy 64/633' (2010) UN Doc A/64/633, 1; The HIPPO Report (ibid.), para 23; and M A Rudderham, 'Canada and United Nations Peace Operations: Challenges, Opportunities, and Canada's Response' (2008) 63(2) *International Journal* 359, 363. See also, Peter (n 25), 353–357.
42 UNGA, 'Report of the Secretary General on Global Field Support Strategy 64/633' (2010) UN Doc A/64/633, 1.
43 The HIPPO Report (n 20), para 23.
44 See, generally, Haidi Willmot and Scott Sheeran, 'The Protection of Civilians Mandate in UN Peacekeeping Operations: Reconciling Protection Concepts and Practices' (2013) 95(891 892) *International Review of the Red Cross* 517.
45 New Horizons (n 7), 23.
46 The Brahimi Report (n 26), para 77.

The wide-ranging nature of these tasks – tasks that reflect the relationship between peacebuilding and peacekeeping – can be seen in those Security Council resolutions that mandate physical, economic and social reconstruction. The mandating of these tasks is often made in response to determinations of a threat to international peace and security, so that the execution of these tasks can be regarded as a practical means of future conflict prevention. It is a further example of the Security Council's recognition of the relationship between poor socio-economic conditions and instability or conflict. In relation to the situation in Kosovo, the Council, acting under its Chapter VII mandate, encouraged all Member States and International Organisations to contribute to economic and social reconstruction.[47] The Security Council also called upon Member States to provide long-term assistance for the social and economic reconstruction and rehabilitation of Afghanistan and, in establishing the United Nations Assistance Mission in Afghanistan (UNAMA), stressed the contribution of recovery and reconstruction assistance to the transitional authority.[48] UNAMA advances the doctrinal shift, first advanced in the Brahimi Report, of incorporating elements of peacebuilding into peace operations.[49] The Council has continued to stress the importance of a comprehensive approach to address the interconnected security, economic, governance and development challenges in Afghanistan. In recognising that there was no purely military solution to ensure the stability of that State, the Council reaffirmed that Afghanistan's peaceful future lay in the building of a stable, secure and economically sustainable State.[50]

In Resolution 1483, on the rebuilding of Iraq, the Council provided for the creation of conditions in which the Iraqi people could freely determine their own political future[51] as well as the establishment of national and local institutions

47 UNSC Res 1244 (10 June 1999) UN Doc S/RES/1244, para 13.

48 UNSC Res 1401 (28 March 2002) UN Doc S/RES/1401, para 3. The importance of economic reconstruction was emphasised in a number of ensuing resolutions: UNSC Res 1419 (26 June 2002) UN Doc S/RES/1419, para 10; UNSC Res 1378 (14 November 2001) UN Doc S/RES/1378, para 4; UNSC Res 1806 (20 March 2008) UN Doc S/RES/1806, para 4(a); and UNSC Res 1868 (23 March 2009) UN Doc S/RES/1868, para 4(a). See also, UNGA, 'Report of the Secretary General 2002/278' (2002) UN Doc A/56/875-S/2002/278 on the 'Situation in Afghanistan and its Implications for International Peace and Security', paras 94–98. See, also, Jacob S Kreilkamp, 'U.N. Postconflict Reconstruction' (2003) 35(3) *Journal of International Law and Politics* 619, 661; Michael Schoiswohl, 'Linking the International Legal Framework to Building the Formal Foundations of a "State at Risk": Constitution-Making and International Law in Post-conflict Afghanistan' (2006) 39(3) *Vanderbilt Journal of Transnational Law* 819, 823; and Tanya Domenica Bosi, 'U.N. Report: Post-conflict Reconstruction: The United Nations' Involvement in Afghanistan' (2003) 19 *Journal of Human Rights* 819, 819–820.

49 Michael O'Flaherty, 'Future Protection of Human Rights in Post-conflict Societies: The Role of the United Nations' (2003) 3(1) *Human Rights Law Review* 53, 63.

50 UNSC Res 2210 (16 March 2015) UN Doc S/RES/2210, paras 4–6. See, similarly, UNSC Res 2189 (12 December 2014) UN Doc S/RES/2189, preambular para 5; UNSC Res 1974 (22 March 2011) UN Doc S/RES/1974, preambular para 11; and UNSC Res 2041 (22 March 2002) UN Doc S/Res/2041, para 20.

51 UNSC Res 1483 (22 May 2003) UN Doc S/RES/1483, para 4.

for representative governance.[52] In renewing and expanding the mandate of the United Nations Assistance Mission for Iraq (UNAMI), which is a political mission established at the request of the Government of Iraq,[53] the Security Council decided that, in conjunction with the Iraqi Government, the Special Representative of the Secretary-General for Iraq (SRSG) and UNAMI would 'promote, support, and facilitate, . . . [e]conomic reform, capacity-building and the conditions for sustainable development'.[54] More recent tasks have included advising, supporting and assisting the Iraqi authorities to strengthen democratic institutions, advance dialogue (national and regional) and encourage national reconciliation. UNAMI has also been tasked to aid vulnerable groups, strengthen gender equality, promote the protection of human rights and promote judicial and legal reform.[55]

Acting under its Chapter VII mandate, the Council called for reconstruction assistance in Timor-Leste[56] and subsequently called on the international community 'to continue providing essential resources and assistance for the implementation of projects towards sustainable and long-term development in Timor-Leste'.[57] Similarly, it called upon the United Nations Integrated Mission in Timor-Leste (UNMIT) to continue to cooperate and coordinate with UN agencies, funds and programmes as well as all relevant partners to support the Government of Timor-Leste and relevant institutions in designing poverty reduction and economic growth policies.[58] More recently, the Council has recognised:

> the importance of the development plans devised by the Government of Timor-Leste, especially the attention paid to infrastructure, rural development and human resources capacity development, and in this regard, calls upon UNMIT to continue to cooperate and coordinate with the United Nations agencies, funds and programmes, as well as all relevant partners, to support the Government of Timor-Leste and relevant institutions in

52 Ibid, para 8(c).

53 UNSC Res 1500 (14 August 2003) UN Doc S/RES/1500.

54 UNSC Res 1770 (10 August 2007) UN Doc S/RES/1770, para 2(b)(iv). See also, UNSC Res 1483 (22 May 2003) UN Doc S/RES/1483, para 2.

55 See, for example, UNSC Res 1936 (5 August 2010) UN Doc S/RES/1936, preambular para 7; UNSC Res 2169 (30 July 2014) UN Doc S/RES/2169, preambular para 11; and UNSC Res 2233 (29 July 2015) UN Doc S/RES/2233, preambular para 11.

56 UNSC Res 1272 (25 October 1999) UN Doc S/RES/1272, para 13.

57 UNSC Res 1543 (14 May 2004) UN Doc S/RES/1543, para 10. See also, UNSC Res 1599 (28 April 2005) UN Doc S/RES/1599, para 9.

58 UNSC Res 1745 (22 February 2007) UN Doc S/RES/1745, para 10. See also, UNSC Res 1802 (25 February 2008) UN Doc S/RES/1802, para 13; and UNSC Res 1867 (26 February 2009) UN Doc S/RES/1867, para 2. UNMIT had been established by UNSC Res 1704 (25 August 2006), and its mission was completed in accordance with UNSC Res 2037 (22 February 2012). UNMIT was one of a number of UN missions that had been deployed to Timor-Leste; see UNMIT, 'UNMIT Background' <http://www.un.org/en/peacekeeping/missions/past/unmit/background.shtml> accessed 1 September 2016.

> designing poverty reduction, improving education, promotion of sustainable livelihood and economic growth policies.[59]

The Council has also encouraged 'the Government of Timor-Leste to strengthen peacebuilding perspectives in such areas as employment and empowerment, especially focusing on rural areas and youth, as well as local socio-economic development in particular in the agricultural sector'.[60]

UN involvement in Haiti goes back to 1994, and a series of peacekeeping operations have been deployed there in the intervening decades.[61] Perhaps some of the clearest examples of reconstruction as an element of collective security can be seen in Council resolutions regarding the situation in Haiti. In UNSC Resolution 1212 (1998), the Council underlined the fact that political reconciliation and economic reconstruction efforts remained key to the stability and security of Haiti.[62] In 2004, the Council determined that the situation in Haiti constituted a threat to international peace and security, leading to the establishment of the United Nations Stabilisation Mission in Haiti (MINUSTAH).[63] The Council has made some quite specific statements regarding the role of MINUSTAH. For example, it has called upon MINUSTAH, in close collaboration with the Haitian Government, to pursue its community violence reduction approach.[64] It has requested the UN Country Team and other actors to complement security and development operations, undertaken by the Government of Haiti with the support of the Mission, with activities aimed at effectively improving the living conditions of the concerned populations, in particular women and children.[65] The Council also encouraged MINUSTAH to continue assisting the Government of Haiti in providing adequate protection to the civilian population, with particular attention to the needs of internally displaced persons and other vulnerable groups, especially women and children, including through joint community policing in the camps.[66] More recently, it has requested, in coordination with the UN Country Team, the continuing implementation of quick-impact projects that contribute to building

59 UNSC Res 1969 (24 February 2011) UN Doc S/RES/1969, para 15 (original emphasis). See also, UNSC Res 2037 (23 February 2012) UN Doc S/RES/2037, para 14.

60 Ibid., para 16; and UNSC Res 2037 (23 February 2012) UN Doc S/RES/2037, para 16.

61 The United Nations Mission in Haiti (UNMIH), the United Nations Support Mission in Haiti (UNSMIH), the United Nations Transition Mission in Haiti (UNTMIH) and the United Nations Civilian Police Mission in Haiti (MIPONUH).

62 UNSC Res 1576 (29 November 2004) UN Doc S/RES/1576, preambular para 3; UNSC Presidential Statement UN Doc 4 (2009) S/PRST/2009/4, 1; UNSC Res 2180 (14 October 2014) UN Doc S/RES/2180, preambular para 13; and UNSC Res 2243 (14 October 2015) UN Doc S/RES/2243, preambular para 19.

63 The Stabilisation mission was established by UNSC Res 1542 (30 April 2004). It was the fifth mission deployed to Haiti; see MINUSTAH, 'MINUSTAH Background' <http://www.un.org/en/peacekeeping/missions/minustah/background.shtml> accessed 1 September 2016.

64 UNSC Res 2119 (10 October 2013) UN Doc S/RES/2119, para 23.

65 UNSC Res 2180 (14 October 2014) UN Doc S/RES/2180, para 18.

66 See, for example, UNSC Res 2180 (14 October 2014) UN Doc S/RES/2180, para 22; and UNSC Res 2243 (14 October 2015) UN Doc S/RES/2243, para 27.

a secure and stable environment, and enhance national ownership and the trust of the Haitian population towards MINUSTAH, particularly in the priority areas identified by the Mission's leadership, and consistent with the Government of Haiti's priorities.[67]

The mandates of a number of missions deployed to Africa reflect a similar approach. The United Nations–African Union Mission in Darfur (UNAMID) was tasked with contributing to a secure environment for economic reconstruction and development.[68] To achieve that goal, it was to contribute to the creation of the necessary security conditions for the provision of humanitarian assistance.[69] The mandate of the United Nations Support Mission in Libya (UNSMIL), an integrated special political mission, which was established under Chapter VII,[70] included undertaking to support, on request, the provision of essential services, and delivery of humanitarian assistance in accordance with humanitarian principles.[71] In relation to a number of other situations, the Council has made reference to the role of the Peacebuilding Commission in peacekeeping operations. In relation to the situation in the Central African Republic (CAR), the Council requested that the United Nations Integrated Peacebuilding Office in the Central African Republic (BINUCA) continue to support the peacebuilding processes in that State.[72] The Council requested the Peacebuilding Commission, with support from the United Nations Integrated Office in Burundi (BINUB), to continue to assist the Government of Burundi in laying the foundations for sustainable peace and security, reintegration and long-term development in Burundi, and in mobilising the resources needed to achieve these aims.[73] With regard to the situation in Guinea-Bissau, the Council requested the Peacebuilding Commission to continue to support the implementation of Guinea-Bissau's peacebuilding priorities as well as to continue to provide advice to the Security Council on how to remove critical obstacles to peacebuilding.[74] The Council affirmed that the United Nations Integrated Peacebuilding Office in Guinea-Bissau (UNIOGBIS) and the Special Representative of the Secretary-General would, as a priority area, work with the Peacebuilding Commission in support of Guinea-Bissau's

67 UNSC Res 2243 (14 October 2015) UN Doc S/RES/2243, para 24. See also, UNSC Res 1944 (14 October 2010) UN Doc S/RES/1944, para 8.

68 UNSC Res 1769 (31 July 2007) UN Doc S/RES/1769, para 1; and UNSC 'Report of the Secretary-General and the Chairperson of the African Union Commission on the Hybrid Operation in Darfur 2007/307' (2007) UN Doc S/2007/307/Rev.1, para 54 (e).

69 UNSC Res 1769 (31 July 2007) UN Doc S/RES/1769, para 1; and UNSC, 'Report of the Secretary-General and the Chairperson of the African Union Commission on the Hybrid Operation in Darfur 2007/307' (2007) UN Doc S/2007/307/Rev.1, para 55 (b)(vi).

70 UNSC Res 2144 (14 March 2014) UN Doc S/RES/2144.

71 UNSC Res 2213 (27 March 2015) UN Doc S/RES/2213, para 9(d).

72 UNSC Res 2088 (24 January 2013) UN Doc S/RES/2088, para 6.

73 UNSC Res 1902 (17 December 2009) UN Doc S/RES/1902, para 11 (Burundi); and UNSC Res 1959 (16 December 2010) UN Doc S/RES/1959, para 10. BINUB had been established by UNSC Res 1719 (25 October 2006) UN Doc S/RES/1719, para 1.

74 UNSC Res 2030 (21 December 2011) UN Doc S/RES/2030, para 15; and UNSC Res 1949 (23 November 2010) UN Doc S/RES/1949, para 17.

peacebuilding priorities.[75] In relation to the situation in Liberia, the Council emphasised the need for coherence between, and integration of, peacekeeping, peacebuilding and development, to achieve an effective response to post-conflict situations.[76]

The above paragraphs show that the Security Council has sought to discharge its responsibility to maintain international peace and security by the building up of a conceptually broader peace (or by building a conceptually broader peace), peace that is then to be 'kept' by the deployment of peacekeeping operations. The permeation of peacekeeping operations with peacebuilding mandates suggest that the Council is giving effect to its recognition of the importance of the relationship between it, the General Assembly and the ECOSOC, and the related need to have regard for the economic and social dimensions of peace and security.

However, these developments have presented a number of challenges for peacekeepers engaged in peacebuilding. Peacekeepers are often the largest and most visible international presence on the ground but face unrealistic expectations as to what they can reasonably achieve.[77] National militaries do not traditionally maintain proactive civilian protection doctrines, operating concepts or tactics beyond the requirements of international humanitarian law.[78] Although peacekeeping operations have shown a remarkable capacity to adjust to evolving situations and new demands, such missions are struggling to cope with the spread and intensity of conflicts today, and the lack of unity amongst Member States over their scope and application is thwarting their adaptation.[79] The outcome of such shortcomings has led, on more than one occasion, to the perception that peacekeeping initiatives have only made the situation worse, a view that undermines any (hard-won) credibility on the part of peacekeepers.[80]

In addition, and at a broader level, there is also an inherent tension in any peacebuilding mission. On the one hand, the goal of such missions is the creation of conditions for peaceful self-government. On the other hand, the means for achieving such a goal involves the presence of foreign actors exercising various levels of authority over the domestic affairs of the State. This disjuncture between goals and means raises a larger problem of trying to ensure that peacebuilding

75 UNSC Res 2267 (26 February 2016) UN Doc S/RES/2267, para 3(f); and UNSC Res 2203 (18 February 2015) UN Doc S/RES/2203, para 3(f). Similarly, see UNSC Res 2103 (22 May 2013) UN Doc S/RES/2103, para 1(i).

76 UNSC Res 1938 (15 September 2010) UN Doc S/RES/1938, para 7; UNSC Res 2066 (17 September 2012) UN Doc S/RES/2066, para 16; and UNSC Res 2116 (18 September 2013) UN Doc S/RES/2116, para 17.

77 New Horizons (n 7), 22.

78 Ibid, 20.

79 UNGA, 'Report of the Secretary-General 2015/682' (2015) UN Doc A/70/357-S/2015/682 'The Future of United Nations Peace Operations: Implementation of the Recommendations of the High-level Independent Panel on Peace Operations', para 5.

80 See, for example, Antonia Chayes, '"Chapter VII½": Is Jus Post Bellum Possible?' (2013) 24(1) *European Journal of International Law* 291, 301–304; and Peter (n 25), 353–357.

and peacekeeping missions are perceived as legitimate in the eyes of those that they are trying to help.[81] The legitimacy question can be answered by ensuring that local populations are incorporated into the planning and management of peacebuilding, bearing in mind that such populations may well include minorities whose needs must be weighed against the majority, as well as those parties who have previously been in conflict with each other.[82] In this regard, not only are human rights a core tool not only to identify and address past grievances, but they are also a means to try to avoid future injustices, thereby contributing to building a more sustainable peace.

4 The role of human rights in peacekeeping and peacebuilding

As indicated in Chapter 2, the Security Council has been concerned with the negative impact of humanitarian crises and gross human rights violations – including systemic socio-economic exclusion – upon international peace and security, particularly since the early 1990s. In addition to drawing from the expert advice of Special Rapporteurs and the OHCHR, the Council has gone on to include humanitarian crises and gross human rights violations as an aspect of its determinations as to whether situations comprised a threat to, or breach of, the peace, from this time. The relationship between the Security Council and human rights mechanisms also revealed the role that human rights can play as an early warning system. The recognition of the relationship between peace and security and human rights also manifests itself in peacebuilding policy and peacekeeping mandates, especially in the integration of human rights into the latter.

The need to integrate human rights into peacekeeping operations was first signalled in the Brahimi Report, which stated that the human rights component of a peace operation was critical to effective peacebuilding.[83] The Report went on to recommend a doctrinal shift in the use of, inter alia, human rights experts in complex peace operations to reflect an increased focus on strengthening rule of law institutions and improving respect for human rights in post-conflict environments.[84] The need to re-establish human rights norms, so as to avoid further

81 Paris Roland, 'Post-Conflict Peacebuilding' in Thomas G Weiss and Sam Daws (eds), *The Oxford Companion on the United Nations* (Oxford University Press, Oxford 2009), 404, 422; and Simon Chesterman, *You the People: The United Nations, Traditional Administration and State-Building* (Oxford University Press, Oxford 2004) 127.

82 Paris, ibid, 422–423; Peter (n 25) 353–357; and Han Dorussen and Theodora-Ismene Gizelis, 'Into the Lion's Den: Local Responses to UN Peacekeeping' (2013) 50(6) *Journal of Peace Research* 691.

83 The Brahimi Report (n 26), para 41.

84 Ibid, para 47(b). It also recommended that the OHCHR coordinate and institutionalise human rights fieldwork in peace operations, and that such efforts be supported by the OHCHR. See the Brahimi Report, ibid, paras 56–63. See also, Susan C Breau, 'The Impact of the Responsibility to Protect on Peacekeeping' (2006) 11(3) *Journal of Conflict and Security Law* 429, 430–431.

gross violations of human rights, has also been explained by the Secretary-General as follows:

> It would be a mistake to treat human rights as though there were a trade-off to be made between human rights and such goals as security or development. . . . Strategies based on the protection of human rights are vital for both our moral standing and the practical effectiveness of our actions.[85]

The Secretary-General's decision on 'Human Rights in Integrated Missions' sets out that all UN entities, such as peacekeeping operations, have a responsibility to ensure that human rights are promoted and protected through and within their operations in the field.[86] The findings of the Report of the Secretary-General's Internal Review Panel on United Nations Action in Sri Lanka 2012 (the Petrie Report) once again demonstrated that when responses to situations of conflict, violence and insecurity fail to take into consideration human rights concerns, the protection of the affected people could not be adequately ensured.[87] The Petrie Report also clearly identified the need for human rights information and analysis to be readily available to the UN and Member States as a basis for action and the need to improve UN responsiveness to such situations. The Secretary-General's Human Rights Up Front Plan of Action[88] seeks to respond to these findings. The Action Plan provides a role for the OHCHR, which, together with the Department of Peacekeeping Operations and the Department of Field Support and the Department of Political Affairs, has worked to mainstream further human rights into all aspects of the work of peace missions.[89] More recently, the Secretary-General summarised the relationship as follows:

> Widespread violations of human rights often trigger a United Nations peace operation, and progress in the protection of those rights is a basis for its

85 UNGA, 'Report of the Secretary-General 59/2005' (2005) UN Doc A/59/2005 on 'In Larger Freedom: Towards Development, Security and Human Rights for All', para 140.

86 United Nations, 'Decisions of the Secretary-General – Policy Committee Meeting of 26 October: Decision No. 2005/24 – Human Rights in Integrated Missions' (26 October 2005). See further, UNSG, 'Note of Guidance on Integrated Missions' (2006) <https://www.regjeringen.no/globalassets/upload/UD/Vedlegg/missions/sgnote.pdf> accessed 28 July 2016.

87 United Nations, 'Report of the Secretary-General's Internal Review Panel on United Nations Action in Sri Lanka' (November 2012). <http://www.un.org/News/dh/infocus/Sri_Lanka/The_Internal_Review_Panel_report_on_Sri_Lanka.pdf> accessed 29 July 2016.

88 UNSG, 'Summary of "Human Rights Up Front"' (undated) <http://www.un.org/News/dh/pdf/english/2016/Human-Rights-up-Front.pdf> accessed 1 February 2017. See also, UNSG, Ban Ki-moon, 'Renewing our Commitment to the Peoples and Purposes of the United Nations' (UN Headquarters, 22 November 2013) <http://www.un.org/apps/news/infocus/sgspeeches/statments_full.asp?statid=2068#.v53yujdr1g> accessed 29 July 2016.

89 According to the OHCHR, its role in this regard is to activate available UN human rights tools to bridge existing human rights protection gaps; contribute to a coherent and mutually

> exit . . . Societies with effective, inclusive and accountable institutions are more likely to withstand crises and peacefully manage disputes. Communities that recognize the dignity of each individual stand less chance of fuelling resentments that can manifest in extremism.[90]

In 2014, the Report of the High-level Independent Panel on Peace Operations (the HIPPO Report) acknowledged the efforts to promote and protect human rights as a means for conflict prevention and the prevention of relapse and it firmly supported the Secretary-General's Human Rights Up Front Action Plan, including strengthening prevention and ensuring that the UN takes the best possible actions to protect people during conflict.[91] The HIPPO Report also noted the advancements that had been made as regards human rights monitoring and reporting initiatives, but it also called for the implementation of public reporting, in particular to the Security Council, on human rights to be more fully reflected in the work of all peace operations with human rights mandates. In that regard, the HIPPO Report also noted that although levels of monitoring and reporting were increasing, such initiatives were often dispersed, fragmented and lacking in a coordinated strategic approach to address human rights issues. The recommendation has been for specialist expertise to be included in mission staffing in accordance with the context, overall monitoring and reporting on human rights, and for the protection of civilians to be coherent and reporting requirements to be streamlined.[92] The view was reiterated during the course of the Peacebuilding Architecture Review

---

reinforcing approach within the UN; and systematically review developments in international and customary law to define policy approaches and interventions. In that regard, its aims include strengthening engagement with the Security Council to advocate for due consideration of human rights in its resolutions and the mandates of peace missions and supporting mission planning. See OHCHR, 'OHCHR Management Plan 2014–2017 – Working for your Rights' (2014) 89, 94–95 <http://www2.ohchr.org/english/OHCHR report2014_2017/OMP_Web_version/media/pdf/0_THE_WHOLE_REPORT.pdf> accessed 29 July 2016. Also, the OHCHR supports human rights components of peacekeeping and special political missions by providing strategic and expert advice, technical assistance, operational support and day-to-day backstopping on human rights issues. The Office participates in interdepartmental technical assessment missions directed at the design, establishment and reconfiguration of peace missions. Additionally, the OHCHR contributes to the implementation of technical cooperation activities and projects through its voluntary contributions from donors. In accordance with Security Council resolutions that create the missions, typical functions of a human rights component include the following: monitoring and reporting on the human rights situation and investigating human rights violations; advocating for peace processes to be inclusive, addressing past human rights violations and promoting and protecting human rights; integrating human rights in legislative and institutional reforms, including the rule of law and security sectors reforms; preventing and redressing violations of human rights and international humanitarian law, with a focus on the protection of civilians; building human rights capacities and institutions; and mainstreaming human rights into all UN programmes and activities; ibid, 17.

90 UNGA, 'Report of the Secretary-General 2015/682' (n 79), para 10.

91 The HIPPO Report (n 20), para 76.

92 Ibid, para 247.

2015, as the Advisory Group noted that human rights violations and impunity were also root causes and had to be addressed as early as possible.[93]

Evidence of the integration of human rights into peacekeeping is evident in the Security Council statements and resolutions on peacekeeping, as well as those on the protection of civilians in armed conflict. Many of these mandates had also incorporated elements of economic and social reconstruction. An early example is the United Nations Interim Administration Mission in Kosovo (UNMIK), which was deployed after the Council determined that the situation in the region constituted a threat to international peace and security.[94] Amongst UNMIK's main responsibilities were the protection and promotion of human rights.[95] When establishing UNAMA, in 2002, the Council called for local authorities to contribute to the maintenance of a secure environment and to demonstrate respect for human rights.[96] It went on to call for the full respect for human rights (and international humanitarian law) throughout Afghanistan, and in this regard it requested UNAMA, with the support of the OHCHR, to continue to assist in the full implementation of the human rights provisions of the Afghan constitution and international treaties to which Afghanistan is a State Party.[97] UNAMI's role was greatly expanded in 2007 so that UNAMI, along with the Special Representative of the Secretary-General for Iraq and at the request of the Iraqi Government, was mandated, inter alia, to promote the protection of human rights and judicial and legal reform, in order to strengthen the rule of law in Iraq.[98] The Council has subsequently reaffirmed the importance of UNAMI in promoting and protecting human rights.[99] The Security Council mandated MINUSTAH to support the promotion and protection of human rights in Haiti, to monitor and report on the human rights situation, in cooperation with the OHCHR,[100] and to investigate human rights violations, again in collaboration with the OHCHR.[101]

93 United Nations (n 8), para 39.
94 UNSC Res 1244 (10 June 1999) UN Doc S/RES/1244, para 5.
95 Ibid, para 11(j).
96 UNSC Res 1401 (28 March 2002) UN Doc S/RES/1401, para 4.
97 UNSC Res 1662 (23 March 2006) UN Doc S/RES/1662, para 12. Similarly, see UNGA 'Report of the Secretary-General 2006/145' (2006) UN Doc A/60/712-S/2006/145, para 52(d). See also, UNSC Res 1806 (20 March 2008) UN Doc S/RES/1806, para 4(g); and UNSC Res 1917 (22 March 2010) UN Doc S/RES/1917, para 6(d).
98 UNSC Res 1770 (10 August 2007) UN Doc S/RES/1770, para 2(c).
99 UNSC Res 1830 (7 August 2008) UN Doc S/RES/1830, preambular para 7; UNSC Res 1883 (7 August 2009) UN Doc S/RES/1883, preambular para 7; UNSC Res 1936 (5 August 2010) UN Doc S/RES/1936, preambular para 7; UNSC Res 2001 (28 July 2011) UN Doc S/RES/2001, preambular para 7; UNSC Res 2061 (25 July 2012) UN Doc S/RES/2061, preambular para 7; UNSC Res 2110 (24 July 2013) UN Doc S/RES/2110, preambular para 7; UNSC Res 2169 (30 July 2014) UN Doc S/RES/2169, preambular para 7; and UNSC Res 2233 (29 July 2015) UN Doc S/RES/2233, preambular para 11.
100 UNSC Res 1542 (30 April 2004) UN Doc S/Res/1542, para 7(III)(a) and (b).
101 Ibid, para 8(a). MINUSTAH's human rights mandate was reaffirmed in UNSC Res 1780 (15 October 2007) UN Doc S/RES/1780, para 16; and UNSC Res 1944 (14 October 2010) UN Doc S/RES/1944, para 16.

The Council has gone on to recognise that respect for human rights is essential to Haiti's stability[102] and has called on MINUSTAH to provide monitoring and support in this regard.[103]

Human rights have featured in the mandates of peace operations responding to crises and conflict in Africa. The United Nations Office for West Africa (UNOWA) was the first regional conflict prevention and peacebuilding office of the UN.[104] Subsequently, UNOWA has been charged with enhancing capability within West Africa towards a harmonised subregional approach to peace and security, and as part of that, it was to reinforce cooperation on cross-cutting issues, including the rule of law, economic issues and human rights.[105] The mandate of the Post-Conflict Peace Building Support Office in Guinea-Bissau (UNOGBIS)[106] was revised in 2004 to include, inter alia, support for all efforts to respect the rule of law and human rights, and within the framework of a comprehensive peacebuilding strategy, to actively support efforts of the UN system and Guinea-Bissau's other partners, towards strengthening State institutions and structures to enable them to uphold the rule of law and respect for human rights.[107] UNOGBIS was succeeded by the United Nations Integrated Peacebuilding Office in Guinea-Bissau (UNIOGBIS), and amongst its key tasks were the undertaking of human rights promotion, protection and monitoring activities, and supporting the institutionalisation of respect for the rule of law.[108] The human rights mandate was varied

102 UNSC Res 2012 (14 October 2011) UN Doc S/RES/2012, para 18; and UNSC Res 2243 (14 October 2015) UN Doc S/RES/2243, para 29.

103 UNSC Res 2180 (14 October 2014) UN Doc S/RES/2180, para 24. See also, UNSC Res 2070 (12 October 2012) UN Doc S/RES/2070, para 20; and UNSC Res 2119 (10 October 2013) UN Doc S/RES/2119, para 21. The Council has emphasized that progress in the recovery and reconstruction of Haiti, as well as in Haiti's social and economic development are crucial to achieving lasting and sustainable stability, and has reiterated the need for security to be accompanied by social and economic development: UNSC Res 2243 (14 October 2015) UN Doc S/RES/2243, preambular para 19. The Council also noted with concern that food insecurity could impact the humanitarian situation and stability: UNSC Res 2243 (14 October 2015) UN Doc S/RES/2243, preambular para 15.

104 UNSC, 'Letter Dated 26 November 2001 from the Secretary-General Addressed to the President of the Security Council 2001/1128' (2001) UN Doc S/2001/1128.

105 See, for example, UNSC, 'Letter Dated 28 November 2007 from the Secretary-General Addressed to the President of the Security Council 2007/753' (2007) UN Doc S/2007/753, Annex Mandate and Functions of the United Nations Office for West Africa from January 2008 to December 2010, Function 1.1; UNSC, 'Letter Dated 14 December 2010 from the Secretary-General to the President of the Security Council 2010/660' (2010) UN Doc S/2010/660, Annex Draft mandate of the United Nations Office for West Africa, Objective 2; and UNSC, 'Letter Dated 19 December 2013 from the Secretary-General Addressed to the President of the Security Council 2013/753' (2013) UN Doc S/2013/753, Annex Draft mandate of the United Nations Office for West Africa for 2014–2016, Objective 3, Function 3.2.

106 UNSC Res 1233 (6 April 1999) UN Doc S/RES/1233, para 7.

107 UNSC Res 1580 (22 December 2004) UN Doc S/RES/1580, para 2(a) and (h), respectively.

108 UNSC Res 1876 (26 June 2009) UN Doc S/RES/1876, para 3(h); and UNSC Res 2103 (22 May 2013) UN Doc S/RES/2103, para 1(h).

subsequently so that UNIOGBIS was tasked with assisting national authorities in the promotion and protection of human rights, as well as undertaking human rights monitoring and reporting activities.[109] When the United Nations Mission in Liberia (UNMIL), a Chapter VII operation, was established[110] it was mandated, inter alia, to contribute towards international efforts to protect and promote human rights in Liberia[111] and to ensure an adequate human rights presence, capacity and expertise within UNMIL to carry out human rights promotion, protection and monitoring activities.[112] More recently, the Council has encouraged the Government of Liberia and UNMIL to address the critical gaps that need to be filled in order to facilitate a successful transition, including by prioritising tasks, included in which are the promotion of human rights and reconciliation.[113]

Part of the mandate of UNSMIL has been, in full accordance with the principles of national ownership, to support the Libyan Government's efforts to promote the rule of law, and monitor and protect human rights in accordance with Libya's international legal obligations.[114] The Council went on to decide that UNSMIL would undertake human rights monitoring and reporting.[115] When it was established, the United Nations Assistance Mission in Somalia (UNSOM) was mandated to help build the capacity of the Federal Government of Somalia to promote respect for human rights, including through the provision of Human Rights Advisors.[116] It was also mandated to monitor, help investigate and report to the Security Council on, and help prevent, any abuses or violations of human rights committed in Somalia, with monitoring to be carried out through the deployment of human rights observers.[117]

After determining that the situation in Mali constituted a threat to international peace and security, the Council established United Nations Multidimensional Integrated Stabilization Mission in Mali (MINUSMA).[118] The Mission was

109 UNSC Res 2157 (29 May 2014) UN Doc S/RES/2157, para 1(f); UNSC Res 2203 (18 February 2015) UN Doc S/RES/2203, para 3(c); and UNSC Res 2267 (26 February 2016) UN Doc S/RES/2267, para 3(c).

110 UNSC Res 1509 (19 September 2003) UN Doc S/RES/1509, para 1.

111 Ibid, para 3(l).

112 Ibid, para 3(m). The Council had continued to support UNMIL's role in this regard: see UNSC Res 1836 (29 September 2008) UN Doc S/RES/1836, preambular para 12; UNSC Res 1885 (15 September 2009) UN Doc S/RES/1885, preambular para 14; and UNSC Res 2008 (16 September 2011) UN Doc S/RES/2008, preambular para 16.

113 UNSC Res 2066 (17 September 2012) UN Doc S/RES/2066, para 3. See also, UNSC Res 2190 (15 December 2014) UN Doc S/RES/2190, para 10(e)(i).

114 UNSC Res 2040 (12 March 2012), UN Doc S/RES/2040, para 6(b).

115 UNSC Res 2213 (27 March 2015) UN Doc S/RES/2213, para 9(a).

116 UNSC Res 2102 (2 May 2013) UN Doc S/RES/2102, para 2(d)(i) and (e)(i). See also, UNSC Res 2158 (29 May 2014) UN Doc S/RES/2158, para 1(d)(i) and (e)(i).

117 UNSC Res 2102 (2 May 2013) UN Doc S/RES/2102, para 2(e)(i); and UNSC Res 2158 (29 May 2014) UN Doc S/RES/2158, para 1(d)(i) and (e)(i).

118 MINUSMA was established by UNSC Res 2100 (25 April 2013) UN Doc S/RES/2100, para 7. The Council had previously determined that the situation in Mali constituted a threat to international peace and security and called for intervention, the first manifestation

charged with the promotion and protection of human rights, entailing monitoring, investigating and reporting abuses to the Council. The operation also made provision for the deployment of human rights observers.[119] In terms of humanitarian support, the promotion and protection of human rights was identified as one of MINUSMA's priorities.[120] A number of other operations, which were also established under Chapter VII, include the promotion and protection of human rights, with some of those being tasked with monitoring and reporting roles, including the United Nations Multidimensional Integrated Stabilization Mission in the Central African Republic (MINUSCA),[121] the UN Organization Stabilization Mission in the Democratic Republic of the Congo (MONUSCO),[122] United Nations Mission in Côte d'Ivoire (UNOCI),[123] and the African Union/UN Hybrid operation in Darfur (UNAMID).[124] The Security Council mandated the United Nations Mission in the Republic of South Sudan (UNMISS)[125] to use all necessary means to monitor, investigate, verify, and report publicly and regularly on abuses and violations of human rights.[126]

The inclusion of robust human rights mandates into peacekeeping operations is reflective of the mainstreaming of human rights within the UN. Both throughout the work of the Organisation generally and in the context of peacekeeping operations, human rights must be incorporated into discussion and decision-making, reaffirming the need for the involvement of the High Commissioner and the OHCHR. The inclusion of human rights monitoring and reporting elements within peacekeeping operations at least opens the door for the provision of (accurate) information to inform such decision-making.

---

of that being the establishment of the African-led International Support Mission to Mali (AFISMA) by UNSC Res 2085 (20 December 2012) UN Doc S/RES/2085.

119 UNSC Res 2100 (25 April 2013) UN Doc S/RES/2100, para 16(d).

120 UNSC Res 2164 (25 June 2014) UN Doc S/RES/2164, para 13(c).

121 UNSC Res 2149 (10 April 2014) UN Doc S/RES/2149, para 30; and UNSC Res 2217 (28 April 2015) UN Doc S/RES/2217, para 32(e)(iv). Its predecessor, the UN Integrated Peacebuilding Office in the Central African Republic (BINUCA, which was a field office of the Department of Political Affairs) had also been accorded a human rights promotion and protection mandate: UNSC Res 2121 (10 October 2013) UN Doc S/RES/2121, para 10(d).

122 UNSC Res 2147 (28 March 2014) UN Doc S/RES/2147, para 5(d). This Mission's predecessor, the United Nations Organization Mission in the Democratic Republic of the Congo (MONUC), also made provision for the promotion and protection of human rights: see UNSC Res 1279 (30 November 1999) S/RES/1279, para 5(e).

123 UNSC Res 1528 (27 February 2004) UN Doc S/RES/1528, para 6(n); and UNSC Res 2226 (25 June 2015) UN Doc S/RES/2226, para 19(g).

124 UNSC Res 1769 (31 July 2007) UN Doc S/RES/1769, para 1; UNSC, 'Report of the Secretary-General and the Chairperson of the African Union Commission on the Hybrid Operation in Darfur 2007/307' (2007) UN Doc S/2007/307/Rev.1, para 55 (c)(v), (vi) and (vii); UNSC Res 2003 (29 July 2011) UN Doc S/RES/2003, para 16; UNSC Res 2063 (31 July 2012) UN Doc S/RES/2063, para 15; and UNSC Res 2173 (27 August 2014) UN Doc S/RES/2173, para 20.

125 UNSC Res 1996 (8 July 2011) UN Doc S/RES/1996, para 3(b)(iii).

126 UNSC Res 2223 (28 May 2015) UN Doc S/RES/2223, para 4(b)(i) and (ii).

In addition to the increasing deployment of Chapter VII peace enforcement operations in response to the threat posed by gross human rights violations, as well as peace operations themselves being increasingly tasked with resetting human rights standards, peace operations are also being subject to strict scrutiny for the extent to which they are complying with human rights norms. The Human Rights Due Diligence Policy requires all UN entities involved in supporting security forces to take into account human rights considerations and risks and to adapt their support accordingly. The Security Council has cited the due diligence policy in resolutions regarding peacekeeping.[127] To date, three peacekeeping missions have developed standard operating procedures for implementing the policy (MONUSCO, UNMISS and UNOCI), whilst others are in the process of integrating its principles into existing procedures and developing relevant guidance.[128] The Secretary-General has also called for the implementation of the Policy on Human Rights Screening of UN Personnel,[129] which sets thresholds of prior conduct with regard to human rights that all types of prospective UN personnel must meet. The onus remains primarily on Member States to screen the personnel they nominate or contribute to peacekeeping.[130] Further progress continues to be achieved in the implementation of these two policies, and the importance of adhering to the latter policy has been stressed by the Security Council in a number of resolutions establishing or extending the mandates of peacekeeping operations (such as MINUSMA, UNOCI, MONUSCO, MINUSCA and UNMISS).[131] However, the context of such initiatives – and thus arguably their resulting focus – has been violations of civil and political rights, as the development of these policies came in response to physical and sexual abuse committed by peacekeepers, abuses that were committed against a broader background of acts of torture, murder, rape, enslavement and arbitrary detention.

Substantial progress has been achieved regarding the integration of human rights into peacekeeping operations and political missions over the past 15 years. This includes the integration of human rights into policy, guidance and training for uniformed and civilian staff. Dedicated and sizeable human rights staffing is included in all integrated peace operations, and human rights expertise is often, but not yet always, included in the assessments and planning process for the

127 See, for example, UNSC Res 2102 (2 May 2013) UN Doc S/RES/2102, para 11; and UNSC Res 2223 (28 May 2015) UN Doc S/RES/2223, para 14.

128 UNGA, 'Report of the Secretary-General 68/652' (2013) UN Doc A/68/652 on 'Implementation of the Recommendations of the Special Committee on Peacekeeping Operations', para 86.

129 United Nations, 'Decision No. 2012/18 – Human Rights Screening of United Nations Personnel' (11 December 2012) <http://repository.un.org/handle/11176/387395> accessed 7 October 2016.

130 UNGA, 'Report of the Secretary-General 68/652' (n 128), para 87.

131 UNGA, 'Report of the Secretary-General 69/642' (2014) UN Doc A/69/642 on 'Implementation of the Recommendations of the Special Committee on Peacekeeping Operations', paras 105–106.

establishment and review of peace operations.[132] Of themselves, peacekeeping operations are not instruments to claim individual human rights, but the elaboration of the Charter's references to human rights by the International Bill of Rights and other core UN (and regional) treaties indicates that the standards set, and elaborated upon, by this treaty framework are the ones that underpin the meaning and content of human rights as integrated into peace operations. It is these standards that also inform the work of the High Commissioner for Human Rights and the work of the Human Rights Council, including the work of the Special Rapporteurs, Commissions of Inquiry and the Universal Periodic Review. On this basis, the role of economic and social rights in peacebuilding and peacekeeping must be given its due recognition, a recognition which would strengthen the efforts of the UN, and the Security Council, to achieve its aim of maintaining international peace and security and promoting better standards of life in larger freedom. Unfortunately, as the ensuing section shows, economic and social rights are still marginalised in the quest for peace.

5 Peacebuilding critiqued: The marginalisation of socio-economic conditions as an aspect of peacebuilding

Although the Security Council increasingly advances peacebuilding and peacekeeping as interrelated initiatives, in which economic and social reconstruction and human rights are progressively emphasised, these initiatives have, nonetheless, been criticised for their emphasis on building a liberal peace[133] and for their exclusion of economic and social rights.[134] Liberal peacebuilding is premised on the view that 'democratic institutions and market mechanisms will ultimately provide the stable foundations for peace, both internally and externally'.[135] Thus,

132 The HIPPO Report (n 20), para 245.

133 Edward Newman, Roland Paris and Oliver P Richmond (eds), *New Perspectives on Liberal Peacebuilding* (United Nations University Press, Tokyo 2009); Susanna Campbell, David Chandler and Meera Sabaratnam (eds), *A Liberal Peace? The Problems and Practices of Peacekeeping* (Zed Books, London 2011); Oliver Richmond (ed), *Advances in Peacebuilding: Critical Developments and Approaches* (Palgrave Macmillan, London 2010); Roland Paris, 'Saving Liberal Peacebuilding' (2010) 36(2) *Review of International Studies* 337; Roger Mac Ginty, *International Peacebuilding and Local Resistance: Hybrid Forms of Peace* (Palgrave Macmillan, New York 2011); Oliver Richmond, *A Post-Liberal Peace* (Routledge, London 2011); Oliver P Richmond and Jason Franks, 'Liberal Peacebuilding in Timor Leste: The Emperor's New Clothes?' (2008) 15(2) *International Peacekeeping* 185; Oliver P Richmond and Roger Mac Ginty, 'Where Now for the Critique of the Liberal Peace?' (2015) 50(2) *Cooperation and Conflict* 171; and Shahar Hameiri, 'The Crisis of Liberal Peacebuilding and the Future of Statebuilding' (2014) 51(3) *International Politics* 316.

134 Sylvia Maus, 'Jus Post Bellum a la United Nations: Human Rights, UN Peace Operations, and the Creation of International Law' (2014) 32 *Wisconsin International Law Journal* 675, 691.

135 Thomas J Biersteker, 'Prospects for the UN Peacebuilding Commission' (2007) 2(2) *Disarmament Forum* 37, 39; and Robert Jenkins, *Peacebuilding: From Concept to Commission* (Routledge, London 2008) 13.

liberal-democratic societies are the preferred outcome for UN peacebuilding because such societies are believed to be inherently more peaceful than other kinds of societies. However, it is further argued that the successful establishment of such societies is also the least likely outcome.[136] Of greater concern is the belief that the emphasis on the (unrealistic) goal of instant liberalisation has been regarded as sowing the seeds of conflict. Such outcomes are perhaps not unsurprising, as peacebuilding entails 'the impossible dream of attempting to engineer in years what took centuries for West European states'.[137]

Liberal peacebuilding has also been criticised for its tendency to simply reinforce the *status quo* where power is concentrated in elite social and economic groups. At best, such outcomes allow the underlying symptoms of conflict to remain unaddressed; at its worst, the maintenance of the *status quo* amplifies tensions in post-conflict societies that are already riven by inequality, thereby undermining any gains by liberalism's self-help approach to equality. Similarly, liberal peacebuilding has been criticised for failing to respond to the 'pervasive threats of indirect violence', such as 'the war-aggravated poverty that strips clothing from people's backs, destroys their shelter and excludes from their lives basic nutrition, jobs and access to clean water'.[138] A further recurring criticism of peacebuilding is its lack of local legitimacy, and the absence of a deep engagement with local politics, the local economy and local actors.[139]

However, critiques of liberal peacebuilding have themselves been critiqued,[140] for being based on flawed information and failing to make important distinctions,[141] with the result that such criticisms really only serve to distract attention from many of the highly problematic consequences of contemporary peacebuilding practices.[142] In an attempt to save liberal peacebuilding, it has been argued that:

> denunciations of liberal peacebuilding are both unwarranted and imprudent. They are unwarranted because such missions, in spite of their many flaws, have done more good than harm; and they are imprudent because the failure

136 Michael Barnett, Songying Fang and Christoph Zurcher, 'Compromised Peacebuilding' (2014) 58(3) *International Studies Quarterly* 608, 608–609.

137 Ibid, 609.

138 David Roberts, 'Post-conflict Peacebuilding, Liberal Irrelevance and the Locus of Legitimacy' (2011) 18(4) *International Peacekeeping* 410, 412. See also, Dorussen (n 82).

139 See generally, Campbell (n 133); Oliver P Richmond and Audra Mitchell (eds), *Hybrid Forms of Peace: From Everyday Agency to Postliberalism* (Palgrave Macmillan, Basingstoke 2012); Roger Mac Ginty and Oliver P Richmond, 'The Local Turn in Peace Building: A Critical Agenda for Peace' (2013) 34(5) *Third World Quarterly* 763; Vivienne Jabri, 'Peacebuilding, the Local and the International: A Colonial or a Postcolonial Rationality?' (2013) 1(1) *Peace-building* 3; and Oliver P Richmond, 'Resistance and the Post-liberal Peace' (2010) 38(3) *Millennium* 665.

140 See, for example, Richmond and Ginty (n 133); and Paris, 'Saving Liberal Peacebuilding' (n 135).

141 Paris, ibid, 347.

142 Hameiri (n 133), 318.

> of the existing peacebuilding project would be tantamount to abandoning tens of millions of people to lawlessness, predation, disease and fear.[143]

Nonetheless, the critique of liberal peacebuilding remains valuable as it reinforces the need to re-evaluate current approaches to peacebuilding,[144] especially since alternative approaches that seek to explore the challenges of the current focus of peacebuilding can offer alternative, complementary pathways.[145]

Similar criticisms have been levelled at transitional justice, criticisms which are worth considering because of the relationship between peacebuilding and transitional justice. Concerns have been expressed that transitional justice – like peacebuilding – has been captured by a liberal model of transitional justice that emphasises individual criminal responsibility[146] and, as a result, civil and political rights.[147] A liberal approach to transitional justice may mean that:

> even with trials and reparations, if economic and social inequalities go unaddressed and the grievances of the poor and marginalized go unheard, we are left with only uncertain guarantees of nonrepetition. It is like treating the symptoms while leaving the underlying illness to fester.[148]

The consequences of a liberal approach to transitional justice further contributes to the view that economic and social rights are not 'real rights' but mere aspirations granting de facto impunity to the architects and authors of economic violence.[149]

Although UN peacebuilding and peacekeeping do recognise the link between socio-economic conditions to the maintenance of peace and security, it may be that such efforts are critiqued because they are executed in the context of attempts to create liberal democracies that favour marketisation, which is an approach that

143 Paris, 'Saving Liberal Peacebuilding' (n 133), 338.

144 Ibid, 340.

145 Catherine Goetze and Berit Bliesemann De Guevara, 'Cosmopolitanism and the Culture of Peacebuilding' (2014) 40(4) *Review of International Studies* 771; and Shaun Goldfinch and Karl Derouen Jr, 'In It for the Long Haul? Post-conflict Statebuilding, Peacebuilding, and the Good Governance Agenda in Timor-Leste' (2014) 34(2) *Public Administration and Development* 96.

146 See, for example, Diane F Orentlicher, 'Settling Accounts: The Duty to Prosecute Human Rights Violations of a Prior Regime' (1991) 100(8) *The Yale Law Journal* 2537; and Diane F Orentlicher, 'Addressing Gross Human Rights Abuses: Punishment and Victim Compensation' (1994) 26 *Studies in Transnational Legal Policy* 425.

147 Louise Arbour, 'Economic and Social Justice for Societies in Transition' (2007) 40(1) *Journal of International Law and Politics* 1, 3.

148 Lisa J Laplante, 'Transitional Justice and Peace Building: Diagnosing and Addressing the Socioeconomic Roots of Violence through a Human Rights Framework' (2008) 2(3) *The International Journal of Transitional Justice* 331, 333.

149 Dustin N Sharp, 'Introduction: Addressing Economic Violence in Times of Transition' in Dustin N Sharp (ed), *Justice and Economic Violence in Transition* (Springer, New York 2014) 13.

favours the *status quo* and does not adequately account for economic and social marginalisation as a driver of conflict. Peacebuilding efforts in Iraq and Afghanistan are advanced as the prime examples of such failures, where earlier attempts to establish liberal democracies and market economies had failed miserably, leading to widespread brutal violence.[150] Thus, there seems to be a mismatch between UN policy and the execution of that policy. The marginalisation of improved economic and social conditions for all as an aspect of conflict prevention in post-conflict societies is facilitated by the misapprehension of the role of economic and social rights and their capacity to underpin the economic and social recovery of States emerging from conflict, a recovery which must be informed by human rights, which include economic and social rights as a means to ensure citizenship and to build a more secure and stable order.

6 Conclusion

UN peacebuilding policy shows that the Organisation understands that peace and security, development and human rights can play a central role in the maintenance of international peace and security. In terms of peacekeeping and peacebuilding, the Security Council continues to recognise that development, peace and security, and human rights are interlinked and mutually reinforcing.[151] The Security Council's mandate to maintain international peace and security has evolved to become one that requires more proactive measures to advance economic and social development and human rights, not only as ends in themselves, but also as a means to avoid conflict. The basis for this approach comes from a shift away from the logic of resolution and towards one of prevention. The shift towards the logic of conflict prevention is noteworthy given that the changing mindset suggests that economic and social development, with its overlap with human rights considerations, is being accorded a greater degree of significance by the Security Council as it seeks to perform its role of maintaining international peace and security.

For their part, peacekeeping operations are becoming increasingly complex, as many operations are charged with putting peacebuilding principles into effect. Peacekeeping mandates increasingly reveal requirements for peacekeepers to facilitate, or engage in, economic and social reconstruction. The integration of human rights into peacekeeping operations also means that peacekeepers have a role to prevent civilian populations from human rights abuses, and to monitor and report on human rights abuses by either local actors and, indeed, their own personnel. If peacekeepers are the UN's most visible tool for conflict prevention, these developments are to be welcomed. However, they are also a matter for concern because these wide-ranging peacekeeping mandates result in efforts that too often 'have been fragmented and unequal to the task'.[152] At the risk of adding to

150 Hameiri (n 133), 319.
151 UNSC Res 2282 (27 April 2016) UN Doc S/RES/2282, preambular para 4.
152 UNGA, 'Report of the Secretary-General 2015/682' (n 79), para 5.

such concerns is the need for peacekeeping to demonstrate a broader approach to the promotion and protection of human rights and to respond to violations of economic and social rights, and to ensure that peacekeepers do not themselves violate these rights.

One of the reasons for adopting a broader approach is that it can help to allay some of the concerns expressed about current peacebuilding and peacekeeping endeavours. Critiques of peacebuilding and transitional justice, to the extent that the latter informs the former, are a reminder of the importance that is to be attached to improving economic and social conditions as a means to ensure citizenship. As elaborated in Chapter 1, this conceptualisation of citizenship is not solely based upon political participation, but it is also based on the provision of basic services and the elaboration of social citizenship, and is an important factor to securing a stable order, both domestically and internationally. Not only that, these endeavours have been given a legal basis in international and domestic human rights law. Chapters 2 and 3 show that, at a broad level, the UN and the Security Council recognise this relationship. It is the execution of this relationship that has led to the criticism that peacebuilding has been captured by liberal and neo liberal agendas. It is at this point that the need to understand the particular role and contribution of economic and social rights within peacekeeping becomes important to allow for a recalibration of peacebuilding and peacekeeping which more fully incorporates economic and social rights.

4 Economic and social rights in peacebuilding and peacekeeping

A measurable legal basis for the economic and social dimensions of peace

1 Introduction

There is an evolving jurisprudence at the regional and international level that considers the issue of States' human rights obligations arising from its peace operations. Such considerations are based on the recognition that States contributing to peacekeeping operations must give extraterritorial effect to those obligations. Although such developments are to be welcomed, these strands of jurisprudence deal almost exclusively with violations of civil and political rights, even though the failure to strengthen the protection of economic and social rights 'undermines the sought-after stability and human security post-conflict (including food, health, gender and physical security)'.[1] This dearth of consideration of the extraterritorial application of economic and social rights has its roots in the marginalisation of economic and social rights, which was detailed in Chapter 1. Such marginalisation continues to persist even though, as Chapters 2 and 3 show, the UN understands that the (re-)establishment of peace and security, human rights and economic and social progress, as underpinned by equality, are all interlinked. Such marginalisation also persists in spite of the fact that post-conflict societies themselves are often prime examples of the fact that, just like schools and hospitals, fully operational judicial and electoral systems require substantial resources for their establishment and on-going functioning. Peacekeeping operations that work to protect and to realise economic and social rights support their own legitimacy, and they can also support efforts to maintain a peace that goes beyond the current confines of liberal peacebuilding.

In light of these developments, this chapter will explore the extraterritorial application of economic and social rights. It will canvass current developments in the extraterritorial application of economic and social rights. The chapter will also

1 Christine Chinkin, *The Protection of Economic, Social and Cultural Rights Post Conflict* (Paper series commissioned by OHCHR, 2009) 4, <www2.ohchr.org/english/issues/women/docs/Paper_Protection_ESCR.pdf> accessed 5 August 2016. See also, M G Kaladharan Nayar, 'Human Rights and Economic Development: The Legal Foundations' (1980) 2(3) *Universal Human Rights* 55.

consider the extraterritorial application of human rights in the context of peacekeeping operations. Even though the latter developments have resulted from violations of civil and political rights, the interrelated and interdependent nature of human rights means that such developments are important to a discussion on the extraterritorial application of economic and social rights. Following on from these analyses, Chapter 4 details the extraterritorial quality of the rights to food, water and health as core survival rights. It also considers the extraterritorial effect of the rights to education and work. These two rights are considered because of the role of the right to education towards the achievement of peace and, as indicated in Chapter 1, worker's rights underpin efforts to maintain international peace and security. Chapter 4 then turns to how human rights indicators can be used to measure the extent to which contributing States are meeting their obligations stemming from each of these rights; indicators measuring the rights to equality and non-discrimination are also considered as a reminder of the essential role of these two rights in the effective realisation of economic and social rights.

Chapter 4 shows that contributing States' extraterritorial obligations extend to economic and social rights, and the acts and omissions that comprise these obligations are measureable, both practically and legally. This approach can be used to affirm contributing States' efforts to improve socio-economic conditions and indicate where and how improvements could be made.

2 The extraterritorial application of economic and social rights

Although peacekeeping operations are subsidiary organs of the Security Council, they retain their status as organs of their contributing States and they remain bound by those States' domestic and international legal obligations, including those that have extraterritorial effect. A key source of extraterritorial obligations for the military of contributing States is international humanitarian law,[2] in particular the laws of occupation which are designed to limit the powers of the occupier.[3] Part III, Section III of Geneva Convention IV provides greater clarity on the rights and responsibilities of Occupying Powers towards the civilian population.[4] The socio-economic nature of the obligations of Occupiers can be seen in provisions such as Article 55 of Geneva Convention IV which states, 'to the fullest extent of the means available to it, the Occupying Power has the duty of ensuring the food and medical supplies of the population' and Article 56 which places similar obligations on the Occupying Power to ensure the provision of

2 UN Secretariat, 'Secretary-General's Bulletin: Observance by United Nations Forces of International Humanitarian Law' (6 August 1999) UN Doc ST/SGB/1999/13, para 1.1.

3 Convention Respecting the Laws and Customs of War on Land (Hague – IV) (signed 18 October 1907, entered into force 26 January 1910) (1907) 36 Stat. 2277, Article 43.

4 Geneva Convention Relative to the Protection of Civilian Persons in Time of War Geneva Convention IV (signed 12 August 1949, entered into force 21 October 1950) 75 UNTS 287.

medical services and sanitation.[5] Consequently, Occupiers are under a responsibility to guarantee the civilian population's human security[6] and lend further credence to the assertion that:

> Today many of us would no longer distinguish between 'security' and economic and social issues, arguing that human security is as critical as state security and that the two are inextricably intertwined.[7]

Occupiers are also subject to the limitations and responsibilities increasingly imposed by international human rights standards,[8] though the laws of occupation remain *lex specialis.*

Ultimately, however, the laws of occupation are of limited assistance in the majority of current post-conflict situations, as the bulk of the, very detailed, rules only apply to armed conflicts of an international character.[9] Conflicts not of an international character are governed either by Common Article 3 of the Geneva Conventions, which merely requires States to maintain minimum humane standards of treatment, or for those ratifying States, Part VI of Additional Protocol II will also apply.[10] A further limitation of the laws of occupation is that the current collective security regime means that peacekeeping operations need not be established in response to armed conflict, and Chapter VII peace enforcement operations may not necessarily constitute an occupation of territory by a foreign power and thus may not trigger the laws of occupation. Consequently, these laws may be inadequate to deal with the demands of peacebuilding and post-conflict reconstruction in particular,[11] though their provisions are still pertinent to estab-

5 For example, regarding Iraq, the UK and the US stated that they would, 'strictly abide by their obligations under international law, including those relating to the essential humanitarian needs of the people of Iraq': UNSC 'Letter Dated 8 May 2003 from the Permanent Representatives of the United Kingdom of Great Britain and Northern Ireland and the United States of America to the United Nations Addressed to the President of the Security Council' (8 May 2003) UN Doc S/2003/538. The recognition of the occupation of Iraq in UNSC Res 1483 (22 May 2003) UN Doc S/RES/1483 and UNSC Res 1511 (16 October 2003) UN Doc S/RES/1511 had the effect of binding the Coalition Provisional Authority by the Hague Regulations and the Geneva Conventions. See Carsten Stahn, 'Jus Ad Bellum', 'Jus in Bello' . . . 'Jus Post Bellum'? – Rethinking the Conception of the Law of Armed Force' (2006) 17(5) *European Journal of International Law* 921, 929.

6 Jennifer Moore, 'Collective Security with a Human Face: An International Legal Framework for Coordinated Action to Alleviate Violence and Poverty' (2004) 33(1) *Denver Journal of International Law and Policy* 43, 67–69.

7 Ibid, 52 citing Anne-Marie Slaughter, 'The Value of Spirited Debate' (2004) *Newsletter of the American Society of International law* 8.

8 See *Legal Consequences of the Construction of a Wall* (Advisory Opinion) [2004] ICJ Rep 136 (the *Israeli Wall* Advisory Opinion), 136, para 114; and *Armed Activities on the Territory of the Congo (DRC v Uganda)* (Judgment) [2005] ICJ Rep 168 (the *Congo* case), para 178.

9 Geneva Convention IV (n 4), Common Article 2.

10 Protocol Additional to the Geneva Conventions of 12 August 1949, and Relating to the Protection of Victims of Non-International Armed Conflicts (Protocol II) (adopted 8 June 1977, entered into force 7 December 1978) 1125 UNTS 609.

11 Kirsten Boon, 'The Future of the Law of Occupation' (2008) 46 *Canadian Yearbook of International Law* 107, 110–114.

lishing a peace and security that encompasses more than the absence of armed conflict. It is in such post-conflict situations that States' obligations under international human rights law have taken on an added significance as a wide range of human rights can now be said to colour the obligations of contributing States in a post-conflict environment.

The obligations that flow from ratification of human rights treaties tend to be limited to those within the territory or jurisdiction of the State. However, it is being increasingly recognised that human rights can have extraterritorial application, meaning that States have an extraterritorial obligation to avoid acts or omissions that would negatively affect the enjoyment of rights of individuals and groups in third States. Whilst this view is not without controversy, there is logic in the view that prohibiting acts and omissions 'at home' but allowing a State to carry out such acts and omissions that have a negative impact 'abroad' is somewhat contrary to the object and purpose of human rights treaties generally. The extraterritorial application of economic and social rights has been increasingly recognised in the Covenant's own interpretive tools, other 'soft law' principles, and in the literature, which has sought both to expand and to refine State Parties' obligations stemming from the ICESCR.[12]

The extraterritorial quality of economic and social rights can be traced to the UN Charter's provisions regarding international economic and social cooperation, and particularly the provisions of Articles 55 and 56. Article 28 of the Universal Declaration also states, 'Everyone is entitled to a social and international order in which the rights and freedoms set forth in this Declaration can be fully realized'.[13] Similarly, Article 2(1) of the ICESCR places States Parties under an international legal obligation 'to take steps, individually and through international assistance

12 Claire Breen, 'The Edges of Extraterritorial Jurisdiction: The Integration of Economic, Social and Cultural Rights into Peace Support Operations' (2012) 16 *Journal of International Peacekeeping* 47, 60–71. See, generally, Malcolm Langford and others (eds), *Global Justice, State Duties: The Extraterritorial Scope of Economic, Social and Cultural Rights in International Law* (Cambridge University Press, New York 2013); Mark Gibney and Sigrun Skogly (eds), *Universal Human Rights and Extraterritorial Obligations* (University of Pennsylvania Press, Philadelphia 2010); Fons Coomans and Menno T Kamminga (eds), *Extraterritorial Application of Human Rights Treaties* (Intersentia, Antwerp 2004); and Wouter Vandenhole, 'Economic, Social and Cultural Rights in the CRC: Is There a Legal Obligation to Cooperate for Development?' (2009) 17(1) *International Journal of Children's Rights* 23. The on-going strong resistance to the notion of binding extraterritorial obligations can be seen in the context of States' continued resistance to accepting any form of binding obligation to engage in international cooperation and provide international assistance: see Fons Coomans, 'The Extraterritorial Scope of the International Covenant on Economic, Social and Cultural Rights in the Work of the United Nations Committee on Economic, Social and Cultural Rights' (2011) 11(1) *Human Rights Law Review* 1; and Monica Hakimi, 'State Bystander Responsibility' (2011) 21(2) *European Journal of International Law* 341. Similarly, the ebb and flow of this resistance can be seen in the discussion around States' ETOs and multinational corporations: see Aoife Nolan, 'Addressing Economic and Social Rights Violations by Non-State Actors through the Role of the State: A Comparison of Regional Approaches to the "Obligation to Protect"' (2009) 9(2) *Human Rights Law Review* 225.

13 Universal Declaration of Human Rights (adopted 10 December 1948) UNGA Res 217 A(III) (the UDHR or the Declaration).

and co-operation'.[14] This aspect of Article 2(1) is a broad concept which can also give rise to obligations that include aspects of a State's foreign policy, such as military and security cooperation to the extent that such matters impact on the enjoyment of human rights in other States.[15] This is relevant because peacekeeping operations, as an aspect of a State's foreign policy, raise issues for extraterritoriality of economic and social rights. The extraterritorial quality of Article 2(1)'s obligations is supported by the fact that Article 2(1), unlike its sister provision in the ICCPR,[16] makes no restrictive reference to territory or jurisdiction. Article 2 of the Optional Protocol to the ICESCR makes no reference to territory either, as it allows communications to be submitted by or on behalf of individuals or groups of individuals under the jurisdiction of a State Party.[17]

The CESCR (or the Committee) has referred to 'the extent to which the various rights are, or are not, being enjoyed by all individuals within its territory or under its jurisdiction'.[18] It has also identified the potential for the extraterritorial effect of State Parties' obligations under the Covenant with its statement that it:

> wishes to emphasize that in accordance with Articles 55 and 56 of the Charter of the United Nations, with well-established principles of international law, and with the provisions of the Covenant itself, international cooperation for development and thus for the realization of economic, social and cultural rights is an obligation of all States. It is particularly incumbent upon those States which are in a position to assist others in this regard.[19]

Other 'soft law' interpretive instruments such as the Limburg Principles[20] and the Maastricht Guidelines[21] also make reference to, or imply, the extraterritorial nature of States' obligations.

14 International Covenant on Economic, Social and Cultural Rights (adopted 16 December 1966, entered into force 3 January 1976) 993 UNTS 3 (ICESCR).
15 Sigrun I Skogly, 'The Right to Adequate Food: National Implementation and Extraterritorial Obligations' (2007) 11 *Max Planck Yearbook of the United Nations* 339, 347.
16 International Covenant on Civil and Political Rights (adopted 16 December 1966, entered into force 23 March 1976) 999 UNTS 171 (ICCPR), Article 2(1).
17 Optional Protocol to the International Covenant on Economic, Social and Cultural Rights (adopted 10 December 2008, entered into force 5 May 2013) UNGA Res 117 (8 December 2008) UN Doc A/RES/63/117 (ICESCR Optional Protocol).
18 CESCR, 'General Comment 1, Reporting by States Parties' in 'Compilation of General Comments and General Recommendations Adopted by Human Rights Treaty Bodies' (2003) UN Doc HRI/GEN/1/Rev.6, para 3.
19 CESCR, 'General Comment 3, The Nature of States Parties' Obligations' in 'Compilation of General Comments and General Recommendations Adopted by Human Rights Treaty Bodies' (2003) UN Doc HRI/GEN/1/Rev.6, para 14.
20 UNCHR, 'Note Verbale Dated 86/12/05 from the Permanent Mission of the Netherlands to the United Nations Office at Geneva Addressed to the Centre for Human Rights' (8 January 1987) UN Doc E/CN.4/1987/17, Annex (the Limburg Principles) reprinted in (1987) 9(2) *Human Rights Quarterly* 122.
21 The Maastricht Guidelines on Violations of Economic, Social and Cultural Rights, Maastricht, 22–26 January 1997 (the Maastricht Guidelines) reprinted in (1998) 20(3) *Human Rights Quarterly* 691. The extraterritorial nature of the Covenant's obligations can be inferred from

The extraterritorial nature of the Covenant's rights has been further supported by the Maastricht Principles on Extraterritorial Obligations of States in the Area of Economic, Social and Cultural Rights 2012.[22] These Principles were adopted by 40 experts to clarify the extraterritorial obligations of States on the basis of existing international law. They affirm that the obligations to respect, protect and fulfil extend extraterritorially and that States must ensure the right to a remedy.[23] Whilst these Principles are far from being a source of binding obligations for States, they have informed the field of interpretation of economic and social rights.[24] According to the Principles, extraterritorial obligations include 'obligations relating to the acts and omissions of a State, within or beyond its territory, that have effects on the enjoyment of human rights outside of that State's territory'.[25] The meaning of jurisdiction encompasses the test of States' authority or effective control, but it also includes, more broadly, situations where States' acts or omissions have foreseeable effects or where States are in a position to exercise decisive influence or to take measures to realise economic, social and cultural rights extraterritorially.[26] Most significant, in the context of this chapter, is Principle 18, which provides that 'A State exercising effective control over persons outside its national territory must respect, protect and fulfil economic, social and cultural rights of those persons.'

The extraterritorial application of obligations under the ICESCR has been considered by the International Court of Justice (the ICJ or the Court) which, in its *Israeli Wall* Advisory Opinion, noted that the construction of the wall had resulted in serious repercussions for agricultural production, and increasing

Guideline 17 which refers to the imputability of conduct to States exercising effective control, albeit in situations of colonialism, other forms of alien domination and military occupation.

22 ETO Consortium, 'Maastricht Principles on Extraterritorial Obligations of States in the Area of Economic, Social and Cultural rights' (FIAN International, Heidelberg 2013) (the Maastricht Principles) <http://www.etoconsortium.org/nc/en/main-navigation/library/maastricht-principles/?tx_drblob_pi1%5BdownloadUid%5D=23> accessed 1 October 2016.

23 Olivier De Schutter and others, 'Commentary to the Maastricht Principles on Extraterritorial Obligations of States in the Area of Economic, Social and Cultural Rights' (2012) 34(4) *Human Rights Quarterly* 1084 (Commentary to the Maastricht Principles). See also, Fons Coomans, 'Situating the Maastricht Principles on Extraterritorial Obligations of States in the Area of Economic, Social and Cultural Rights' (Maastricht Faculty of Law Working Paper, 2013) <http://ssrn.com/abstract=2256836> accessed 13 August 2016. Some hesitance has been expressed in relation to the ETO Principles, stemming from their vague legal status and unclear legal basis for ETOs, as well as the lack of elaboration on what exactly must be done by which foreign State: see Wouter Vandenhole, 'Beyond Territoriality: The Maastricht Principles on Extra-Territorial Obligations in the Area of Economic, Social and Cultural Rights' (2011) 29(4) *Netherlands Quarterly of Human Rights* 429.

24 The Principles have featured in a number of Reports of Special Rapporteurs, such as, UNGA 'Report of the Special Rapporteur on the Human Right to Safe Drinking Water and Sanitation, Catarina de Albuquerque' (2014) UN Doc A/HRC/27/55, para 70; and UNGA 'Report of the Special Rapporteur on the Human Right to Safe Drinking Water and Sanitation 68/264, Catarina de Albuquerque' (2013) UN Doc A/68/264, para 46.

25 The Maastricht Principles (n 22), Principle 8(a).

26 Ibid, Principle 9. Principle 14 requires States to conduct prior assessment, with public participation, of the risks and potential extraterritorial impacts of their laws, policies and practices on the enjoyment of economic, social and cultural rights.

difficulties for the population concerned regarding access to health services, educational establishments and primary sources of water.[27] Although it determined that the rights in the ICESCR, unlike those of the ICCPR,[28] are 'essentially territorial',[29] the Court did note that the essential territoriality of economic and social rights was not to be read as precluding the extraterritorial application of the Covenant 'to territories over which a State party has sovereignty and to those over which that State exercises territorial jurisdiction'.[30] The Court was of the view that Israel was under an obligation not to raise obstacles in the exercise of rights that had been transferred to the Palestinian authorities.[31] In the *Congo* case, the ICJ referred to its *Israeli Wall* Advisory Opinion but concluded, more broadly, that 'international human rights instruments are applicable "in respect of acts done by a State in the exercise of its jurisdiction outside its own territory" particularly in occupied territories'.[32] The equivocal statement by the Court that Uganda was responsible for acts by its military that violated any international human rights law and international humanitarian law and for any lack of vigilance in preventing such violations as committed by other actors present in the occupied territory may also mean, respectively, that extraterritorial obligations encompass the negative obligation to respect and the positive obligation to protect.[33]

After recognising the extraterritorial nature of States' obligations under the ICESCR, the Court turned to the question of when that quality comes into effect. The view of the ICJ in the *Israeli Wall* Advisory Opinion suggests that the threshold would only be reached in exceptional circumstances, such as military occupation.[34] However, in the *Congo* case, the Court concluded that international human rights instruments are applicable when States exercise jurisdiction outside of their own territory, *particularly* in occupied territories.[35] This view suggests that there may be situations other than military occupation in which extraterritorial jurisdiction may be exercised. The question of what comprises extraterritorial jurisdiction and what set of circumstances comprises effective control for the purposes of Article 1 of the European Convention on Human Rights (the ECHR)[36] has been elaborated upon by the European Court of Human Rights

27 *Israeli Wall* Advisory Opinion (n 8), para 133.
28 ICCPR (n 16), Article 2(1).
29 *Israeli Wall* Advisory Opinion (n 8), para 112. See Marko Milanović, 'From Compromise to Principle: Clarifying the Concept of State Jurisdiction in Human Rights Treaties' (2008) 8(3) *Human Rights Law Review* 411; John Cerone, 'Human Dignity in the Line of Fire: The Application of International Human Rights Law During Armed Conflict, Occupation, and Peace Operations' (2006) 39 *Vanderbilt Journal of Transnational Law* 1447.
30 *Israeli Wall* Advisory Opinion (n 8), para 112.
31 Ibid.
32 The *Congo* case (n 8), para 216.
33 Ibid, para 179; and Breen (n 12), 68.
34 *Israeli Wall* Advisory Opinion (n 8), para 112. See Cerone (n 29), 1495.
35 The *Congo* case (n 8), para 216.
36 ECHR, Article 1 provides, 'The High Contracting Parties shall secure to everyone within their jurisdiction the rights and freedoms defined in Section I of this Convention'. For a general overview of the extraterritorial application of the ECHR and other international human rights law instruments, see Coomans and Kamminga (n 12); Marko Milanović,

(the ECtHR), particularly in the context of Contracting Parties which had contributed to UN peacekeeping missions, as well as NATO-led but Security Council mandated operations. The ECtHR's reasoning has been varied, and not always consistent, but has found that effective control can be exercised in exceptional cases.[37] The ECtHR has found that extraterritorial jurisdiction arises from the fact of control, whether lawful or unlawful, rather than the principles of general international law regarding jurisdiction.[38] The threshold for effective control has also been found where the respondent State was exercising all or some of the public powers normally to be exercised by a government[39] or where the Contracting State exercised authority and control over an individual abroad through its agents or where it exercised effective control of an area outside its national territory.[40] Effective control was found to exist where the armed forces of a Contracting State had exclusive control over a detention facility[41] and, on the basis that a State retained full command over its military personnel during their participation, in a multinational peace operation.[42] The Inter-American Commission on Human Rights has determined that the Inter-American Convention on Human Rights has extraterritorial effect in instances where ratifying States were found to exercise control over the individuals whose rights were allegedly violated,[43] an approach which now resonates with Principle 18 of the Maastricht Principles and the *Jaloud* case from the ECtHR.

The UN Human Rights Committee has recognised that the extraterritorial application of human rights treaties may attach to States that contribute to peace operations.[44] The Security Council has also stressed the responsibility of parties

---

Extraterritorial Application of Human Rights Treaties: Law, Principles, and Policy (Oxford University Press, Oxford 2011); Karen Da Costa, *The Extraterritorial Application of Selected Human Rights Treaties* (11 Graduate Institute of International and Development Studies, Martinus Nijhoff Publishers, Leiden 2013); and Samantha Besson, 'The Extraterritoriality of the European Convention on Human Rights: Why Human Rights Depend on Jurisdiction and What Jurisdiction Amounts To' (2012) 25(4) *Leiden Journal of International Law*, 857, 872.

37 *Bankovic and Others v Belgium and Others* (App no. 52207/99) (2007) 44 EHRR SE5, paras 59–61. Compare, *Loizidou v Turkey* (App no. 15318/89) (1995) 20 EHRR 99 where a broader approach had been taken by the ECtHR.

38 *Behrami and Behrami v France* and *Saramati v France and Others* (App nos 71412/01 and 78166/01) (2007) 45 EHRR SE10. Compare, *Issa v Turkey* (App no. 31821/96) (2004) 41 EHRR 567; and *Ilascu and Others v Moldova and Russia* (App no. 48787/99) (2004) 40 EHRR 1030.

39 *Bankovic and Others v Belgium and Others* (n 37), para 71. However, this view has been criticised. See Milanović (n 29), 419.

40 *Al-Skeini v The United Kingdom* (App no. 55721/07) (2011) 53 EHRR 18, paras 130–148.

41 *Al-Jedda v The United Kingdom* (App no. 27021/08) (2011) 53 EHRR 23, para 86. See also, *Hassan v The United Kingdom* (App no. 29750/09) ECHR 16 September 2014.

42 *Jaloud v The Netherlands* (App no. 47708/08) ECHR 20 November 2014, para 143.

43 *Coard et al v United States* (Case 10.951, Report No. 109/99) (1999) IACHR; and *Alejandre et al v Cuba* (Case 11.589, Report No. 86/99) (1999) IACHR.

44 In relation to Article 2(1) of the ICCPR, the Committee has stated:

> a State party must respect and ensure the rights laid down in the Covenant to anyone within the power or effective control of that State Party, even if not situated within the

to armed conflict to respect, protect and meet the basic needs of civilian populations within their effective control.[45] It must be acknowledged that much of the jurisprudence to date has dealt with violations of civil and political rights. Nonetheless, the division between civil and political rights and economic and social rights is not 'water tight', as elaborated in Chapter 1.

In essence, therefore, jurisdiction, in the context of human rights treaties, is primarily territorial but it may be exercised extraterritorially. The effect of establishing jurisdiction is that it allows an individual or a group to claim that their rights under the ICESCR[46] were breached by a foreign State or, in the context of peacekeeping operations, by a contributing State. In such situations, jurisdiction is dependent on the existence of an element of control that a State exercises over persons or territory. What constitutes 'control' has been interpreted variously, but there is increasing consideration of the fact that it applies to peacekeeping operations. Establishing the requisite level of control allows a further, but separate, question to be asked, which is whether a contributing State may be held to be accountable for a failure to respect, protect and fulfil economic and social rights,[47] a matter that will be revisited in Chapter 5.

> territory of the State Party . . . This principle also applies to those within the power or effective control of the forces of a State Party acting outside its territory, regardless of the circumstances in which such power or effective control was obtained, such as forces constituting a national contingent of a State Party assigned to an international peace-keeping or peace-enforcement operation.

See HRC, 'General Comment 31, Nature of the General Legal Obligation on States Parties to the Covenant' (2004) UN Doc CCPR/C/21/Rev.1/Add.13, para 10. The Committee has also stated, in its State Party Reports, that extraterritorial application of the Covenant should also be extended to all individuals who are subject to the jurisdiction of a State when the military personnel of that State are serving abroad, particularly in the context of peacekeeping and peace restoration missions, NATO military missions or belligerent occupation. See HRC 'Consideration of Reports submitted by States Parties under Article 40 of the Covenant: Concluding Observations of the Human Rights Committee on Poland' (2 December 2004) UN Doc CCPR/CO/82/POL, para 3; HRC, 'Consideration of Reports Submitted by States Parties under Article 40 of the Covenant: Concluding Observations of the Human Rights Committee on Belgium' (12 August 2004) UN Doc CCPR/CO/81/BEL, para 6; HRC, 'Consideration of Reports Submitted by States Parties under Article 40 of the Covenant: Concluding Observations of the Human Rights Committee on Germany' (4 May 2004) UN Doc CCPR/CO/80/DEU, para 11; UNGA, 'Report of the Human Rights Committee on Iraq' (1991) UN Doc A/46/40, para 652; and UN Docs CCPR/C/SR.1080–1082. See further, Egbert W Vierdag, 'The Legal Nature of the Rights Granted by the International Covenant on Economic, Social and Cultural Rights' (1978) 9 *Netherlands Yearbook of International Law* 69; and Martin Scheinin, 'Economic and Social Rights as Legal Rights' in Asbjørn Eide, Catarina Krause and Allan Rosas (eds), Economic, Social and Cultural Rights: A Textbook (2nd edn, Martinus Nijhoff, Dordrecht and London 2001).

45 UNSC Presidential Statement UN Doc 3 (2014) S/PRST/2014/3, 4.

46 ICESCR Optional Protocol (n 17), Article 2. See further, Skogly (n 15); and Christian Courtis and Magdalena Sepúlveda, 'Are Extra-Territorial Obligations Reviewable under the Optional Protocol to the ICESCR?' (2009) 27(1) *Nordic Journal on Human Rights* 54.

47 See Aurel Sari, 'Jurisdiction and International Responsibility in Peace Operations: The Behrami and Saramati Cases' (2008) 8(1) *Human Rights Law Review* 151. See also, John

As noted in Chapter 1, States' obligations have been disaggregated into obligations that must be realised immediately, minimum core rights and rights that may be achieved progressively through a typology of respecting, protecting and fulfilling the rights contained in the Covenant. This typology has been repeated in relation to the extraterritorial obligations of States on the basis that 'there is no reason to conclude that this explanation, specifying the nature of state parties' obligations, is limited to domestic obligations'[48] and excludes rights-holders that are non-nationals residing in a third State's territory.[49] The extraterritorial obligation to respect is the least controversial,[50] 'in so far as the international community as a whole has an obligation to take cognizance of human rights in its interactions, it is axiomatic that States parties have a similar duty to respect the realisation of the rights of other countries'.[51] According to the Maastricht Principles, the obligation to respect means the obligation not to interfere with the enjoyment of economic and social rights, as well as the positive obligation to take joint and separate action, through international cooperation, to establish institutional arrangements to respect economic and social rights.[52] The obligation to respect also encompasses States' own behaviour as well as any of its behaviour that facilitates breaches by other States or organisations,[53] rendering explicit the obligation imposed by Article 56 of UN Charter.[54] Such positive and negative obligations must then inform the activities of contributing States as they discharge their obligations that stem from human rights mandates of peace operations.

The obligation to protect, in the extraterritorial context, poses a number of challenges to fundamental international legal principles. The obligation to protect requires positive action whereby States must ensure that their own agents or non-State actors, such as transnational corporations, groups or individuals, do not infringe upon the rights and freedoms being enjoyed in third States.[55] This

Cerone, 'Minding the Gap: Outlining KFOR Accountability in Post-conflict Kosovo' (2001) 12(3) *European Journal of International Law* 469.

48 Margot E Salomon, *Global Responsibility for Human Rights: World Poverty and the Development of International Law* (Oxford University Press, Oxford 2007) 190. See also, Magdalena Sepulveda Carmona, 'The Obligation of "International Assistance and Cooperation" under the International Covenant on Economic, Social and Cultural Rights: A Possible Entry Point to a Human Rights Based Approach to Millennium Development Goal 8' (2009) 13(1) *The International Journal of Human Rights* 86.

49 See Sigrun I Skogly, 'The Obligation of International Assistance and Co-operation in the International Covenant on Economic, Social and Cultural Rights' in Morten Bergsmo and Asbjørn Eide (eds), *Human Rights and Criminal Justice for the Downtrodden: Essays in Honour of Asbjørn Eide* (Martinus Nijhoff Publishers, Leiden 2003) 419–420; and Salomon, ibid, 189–195.

50 Amanda Cahill-Ripley, 'Protecting Rights in the Face of Scarcity: The Right to Water' in Gibney (n 12), 194, 197.

51 Matthew C R Craven, *The International Covenant on Economic, Social, and Cultural Rights: A Perspective on Its Development* (Clarendon Press, Oxford 1995) 148.

52 The Maastricht Principles (n 22), Principle 19; and Commentary to the Maastricht Principles (n 23), 1127.

53 The Maastricht Principles (n 22), Principles 19, 20 and 21.

54 Commentary to the Maastricht Principles (n 23), 1127.

55 The Maastricht Principles (n 22), Principle 23. Wouter Vandenhole, 'EU and Development: Extraterritorial Obligations under the International Covenant on Economic, Social

obligation encompasses the obligation to regulate (Principle 24) which includes situations where States fail to adopt regulations, or to implement them effectively, where such a failure is in violation of the human rights undertakings of those States. It is perhaps this aspect of the obligation to protect that is the most problematic because the obligation to regulate must be balanced with the UN Charter's prohibition on intervention into the domestic affairs of the territorial State or interference with its sovereign rights and the principle of equality of all States.[56] In accordance with this view then, States contributing to peacekeeping operations that are mandated to promote and protect human rights, and to support national authorities in this regard, such as UNMIK,[57] UNAMA,[58] UNAMI,[59] UNMIL[60] and UNSMIL,[61] would be under a positive obligation to act to promote human rights. However, there are other ways in which States can seek to influence the conduct of private actors including through the use of indicators to monitor progress.[62] This requirement also raises some issues for States' obligations, as the obligation to monitor is an increasing element of the human rights mandates of peacekeeping operations,[63] a point that will be revisited in Chapter 5. Finally, the obligation to protect also includes the obligation to cooperate which has largely been interpreted to encompass the obligation to provide an effective remedy.[64]

The most controversial of all extraterritorial obligations – both politically and legally – is the obligation to fulfil human rights in the jurisdiction of a third State.[65]

---

and Cultural Rights' in Wouter Vandenhole, Arne Tostensen and Margot E Salomon (eds), *Casting the Net Wider: Human Rights, Development and New Duty-bearers* (Intersentia, Antwerp 2007); and Takele Soboka Bulto, 'Towards Rights-Duties Congruence: Extraterritorial Application of the Human Right to Water in the African Human Rights System' (2011) 29(4) *Netherlands Quarterly of Human Rights* 491.

56 Commentary to the Maastricht Principles (n 23), 1133–1137; and The Maastricht Principles (n 22), Principle 25(d).

57 UNSC Res 1244 (10 June 1999) UN Doc S/RES/1244, para 11(j).

58 UNSC Res 1401 (28 March 2002) UN Doc S/RES/1401, para 4.

59 UNSC Res 1770 (10 August 2007) UN Doc S/RES/1770, para 2(c).

60 UNSC Res 1509 (19 September 2003) UN Doc S/RES/1509, para 3(l).

61 UNSC Res 2144 (14 March 2014) UN Doc S/RES/2144, para 6(b).

62 See the Maastricht Principles, (n 22), Principle 26; and Commentary to the Maastricht Principles (n 23), 1144.

63 See, for example, UNSC Res 1509 (n 60), para 3(m) (UNMIL); UNSC Res 2103 (22 May 2013) UN Doc S/RES/2103, para 1(g) (UNIOGBIS); UNSC Res 2144 (n 61), para 6(b) (UNSMIL); UNSC Res 2217 (28 April 2015) UN Doc S/RES/2217, para 32(e)(iv) (MINUSCA); UNSC Res 2147 (28 March 2014) UN Doc S/RES/2147 paras 5(d) and 31 (MONUSCO); and UNSC Res 2226 (25 June 2015) UN Doc S/RES/2226, para 19(g) (UNOCI). See Chapter 3, footnotes 95–128 and accompanying text.

64 Commentary to the Maastricht Principles (n 23), 1145.

65 Craven (n 51), 149; Sigrun I Skogly, *Beyond National Borders: States' Human Rights Obligations in International Cooperation* (Intersentia, Antwerp, Oxford 2006) 71; and Cahill-Ripley (n 50), 198. Margot E Salomon, 'Legal Cosmopolitanism and the Normative Contribution of the Right to Development' (LSE legal Studies Working Paper 16/2008) (2008) 6 <http://papers.ssrn.com/sol3/papers.cfm?abstract_id=1272582> accessed 22 August 2016.

It has been closely aligned with Articles 55 and 56 of the Charter and the principles of inter-State cooperation.[66] The obligation to fulfil may also include other measures that directly support the enjoyment of economic and social rights of individuals found on another State's territory.[67] In other words, the obligation to fulfil requires the State to provide life sustaining resources, free of charge, to those who cannot afford to pay for those and who are in a third State that cannot by itself provide the bare necessities of life for individuals and groups within its territory. However, the scope of this duty is also limited by the obligation to respect the sovereignty of the territorially competent State. A State is not relieved of its extraterritorial obligation to fulfil simply because it lacks resources; it may be held internationally responsible also for a failure to seek to mobilise the necessary resources globally.[68] The question of resourcing is dealt with similarly to the territorial context so that, in fulfilling economic and social rights extraterritorially, States must prioritise core obligations and move as expeditiously and effectively as possible towards the full realisation of the rights.[69] The obligation to fulfil also means that States must avoid any retrogressive measures or else demonstrate that such measures are duly justified by reference to the full range of human rights obligations after a comprehensive examination of alternatives.[70] This set of obligations is only a tangential matter for States contributing to peacekeeping operations, as the latter tend to be mandated to support and facilitate the provision of humanitarian assistance,[71] which may be supplied by States, either on their own or with others. However, to the extent that they may be involved in decision-making on matters of humanitarian assistance, States must prioritise the protection of minimum core rights, and avoid retrogressive decisions or justifying such decision-making.

As indicated in Chapter 3, some peace operations are specifically mandated to promote and protect human rights, an action that serves to reinforce the significance of human rights to the maintenance of international peace and security. However, Chapter 3 also showed that, even in the absence of an explicit human rights mandate, the promotion and protection of human rights remained

66 The Maastricht Principles (n 22), Principle 28.
67 Commentary to the Maastricht Principles (n 23), Principle 28, 1145–1146.
68 The Maastricht Principles (n 22), Principle 31. See Commentary to the Maastricht Principles (n 23), 1151–1152.
69 The Maastricht Principles (ibid.), Principle 32(b).
70 Ibid, Principle 32(d).
71 See, for example, UNSC Res 1542 (30 April 2004) UN Doc S/RES/1542, para 9 (MINUSTAH); UNSC Res 1662 (23 March 2006) UN Doc S/RES/1662, para 3 (Afghanistan); UNGA, 'Report of the Secretary-General 2006/145' (2006) UN Doc A/60/712-S/2006/145, para 52(f) (UNAMA); UNSC Res 1769 (31 July 2007) UN Doc S/RES/1769, para 1 (UNAMID); UNSC, 'Report of the Secretary-General and the Chairperson of the African Union Commission on the Hybrid Operation in Darfur' (2007) UN Doc S/2007/307/Rev.1, para 55 (b)(vi) (UNMID); UNSC Res 2213 (27 March 2015) UN Doc S/RES/2213, para 9(d) (UNSMIL); UNSC Res 2223 (28 May 2015) UN Doc S/RES/2223, para 4(c)(i) (UNMISS); UNSC Res 2164 (25 June 2014) UN Doc S/RES/2164, para 13(c) (MINUSMA); and UNSC Res 2149 (10 April 2014) UN Doc S/RES/2149, para 30(c) (MINUSCA).

a critical aspect of peacekeeping operations. When peacekeeping operations are mandated to support the delivery of humanitarian assistance and/or to undertake or support recovery and reconstruction activities, some of these activities may raise specific issues in terms of substantive economic and social rights. These obligations must then frame the conduct of contributing States.

3 The extraterritorial application of the rights to food and water, health, education and work by contributing States

Whilst the basis for a discussion on the extraterritoriality of economic and social rights lies with Article 2, the wording of a number of the ICESCR's substantive rights also reveals extraterritorial characteristics. When Article 2(1) is read together with Articles 6 and 7, 11, 12 and 13, for example, these characteristics become more apparent.

In relation to the right to food, Article 11(1) notes the essential importance of international cooperation, based on free consent, to the realisation of the right to an adequate standard of living, from which the rights to food and water have been elaborated. Article 11(2) obliges States, acting either individually and through international cooperation, to realise the specific right of everyone to be free from hunger. The extraterritorial qualities of the right to food were first elaborated by the CESCR in General Comment 12 in the context of States' international obligations.[72] Drawing from the spirit of Article 56 of the Charter, the CESCR stated that the specific provisions contained in Articles 2(1) and 11 of the Covenant meant that States should recognise the essential role of international cooperation and comply with their commitment to take joint as well as separate action to achieve the full realisation of the right to adequate food. According to the Committee, the implementation of this right meant that States should take steps to respect the enjoyment of the right to food in other countries, to protect that right, to facilitate access to food and to provide the necessary aid when required. Furthermore, States should, in international agreements whenever relevant, ensure that the right to adequate food is given due attention and consider the development of further international legal instruments to that end.[73] Realisation of the right to food also means that States (and International Organisations) have a joint and individual responsibility, in accordance with the Charter, to cooperate in providing disaster relief and humanitarian assistance in times of emergency. Each State should contribute to this task in accordance with its ability.[74] Such emergency aid must always be provided in ways that do not adversely affect local producers and markets, and it should be organised in such a manner

72 CESCR, 'General Comment 12, Right to Adequate Food' in 'Compilation of General Comments and General Recommendations Adopted by Human Rights Treaty Bodies' (2003) UN Doc HRI/GEN/1/Rev.6, 62.

73 Ibid, para 36.

74 Ibid, para 38.

so as to facilitate the beneficiaries' return to food self-reliance. Such food aid must also be safe and culturally acceptable to the recipient population.[75]

The Special Rapporteur on the Right to Food[76] has also elaborated the extraterritorial obligation to respect, protect and fulfil this right.[77] According to the Special Rapporteur, the extraterritorial obligation to respect the right to food is simply an obligation to 'do no harm' which requires States to ensure that their policies and practices do not lead to violations of the right to food for people living in other countries. For example, food and water should never be used to exert political or economic pressure.[78] This 'resource-light' obligation may come into play as contributing States seek to fulfil their mandate to assist national authorities to devise law and policy to realise the right to food. The extraterritorial obligation to protect (or to ensure) the right to food was elaborated mainly in relation to States' obligations to ensure transnational corporations, as non-State actors, did not violate the right to food of people living in other countries. However, the obligation to protect does also extend to the (contributing) States' own citizens (such as peacekeepers) acting to protect the rights of the inhabitants of other countries.[79] Referring to Article 28 of the Universal Declaration, the Special Rapporteur explained that the obligation to fulfil (to provide and to facilitate) the right to food meant that all countries should cooperate to provide an enabling environment for the realisation of the right to food in all countries. In the context of emergencies, the Special Rapporteur declared that governments have an obligation to provide assistance, to the extent that their resources permit, when individuals are suffering in another country. He reiterated the views expressed in General Comment 12 regarding the need to support local markets and food self-reliance, in the provisions of food aid where such aid must also be safe and culturally acceptable.[80]

In 2008, the Special Rapporteur further explained States' extraterritorial obligations stemming from the right to food and stated that the primary responsibility to ensure human rights always rests with national governments but that in such a globalised and interconnected world, the actions taken by one government may have negative impacts on the right to food of individuals living in other countries.[81] The Special Rapporteur has returned to the issue of extraterritorial obligations of the right to food, observing that the CESCR has stated that the duties associated with the right to food extend to all situations, whether located on a State's national territory or abroad, where a State may exercise influence without infringing on the sovereignty of the territorial State. He noted that this

75 Ibid, para 39.
76 Established by UNCHR Res 10 (2000) UN Doc E/CN.4/RES/2000/10.
77 UNESC, 'Report of the Special Rapporteur on the Right to Food, Jean Ziegler 2006/44' (2006) UN Doc E/CN.4/2006/44, paras 35–38.
78 Ibid, para 35.
79 Ibid, para 36.
80 Ibid, paras 37–38.
81 UNGA, 'Report of the Special Rapporteur on the Right to Food, Jean Ziegler 7/5' (2008) UN Doc A/HRC/7/5, para 21.

approach had been affirmed in the Maastricht Principles as well as in the Guiding Principles on Extreme Poverty and Human Rights. Unfortunately, the mechanisms allowing victims of violations of the right to food in extraterritorial situations are often regarded as being non-existent or hardly accessible in practice.[82]

States' extraterritorial obligations have also been identified in the context of the right to water. According to the CESCR, States have to respect the enjoyment of the right in other countries.[83] The obligation to respect encompasses direct or indirect interference with the right to water. This obligation relates to the effects of State actions in relation to individuals and groups in another State, but it also relates to a State's action or omission which would deprive another State of the ability to realise the right to water for persons in its jurisdiction.[84] The obligation to protect the right to water extraterritorially means that States must prevent their own citizens (and companies) from violating the right to water of individuals and communities in other countries.[85] The obligation to fulfil the right to water extraterritorially means that 'depending on the availability of resources, States should facilitate realization of the right to water in other countries, for example through provision of water resources, financial and technical assistance, and provide the necessary aid when required'.[86] The issue of the extraterritorial obligation to fulfil the right to water also arises in the context of core obligations, as the Committee, for the avoidance of any doubt, emphasised that States, and other actors in a position to assist, must provide 'international assistance and cooperation, especially economic and technical, which enables developing countries to fulfil their core obligations'.[87] According to this statement, States are under the extraterritorial obligation to assist, and cooperate with, developing States to ensure that the latter can provide access to the minimum essential amount of water that is sufficient and safe for personal and domestic use to prevent disease in a non-discriminatory and safe manner. Assistance and cooperation also extends to enabling developing States to adopt and implement a national water strategy and plan of action, which is reviewed periodically on the basis of a participatory and transparent process. The review process should include methods, such as the right to water indicators and benchmarks, allowing the State to monitor the extent of the realisation, or the non-realisation, of the right to water. States must also help with the adoption of relatively low-cost targeted water programmes to protect vulnerable and marginalised groups and to take measures to prevent, treat and control diseases linked to water, in particular ensuring access to adequate sanitation. As these obligations fall within the realms of core obligations, they are extraterritorial obligations of

82 UNGA, 'Interim Report of the Special Rapporteur on the Right to Food, Olivier de Schutter 68/288' (2013) UN Doc A/68/288, para 19.

83 CESCR, 'General Comment 15, The Right to Water' in 'Compilation of General Comments and General Recommendations Adopted by Human Rights Treaty Bodies' (2003) UN Doc HRI/GEN/1/Rev.6, para 31.

84 Ibid.

85 Ibid, para 33.

86 Ibid, para 34.

87 Ibid, para 38.

immediate effect. The disastrous consequences of the failure to meet such obligations have been demonstrated by the cholera epidemic in Haiti, where inadequate sanitation conditions at the Mirebalais MINUSTAH camp led to the contamination of one of the main water sources in Haiti with human faecal waste and the consequent spread of cholera across the population of Haiti.[88]

The Special Rapporteur on the right to safe drinking water and sanitation[89] has also addressed the issue of the extraterritorial application of the right to water. According to the Special Rapporteur, the Maastricht Principles underscore the obligation of States to avoid causing harm extraterritorially and States must desist from acts and omissions that create a real risk of nullifying or impairing the enjoyment of economic, social and cultural rights extraterritorially.[90] The Special Rapporteur went on to identify a number of State actions that could give rise to violations of extraterritorial obligations stemming from the right to water, ranging from the actions of transnational companies to the development context, sanctions and climate change.[91] Most notably, the Special Rapporteur referred to the fact that both the Human Rights Committee and the CESCR had expressed concern about the denial by Israel of access to water and sanitation and about the destruction of infrastructure in the Occupied Palestinian Territory. The Special Rapporteur recommended that increased attention be paid to violations of extraterritorial obligations.[92]

As regards the right to health, General Comment 14 elaborates upon the obligations stemming from Article 12, obligations which encompass extraterritorial obligations such as the requirement for States to respect the enjoyment of the right to health and to protect this right by preventing third parties from violating it in other States where they have legal or other influence. States must also ensure that the right to health is given due attention in international agreements and that their actions as members of International Organisations take due account of the right to health.[93] Depending on the availability of resources, States should

88 Alejando Cravioto and others, (2012) *Final Report of the Independent Panel of Experts on the Cholera Outbreak in Haiti*, 23. <http://www.un.org/News/dh/infocus/haiti/UN-cholera-report-final.pdf> accessed 12 October 2016.

89 UNCHR Res 10 (n 76).

90 UNGA, 'Report of the Special Rapporteur on the Human Right to Safe Drinking Water and Sanitation, Catarina de Albuquerque 68/264' (2013) UN Doc A/68/264, para 46.

91 UNGA, 'Report of the Special Rapporteur on the Human Right to Safe Drinking Water and Sanitation, Catarina de Albuquerque 27/55' (2014) UN Doc A/HRC/27/55, para 72.

92 Ibid, para 73, referring to HRC 'Consideration of Reports Submitted by States Parties under Article 40 of the Covenant: Concluding Observations of the Human Rights Committee on Israel' (3 September 2010) UN Doc CCPR/C/ISR/CO/3, para 18; and UNESC, 'Consideration of Reports Submitted by States Parties under Articles 16 and 17 of the Covenant: Concluding Observations of the Committee on Economic, Social and Cultural Rights on Israel' (16 December 2011) UN Doc E/C.12/ISR/CO/3, para 29.

93 CESCR, 'General Comment 14, The Right to the Highest Attainable Standard of Health' in 'Compilation of General Comments and General Recommendations Adopted by Human Rights Treaty Bodies' (2003) UN Doc HRI/GEN/1/Rev.6, para 39. See also, William Newbrander, Ronald Waldman and Megan Shepherd-Banigan, 'Rebuilding and

facilitate access to essential health facilities, goods and services in other countries, wherever possible, and provide the necessary aid when required.[94] With regard to what is entailed in relation to this facilitating role, footnote 27 of General Comment 14 on the right to health directs States to their international obligations contained in paragraph 45. Using language similar to that on the right to water, the General Comment states:

> For the avoidance of any doubt . . . it is particularly incumbent on States parties and other actors in a position to assist, to provide 'international assistance and cooperation, especially economic and technical' which enable developing countries to fulfil their core and other obligations indicated in paragraphs 43 and 44.[95]

States' core obligations, as identified in paragraph 43, include at least the obligation to ensure, on a non-discriminatory basis: the right of access to health facilities, goods and services and equitable distribution thereof, especially for vulnerable or marginalised groups; access to the minimum essential, nutritionally adequate and safe food as well as freedom from hunger to everyone; and access to basic shelter, housing and sanitation, and an adequate supply of safe and potable water. States must also provide essential drugs and they must adopt and implement a national public health strategy and plan of action, which is to be periodically reviewed, on the basis of a participatory and transparent process using methods such as the right to health indicators and benchmarks. Paragraph 44 identifies obligations of comparable priority as the obligation to ensure reproductive, maternal (pre-natal as well as post-natal) and child health care. States must provide immunisation against the major infectious diseases occurring in the community, as well as education and access to information concerning the main health problems in the community, including methods of preventing and controlling them. States must introduce measures to prevent, treat and control epidemic and endemic diseases and, finally, they must provide appropriate training for health personnel. These latter obligations around the prevention, treatment and control of disease are particularly pertinent in the context of the cholera epidemic in Haiti, the cause of which has been linked to UN peacekeepers from Nepal.[96] It raises the question of whether the introduction and failure to treat and control the disease adequately is a failure of Nepal's extraterritorial obligations stemming from the right to health and, indeed, other ratifying States that failed to provide economic and technical assistance to either Nepal, which may have been struggling to meet this obligation due to inadequate financial resources, or Haiti, which was most certainly struggling on this basis.

Strengthening Health Systems and Providing Basic Health Services in Fragile States' (2011) 35(4) *Disasters* 639, 642.

94 CESCR, ibid.

95 Ibid, para 45.

96 Cravioto (n 88), 4. Ralph Frerichs, 'Nepalese Origin of Cholera Epidemic in Haiti' (2012) 18(6) *Clinical Microbiology and Infection* E158, E158–E163.

The Special Rapporteur on the Right to Health has considered the extraterritorial application of the right to health in the context of Article 2(1)'s requirements regarding international cooperation and assistance, with a particular focus on the relationship between low-income and high-income States.[97] According to the Special Rapporteur, speaking in response to Sweden's unwillingness to accept that it has a legal obligation of international assistance and cooperation:[98]

> if there is no legal obligation underpinning the human rights responsibility of international assistance and cooperation, inescapably all international assistance and cooperation fundamentally rests upon charity. While such a position might have been tenable in years gone by, it is unacceptable in the twenty-first century.[99]

As noted in Chapter 1, the Special Rapporteur on the right to education challenged the invisibility of this right in the context of emergencies and humanitarian crises.[100] According to the Special Rapporteur, the Minimum Standards for Education in Emergencies, Chronic Crises and Early Reconstruction (2004), which had been elaborated by the Inter-Agency Network for Education in Emergencies, offered a harmonised framework of principles and paths of action to all actors who may be involved in the provision of education during emergencies, for them to coordinate their educational activities and, even more importantly, to promote the acceptance of responsibilities.[101]

Violations of all of the above rights can have a cumulative effect in relation to the right to work. Improvements in security, the elimination or mitigation of hazardous or unsanitary working conditions, and improved access to adequate health and education systems can positively impact the right to work, which also entails the right to decent work. In terms of the right to work, the CESCR has stated that States Parties should recognise the essential role of international cooperation and comply with their commitment to take joint and separate action to achieve the full realisation of the right to work.[102] Although much of the context for this view relates to international and regional lending institutions and structural

97 UNGA, 'Report of the Special Rapporteur on the Right of Everyone to the Enjoyment of the Highest Attainable Standard of Physical and Mental Health, Paul Hunt, Addendum, Missions to the World Bank and the International Monetary Fund in Washington, D.C. (20 October 2006) and Uganda (4–7 February 2007) 7/11' (2008) UN Doc A/HRC/7/11/Add.2, paras 18 and 132.

98 Ibid, para 132.

99 Ibid, para 133.

100 UNGA, 'Report of the Special Rapporteur on the Right to Education, Vernor Muñoz 8/10' (2008) UN Doc A/HRC/8/10, paras 14, 31–35.

101 Ibid, paras 64–65.

102 CESCR, 'General Comment 18, Article 6: The Equal Right of Men and Women to the Enjoyment of all Economic, Social and Cultural Rights' (2006) UN Doc E/C.12/GC/18, para 29.

adjustment programmes, the comment that the obligations stemming from the right to work means that States Parties should endeavour to promote the right to work in other countries[103] does not preclude contributing States' obligations stemming from the extraterritorial application of economic and social rights.

The requirement that core obligations – but also all Covenant obligations – be extended to vulnerable and marginalised groups reiterates the international (legal) recognition of the relationship between marginalisation and conflict. The rights to equality and non-discrimination underpin any analysis of economic and social rights as States move to rebuild economic and social infrastructures such as water services, food networks, health care services and educational facilities so that in meeting its minimum core obligations under these rights, a State has to ensure access on a non-discriminatory basis. As noted in Chapter 1, non-discriminatory access to all facilities, goods and services relating to food, water and health, as survival rights, and education and work at a broader level, is essential to mitigate tensions and the prevention of violent conflict. Similarly, the UN Committee on the Elimination of Racial Discrimination, held in several of its concluding observations that the insufficient implementation of the Convention on the Elimination of All Forms of Racial Discrimination[104] 'contributes very significantly to the dangerous escalation of tension'[105] in different countries and regions.

The inclusion of the detailed nature of States' obligations may be seen as a further barrier – or a further reason – for excluding the legal rights language from the practice of States' peace operations. In the context of the right to water, it has been noted that '[i]ncorporation of rights language can increase expectations (which may be hard to meet in reality), and too much rights-talk may dominate water debates and consume already overstretched resources.'[106] However, rights are not to be confined to academic or theoretical discussion, and the above detail reveals that economic and social rights can have a very

103 Ibid, para 30.

104 International Convention on the Elimination of All Forms of Racial Discrimination (adopted 7 March 1966, entered into force 4 January 1969) 660 UNTS 195.

105 See, for example, CERD, 'Concluding Observations of the Committee on the Elimination of Racial Discrimination: Israel' (1998) UN Doc CERD/C/304/Add.45, para 4. CERD, 'Concluding Observations of the Committee on the Elimination of Racial Discrimination: Israel' (2012) UN Doc CERD/C/ISR/CO/14–16, paras 24–29; CERD, 'Concluding Observations of the Committee on the Elimination of Racial Discrimination: Georgia' (2011) UN Doc CERD/C/GEO/CO/4–5, para 14; and CERD, 'Concluding Observations of the Committee on the Elimination of Racial Discrimination: Kyrgyzstan' (2013) UN Doc CERD/C/KGZ/CO/5–7, para 10. See also, for example, CRC, 'Concluding Observations of the Committee on the Rights of the Child: New Zealand' (2016), UN Doc CRC/C/NZL/CO/5, para 15(b); CRC, 'Concluding Observations of the Committee on the Rights of the Child: Guatemala' (2010) UN Doc CRC/C/GTM/CO/3–4, paras 40–42; and CRC, 'Concluding Observations of the Committee on the Rights of the Child: Ireland' (2016) UN Doc CRC/C/IRE/CO/3–4, paras 69–70.

106 Anna F S Russell, 'International Organizations and Human Rights: Realizing, Resisting or Repackaging the Right to Water?' (2010) 9(1) *Journal of Human Rights* 1, 12.

practical effect. This detail clarifies what States can do and it may reflect aspects of State practice already. Furthermore, any thinking that rights fall outside peace operations mandates can be put to one side given the UN's mainstreaming of human rights and its recognition of the link between rights violations and conflict, as well as the inclusion of specific human rights mandates in peace operations. All of these developments further serve to counter the argument that economic and social rights are not real rights in a broader environment where human rights may not be fully embraced. There is a final element stemming from the extraterritorial application of economic and social rights, which is that the legal discourse rights underpinning the rights to health, food and water, for example, could benefit from ensuring that such application is well informed by the technical knowledge associated with these fields.

4 Measuring the impact of economic and social rights in peacekeeping operations: The added value of human rights indicators

As indicated in Chapter 3, it is increasingly clear that peace operations are mandated to monitor and report on the promotion and protection of human rights. Chapters 2 and 3 also indicated that the OHCHR can assist both peacekeeping operations and the Security Council to monitor human rights through a variety of means such as the use of Special Procedures, fact-finding, the Universal Periodic Review and treaty-monitoring bodies. The gathering of accurate information is important to decision-making in terms of assessing the activities of contributing States, peacekeeping operations themselves and the work of the Security Council. These entities – both separately and together – work towards the goal of maintaining international peace and security, a goal that is informed by the realisation of human rights, and economic and social rights in particular.

Peace operations face a multitude of challenges as they seek to put into effect Security Council resolutions, which provide the legal basis for policy and practical responses. From the perspective of international law, the Security Council resolutions creating any given peace operation may be examined to reveal that operation's primary goals, which may be both generic and mandate-specific. Once the goals are identified, strategies to achieve these goals must be identified. These strategies should also draw from programming and policy mechanisms that reflect the particularities of the mission and the host State. However, Security Council mandates are often vaguely worded and may reflect not only political compromise but also the broader work of the UN, which spans defence, development and human rights, each of which have their own measurement practices which may be informed by the different objectives of each area. It has been argued that 'the short-term focus that military involvement lends to the delivery of development assistance can have a negative impact on development, thus militating against combining development and security policies that involve military intervention'.[107] At the organisational level, the upshot is often confused and disparate measurements of progress that present a real difficulty in developing a single range of core indicators,[108] difficulties which may well reverberate at the level of the contributing State.

Further challenges accompany the requirement to monitor human rights. Both the nature of the peacekeeping operation mandates and operational issues, such as the different levels of authority that may be exercised by contributing States over a territory or zone where they are deployed, may impact upon the extent to which a State can meet its human rights obligations. Situations such as these have the potential to be further complicated if units of different contributing States operate together,[109] especially, for example, where some contributing States have ratified the ICESCR, and others have not. A further issue that have to be taken into account when monitoring human rights in peacekeeping operations is that there are a number of factors, many of which are outside the control of the operations, such as international events, restrictions imposed by target States, available resources and national policies, all of which can impact upon the extent to which a mission's goal is achieved.[110] These measurements are, in turn, influenced by other such factors, such as societal wealth, education and related demographics, so the context of the conflict and the nature of the pre- and post-conflict society must also be taken into account. Poor economic conditions may increase the potential for renewed fighting, as lawlessness and group-based grievances are associated with higher levels of violence. The concentration of poverty in some sectors of society can reinforce the ethnic or other cleavages that gave rise to the conflict in the first place. Poorer States also tend to recover more slowly from conflict, a problem compounded by the impact of the conflict itself on the economy and, as well as the destruction of infrastructure and industry, the disruption of agriculture and mass displacement of portions of the population. Added to these challenges is the observation that the fragmentation of society that results from foreign military intervention makes it difficult if not impossible to address the inequalities that lead to conflict and violent extremism.[111] Such

107 Graham Mayeda, 'Legal Aspects of the Security-Development Nexus: International Administrative Law as a Check on the Use of Development Assistance in the War on Terror' (2012) 13(1) *Chicago Journal of International Law* 71, 88, citing Frances Stewart, 'Development and Security' (CRISE Working Paper 3, 2004) <http://www3.qeh.ox.ac.uk/pdf/crisewps/workingpaper3.pdf> accessed 25 August 2016. See also, Frances Stewart, 'Horizontal Inequalities in Kenya and the Political Disturbances of 2008: Some Implications for Aid Policy' (2010) 10(1) *Conflict, Security & Development* 133.

108 Jake Sherman, 'Measuring Effectiveness in Peace-building and State-building' in Sarah Jane Meharg (ed), *Measuring What Matters In Peace Operations and Crisis Management* (Queen's Policy Study Series, McGill-Queen's University Press, Montreal 2009), 251.

109 Breen (n 12), 75–77.

110 Paul Francis Diehl and Daniel Druckman, *Evaluating Peace Operations* (Lynne Rienner Publishers, Boulder 2010) 27.

111 Mayeda (n 107), 87. See also, Marianne Dahl and Bjørn Høyland, 'Peace on Quicksand? Challenging the Conventional Wisdom about Economic Growth and Post-conflict Risks' (2012) 49(3) *Journal of Peace Research* 423, 423–429.

factors increase the pressures on peace operations and they must be factored into evaluations of their success.[112] In other words, decisions by peacekeepers can progress, or undermine, the mission's mandate as set down by the Security Council, a situation that reaffirms the need to subject such operations to some practical and legal scrutiny.

Difficulties such as these do little to lessen the heavy, and sometimes warranted, criticism that has been levelled at a process of accountability that starts with the Security Council mandate establishing the peace operation.[113] From the perspective of international law, however, an operation's mandate cannot be ignored and while it may require some effort to value an operation's mandate, it is a valid assessment of peacekeeping success,[114] which has, in general, been marginally successful.[115] The requirement to monitor and report once again raises the issue of the dual nature of peace operations as the requirement to report is placed on peace operations as subsidiary organs of the Security Council, as well as contributing States through their ratification of human rights treaties, such as the ICESCR.

5 Human rights indicators as a measure of compliance of contributing States' extraterritorial obligations

The accountability of States, generally, has been facilitated by the development of human rights indicators and benchmarks.[116] The normative framework developed by the CESCR has placed such monitoring at its centre, especially in relation to core rights, where monitoring is an obligation of immediate effect.

There are a number of challenges associated with the development and use of the human rights indicators as abstract legal norms that need to be translated into measureable units. This is a complex exercise covering many interrelated issues, as it may be necessary to take a wide range of factors into account in the process of gathering and disseminating a great amount of information. Inevitably, such

112 Deployment benchmarks have been established without fully taking into consideration the excessively difficult environment for mission deployment (such as gaps in transportation infrastructure and limited sources of specialised human and material resources). See, generally, Department of Peacekeeping Operations and Department of Field Support, 'A New Partnership Agenda Charting a New Horizon for UN Peacekeeping' (A Non-Paper, 2009) 23 <http://www.un.org/en/peacekeeping/documents/newhorizon.pdf> accessed 21 July 2016 (New Horizons).

113 Duane Bratt, 'Assessing the Success of UN Peacekeeping' (1996) 3(4) *International Peacekeeping* 64, 67.

114 Ibid.

115 Ibid, 71.

116 Audrey R Chapman, 'A "Violations Approach" for Monitoring the International Covenant on Economic, Social and Cultural Rights' (1996) 18(1) *Human Rights Quarterly* 24; and Gauthier de Beco, 'Human Rights Indicators for Assessing State Compliance with International Human Rights' (2008) 77(1–2) *Nordic Journal of International Law* 23, 27–28. Data sources that measure States' performance in response to ESR include the Physical Quality of Life Indicators, Human Development Indicators and Human Poverty Index.

challenges will be greater for contributing States in the post-conflict environment. However, such challenges must be responded to, as contributing States are legally obliged to do so as a consequence of ratifying the ICESCR. The lives of local populations may have been improved by, for example, the maintenance or construction of approximately 3,000 kilometres of roads between 2012 and 2014 and the completion of more than 100 water projects in four different missions,[117] but as indicated in Chapter 1, quick-impact projects such as these can undermine the credibility of the peace that is being built and the legitimacy of peacekeepers. This observation brings us back to the broader relationship that exists between peacebuilding and peacekeeping, where the latter is informed by elements of the former. It is at this point that the need to assess the activities of peace operations for their impact on economic and social rights, both in terms of activities that have happened in the past as well as planned future activities. Such an analysis can be enhanced if the initial planning and the long-term value of such projects is informed by economic and social rights.

As indicated in Chapter 1, there are two broad indicator frameworks that are favoured by the OHCHR; the structure-process-outcome framework and the AAAQ/AAAA framework.[118] The ensuing sections will consider the extent to which the assessment of reconstruction activities may be recast and refined using indicators measuring economic and social rights.[119]

5.1 *Structural, process and outcome indicators measuring the rights to food, health and work*

One of the easiest ways that a contributing State can demonstrate that it is meeting its extraterritorial obligations to respect, protect and fulfil the rights to food, health and work is to indicate what relevant treaties it has ratified. Once these legal obligations are identified, the extent to which States are meeting their obligations can be measured by utilising a further structural indicator examining if, and to what extent, contributing States have formulated policies to guarantee these rights. Such policies would naturally have to reflect the post-conflict environment but, at a minimum, they would have to be non-discriminatory and not contravene local policies governing the rights to food, water, health and life. The number of registered and/or active NGOs engaged in the promotion and protection of economic and social rights generally, or the rights to food and

117 UNGA, 'Report of the Secretary-General 69/642' (2014) UN Doc A/69/642 on 'Implementation of the Recommendations of the Special Committee on Peacekeeping Operations', para 66.

118 See also, The RTE Project Indicators which can be found at Right to Education Project, 'The Right to Education: Indicators (May 2013) <http://www.right-to-education.org/sites/right-to-education.org/files/resource-attachments/RTE_List_Right_to_Education_Indicators_May_2013.pdf> accessed 9 September 2016.

119 See, generally, Claire Breen, 'Progressing Towards Peace? States' Extraterritorial Obligations in Peace Operations and the Added Value of Human Rights Indicators' (2015) 9 (2) *Human Rights and International Legal Discourse* 123.

health in particular, comprises a further structural indicator.[120] In the context of a post-conflict environment, the extent to which a State's national contingent has achieved its broader goals of conflict abatement, containment and/or settlement may serve the dual purpose of facilitating the presence of NGOs. Thus, the achievement of such security-orientated goals can also serve as an indicator of the extent to which a State is meeting its extraterritorial obligations in the course of its contribution to a peacekeeping operation. As indicated in Chapter 3, several Security Council resolutions have mandated peace operations to assist national authorities to adopt legislation and policy consonant with international human rights law. Structural indicators measuring the adoption of human rights law and policies in the target State may be evidence of a contributing State meeting its extraterritorial obligation not to facilitate the violation of economic and social rights in a third State.

Bearing in mind that process indicators help to assess the extent to which States are implementing their extraterritorial human rights obligations on the ground during peacekeeping operations, nutrition levels, as one process indicator, may reveal the proportion of the targeted population that was brought above the minimum level of dietary energy consumption, covered under public nutrition supplement programmes and/or provided with improved sources of drinking water. In terms of measuring the actual impact of States' strategies, nutrition levels acting as outcome indicators can help to reveal the impact of their national contingents by measuring the prevalence of underweight and stunted children under five years of age and/or the proportion of adults with a body mass index (BMI) under 18.5.[121] These indicators could inform the other more basic indicators of the impact of peacekeeping operations, particularly in the short term, which may be measured by the delivery of humanitarian assistance, including the tonnage of food delivered and death rates due to starvation. Food availability is a further process indicator which can be used to measure any increases in the amount of arable land being made available. As national contingents may be charged with demining, States' efforts in this regard may also be used as a process indicator measuring the availability of food, particularly in rural or agricultural areas.[122] Whether and to what extent States' extraterritorial obligations are being implemented can also be measured by looking at food accessibility, measuring the coverage of programmes to secure access to productive resources for target groups, the proportion of the population that is undernourished or was brought above the poverty line and/or the average household expenditure on food in the targeted population. In terms of food availability as an outcome indicator, States' requirement of non-discrimination means that the estimated access of women and girls to adequate food within households must also be measured.

120 OHCHR, 'Human Rights Indicators: A Guide to Measurement and Implementation' (2012) UN Doc HR/PUB/12/5, 89 and 90 <http://www.ohchr.org/Documents/Publications/Human_rights_indicators_en.pdf> accessed 25 August 2016.

121 Ibid, 89.

122 Ibid.

As an aspect of their contribution to peace operations, States' national contingents often engage in post-conflict reconstruction activities, such as well digging and demining. Data on the number of wells dug or hectares demined, as well as the broader impact of such activities, are also relevant when seeking to measure whether a State is meeting its extraterritorial obligations stemming from the right to health. For example, process indicators relating to the natural environment can take into account the number of wells drilled and the amount of potable water produced. These measurable activities may then facilitate the utilisation of other process indicators measuring the proportion of the targeted population that was extended access to improved drinking water or sanitation. Similarly, data on the number of hectares demined may be used as a process indicator relating to the occupational environment, measuring the extent to which the population is able to live in or work near previously hazardous conditions such as minefields. Data measuring the prevalence of deaths, injuries, diseases and disabilities caused by an unsafe natural and occupational environment,[123] and data measuring any reductions in such negative outcomes stemming from a State's post-conflict reconstruction activities, could also be regarded as outcome indicators measuring the practical effect of a State's policies in this regard.

The presence and efforts of skilled health personnel in a peace operation may support process indicators on sexual and reproductive health such as the extent of antenatal care coverage and any increase in the proportion of adults of reproductive age using contraception. The impact of States' efforts in this regard can be measured using outcome indicators such as the proportion of live births with low birth-weight, as well as perinatal and maternal mortality ratios. The extent to which a State is putting into effect its obligations under the right to health can also be measured using process indicators measuring child mortality, drawing on data such as the proportion of children covered under programmes for regular medical check-ups in the reporting period, exclusively breastfed during the first six months and/or covered under a public nutrition supplement programme. The actual effect of the State's endeavours can be measured using outcome indicators such as infant and under-five mortality rates and the proportion of underweight children under five years of age.[124]

The prevention and control of disease can be an important aspect of peacekeeping operations, especially when responding to humanitarian crises in the short term. Thus, national contingents should engage in awareness-raising programmes on the transmission of diseases and/or apply effective preventive measures against diseases. Data on the percentage of the population that is targeted by such programmes or immunised against vaccine-preventable diseases, or the proportion of disease cases detected and cured, constitute some of the data that national contingents can gather to indicate to what extent States are putting their obligations into effect. Most of these efforts rely on accessibility to health facilities and essential medicines. Process indicators measuring primary health care and

123 Ibid, 90.
124 Ibid.

medicines, therefore, include improvement in the number of primary health care facilities and personnel therein. Such improvements may stem from the number of clinics built and staffed by national contingents. The impact of such endeavours can also be measured by the proportion of the population accessing affordable health care and essential medicines or rates of discrimination stemming from the refusal to provide medical consultations to a target group.

The actual impact of States' policies around food availability and food accessibility can be considered using outcome indicators measuring, for example, death rates, including infant and under-five mortality rates, associated with malnutrition and the prevalence of malnutrition, which could be further disaggregated along gender lines.[125] Similarly, the actual impact of outcome indicators measuring the impact of such initiatives include rates of prevention, treatment and control of disease, and the accessibility of health facilities and medicines, the death rates associated with and prevalence of communicable and non-communicable diseases, and life expectancy at birth or age one and health-adjusted life expectancy.[126] Two final observations about States' extraterritorial obligations arising from the right to health can be made at this point. Firstly, violations stemming from denying or limiting equal access to health services and people's participation in health-related matters, including means of maintaining sexual and reproductive health, and from limiting access to health services as a punitive measure are not only a violation of the ICESCR, but, where they take place during armed conflicts, they also constitute a violation of international humanitarian law.[127] Secondly, it is clear that the right to health is dependent upon other rights, an interrelationship that can be seen in States' obligations to ensure access to the minimum essential nutritionally adequate and safe food, to basic shelter, to housing and sanitation, and to an adequate supply of safe and potable water.[128]

Process indicators measuring the right to safe and decent work include effective support to (re-)enter the labour market rates by education level. The proportion of workers who moved from precarious to stable contracts during the reporting period can be used as a process indicator measuring just and safe working conditions, whilst the proportion of children in productive activity is a process indicator measuring levels of protection from forced labour and unemployment. Outcome indicators measuring the right to safe and decent work include employment to population ratio by sex, target group and education level, or the numbers of women in wage employment in the non-agricultural sector. Outcome indicators measuring forced labour and unemployment include counting instance of the worst forms of child labour, domestic work and work of migrants, and human trafficking and reports of violations of the right to work, including forced labour, discrimination and unlawful termination of employment and the proportion of

125 Ibid, 89.

126 Ibid, 90.

127 CESCR, 'General Comment 14' (n 93), para 34; and Sylvain Vite, 'The Interrelation of the Law of Occupation and Economic, Social and Cultural Rights: The Examples of Food, Health and Property' (2004) 90(871) *International Review of the Red Cross* 629.

128 CESCR, 'General Comment 14', ibid, para 43(b) and (c).

victims who received adequate compensation. Outcome indicators measuring the right to safe and just working conditions can include incidences of occupational hazards, including acts of violence, personal injury, disease or death (or other target groups), the ratio of women's wages to men's by sector (e.g., senior officials, managerial positions in public/private service) and the proportion of identified positions held by women and members of other target groups.[129]

5.2 *The rights to water and education: The AAAQ and AAAA frameworks and the use of indicators*

The OHCHR has identified indicators measuring access to water but they only appear in the context of other economic and social rights. In terms of the right to adequate food, water appears as a process indicator, namely the proportion of the targeted population that was extended access to an improved drinking water source.[130] Similarly, as regards the right to health, the proportion of the targeted population that was extended access to an improved drinking water source and/ or improved sanitation is identified as a process indicator.[131] In the context of the right to adequate housing, water appears as a process indicator measuring accessibility in relation to, for example, the share of public expenditure on the provision and maintenance of services such as sanitation and water supply, as well as the proportion of the population that was provided with access to improved drinking water sources and improved sanitation.[132] However, water is also identified as an outcome indicator for the right to adequate housing, again in terms of accessibility to services, in particular, the proportion of the population using an improved drinking water source (public or private) and sanitation facility. Access to water also features as an outcome indicator seeking to measure the proportion of the household budgets of the target population group spent on water supply and sanitation.[133] The OHCHR Guidelines also identify water as an aspect of the rights to equality and non-discrimination where, as a process indicator, it seeks to measure the proportion of the population that has been extended sustainable access.[134] The proportion of the population using an improved drinking water facility has also been identified as a process indicator measuring the right to life.[135]

Elsewhere, the CESCR has stated that the indicators measuring the right to water should address the different components of adequate water, such as sufficiency, safety and acceptability, affordability and physical accessibility. These indicators should be disaggregated by the prohibited grounds of discrimination and cover all persons residing in the State Party's territorial jurisdiction or under their

129 OHCHR (n 120), 95.
130 Ibid, 89.
131 Ibid, 90.
132 Ibid, 94.
133 Ibid.
134 Ibid, 100.
135 Ibid, 101.

control.[136] Indicators measuring the availability of water could measure whether water is available continuously and, if it is not, whether the amount of water that is available meets the World Health Organisation (WHO) guidelines. Availability, as an indicator, can measure the extent to which essential levels of drinking water is prioritised over other uses.[137] In terms of accessibility of water and sanitation, physical accessibility can be measured in terms of the percentage of the targeted population which has improved access to drinking water and sanitation facilities, including the numbers of sources and facilities and whether the numbers of individuals sharing them reflects an equitable distribution.[138] Other factors to be considered are the proximity of water sources and sanitation facilities, the waiting time and whether security is present en route to and at these sources and facilities. In other words, such data should reveal how many more toilets and drinking water sources there are in households and/or communities; if there are schools and hospitals, accessibility can capture data on how many of these facilities have sanitation facilities. Indicators measuring economic accessibility or affordability include the percentage of the household budget spent on drinking water and sanitation, numbers of water disconnections in a given year because the service became unaffordable, and whether low-income groups are provided with economic assistance.[139]

Acceptability of drinking water measures issues such as colour, odour and taste, whilst acceptability in relation to sanitation can measure the location and privacy of sanitation facilities, the levels of comfort and dignity with which they can be used.[140] Data in support of this indicator could include the percentage of the population that report their satisfaction and/or the number of complaints received about odour, taste or quality.[141] Quality as an indicator can measure the extent of open defecation, the presence and number of facilities that manage excreta safely, the numbers of households and educational and health facilities that have sanitation facilities, handwashing devices and soap, and menstrual hygiene management.[142] In relation to drinking water, quality can be measured by counting the number of households that have safe water, whether from source or treated water that is free from microorganisms, chemical substances and radiological hazards, which can be measured by WHO guidelines. Water quality can also be measured by the prevalence of waterborne diseases.[143] Indicators measuring water quality

136 CESCR, 'General Comment 15' (n 83), para 53.

137 Oscar Flores Baquero, Alejandro Jiménez Fernandez de Palencia and Agusti Pérez Foguet, 'Reporting Progress on the Human Right to Water and Sanitation through JMP and GLAAS' (2015) 5(2) *Journal of Water Sanitation and Hygiene for Development* 310, 315.

138 Mads Holst Jensen, Marie Villumsen and Thomas Døcker Petersen, *The AAAQ Framework and the Right to Water: International Indicators for Availability, Accessibility, Acceptability and Quality* (The Danish Institute for Human Rights, Copenhagen 2014) 31.

139 Baquero (n 137), 315 and 316.

140 Ibid, 317.

141 Jensen (n 138), 31.

142 Baquero (n 137), 316.

143 Jensen (n 138), 31.

also include the presence or absence of policies and regulations for pollution, as well as risk management plans.

All of these indicators should facilitate the provision of disaggregated data measuring the attention paid to marginalised and vulnerable groups in strategies and plans, and the percentage by which inequities have been reduced in relation to particular groups.[144] In other words, data should reflect the extent to which women, children and persons with disabilities, for example, actually use household and/or public facilities and what barriers might explain their lack of use. One particular area where individual inequalities and the lack of attention to women's and girl's needs is starkly apparent is menstrual hygiene. Women and girls are often forced to hide the fact they menstruate, which means that they limit their movements and social activities during menstruation. Girls may be taken out of school or workplaces, or they may choose not to attend because there are no facilities for hygienically managing menstruation. In this way, menstrual hygiene could be used as a proxy for information about discrimination against women and girls in sanitation and hygiene. Targets and indicators should be crafted to capture the presence and numbers of menstrual sanitation facilities in households, schools, hospitals and workplaces.[145]

In terms of the right to education, availability examines whether education is generally available in terms of schools, infrastructure and teaching materials.[146] The availability of education can, for instance, be measured by enrolment ratios. The budget allocated to education also reflects efforts made by States to make education generally available.[147] Accessibility focuses on the various physical, economic, administrative, gender and socio-economic obstacles to accessing education, and the numbers of out-of-school children, with a special focus on vulnerable groups. Indicators can measure the extent to which minimum standards for quality, safety or environmental health are being enforced and the extent to which barriers to education, such as poverty-induced obstacles and the opportunity cost of education and transportation are being eliminated.[148] Acceptability evaluates the various aspects of the content of education, and indicators of this type can measure skills, tolerance, qualification of teachers, gender, religion and language.

144 Baquero (n 137), 317.

145 Inga T Winkler, Margaret L Satterthwaite and Catarina De Albuquerque, 'Treasuring What We Measure and Measuring What We Treasure: Post-2015 Monitoring for the Promotion of Equality in the Water, Sanitation, and Hygiene Sector' (2014) 32(3) *Wisconsin International Law Journal* 547, 585–586.

146 Gauthier de Beco, 'Human Rights Indicators: From Theoretical Debate to Practical Application' (2013) 5(2) *Journal of Human Rights Practice* 380, 388.

147 Gauthier de Beco, 'Right to Education Indicator Based on the 4 A framework: Concept Paper for The Right to Education Project' (May 2009), 7 <http://www.right-to-education.org/sites/right-to-education.org/files/resource-attachments/RTE_RTE_indicators_Concept_Paper_De%20Beco_2010.pdf> accessed 12 September 2016.

148 CHR, 'Annual Report of the Special Rapporteur on the Right to Education, Katarina Tomasevski, Submitted Pursuant to Commission on Human Rights Resolution 2001/99' (2002) UN Doc E/CN.4/2002/60, 13.

Fourthly, adaptability concerns the needs of special categories of children such as working children, child soldiers, child prisoners, minority children, children with disabilities or children caught up in armed conflict.[149]

5.3 *'Survival' rights and the right to life*

As the previous paragraphs indicate, indicators measuring the right to food and access to adequate health care, health and nutrition are also illustrative indicators for the right to life. Similar structural indicators can be identified, such as treaty ratification, domestic law and policy measures and the presence of NGOs.[150] The overlap between the rights to food and health can also be seen in the use of process indicators for the right to life, such as the proportion of the population using an improved drinking water source or sanitation facility[151] that resulted from a national contingent's project. Further process indicators include data on the proportion of the population that is below the minimum level of dietary energy consumption and/or receiving a public nutrition supplement programme that may fall under the auspices of a national contingent. Further, process indicators include the number of: births attended by skilled health personnel (peace operation personnel or those whose presence is facilitated by the presence of a national contingent); one-year-olds immunised (as a result of the presence of a national contingent); and cases of diseases detected and cured. Outcome indicators for the right to life based on health and nutrition could also include infant and under-five mortality rates, the maternal mortality ratio, life expectancy at birth and age one, and the prevalence of death rates associated with communicable and non-communicable diseases.[152] Thus, States' extraterritorial efforts to protect and promote the rights to health and food as an aspect of the activities of their national contingents in peace operations can impact on this 'supreme' right.[153] Once again, the cholera epidemic in Haiti is stark evidence of the impact

149 de Beco (n 146), 388–389; and de Beco (n 116), 20–21.

150 OHCHR (n 120), 101.

151 The extraterritorial nature of the right to water has also been elaborated in CESCR, 'General Comment 15' (n 83), para 53: 'Indicators should address the different components of adequate water (such as sufficiency, safety and acceptability, affordability and physical accessibility), be disaggregated by the prohibited grounds of discrimination, and cover all persons residing in the State party's jurisdiction or under their control. . . .' Accordingly, the obligation to respect, as an aspect of the right to water, for example, means that States must refrain from engaging in any practice or activity that denies or limits equal access to adequate water; arbitrarily interferes with customary or traditional arrangements for water allocation; or unlawfully diminishes or pollutes water, limits access to, or destroys, water services and infrastructure as a punitive measure: para 21. The obligation to respect also means that during armed conflicts, emergency situations and natural disasters, the right to water embraces those obligations by which States Parties are bound under international humanitarian law: para 22.

152 OHCHR (n 120), 101.

153 Breen (n 119); and HRC, 'General Comment 6, Article 6' in 'Compilation of General Comments and General Recommendations Adopted by Human Rights Treaty Bodies'

of a failure to secure these rights on the right to life given that the estimated death toll measures in the thousands, if not the tens of thousands.[154]

5.4 Indicators on the rights to equality and non-discrimination

Disaggregated data is needed to unmask the direct and indirect discrimination that has a negative effect on economic and social rights. The OHCHR has identified structural, process and outcome indicators to measure the extent to which the rights to equality and non-discrimination inform economic and social rights, such as the rights to food, water, health and education. In a, by now, familiar fashion, structural indicators include the number of international treaties that have been ratified and the number of domestic laws and policies that have been adopted. They also include the establishment of a body dedicated to promoting the rights to equality and non-discrimination, as well as the number of NGOs involved in the promotion and protection of these rights. Structural indicators measuring equality of access to food, water, health, education and work include timeframes and coverage of policies providing protection from discrimination in regards to these rights.[155]

Process indicators should be designed to measure the proportion of the targeted populations (such as girls) in education or the number of buildings (including schools and hospitals) that provide facilities to persons with physical disabilities, or the proportion of the targeted population that was extended sustainable access to improved water sources, sanitation, and waste disposal. In terms of the right to work, process indicators can measure the time spent by women in unpaid domestic work and caregiving, the number of migrant workers who initiate a complaint reporting discrimination and abuse at work or the number of government contractors, for example, that conform with certified discrimination-free workplace practices.[156] Outcome indicators can measure literacy rates amongst youth within a targeted population, or births, mortality and life expectancy rates within a targeted group. Outcome indicators can measure the proportion of the targeted population in employment and any wage gaps that they experience. Outcome indicators measuring the negative impact of discrimination and inequality on the realisation of these economic and social rights can also inform the measurement of the numbers of the targeted population that are living below the national poverty line.[157]

(1994) UN Doc HRI/GEN/1/Rev.1, para 1. These types of indicators can also feed into the broader long-term question as to whether the quality of life has improved as economists and social scientists draw from an array of similar indicators when answering this question, such as infant mortality, life expectancy, housing availability, safety provisions and population density. See Patrice Flynn, Jon Lickerman and Hazel Henderson, *Calvert-Henderson Quality of Life Indicators* (Calvert Group, Maryland 2000).

154 Francisco J Luquero and others, (2016) 'Mortality Rates during Cholera Epidemic, Haiti, 2010–2011' 22(3) *Emerging Infectious Diseases* 410, 410–416.

155 OHCHR (n 120), 100.

156 Ibid.

157 Ibid.

As indicated in Chapter 1, the realisation of the rights to equality and non-discrimination may also involve the adoption of special measures. Participation in decision-making has also been identified as a core measure to ensure the realisation of economic and social rights in their own right but also their realisation in a non-discriminatory manner. In terms of the crossover with peacekeeping operations, local involvement in decision-making is key to ensuring the success of these operations. The OHCHR has identified the measurement of timeframes and the number of policies ensuring or accelerating equality in the enjoyment of human rights. Process indicators can measure the proportion of the targeted population receiving training as a manifestation of policies on preferential treatment or the number of education institutions promoting understanding on human rights. Outcome indicators can measure the number of relevant or senior positions in the public and private sectors held by members of the targeted group or they could measure the numbers amongst the targeted population that hold seats in local or subnational bodies.[158]

6 Conclusion

Peacekeepers, particularly those that are a part of multidimensional operations engaged in peacebuilding, perform an increasing array of tasks that impact on socio-economic conditions in target States. For contributing States, these tasks may be informed by obligations stemming from economic and social rights if it can be established that the contributing State had effective control so that it was in a position to secure those rights, rights that can be distilled into the core minimum obligations to respect, to protect and to fulfil. The obligation to respect requires States to refrain from actions or omissions that violate human rights treaties. Such obligations are of immediate effect and can take place during peace operations, such as the avoidance of discrimination in the allocation of goods and services, including access to water, food or medical treatment. The obligation to protect requires positive actions, which may take place in the medium term and so can run through the course of an operation and be an end goal of that operation. Finally, the obligation to fulfil also tends to require positive actions, typically in the longer term, and can provide an overall measurement of the extent to which human rights have been achieved and thus be an indicator for an exit strategy.

States that claim that they are unable to fulfil their extraterritorial obligations for reasons beyond their control must therefore show that 'every effort has been made to use all resources that are at [their] disposition in an effort to satisfy, as a matter of priority, those minimum obligations'.[159] Such efforts can be measured through the use of structure-process-outcome indicators informed, where possible, by data relating to economic and social rights prior to the conflict, so as to

158 Ibid.

159 CESCR, 'General Comment 3, The Nature of States Parties' Obligations' in 'Compilation of General Comments and General Recommendations Adopted by Human Rights Treaty Bodies' (2003) UN Doc HRI/GEN/1/Rev.6, para 10.

illustrate the extent to which human suffering was reduced post-conflict, both immediately and in the longer term. The issue of whether States, through their contributions to peace operations, have met their obligations stemming from the ICESCR can be determined through the use of indicators and benchmarks. The use of economic and social rights indicators to measure States' extraterritorial obligations in peacekeeping operations adds value. They allow the identification of specific activities that may be undertaken by peacekeepers, which can then be viewed through the lens of specific rights. The outcome of this process permits an assessment of whether the activities of contributing States correlate with their obligations stemming from the extraterritorial application of economic and social rights. It also eases in recognition of the need to consider such rights as States plan their contribution to a peacekeeping operation, review that contribution and ultimately assess its success.

The flexible, but still obligatory, language underpinning the protection and promotion of economic and social rights correlates with the need to recognise the different phases of a peace operation and the different requirements of each phase, particularly in complex peace operations. The variability of the role and requirements of a peace operation resonates with economic and social rights obligations that traverse the requirements of immediacy, core rights and progressive realisation. For example, although there is some merit in the contention that the provision of water, electricity and other public goods ought to be excluded because 'they are well removed from the actual duties of the peace operation and therefore it would be hard to link operational performance to outcomes',[160] in the short term, the provision of such services may well fall to a peace operation in the absence of any national or local actors capable of such service provision. These types of initiative are one area where peacekeeping operations, in the short and medium term, can exercise a high degree of control and exhibit a high degree of success. They are also initiatives that will have consequences for the promotion and protection of the human rights of the local population in the medium and long term.

160 Diehl (n 110), 107.

5 Reimagining peace and security in the post-conflict environment

1 Introduction

The preceding chapters have illustrated that the importance of human rights and economic and social reconstruction aimed at addressing the root causes of war and building a sustainable peace – from strengthening relationships between key UN bodies to imbuing complex peace operations with peacebuilding and human mandates – is well recognised.[1] This work has sought to add to these policy developments, their manifestation in international legal mechanisms and the ensuing scholarly literature by drawing attention to the often overlooked ability of economic and social rights to act as a fulcrum around which such endeavours should revolve. After having set out the normative content and ensuing obligations stemming from economic and social rights, this work has elaborated on the application of the rights and the obligations in the extraterritorial context of peace operations, has emphasised the requirement to monitor, and has suggested methods by which this obligation can be discharged by identifying developments in the context of States' territorial obligations and extrapolating their application in the extraterritorial context.

This enquiry leads us to the question of 'where to from here', as some form of analytical framework must be constructed so that scholarship can intersect with the realms of policy, which in turn can contribute to the discourse of a reimagined peace and security. A key challenge to the creation of such a framework is the need to bridge further the international policy elements of peacebuilding and peacekeeping with the international and domestic legal elements of human rights, and in particular economic and social rights. The previous chapter indicated one way of bridging policy and law with its elaboration of contributing States' extraterritorial obligations stemming from ICESCR ratification. This chapter opens with a consideration of the theory of *jus post bellum*, which calls for post-conflict endeavours to be framed in terms of State obligations. The relationship between peacebuilding and *jus post bellum* reflects a view of States' post-conflict obligations in an environment which is no longer populated solely by States, where the boundaries of conflict and peace are blurred and where the notions of peace and

1 UNSC, 'Report of the Secretary-General 2004/616' (2004) UN Doc S/2004/616, para 4.

security are being reconfigured by non-State actors such as the UN, where the efforts of all involved are increasingly informed by human rights and where economic and social rights, in particular, must play an increasing part.

Jus post bellum theory signals that the rights and responsibilities of parties to a conflict do not end at the conflict's termination but that such rights and obligations continue through the post-conflict phase. The re-emergence of *jus post bellum* theory serves to highlight the rules and principles that currently underpin post-conflict activities and raises the question of whether post-conflict peacebuilding is to be regarded as *jus post bellum* in Security Council peacekeeping operations. One view is that 'peacebuilding represents the operational manifestation of the abstract concept of *jus post bellum*'.[2] However, such developments have 'raised many questions regarding the applicable legal framework, in terms of both the rights and obligations of the actors involved in the post-conflict phase and the content of reconstruction and reform',[3] leading some to negate the existence of such a legal framework.[4] Whilst the questioning of the current existence of a legal framework for post-conflict reconstruction has merit, the increasing amount of peacekeeping operations which themselves have increasingly complex reconstruction and peacebuilding mandates means that the questions posed by *jus post bellum* cannot be ignored. In the context of this work, these questions must also be addressed amid the concerns that have been expressed at the narrow conceptualisation of peace and the marginalisation of economic and social justice, and the related marginalisation of economic and social rights.

To respond to such questions, the chapter turns to a consideration of the concepts of positive peace and human security. Positive peace calls for the establishment of a peace that is more than the absence of armed conflict but which also brings to an end structural and cultural violence. The notion of human security seeks to put the security of the individual on an equal footing with that of the State, so that the individual is protected from severe and pervasive threats and is empowered to act on his/her own behalf. The concepts of positive peace and human security echo aspects of *jus post bellum* theory that call for steps to be taken to mitigate risks to States emerging from conflict, risks such as those identified in Chapter 1. Calls to move beyond the *status quo ante*, as advocated by some interpretations of *jus post bellum*, resonate with the UN's recognition of

2 Melissa Labonte, 'Jus Post Bellum, Peacebuilding, and Non-State Actors: Lessons from Afghanistan' in Eric A Heinze and Brent J Steele (eds), *Ethics, Authority, and War: Non-State Actors and the Just War Tradition* (Palgrave Macmillan, New York 2009) 215.

3 Eric de Brabandere, 'The Responsibility for Post-conflict Reforms: A Critical Assessment of Jus Post Bellum as a Legal Concept' (2010) 43(1) *Vanderbilt Journal of Transnational Law* 120. See also, Antonia Chayes, 'Chapter VII½: Is Jus Post Bellum Possible?' (2013) 24(1) *European Journal of International Law* 291.

4 See, generally, Eric de Brabandere, 'The Concept of Jus Post Bellum in International Law: A Normative Critique' in Carsten Stahn, Jennifer S Easterday and Jens Iverson (eds), *Jus Post Bellum: Mapping the Normative Foundations* (Oxford University Press, Oxford 2014) 123; and Chayes (ibid), 293–296.

the need to build a more sustainable peace, as indicated in Chapters 2 and 3 that emphasised the need to mitigate economic and social inequality. The highlighting of economic and social rights throughout this work is aimed at contributing to the re-orientation of the notions of violence and peace and security in the post-conflict phase so as to facilitate the achievement of positive peace and human security.

This chapter considers the potential impact of these concepts upon the workings of the Security Council because the Council is primarily responsible for the maintenance of international peace and security. Council resolutions are, for the most part, the genesis of peacebuilding mandates and peacekeeping operations, though such language is often carefully couched in terms of whether it puts Member States under an obligation or otherwise.[5] Although some of the steps already taken by the Council to engage with broader concepts of peace and security as well as post-conflict obligations are to be acknowledged, the chapter considers the possibility of whether the Security Council is obliged to do more. It considers whether the Council should incorporate broader post-conflict obligations into its peacebuilding and peacekeeping mandates in a manner that is more considered and consistent and whether economic and social rights should play a more visible part in peacebuilding and peacekeeping mandates.

Focusing on the issue of Security Council obligations raises the issue if, and to what extent, the UN (and thus the Security Council) is bound by such obligations. Stemming from that issue is the further question of the consequences of a failure to meet any such obligations. The latter question of accountability is dealt with from the perspective of responsibility in international law, which would suggest that International Organisations such as the UN should be accountable for internationally wrongful acts. However, the value of such an approach has to contend with the privileges and immunities afforded to the UN by the Charter, as well as the privileges and immunities conferred on the Organisation by the Convention on the Privileges and Immunities of the UN.[6] The reality of this approach is spelt out in the response of the UN to questions of its responsibility for the cholera epidemic in Haiti, in which it denied any legal responsibility for its acts and omissions that are clear violations of the (admittedly State-centric) obligations to respect, protect and fulfil the right to health, water and sanitation, as well as the right to life. Limitations on the accountability of the UN for breaches of international law brings this chapter to the question of the accountability of contributing States, which is addressed in terms of State Responsibility in international law and in terms of the ICESCR's own complaints mechanism. This approach reaffirms the justiciable nature of economic and social rights, which should serve to influence contributing States' understanding of their extraterritorial obligations stemming from such rights.

5 See, generally, Samantha Besson, 'The Bearers of Human Rights' Duties and Responsibilities for Human Rights: A Quiet (R)Evolution?' (2015) 32(1) *Social Philosophy and Policy* 244.

6 Convention on the Privileges and Immunities of the United Nations (adopted 13 February 1946, entered into force 17 September 1946) 1 UNTS 15.

This chapter's examination of the complex issues of accountability for breaches of international law, including violations of economic and social rights, is ultimately confined to reiterating a core theme in this work and that is the need to recognise the centrality of economic and social rights to the maintenance of international peace and security. Where violations of such rights undermine such efforts to maintain international peace and security, they should be addressed inasmuch as violations of civil and political rights are addressed. The question of post-conflict obligations to build a broader and more enduring peace that has the individual at its centre is not entirely baseless. At a minimum, it underpins the need for a more nuanced approach to international peace and security on the part of the Security Council, an approach that reflects the permeation of the UN Charter by the need to advance economic and social justice and to protect human rights.

2 *Jus Post Bellum* as a philosophical construct

Jus post bellum theory signals that the rights and responsibilities of parties to a conflict do not end at the conflict's termination but that such rights and obligations continue through the post-conflict phase. *Jus post bellum* can be understood as a largely philosophical concept, which, like many philosophical concepts, may ultimately guide the role of international law in post-conflict societies. References to *jus post bellum* can be identified in the evolution of just war theory, historically.[7]

7 See for example, Carnes Lord (tr), *Aristotle's Politics* (2nd edn, Chicago University Press, Chicago 2013); and Miriam Griffin (tr), *Cicero: On Duties* (Cambridge Texts in the History of Political Thought, Cambridge University Press, Cambridge 1991). Christian theologians predominately have been identified in the emergence of just war theory and *jus post bellum*, in particular: Henry Bettenson (tr), *St Augustine: Concerning the City of God Against Pagans* (2nd edn, Penguin Books, London 1984); Anthony Pagden and Jeremey Lawrence (eds), *Vitoria: Political Writings* (Cambridge Texts in the History of Political Thought, Cambridge University Press, Cambridge 1991) 303; and Gwladys L Williams (tr), 'The Three Theological Virtues' in James Brown Scott (ed), *The Classics of International Law* (Clarendon Press, Oxford 1944) 20. The just war theory has also been considered in other religious traditions. See generally, Paul Robinson (ed), *Just War in Comparative Perspective* (Ashgate, Surrey 2003); and Peggy Morgan and Clive Lawton (eds), *Ethical Issues in Six Religious Traditions* (Edinburgh University Press, Edinburgh 1996) 44–47, 88–90, 123–125, 165–167 and 255–256. In terms of international law, see Francis W Kelsey (tr), 'Hugo Grotius on the Law of War and Peace' in James Brown Scott (ed), *The Classics of International Law* (Carnegie Institution of Washington, Washington DC 1925); Charles Ghequiere Fenwick (tr), *The Law of Nations, or, the Principles of Natural Law Applied to the Conduct and the Affairs of Nations and of Sovereigns* (vol III, Carnegie Institution of Washington, Washington DC 1916) 344; and William Hastie (tr), *The Philosophy of Law: An Exposition of the Fundamental Principles of Jurisprudence as the Science of Right* (Clark, Edinburgh 1887) 218–222. *Jus post bellum* has equally been considered in recent military strategy, according to General William Tecumseh Sherman, in a speech delivered in St Louis in 1865, 'The legitimate object of war is a more perfect peace,' quoted in Basil Henry Liddell-Hart, *Sherman: Soldier, Realist, American* (Dodd, Mead and Company, Boston 1929) 425. Echoing this tradition, Liddell-Hart wrote, 'The object in war is a better state of peace': see Basil Henry Liddell-Hart, *Strategy* (Praeger Paperbacks, New York 1954) 338.

The discourse on *jus post bellum* and post-conflict reconstruction has also been elaborated upon, more recently, by theorists and theologians. Perhaps most significantly, in the current context, is the principle of restoration, according to which the victors must not only 'return to the fields of battle and help remove the instruments of war', they must also assist in rebuilding the social infrastructure of the vanquished nation.[8] Such activities are premised on the notion that 'most often it is those who are least able to fend for themselves who are affected the greatest in the aftermath of war – the children, the sick and the elderly'.[9]

Recent moral and ethical considerations of just war theory also underpin theories of *jus post bellum*.[10] Philosophically, linkages between *jus ad bellum* and *jus post bellum* have been made[11] so that the 'declared ends that justify a war impose obligations on belligerent powers to try, even after the conclusion of the war, to bring about the desired outcome'.[12] Similar philosophical linkages have been made between *jus post bellum* and *jus in bello*, as the latter's requirement of proportionality calls for restraint in combat so that both total war and total conquest are to be regarded, at the very least, as suspect.[13] The tripartite nature of just war theory is further elaborated with the view that if a war has a just cause, and is fought justly, the war still must lead to a just post-war settlement[14] because:

> the way a war is fought and the deeds done in ending it live on in the historical memory of societies and may or may not set the stage for future war. It is always the duty of statesmanship to take this longer view.[15]

Although *jus post bellum* has been regarded as 'the least developed part of just war theory',[16] a number of general themes that underpin *jus post bellum* theory can be identified. One, the notion of just cause for termination permits the State(s) that resorted to armed force to seek 'termination of the just war in question if there has been a reasonable vindication of those rights whose violation grounded the resort to war in the first place'.[17] Two, acceptance of the terms of surrender means not only the cessation of hostilities but also means renouncing the gains of

8 Michael J Schuck, 'When the Shooting Stops: Missing Elements in Just War Theory' (1994) 111(30) *Christian Century* 982, 983.
9 Anthony Di Meglio, 'The Evolution of the Just War Tradition: Defining Just Post Bellum' (2005) 186 *Military Law Review* 116, 137.
10 Michael Walzer, *Just and Unjust Wars: A Moral Argument with Historical Illustrations* (3rd edn, Basic Books, New York 2000).
11 Brian Orend, 'Jus Post Bellum' (2000) 33(1) *Journal of Social Philosophy* 117; and Gary Bass, 'Jus Post Bellum' (2004) 32(4) *Philosophy and Public Affairs* 384.
12 Bass, ibid, 386.
13 Ibid, 390–392.
14 Ibid, 389.
15 John Rawls, *The Law of Peoples* (Harvard University Press, Cambridge 1999) 96.
16 Michael Walzer, *Arguing about War* (Yale University Press, New Haven 2004) 161.
17 Brian Orend, *War and International Justice: A Kantian Perspective* (Wilfrid Laurier University Press, Waterloo, Ontario 2000) 269. See also, Brian Orend, 'Jus Post Bellum: The Perspective of a Just-War Theorist' (2007) 20(3) *Leiden Journal of International Law* 573;

aggression as well as submission to reasonable principles of punishment, including compensation, war crimes trials, and perhaps rehabilitation.[18] Three, the object in war is a better state of peace,[19] meaning greater territorial security as well as a greater degree of safety for ordinary men and women and their domestic self-determinations. Simply returning to the *status quo ante bellum* would be morally and legally problematic since such circumstances may have been the justification for the initiation of the war in the first place.[20] As such, *jus post bellum* gives rise to a series of obligations ranging from the simple to the complex. At its simplest, a 'minimalist' view of *jus post bellum* permits a victorious State to choose merely to settle for the restoration of the *status quo*.[21] In contrast, the more complex or 'maximalist' interpretation of *jus post bellum* advances the view that:

> victors have a moral and legal obligation to do more than merely satisfy their own rights afterwards. They must also remove the seeds of potential future war by punishing those guilty of initiating aggressive war and positively assisting the civilian population in the building of legitimate and peaceful government institutions and in the rebuilding of the domestic economy.[22]

Attempts to respond to such complexity allow the identification of further principles, which to varying degrees resonate with UN post-conflict peacebuilding. One, as noted above, the principle of rights vindication has been expanded to mean that the post-conflict settlement should secure those basic rights the violation of which triggered the war. Although the human rights to life and liberty and community entitlements to territory and sovereignty have been identified in this context,[23] violations of economic and social rights that permeate this book must also be taken into account. Two, according to the principle of proportionality, the terms of any peace settlement should be measured,[24] reasonable and proportional to the end of rights vindication so that 'the people of the defeated Aggressor never forfeit their human rights'.[25] The related principle of publicity requires

---

and Alex Bellamy, 'The Responsibilities of Victory: Jus Post Bellum and the Just War' (2008) 34(4) *Review of International Studies* 601.

18 Orend, 'War and International Justice', ibid.

19 Liddell-Hart (n 7), 338.

20 Di Meglio (n 9), 138.

21 Orend, 'Jus Post Bellum: The Perspective of a Just War Theorist' (n 17), 603.

22 Bellamy (n 17), 618.

23 Orend, 'Jus Post Bellum: The Perspective of a Just-War Theorist' (n 17), 580. See also, Rawls's just war theory emphasising the restoration of the sovereignty of the aggressor nations: Rawls (n 15), 98. Re *jus post bellum*, see similarly, Bass's call for restraint in conquest: Bass (n 11), 390; and Bellamy (n 17), 602–605.

24 Orend 'Jus Post Bellum: The Perspective of a Just-War Theorist' (n 17), 580; and Brian Orend, 'Justice after War' (2002) 16(1) *Ethics and International Affairs* 43, 47.

25 Orend, *War and International Justice* (n 17), 270. See also, Rawls's view that, 'The enemy's people are not to be held as slaves or serfs after surrender, or denied in due time their full liberties': Rawls (n 15), 98.

that such a reasoned settlement must then be publicly proclaimed.[26] Three, the principle of discrimination dictates that a distinction needs to be made between the defeated leaders, soldiers and civilians. Not only should civilians be entitled to reasonable immunity from punitive post-war measures, but sweeping socio-economic sanctions, as part of post-war punishment, should also be prohibited.[27] Four, according to the principle of punishment, the leaders of the aggressor regime, in particular, should face fair and public international trials for war crimes for reasons of deterrence, atonement and rehabilitation, and recognition of the aggressor's victims.[28] However, such a focus on criminal justice echoes those critiques of the liberal models of peacebuilding and transitional justice, which would regard this approach as being unduly narrow. Proper punishment also includes the requirement that an aggressor State provides restitution to the victim State for 'at least some of the costs incurred during the fight for its rights'.[29] Five, the principle of compensation also allows for the mandating of financial restitution, as an aspect of punishment. This principle, too, is subject to the tenets of proportionality and discrimination so that civilians of the Aggressor State retain their claims to human rights fulfilment.[30] Similarly, the payment of reparations must be 'compensatory not vindictive'.[31]

The above principles are indicative of the victor's rights and the limits upon those rights. However, it is the principle of rehabilitation, encompassing the concept of post-conflict reconstruction, which throws into sharp relief a core issue of just war theory: the extent to which the victors are obliged to go beyond a restoration of the *status quo ante*. The principle of rehabilitation permits, or even requires, the aggressor State to engage in some demilitarisation and political rehabilitation, depending on the nature and severity of the aggression it committed and the threat that it would continue to pose in the absence of such measures.[32] Similarly, a restrictive view of rehabilitation, for example one that is merely pedagogical or reformist, allows for sweeping internal political reconstruction only in the most severe cases, such as genocide.[33] In cases involving the latter, political reconstruction can be regarded as being a *jus post bellum* duty:[34]

> When the victorious State fails to assist in reconstruction in such post-genocidal cases, it calls into question its claim to have waged a just war of

26 Orend, 'Jus Post Bellum: The Perspective of a Just-War Theorist' (n 17), 580.
27 Ibid.
28 Ibid. See also, Di Meglio (n 9), 154–155; and Bass (n 11), 404–406.
29 Orend, 'Justice after War' (n 24), 47.
30 Ibid, 48.
31 Bass (n 11), 409.
32 Orend, 'Jus Post Bellum: The Perspective of a Just-War Theorist' (n 17), 581; and Orend (n 11), 128–129. Similarly, Bass (n 11), 390–392. See also, Manuela Melandri, 'The State, Human Rights and the Ethics of War Termination: What Should a Just Peace Look Like? A Critical Appraisal' (2011) 7(3) *Journal of Global Ethics* 241.
33 Bass (n 11), 396; Orend, 'Justice after War' (n 24), 47; and Di Meglio (n 9), 148–149.
34 Bass, ibid, 396, 397–398.

> humanitarian intervention, for it has failed to finish what it began in waging the war.[35]

At its broadest, post-conflict reconstruction, as informed by *jus post bellum* theory, permits total regime change which links the concept of punishment to the criterion of just cause for termination. On the basis of this connection, *jus post bellum* theory contends that forcible regime change is permitted provided that (i) the war itself was just and conducted properly; (ii) the target regime was illegitimate and thus had forfeited its State rights; (iii) the goal of the reconstruction is to be a minimally just regime; and (iv) respect for *jus in bello* and human rights is to be integral to the transformation process itself. In such situations, the moral basis for permitting forcible regime change is thus fulfilled because: (i) the transformation violates neither State nor human rights; (ii) its expected consequences are very desirable, namely, satisfied human rights for the local population and increased international peace and security for everyone; and (iii) the post-war moment is especially promising regarding the possibilities for reform.[36]

The issues of rehabilitation and restoration are not confined to political matters. The question of economic restoration raises issues around the obligations of the victors to assist in the restoration of a shattered economy and society to its pre-war status.[37] The failure to provide some small measure of economic rehabilitation to war-torn economies may make it difficult to secure basic subsistence rights, as 'not even those who were responsible for the war should be allowed to starve to death'.[38] The issue of economic reconstruction may also draw from the *jus post bellum* principles of compensation, restitution and reparations.[39] The requirements around rehabilitation and restoration, both political and economic, must be balanced with the duty to respect, as far as possible, the sovereignty of the defeated State and to seek the consent of the latter in any reconstruction project.[40] The end of war must entail the restoration of national sovereignty,[41] with sovereignty not just meaning territorial sovereignty but also the sovereignty of a justly governed people. A successful outcome of such an approach would see a post-conflict situation in which:

> all aspects of political, economic, and social life are returned to the control of the indigenous population. Interim political authorities are eventually replaced by elected officials, and these political figures assume full responsibility for security, critical infrastructure, and nation building.[42]

35 Ibid, 401.

36 Orend, 'Jus Post Bellum: The Perspective of a Just-War Theorist' (n 17), 583.

37 Bass (n 11), 406–407 wherein he compares the question to the principle of restoration identified by Schuck, (n 8).

38 Robert E Williams and Dan Caldwell, 'Just War Theory and the Principles of Just Peace' (2006) 7(4) *International Studies Perspectives* 309, 318.

39 Bass (n 11), 409.

40 Ibid, 392.

41 Ibid, 395.

42 Louis V Iasiello, 'Jus Post Bellum: The Moral Responsibilities of Victors in War' (2004) 57(3/4) *Naval War College Review* 33, 44.

As such, *jus post bellum* theory emphasises a preference for the end to war, 'with governments in power in the defeated States that are chosen by the people they rule – or at least recognised by them as legitimate – and that are visibly committed to the welfare of those same people (all of them)'.[43]

Responsibility for reconstruction falls on a number of parties. The establishment of a more just social and political order is ultimately a political decision, which may take into account the best advice of the military[44] and other actors, including NGOs and private agencies.[45] Such political decision-making must adhere to legal standards. These standards are, unfortunately, rather erratic, and the contribution of *jus post bellum* could, therefore, be advantageous for a number of reasons. Firstly, a discussion of justice during the termination phase of war would mirror the conception of war having a beginning, a middle and an end (however blurred these phases may be). Secondly, it would facilitate the consideration of war in a deep and comprehensive way. In addition, greater consideration of *jus post bellum* could serve to restrain war termination and not only curtail fighting on the ground but avoid future bloodshed by underscoring the need for a just peace settlement. Such greater consideration could also provide firm and objective guidelines to measure achievements and to create timelines for both progress and eventual withdrawal, which is advantageous to victors.[46] The overall benefit of *jus post bellum* theory is that it:

> forces just-war theory and international law to confront deeper and longer-term issues of international justice at the conclusion of conflict, and refuses to treat wars as isolated, atomic units to be each evaluated using rules and laws but then considered 'closed' after that – as if wars do not have profound rippling effects, through both time and space, into the future and in to other countries and regions.[47]

Jus post bellum theory highlights the need for a normative framework to minimise even potential violations of international law during the post-conflict

43 Walzer (n 16), 164.

44 Doug McCready, 'Ending the War Right: Jus Post Bellum and the Just War Tradition' (2009) 8(1) *Journal of Military Ethics* 66, 68.

45 Di Meglio (n 9), 150–151.

46 Orend, 'Jus Post Bellum: The Perspective of a Just-War Theorist' (n 17), 575–577; and Orend, *War and International Justice* (n 17), 226.

47 Orend, 'Jus Post Bellum: The Perspective of a Just-War Theorist' (n 17), 575. However, the concept of *jus post bellum* has itself been criticised as not actually adding to a complete ethics of war because the normative principles that govern the termination of war remain omitted. *Jus terminatio* governs the transition from a state of war back into a state of peace, and its central concerns are when it is obligatory to terminate a state of war and how this can be done in the morally best way. *Jus post bellum* is distinguished as governing conduct in the subsequent post-war state. See David Rodin, 'First View: Ending War' (2011) 25(3) *Ethics & International Affairs* 59; and David Rodin, 'Two Emerging Issues of Jus Post Bellum: War Termination and the Liability of Soldiers for Crimes of Aggression' in Carsten Stahn and Jann K Kleffner (eds), *Jus Post Bellum: Towards a Law of Transition from Conflict to Peace* (T M C Asser Press, The Hague 2008) 53–75. See also, Darrell Mollendorf, 'Jus ex Bello' (2008) 16(2) *Journal of Political Philosophy* 123.

peacebuilding phase and to increase accountability when violations do occur. It emphasises the importance of principles of justice and legitimacy in post-conflict efforts. *Jus post bellum* theory also highlights the need to reconsider approaches to the maintenance of international peace and security, which would necessarily impact upon peacebuilding and peacekeeping mandates.

Although the overall concept of post-conflict rules is instructive, the language of victor and vanquished, retribution and reparations signal the State-centric nature of the propositions of *jus post bellum*. The overall practice of the Security Council to date, the contents of just war theory generally and *jus post bellum*, in particular, do not fit comfortably into current international law with its emphasis on *jus contra bellum* as enshrined in Articles 2(4) and 51 of the UN Charter, and the State-centric legal regime of *jus in bello* enshrined in international humanitarian law, which is increasingly being informed by the equally State-centric body of international human rights law. Consequently, any legal basis for the incorporation of such considerations remains largely lacking, and *jus post bellum* theory remains an ethical and moral tool[48] that may inform post-conflict obligations in spite of the fact that, in the context of collective security, such a framework could serve to maximise the perception of legitimacy of the UN and of international law as a system.[49]

A second challenge is that much of the theory is derived from war laws with their emphasis on just war and the conduct of the war itself. The context for such analyses has been inter-State conflict, which has given a certain shape and form to the principles of *jus post bellum*. However, given that it is responses to intra-State conflict that largely underpin UN peacebuilding and peacekeeping policy and action, the question of the relevance of the questions and issues raised by *jus post bellum* theory to peacebuilding and peacekeeping as conducted by an International Organisation needs to be considered. A further, and related, consideration is the impact of human rights as an aspect of peacebuilding and peacekeeping operations. Inasmuch as the jurisprudence on extraterritorial rights is indicative of the expansion of human rights, such jurisprudence can also be regarded as post-conflict jurisprudence 'of sorts', given the increasing number of human rights cases being considered by the ECtHR that originate from post-conflict situations.[50]

Whilst the current discussion has many limits, the actual discussion itself is a further element in the on-going and evolving discussion securing a more sustainable peace. There is merit in the concern expressed at the view that States and International Organisations that have actively participated in the *jus ad bellum* stage of a conflict would then have responsibilities in the post-conflict phase, because of its potential to reintroduce just war theory into international law

48 Chayes (n 3), 296.

49 Bellamy (n 17), 615–616; and Liliana Lyra Jubilut, 'Towards a New Just Post Bellum: The United Nations Peacebuilding Commission and the Improvement of Post-conflict Efforts and Accountability' (2011) 20(1) *Minnesota Journal of International Law* 26, 51–52.

50 Guglielmo Verdirame, 'What to Make of Jus Post Bellum: A Response to Antonia Chayes' (2013) 24(1) *European Journal of International Law* 307, 308.

which today, with its identification of States' use of force in self-defence or collective security to maintain or restore international peace and security, falls well short of identifying such responsibilities. Articles 39 and 42 of the Charter have been identified as providing the most tentative of bases for such obligations,[51] the concepts of peacebuilding and post-conflict reconstruction derived from Chapters VI and VII of the UN Charter, rather than any question of obligations of victors. As illustrated in Chapters 2 and 3, these concepts were not underpinned by any discussions on the legality of the use of armed force. For example, the Report of the International Commission on Intervention and State Sovereignty (ICISS) advanced the view that the UN has a subsidiary responsibility to prevent, protect and rebuild a State so that the latter can counter those circumstances which necessitated the intervention,[52] with the level of responsibility presumably being commensurate with the level of intervention. Similarly, the *Report of the High-level Panel on Threats, Challenges and Change* noted in relation to the establishment of the Peacekeeping Commission that:[53]

> today, in an era when dozens of States are under stress or recovering from conflict, there is a clear international obligation to assist States in developing their capacity to perform their sovereign functions effectively and responsibly.[54]

The Report goes further and details UN obligations as well as recommendations on how to meet them. Some of these obligations devolve to the Security Council on the basis that 'even if its peace and security institutions played no part in initiating, or intervening, in the war',[55] 'those charged with global responsibilities for international peace and security ought to acquire a responsibility to help rebuild after war, thus helping to remove the seeds of future conflict'.[56]

Thus, concerns about the question of a direct transposition of such obligations onto intervening States and organisations may be misguided and should not preclude the contribution of such theory to peacebuilding and peacekeeping policy in an attempt to construct a more sustainable peace. Having said that, however, the question of whether, and to what extent, International Organisations such as the UN, are under such obligations is a point to which this chapter will return.

51 Chayes (n 3), 292–293.

52 ICISS, 'The Responsibility to Protect: Report of the International Commission on Intervention and State Sovereignty' (International Development Research Centre, Ottawa 2001) 39–44.

53 UNSC Res 1645 (20 December 2005) UN Doc S/RES/1645; and UNGA Res 60/180 (30 December 2005) UN Doc A/RES/60/180.

54 United Nations, 'A More Secure World: Our Shared Responsibility, Report of the Secretary-General's High-level Panel on Threats, Challenges and Change' (2004), para 261 <http://www.un.org/en/peacebuilding/pdf/historical/hlp_more_secure_world.pdf> accessed 15 July 2016.

55 Bellamy (n 17), 616.

56 Ibid, 623.

3 Positive peace and human security as collective security

As the previous section indicates, the existence and extent of post-conflict obligations is a matter of some concern from the theoretical perspective of what ought to be achieved. This section seeks to provide a different perspective on why post-conflict peace, and security more generally, are in need of realignment. The need for realignment requires the critiques of liberal peacebuilding and transitional justice to be revisited, as much of the critiques levelled at these mechanisms stem from the narrow nature of the peace and security that they seek to (re-)establish. The favouring of a narrow liberal peace means that the more endemic causes of conflict resulting from economic and social inequality will not be properly addressed, an outcome which is contrary to nearly two decades of UN policy in this regard. It also means that economic and social rights will continue to be marginalised, as the focus on violations of civil and political rights means that there is less explicit concern with situations and actions that comprise violations of economic and social rights and which underpin and promote socio-economic inequality. Similar criticisms have been levelled at transitional justice mechanisms on the basis that they fail to address the structural causes that led to such violence and the general failure to prosecute for massive violations of economic and social rights,[57] and the failure to account for religion, culture, economics and local tradition, which are, themselves, elements of the human rights discourse.[58] Such an approach also allows economic and structural violence, including violations of economic and social rights, to be overlooked.[59]

Thus, the relationship between human rights, peace, peacebuilding and transitional justice brings us to consider what is meant by peace. To date, peace tends to be defined narrowly in terms of 'negative peace' and the absence of conflict and/or direct violence, and where responding to civil and political rights violations is the primary concern. The liberal peace project's emphasis on negative peace overlooks the more indirect forms of violence, including forms of structural violence such as poverty, corruption, social and economic inequalities, and other forms of social injustice. In contrast, positive peace is aimed at ending indirect structural and cultural violence (indirect violence) that threatens the economic, social and cultural well-being and identity of individual human beings and groups. Positive peace seeks to create political, economic and social conditions that support sustainable justice and security and in which individuals can realise their full potential.[60]

57 However, see Louise Arbour, 'Economic and Social Justice for Societies in Transition' (2007) 40(1) *Journal of International Law and Politics* 1, 16–17.

58 Dustin N Sharp, 'Addressing Economic Violence in Times of Transition: Toward a Positive Peace Paradigm for Transitional Justice' (2012) 35(3) *Fordham International Law Journal* 780, 783.

59 Arbour (n 57), 4–5.

60 Johan Galtung, 'Violence, Peace and Peace Research' (1969) 6(3) *Journal of Peace Research* 167, 183.

As indicated in Chapters 2 and 3, the need to formulate the concept of peace more broadly has already been translated into the UN's policy endeavours because, according to the Secretary-General, the aim of the UN had to be, 'in the largest sense, to address the deepest causes of conflict: economic despair, social injustice and political oppression'.[61] When he revisited the concept, the Secretary-General stated that 'every step towards reducing poverty and achieving broad-based economic growth – is a step toward conflict prevention',[62] so that what is actually needed is 'a comprehensive strategy that incorporates but is broader than coercive measures'.[63] Such views reinforce the need for the creation and maintenance of a positive peace that entails law and policy to address economic violence, structural violence and the creation of social justice. It should also allow for a more balanced approach to be struck between civil and political rights and economic and social rights. Positive peace allows for the legacies of economic violence to be dealt with, an approach that should inform peacebuilding initiatives associated with post-conflict reconstruction. Peacebuilding efforts must address political and material rights and they must go beyond the provision of only the very basic of public services to create more equal forms of citizenship.[64]

However, inasmuch as the understanding of peace may need to be adjusted, so too should the understanding of security. The predominance of intra-State conflict and/or organised violence,[65] as well as the overall upward trend in the numbers of peace support operations,[66] indicates that the maintenance of security ought no longer to be measured solely in terms of inter-State security. The complexity of the issue is also compounded as:

> intrastate civil wars are still fought in what we might call a state-laden context: they are fought either over which group gets to control the existing state or over which group gets to have a new state. Thus, there are always state-to-state issues involved in contemporary armed conflict.[67]

Post-conflict peacebuilding and peacekeeping initiatives ought to facilitate an understanding of security that is broader than State security, with its emphasis

61 UNGA, 'Report of the Secretary General 24111' (1992) UN Doc A/47/277-S/24111, para 15.

62 UNGA, 'Report of the Secretary General 54/2000' (2000) UN Doc A/54/2000, para 202.

63 United Nations (n 54), para 148.

64 Oliver P Richmond, 'The Impact of Socio-Economic Inequality on Peacebuilding and State-building' (2014) 16(4) *Civil Wars* 449, 457.

65 Erik Melander, Therése Pettersson and Lotta Themnér, 'Organized Violence, 1989–2015' (2016) 53(5) *Journal of Peace Research* 727.

66 Stockholm International Peace Research Institute, 'Data and Trends for Multilateral Peace Operations' (Number of Peace Operations, 2006–2015, undated) <https://www.sipri.org/research/conflict-and-peace/peace-operations-and-conflict-management/data-and-trends-multilateral-peace-operations> accessed 17 September 2016.

67 Orend, *War and International Justice* (n 17), 9.

on the military defence of State interests and territory.[68] The broader approach to security, that is, human security, allows greater emphasis to be placed on people's security including 'safety from chronic threats such as hunger, disease, and repression, [as well as] protection from sudden and harmful disruptions in the patterns of daily life',[69] because 'the security of people must be regarded as a goal as important as the security of states'.[70] Human security has also been described as an approach that encompasses the protection of people 'from severe and pervasive threats, both natural and societal, and empowering individuals and communities to develop the capabilities for making informed choices and acting on their own behalf'.[71] The concept was given further recognition by the 2005 World Summit Outcome Document, which stressed:

> the right of people to live in freedom and dignity, free from poverty and despair. We recognize that all individuals, in particular vulnerable people, are entitled to freedom from fear and freedom from want, with an equal opportunity to enjoy all their rights and fully develop their human potential.[72]

Three general versions of human security have been identified:

> a narrow approach that relies on natural rights and the rule of law anchored in basic human rights; a humanitarian approach that understands human security as a tool for deepening and strengthening efforts to tackle issues such as war crimes or genocide and finally preparing the ground for humanitarian intervention; and a broad approach that links human security with the state of the global economy, development, and globalization.[73]

68 United Nations Development Programme, *Human Development Report 1994* (UNDP, New York 1994) 22 and 24; and Roland Paris, 'Human Security: Paradigm Shift or Hot Air' (2001) 26(2) *International Security* 87.

69 UNDP, ibid, 23.

70 Commission on Global Governance, *Our Global Neighbourhood: Report of the Commission on Global Governance* (Oxford University Press, Oxford 1995) <http://www.gdrc.org/u-gov/global-neighbourhood/chap3.htm> accessed 2 February 2017.

71 Sadako Ogata and Johann Cels, 'Human Security: Protecting and Empowering the People' (2003) 9(3) *Global Governance* 273, 274. See also, Commission on Human Security, *Human Security Now: Protecting and Empowering the People* (Commission on Human Security, New York 2003). Unsurprisingly, the concept has proven controversial. Advocates regard human security as a timely, necessary and helpful expansion of traditional security concerns and either a paradigm shift and dramatic departure from traditional security concepts or a useful tool for shaping foreign policy. Its critics regard it as too universalistic, conceptually flawed, impracticable and contrary to national interests with the potential of being captured by ideology. See Gerard Oberleitner, 'Human Security: A Challenge to International Law' (2005) 11(2) *Global Governance* 187.

72 UNGA, '2005 World Summit Outcome 60/L.1' (2005) UN Doc A/60/L.1, para 143.

73 Oberleitner (n 71), 187–188, citing Fen Osler Hampson and John Hay, 'Human Security: A Review of the Scholarly Literature' (2002) 1(2) *Human Security Bulletin* 4.

These categories are also more generally refined into broad approaches and narrow approaches to human security. The broad version draws upon the United Nations Development Programme's (UNDP) vision of human security which not only focuses on situations of conflict but is also aimed at ensuring protection against extreme poverty and the provision of human basic needs in economic, health, food, social and environmental terms.[74] The narrow version focuses upon removing the use of, or threat of, force and violence from people's everyday lives through campaigns to ban anti-personnel landmines, to regulate small arms and light weapons and to promote the International Criminal Court.[75] In a manner reflective of the later doctrine of the Responsibility to Protect, this narrow version of human security allows the international community to intervene to protect people in crisis situations when their own States cannot or will not do so. It advances the view that the international community should have stronger enforcement mechanisms to remedy gross human rights violations occurring within a State, one that is not confined by the political machinations of the Security Council. This view proceeds on the premise that insecure citizens make for insecure States and that these insecure citizens need not be the citizens of the State itself. Consequently, the protection of citizens in other States may be a matter of concern for foreign governments.[76]

The correlations between the broad and narrow approaches to human security and Roosevelt's freedom from want and freedom from fear, respectively, as precursors to international peace and security is not to be overlooked.[77] It is also reflective of the interrelationship between international peace and security and the promotion and protection of human rights enshrined in the UN Charter, efforts which can be seen in the work of the Organisation in its peacekeeping efforts, management of refugees and environmental issues. Accordingly, it has been asserted by a former UN High Commissioner for Human Rights that 'the commitment to human security underlines much of the United Nations action in the areas of peace and security, humanitarian assistance, crime prevention and development, among others'.[78] As such, there is ample evidence to support the view that the human security approach 'is well entrenched in the raison d'être of

74 Commission on Human Security (n 71), 6–7.

75 Keith Krause, 'Towards a Practical Human Security Agenda' (Policy Paper 26, Geneva Centre for the Democratic Control of Armed Forces 2007) 3–4 <www.dcaf.ch/content/download/35420/526057/file/PP26.pdf> accessed 26 September 2016.

76 Rhoda Howard Hassmann, 'Human Security: Undermining Human Rights?' (2012) 34(1) *Human Rights Quarterly* 88, 90.

77 Franklin D Roosevelt, 'Annual Message to Congress on the State of the Union' (Speech to the Congress on 6 January 1941) <http://www.presidency.ucsb.edu/ws/?pid=16092> accessed 26 September 2016.

78 Oberleitner (n 71) 192, citing Mary Robinson in a statement from UNCHR 'Effective Functioning of Human Rights Mechanisms: National Institutions and Regional Arrangements' (2000) UN Doc E/CN.4/2002/WP3.

the UN work'.[79] Thus, what is required is a further recalibration of the meaning of security towards that of human security whereby security (and peace) can be viewed in strategic and humanistic terms. Under this concept of security, the focus lies upon the individual and his/her community, rather than upon the State. It affords a greater consideration of threats posed to humankind and to the individual and basic rights like liberty, subsistence and security.[80] A human security approach reinforces the need for protection from threats of physical and structural violence as well as the promotion of sustainable human development and the freedom from want that ought to ensue.[81] Thus, positive peace and human security resonates with *jus post bellum* analysis to reveal three goals in particular:

> (1) physical security for the general population that exceeds the status quo ante bellum; (2) just ordering of society via 'positive assistance,' restoration, and rehabilitation that makes life 'fully human' and emphasizes human capabilities; and (3) the vindication and securing of rights.[82]

In the context of the Responsibility to Protect discourse, although the Charter provisions relating to the use of force and collective security remain largely definitive, there are calls for a reconsideration of the legal content of the norms of peace and security,[83] which emphasise that sovereignty implies a responsibility of the State to protect its citizens from human rights violations. Where a State does not live up to this sovereign responsibility, the international community, it is argued, assumes responsibility to act in its place. Consequently, human rights and human security become intrinsic to sovereignty. Thus, if sovereignty is viewed as something more than a territorial matter, and the interaction of States in the international community, but rather is imbued with the notion of protection of citizens, such protection should not end after the cessation of hostilities but should extend to support the sustainable development of a stable and safe society,[84] to prevent future conflict and thereby to protect civilians.[85] Such views are encompassed in the Responsibility to Protect and, particularly, in the concept

79 Noëlle Quénivet, 'You Are the Weakest Link and We Will Help You! The Comprehensive Strategy of the United Nations to Fight Terrorism' (2006) 11(3) *Journal of Conflict and Security Law* 371, 386.

80 Labonte (n 2), 209.

81 Ibid, 214. Compare, Neil MacFarlane and Yuen Foong Khong, *Human Security and the UN: A Critical History* (University of Indiana Press, Bloomington 2006).

82 Labonte (n 2), 214–215.

83 See, for example, Mehrdad Payandeh, 'With Great Power Comes Great Responsibility? The Concept of the Responsibility to Protect Within the Process of International Lawmaking' (2010) 35(2) *Yale Journal of International Law* 471; and Inger Osterdahl and Esther van Zadel, 'What Will Jus Post Bellum Mean? Of New Wine and Old Bottles' (2009) 14(2) *Journal of Conflict and Security Law* 191.

84 ICISS (n 52), para 5.1–5.31.

85 Ibid, para 5.1. See also Inger Osterdahl, 'The Exception as the Rule: Lawmaking on Force and Human Rights by the UN Security Council' (2005) 10(1) *Journal of Conflict and Security Law* 1.

of the responsibility to rebuild, which resonates with the *jus post bellum* principle of restoration.

Thus, inasmuch as the nature of armed conflict has changed since the establishment of the UN, so too has the understanding of peace and security. *Jus post bellum* theory and the concepts of positive peace and human security complement such endeavours, as various State actors and non-State actors are encouraged to move 'beyond measures designed to help belligerents reach compromise and [include] building political structures that respect human rights, permit self-determination, punish wrongdoers and promote social, economic and legal reconstruction'.[86]

4 Economic and social rights in the post-conflict environment: The importance of accountability

Chapters 2 and 3 outlined the legal bases that have informed not only the Security Council's peacebuilding and peacekeeping policies but which have also had an impact on Security Council peacebuilding and peacekeeping mandates. Chapter 4 has shown the emergence of post-conflict legal obligations 'of sorts', stemming from the extraterritorial application of contributing States' human rights and, in particular, their economic and social rights. The preceding paragraphs of this chapter set out some of theoretical principles which also contribute to an evolving understanding of what is necessary, and why it is necessary, to secure peace in a more enduring fashion. These questions and considerations bring us back to considering the manner in which economic and social rights can play a role in the maintenance of peace and security, a process that requires consideration of: (i) the application and enforcement of these rights as regards the Security Council and (ii) the enforcement of these rights as regards contributing States.

The issue of the application of economic and social rights to the Security Council raises the broader question of the ability of the Security Council to create a more enduring peace in a legal environment dominated by the sovereign equality and territorial integrity of States and the principle of self-determination as enshrined in the Charter,[87] principles that have been reaffirmed by the ICJ.[88]

86 Bellamy (n 17), 615.

87 Charter of the United Nations (adopted 26 June 1945, entered into force 24 October 1945) 1 UNTS XVI (UN Charter), Article 2(1) and 2(4), respectively.

88 The primacy accorded to State sovereignty was clearly established by the ICJ in the *Corfu Channel* case wherein the Court stated that there was no authority for a right of intervention where it would result in the violation of the territorial integrity of a State: *Corfu Channel Case (Merits)* (Judgment) [1949] ICJ Rep 4, 35. This principle was reaffirmed by the Court in *Nicaragua v United States* in which the Court stated, 'The principle of non-intervention involves the right of every sovereign State to conduct its affairs without outside interference; . . . the Court considers that [this right] is part and parcel of customary international law': *Military and Paramilitary Activities in and against Nicaragua (Nicaragua v USA) (Merits)* (Judgment) [1986] ICJ Rep 14, para 202.

This question has, in part, been answered in Chapter 1, which shows that Articles 55(c) and 56 obliges Member States and the UN itself to respect human rights and to take joint and separate action in that regard to promote international peace and security. More generally, and as indicated in Chapter 2, this broader approach reflects the interrelationship between peace and security and the creation of an economic and social order that facilitates peace and security and the realisation of human rights, which is encompassed in the Charter. This relationship not only affords roles for the General Assembly and the ECOSOC in the maintenance of a broader conception of peace, it also requires such roles. Thus, under the UN Charter, peace is no longer limited to a minimalist negative core but increasingly contains positive duties linked to the conditions that make peace practicable. In this way, the Security Council can take a first step towards international peace and security that is informed by the need to improve social and economic conditions, as underpinned by economic and social rights.

Nonetheless, the following remain on-going concerns: (i) the Charter's recognition of the link between peace and security, (ii) the creation of an economic and social order in which human rights are to be realised, (iii) the widening gap between the laws of occupation and the reality of societies transitioning towards peace and (iv) efforts towards a clearer enunciation of post-conflict obligations. One of the main issues is that the respect for State sovereignty and territorial integrity is inherent in the balance that States strike when responding to a post-conflict environment. On the one hand, respect for State sovereignty suggests that only the narrowest range of post-conflict obligations are to be undertaken so as to restore simply the *status quo ante*. On the other hand, evolving views on the laws of occupation and/or the impact of human rights law, especially where the realisation of economic and social rights occupies a central role, indicate that a broader range of post-conflict obligations are increasingly necessary. Related to this point is the recognition that, in theory if not in law, a return to the *status quo ante* may be problematic especially where the circumstances of the *status quo ante* constituted a threat to, or a breach of, the peace.[89] Consequently, a maximalist understanding of *jus post bellum* allows for State sovereignty to be compromised so that less significance is attached to consent (or otherwise) of the target State as regards post-conflict reconstruction. As suggested by *jus post bellum* theory, it may be that this broader approach reflects evolving views on the nature of sovereignty as being something more than territorial sovereignty but also that it encompasses a justly governed people, as signalled in the discourse on the Responsibility to Protect. However, many of these initiatives only come into play when States seek to respond to post-conflict environments, but more could

89 The right of intervention has been recast more recently to draw increasingly upon human rights violations as 'the responsibility of the international community to prevent and punish serious violations of human rights comes into play . . . in the case of "weak" or "failed" states, unable to prevent serious violations from being committed on its territory by private parties': Siobhan Wills, *Protecting Civilians: The Obligations of Peacekeepers* (Oxford University Press, Oxford 2009) 391.

be done at the institutional level from the outset to lay down clear directions to States, both contributing and target, for post-conflict reconstruction. This conclusion raises the question of whether the Security Council is obliged to do more.

There is some legal basis for the proposition that the UN – as an International Organisation dedicated to supervising peace and security, human rights, and the creation of economic and social order to support these endeavours – must itself comply with these obligations, both generally and in the post-conflict environment. In the *Reparations* case,[90] the ICJ stated that the UN was an international person, meaning that it is a subject of international law and is capable of possessing international rights and duties,[91] with such rights and duties being dependent upon 'its purposes and functions as specified or implied in its constituent documents and developed in practice'.[92] In making its determination in the *Effect of Awards* Advisory Opinion, the ICJ drew upon 'the expressed aim of the Charter to promote freedom and justice for individuals and . . . the constant preoccupation of the United Nations Organisation to promote this aim'.[93] In its *Namibia* Advisory Opinion, the ICJ stated that its interpretation of the law could not remain unaffected by the subsequent development of law, through the Charter and by way of customary law. Moreover, it held that an international instrument must be interpreted and applied within the framework of the entire legal system prevailing at the time of the interpretation.[94] The ICJ has also affirmed, in principle, that the UN is bound by customary international law.[95]

With regard to the Security Council in particular, the ICJ has affirmed that the powers conferred upon the Council to maintain international peace and security are limited by the 'fundamental principles and purposes found in Chapter I of the Charter'.[96] However, given that Article 1 is concerned with the peaceful settlement of disputes in conformity with the principles of justice and international law, the enforcement powers conferred upon the Council under Chapter VII would seem to fall outside of this restriction, leaving the Council with wide discretion to respond to a threat to international peace and security once the threshold of

90 *Reparation for Injuries Suffered in the Service of the United Nations* (Advisory Opinion) [1949] ICJ Rep 174.

91 Ibid, 179.

92 Ibid, 180.

93 *Effect of Awards of Compensation Made by the United Nations Administrative Tribunal* (Advisory Opinion) [1954] ICJ Rep 47, 57.

94 *Legal Consequences for States of the Continued Presence of South Africa in Namibia (South-West Africa) Notwithstanding Security Council Resolution 276 (1970)* (Advisory Opinion) [1971] ICJ Rep 16 (*Namibia* Advisory Opinion), para 53; and Elena Katselli, 'Holding the Security Council Accountable for Human Rights Violations' (2007) 1(2) *Human Rights and International Legal Discourse* 301, 320.

95 *Interpretation of the Agreement of 25 March 1951 between the WHO and Egypt* (Advisory Opinion) [1980] ICJ Rep 73, 89–90.

96 *Namibia* Advisory Opinion (n 94), para 110.

Article 39 has been achieved.[97] The powers of the Council must also be considered in light of Article 103, which provides that Member States' obligations under the Charter prevail over those arising from any other international agreement. In determining whether it had to indicate provisional measures in the *Lockerbie* case, the Court held that Security Council resolutions, on the basis of Article 103 of the Charter, preceded all other obligations.[98] On the one hand, such an approach allows the Security Council to respond to post-conflict environments without being confined by a lack of *jus post bellum*. However, some caution is still needed, as Judge Weeramantry noted, in a dissenting opinion in the *Lockerbie* case, that:

> The history of the United Nations Charter . . . corroborates the view that a clear limitation on the plenitude of the Security Council's powers is that those powers must be exercised in accordance with the well-established principles of international law.[99]

The International Criminal Tribunal for the former Yugoslavia (ICTY) Appeals Chamber, in *Tadic*, reviewed the legality of the establishment of the Tribunal. It noted not only that the Security Council was not *legibus solutus* (unbound by law),[100] but that the determinations by the Council regarding the existence of a threat to peace and security 'is not a totally unfettered discretion, as it has to remain, at the very least, within the limits of the Purposes and Principles of the Charter'.[101]

Similarly, the ECtHR has recognised that both Member States and the organs of the UN are bound by *jus cogens* norms which cannot be derogated from,[102] that obligations arising from membership of international bodies are to be adhered to only on provision of equivalent human rights protection,[103] and that participation in International Organisations does not exempt Member States from responsibility for violations of the ECHR as a consequence of compliance with their other international commitments.[104] Nonetheless, in *Al-Jedda*, the

97 Bernd Martenczuk, 'The Security Council, the International Court and Judicial Review: What Lessons from Lockerbie' (1999) 10(3) *European Journal of International Law* 545.

98 *Questions of Interpretation and Application of the 1971 Montreal Convention arising from the Aerial Incident at Lockerbie (Libyan Arab Jamahiriya v United Kingdom)* (Provisional Measures) [1992] ICJ Rep 3 (*Lockerbie* Provisional Measures Case), para 39.

99 Ibid, Dissenting Opinion of Judge Weeramantry, 65.

100 *Prosecutor v Dusko Tadic (Decision on the Defence Motion for Interlocutory Appeal on Jurisdiction)* ICTY-94-1-AR72 (2 October 1995), para 28.

101 Ibid, para 29.

102 T-306/01 *Yusuf and Al Barakaat International Foundation v Council and Commission* [2005] ECR II-3533; T-315/01 *Kadi v Council and Commission* [2005] ECR II-3649; *Behrami* and *Behrami v France and Saramati v France and Others* (App nos 71412/01 and 78166/01) (2007) 45 EHRR SE10; and Joined Cases C-402 & 415/05 *Kadi v Council and Commission* [2008] ECR I-6351. See Elena Katselli, 'International Peace and Security, Human Rights and the Courts: A Critical Re-Appraisal' (2012) 16(1) *The International Journal of Human Rights* 257.

103 *M & Co v The Federal Republic of Germany* (App no. 13258/87) (1999) DR 64; and *Waite and Kennedy v Germany* (App no. 26083/94) (2000) 30 EHRR 261.

104 *Matthews v United Kingdom* (App no. 24833/94) (1999) 28 EHRR 361, paras 26–35; and *Bosphorus Hava Yollari Turizm v Ireland* (App no. 45036/98) (2006) 42 EHRR 1, para 156.

ECtHR held that where the text of a Security Council resolution is ambiguous, the resolution must be interpreted in a manner that is most harmonious with the European Convention and which avoids any conflict of obligations.[105] According to the ECtHR:

> In the light of the United Nations' important role in promoting and encouraging respect for human rights, it is to be expected that clear and explicit language would be used were the Security Council to intend States to take particular measures which would conflict with their obligations under international human rights law.[106]

Such views suggest that Article 103 cannot be interpreted so as to allow the Council to violate customary international law or to allow Council resolutions to prevail over inconsistent treaty obligations.[107] This approach does little to support efforts to secure broader and more enduring peace and security, although the recognition of non-discrimination as *jus cogens* could serve as a tool to consider violations of economic and social rights.

Similarly, according to the UN Special Rapporteur on the Right to Food, it is clear that International Organisations are bound by international law with regard to the human right to food,[108] a view which has been supported by the General Assembly.[109] The Special Rapporteur has also identified a legal framework for the responsibilities of International Organisations, based on the three levels of obligations to respect, protect and support the fulfilment of the right to food.[110] Although much of the context of the framework relates to the work of the World Bank and the International Monetary Fund, the comments of the Special Rapporteur are not confined to these bodies, and the elaboration of such obligations can extend to other UN bodies and their subsidiary organs such as peacekeeping operations. Principle 16 of the Maastricht Principles also states that these principles also extend to the human rights obligations of International Organisations under, inter alia, general international law and international agreements to which they are parties.[111]

105 *Al-Jedda v The United Kingdom* (App no. 27021/08) (2011) 53 EHRR 23, para 102.

106 Ibid.

107 Katselli (n 94), 320–323. See generally, Bardo Fassbender, 'Uncertain Steps into a Post-Cold War World: The Role and Functioning of the UN Security Council after a Decade of Measures against Iraq' (2002) 13(1) *European Journal of International Law* 273; Jose E Alvarez, 'Judging the Security Council' (1996) 90(1) *American Journal of International Law* 1; and Dapo Akande, 'The International Court of Justice and the Security Council: Is There Room for Judicial Control of Decisions of the Political Organs of the United Nations?' (1997) 46(2) *International and Comparative Law Quarterly* 309.

108 UNESC, 'Report of the Special Rapporteur on the Right to Food, Jean Ziegler 2006/44' (2006) UN Doc E/CN.4/2006/44, para 41.

109 UNGA Res 60/165 (2 March 2006) UN Doc A/RES/60/165

110 UNESC (n 108), paras 43–45.

111 ETO Consortium, 'Maastricht Principles on Extraterritorial Obligations of States in the Area of Economic, Social and Cultural Rights' (FIAN International, Heidelberg 2013)<http://www.etoconsortium.org/nc/en/main-navigation/library/maastricht-principles/?tx_drblob_pi1%5BdownloadUid%5D=23> accessed 1 October 2016.

Such views are merely indicative of how the Council should behave given the lack of consensus on whether the ICJ can review decisions of the Council.[112] However, they strengthen the assertion that, because the UN was created under the umbrella of international law, the latter is integral to the Organisation and it influences the evolution and development of the UN's rules and principles. Such assertions extend to the role of the Security Council, which must take into account the purposes and principles of the UN, including the promotion and protection of human rights and the advancement of economic and social progress, as it carries out its responsibility for the maintenance of international peace and security.

If one regards the Security Council not merely as an institutional entity but rather as a body made up of Member States, it can be seen that there is another source of legal obligation and limitation stemming from States' own customary and treaty-based obligations. Such obligations cannot be left at the door of the Council Chamber. It is against this framework that it can be argued that the Council is also bound by international human rights law enshrined, at a minimum, in customary international law.[113] Accordingly, the Security Council ought to be mindful of the negative obligation to respect the rights of the population. In other words, it has an obligation to refrain from acts that deny or limit equal access to rights or constitute arbitrary or unlawful conduct, the former being an obligation that has been found to constitute *jus cogens*.[114]

In addition, according to the CESCR, most Permanent and Non-Permanent Members of the Security Council have ratified the ICESCR and therefore it is incumbent upon them to respect and take account of their treaty obligations.[115] The CESCR emphasised that States Parties to the Covenant have a duty to take human rights considerations into account when deciding and implementing sanctions and, furthermore, to establish effective monitoring mechanisms. It also stressed:

> Although the Committee has no role to play in relation to decisions to impose or not to impose sanctions, it does, however, have a responsibility to

112 Kathleen Renée Cronin-Furman, 'The International Court of Justice and the United Nations Security Council: Rethinking a Complicated Relationship' (2006) 106(2) *Columbia Law Review* 435.

113 Fassbender (n 107); Alexander Orakhelashvili, 'The Impact of Peremptory Norms on the Interpretation and Application of United Nations Security Council Resolutions' (2005) 16(1) *European Journal of International Law* 59; August Reinisch, 'Developing Human Rights and Humanitarian Law Accountability of the Security Council for the Imposition of Economic Sanctions' (2001) 95(4) *American Journal of International Law* 851; and Claire Breen, 'The Edges of Extraterritorial Jurisdiction: The Integration of Economic, Social and Cultural Rights into Peace Support Operations' (2012) 16 *Journal of International Peacekeeping* 47.

114 *Juridical Condition and Rights of the Undocumented Migrants*, Advisory Opinion OC-18/03, IACHR Series A No. 18 (17 September 2003), para 101.

115 CESCR, 'General Comment 8, The Relationship between Economic Sanctions and Respect for Economic, Social and Cultural Rights' in 'Compilation of General Comments and General Recommendations Adopted by Human Rights Treaty Bodies' (2003) UN Doc HRI/GEN/1/Rev.6, para 8.

> monitor compliance by all States parties to the Covenant. When measures are taken which inhibit the ability of a State party to meet its obligations under the Covenant, the terms of sanctions and the manner in which they are implemented become appropriate matters for concern for the Committee.[116]

On this basis, the Security Council is obliged to protect the civilian population, who must not be deprived of essential means of survival. Similarly, the Special Rapporteur on the Right to Water and Sanitation has stated, 'Human rights obligations also apply to actions of States as members of international organizations.'[117] According to the International Law Commission, a State member of an International Organisation would be breaking international law if it caused that organisation to commit an act that would be illegal under international law for a State to carry out itself.[118] Perhaps more bluntly, it has been observed that States are precluded from authorising an International Organisation to do what they are prohibited from doing,[119] and if a Security Council act is found to be unlawful and in contravention of international law and particularly of peremptory norms, such acts are void *ab initio* and States have the right to refuse compliance with the resolution in question.[120]

There is support for the view that the UN, and thus the Security Council and peacekeeping operations as subsidiary organs of the Security Council,[121] is bound by international law. However, a number of challenges remain. The Security Council is increasingly engaging with human rights norms, but the level of protection detailed in human rights treaties does not extend to the UN given that: (i) human rights treaties create obligations for States, albeit obligations which may include the obligation to prevent third parties from violating the treaty provisions; and (ii) the UN's internal rules do not provide the Organisation and/or the Council with the capacity to protect human rights,[122] to the extent that those

116 Ibid, para 9.

117 UNGA, 'Report of the Special Rapporteur on the Human Right to Safe Drinking Water and Sanitation, Catarina de Albuquerque 27/55' (2014) UN Doc A/HRC/27/55, para 70.

118 Ibid, citing the ILC, 'Draft Articles on the Responsibility of International Organizations, with Commentaries' (2011) II *Yearbook of the International Law Commission*, Article 61, para 1.

119 Orakhelashvili (n 113), 68.

120 Ibid, 83.

121 According to the UN's legal counsel, 'As a subsidiary organ of the United Nations, an act of a peacekeeping force is, in principle, imputable to the Organization, and if committed in violation of an international obligation entails the international responsibility of the Organization and its liability in compensation.' See Unpublished letter of 3 February 2004 by the United Nations Legal Counsel to the Director of the Codification Division, cited in International Law Commission, Report of the ILC, GA Official Records, 56th session, Supplement No. 10, 111, UN Doc. A/59/10 (2004).

122 *Vienna Convention on the Law of Treaties between States and International Organizations or between International Organizations* (adopted 21 March 1986, not yet in force) 25 ILM 543, Article 6: 'The capacity of an international organization to conclude treaties is governed by the rules of that organization.' See further, Noëlle Quinivet, 'Binding the United Nations to Human Rights Norms by Way of the Laws of Treaties' (2010) 42(3) *George*

rights are captured in international human rights treaties. The current framework of international human rights law system also makes no provision for forums that could hear claims against International Organisations, as human rights treaties only make provision for individuals and groups to make complaints against States. As noted above, Article 103 of the Charter means that the obligations of the Charter take precedence over any other (human rights) treaty, a point that the Security Council has also highlighted.[123] Furthermore, Article 105 of the UN Charter accords immunity to the UN before national courts and international tribunals. These matters serve to insulate the UN and the Security Council from the breadth of international legal obligations that stem from treaty law, particularly human rights law that includes the right to a legal remedy.[124]

Questions around the responsibility of the UN have arisen most recently in relation to the cholera epidemic in Haiti, as it is thought that the infection was brought into Haiti by UN peacekeepers from Nepal.[125] Efforts to hold the UN responsible for the outbreak have been unsuccessful, as the UN's absolute immunity under Article 29 of the Convention on the Privileges and Immunities of the UN was upheld the United States District Court for the Southern District of New York in 2015.[126] The case was the culmination of efforts which started with a petition that had been lodged with MINUSTAH, in 2013, on behalf of around 5,000 cholera victims who called for a fair and impartial hearing, monetary compensation, preventive action by the UN, a public acknowledgement of UN responsibility and a public apology, a claim that the UN rejected in strong terms.[127] In noting the decision of the court, the Office of the Secretary-General stated that 'The United Nations has a moral responsibility to the victims of the cholera epidemic and for supporting Haiti in overcoming the epidemic and

---

Washington International Law Review 587, 592 (due to lack of provisions for IO accession, 'it is currently impossible for the United Nations, notwithstanding its capacity to enter into treaty relationships, to accede to human rights treaties').

123 See for example, UNSC Res 757 (30 May 1992) UN Doc S/RES/757 (Former Yugoslavia); UNSC Res 917 (6 May 1994) UN Doc S S/RES/917 (Haiti); UNSC Res 1127 (28 August 1997) UN Doc S/RES/1127 (Angola); and UNSC Res 1267 (15 October 1999) UN Doc S/RES/1267 (Afghanistan). See *Lockerbie* Provisional Measures Case (n 98), para 39: 'in accordance with Article 103 of the Charter, the obligations of the Parties in that respect prevail over their obligations under any other international agreement'; Bruno Simma and others (eds), *The Charter of the United Nations: A Commentary* (3rd edn, Oxford University Press, Oxford 2013) 2135.

124 Universal Declaration of Human Rights (adopted 10 December 1948) UNGA Res 217 A(III), Article 8; and International Covenant on Civil and Political Rights (adopted 16 December 1966, entered into force 23 March 1976) 999 UNTS 171, Article 3(2)(a).

125 Alejando Cravioto and others, 'Final Report of the Independent Panel of Experts on the Cholera Outbreak in Haiti' <http://www.un.org/News/dh/infocus/haiti/UN-cholera-report-final.pdf> accessed 12 October 2012.

126 *Georges v United Nations* 84 F Supp 3d 246, 2015 WL 129657, at 4.

127 UN Department of Public Information (New York), 'Haiti Cholera Victims' Compensation Claims "Not Receivable" under Immunities and Privileges Convention, United Nations Tells Their Representatives' (21 February 2013), UN Doc SG/SM/14828.

building sound water, sanitation and health systems.'[128] A spokesperson for the Secretary-General stated also that the UN 'needs to do much more regarding its own involvement in the initial outbreak and the suffering of those affected by cholera'. In response to the question of whether the UN was considering reparations for victims, the response was that the UN's response was not something that was being discussed in terms of reparations and that the UN's legal position regarding the outbreak had not changed.[129] In short, it would seem that the UN is not accepting legal responsibility for its actions, which by recent estimates has resulted in upwards of the deaths of 30,000 Haitians.[130] According to the UN Special Rapporteur on Extreme Poverty and Human Rights:

> the United Nations' existing legal approach of simply abdicating responsibility is morally unconscionable, legally indefensible, and politically self-defeating. The abdication approach is not only unsustainable, it is also entirely unnecessary.[131]

That such a highly critical response should come in relation to the negative impact of peacekeepers on matters of life, health, water and sanitation is notable in the context of this work.

Limitations on the accountability of the UN for violations of international law puts increased focus on contributing States' responsibility for violations of international law and the question of access to a remedy for the injured State and/or the individual whose right was violated. As regards to the question of whether contributing States can be held to be responsible for breaches of international law, there are two approaches. The first is to consider the rules around State Responsibility. The second approach is to consider the ICESCR's own complaints mechanism.

State Responsibility provides that when one State commits an internationally wrongful act against another State, which causes material or moral damage to that State,[132] the wrongful act gives rise to responsibility on the part of the former

128 United Nations, 'Statement Attributable to the Spokesman for the Secretary-General on Haiti' <https://www.un.org/sg/en/content/sg/statement/2016-08-19/statement-attributable-spokesman-secretary-general-haiti> accessed 1 February 2017.

129 United Nations, 'Daily Press Briefing by the Office of the Spokesperson for the Secretary-General' (18 August 2016) <http://www.un.org/press/en/2016/db160818.doc.htm> accessed 12 October 2016.

130 Francisco J Luquero and others, (2016) 'Mortality Rates during Cholera Epidemic, Haiti, 2010–2011' 22(3) *Emerging Infectious Diseases* 410, 410–416.

131 'Report of the Special Rapporteur on Extreme Poverty and Human Rights, Philip Alston' (2016) Advance Unedited Version A/71/40823, para 3. See further, Kirsten Boon, 'The United Nations as Good Samaritan: Immunity and Responsibility' (2016) 16(2) *Chicago Journal of International Law* 341; Thomas G Bode 'Cholera in Haiti: United Nations Immunity and Accountability' (2015) 47 *Georgetown Journal of International Law* 759; Rosa Freedman, 'UN Immunity or Impunity? A Human Rights Based Challenge' (2014) 25(1) *European Journal of International Law* 239.

132 ILC, 'Draft Articles on Responsibility of States for Internationally Wrongful Acts, 53 UN GAOR Supp. (No. 10) at 43, U.N. Doc. A/56/10 (2001), Article 31(2).

and, consequently, the need for reparation.[133] An internationally wrongful act can consist of an act or an omission constituting a breach of an international obligation,[134] regardless of the origin or character of that breach,[135] and includes the breach of a treaty. However, in order for the doctrine of State Responsibility to come into effect, the requirement of imputability or attribution must be satisfied whereby a link must be found to exist between the State and the person(s) that committed the unlawful act or omission so that the acts of the individuals can be assimilated to the State itself. As regards the conduct of national contingents of a contributing State, the most relevant means of establishing attribution stems from Article 4's provision that the conduct of any organ (including a person or entity having that status under the internal law of the State) must be regarded as an act of that State[136] where the conduct arises from the organ's exercising of legislative, executive, judicial or any other function. In this way, if the acts and omissions of national contingents violate a human rights treaty that their State has ratified and such acts or omissions have detrimental effect, then the contributing State will be required to provide reparation. The establishment of such links becomes all the more important given some of the challenges stemming from establishing responsibility for internationally wrongful acts or omissions on the part of International Organisations generally, and in relation to the UN particularly.

State acts and/or omissions as an aspect of State Responsibility raises the question of what acts or omissions would, in fact, comprise such a breach. It is at this point that the normative content of economic and social rights and their ensuing obligations, as elaborated in Chapter 1 and, more particularly in terms of the current analysis, Chapter 4, take on particular significance. In short, a failure to take deliberate, concrete and targeted steps towards the progressive realisation of economic and social rights would comprise a violation of the contributing States' obligations. However, in the interim, such States are also required to realise effectively their minimum core obligations, a requirement that takes into account the resource constraints in the exercise of any extraterritorial jurisdiction that it may exercise. The rules on State Responsibility also provide some defences to States, but if the State is not able to establish any of the circumstances that preclude wrongfulness,[137] the State in question must then provide reparation for the injury

133 Ibid, Article 31(1).

134 Ibid, Article 2.

135 Ibid, Article 12.

136 *Difference Relating to Immunity from a Legal Process of a Special Rapporteur* (Advisory Opinion) [1999] ICJ Rep 62, para 62; *Application of the Convention on the Prevention and Punishment of the Crime of Genocide (Bosnia and Herzegovina v Serbia and Montenegro)* (Merits) [2007] ICJ Rep 43, para 385. See further, Tom Dannenbaum, 'Translating the Standard of Effective Control into a System of Effective Accountability: How Liability Should be Apportioned for Violations of Human Rights by Member State Troop Contingents Serving as United Nations Peacekeepers' (2010) 51(1) *Harvard International Law Journal* 113; and Kjetil Mujezinovic Larsen, *Human Rights Treaty Obligations of Peacekeepers* (Cambridge University Press, Cambridge 2012).

137 ILC (n 132), Chapter V.

caused.[138] In the context of this discussion, a State may be held to be responsible for a breach of the ICESCR's obligations to respect, protect and fulfil if it can be established that the breach can be attributed to the national contingent of a contributing State Party. The ICJ would have jurisdiction to hear such a case, but only if the State in breach and the injured State had accepted the jurisdiction of the Court.

For those States that have ratified it, the Optional Protocol to the ICESCR[139] provides a further avenue of accountability whereby individuals and groups may make a complaint that their rights under the ICESCR were violated, where such violations resulted in a clear disadvantage to the complainant(s) (unless the communication raises a serious issue of general importance).[140] When examining a communication, the Committee can take into account the reasonableness of the steps taken by the State Party bearing in mind the nature of States' obligations and non-discrimination (Article 2), the equal rights of men and women (Article 3) and the question of limitations (Article 4).[141]

The Optional Protocol provides three mechanisms for bringing complaints. One, Article 2 allows an individual or group of individuals under the jurisdiction of a State Party to bring a complaint. In practice, Article 3's requirement that all domestic remedies be exhausted as an aspect of the admissibility of the complaint could present a barrier to individuals or groups in a State where a peacekeeping operation has been deployed and who wish to bring a complaint against a contributing State(s). One solution to this problem is to require complainants to exhaust the effective remedies in the State in which the peacekeeping operation has been deployed.[142] Article 2 does allow a complaint to be brought on behalf of individuals or groups with their consent, or indeed without their consent, if the third party can justify acting without their consent. This aspect of the Protocol could allow a third party, such as an NGO, in the State alleged to have violated the Covenant to bring a complaint, an approach which could overcome some of the practical barriers faced by complainants themselves. The second mechanism is to be found in Article 10's provision for an inter-State communications procedure. This procedure is subject to the 'opt-in provision' of Article 10(1). Article 10 could allow States where peacekeeping operations are deployed to make a complaint that the contributing State is not fulfilling its (extraterritorial) obligations under the Covenant. Three, Article 11(2) provides for an inquiry procedure that is not framed by matters of jurisdiction or territory so that where the Committee receives reliable information, 'indicating grave or systematic violations by a State Party of any of the economic, social and cultural rights set forth in the Covenant',

138 Ibid, Part II, Chapter II.

139 Optional Protocol to the International Covenant on Economic, Social and Cultural Rights (adopted 10 December 2008, entered into force 5 May 2013) UNGA Res 117 (8 December 2008) UN Doc A/RES/63/117.

140 Ibid, Article 4.

141 Ibid, Article 8(4).

142 Alexandre Faite and Jeremie Labbe Grenier, 'Expert Meeting on Multinational Peace Operations: Applicability of International Humanitarian Law and International Human Rights Law to UN Mandated Forces' (Geneva, 11–12 December 2003) 85.

it shall invite that State Party to cooperate in the examination of the information and to submit observations with regard to the information concerned. Despite the high threshold associated with the requirement that such violations must be grave or systematic, this procedure allows the CESCR to receive information from a wide variety of sources, including from States that have neither ratified the ICESCR nor the Optional Protocol. In terms of 'remedies', where a violation of the ICESCR is found, the CESCR can make a recommendation for change with an invitation for the State Party concerned to advise the CESCR of any changes made within six months.[143] These three procedures comprise a further avenue by which alleged violations of economic and social rights can be examined in a sphere where there is scant jurisprudence on the extraterritorial obligations of the ICESCR.[144]

The elaboration of a framework of post-conflict obligations that recognises the importance of economic and social progress for all that draws from the framework of economic and social rights is important in its own right. However, the question of accountability is an important consideration because action that is not informed by some semblance of accountability can facilitate ill-judged peacebuilding and peacekeeping endeavours that undermine the credibility of the UN and contributing States and potentially undermine any gains made in maintaining peace and security.

5 Conclusion

The importance of civil and political, as well as economic and social, reconstruction aimed at addressing the root causes of war and building a sustainable peace is well recognised in theory, policy and law. *Jus post bellum* theory signals that the rights and responsibilities of parties to a conflict do not end at the conflict's termination but that such rights and obligations continue through the post-conflict phase. *Jus post bellum* theory neatly summarises the various considerations that inform the immediate post-conflict environment and related attempts to build a better state of peace. At the policy level, attempts to reconfigure peace and security to include positive peace and human security are evident. Consideration of the concepts of *jus post bellum*, positive peace and human security together provide a template of interrelated post-conflict objectives to be considered by the Security Council. Such a template clarifies that the Council must continue to strive towards a post-conflict environment that, at a minimum, goes further than restoring a level of security commensurate with that in existence prior to the exercise of its powers. Such security must encompass physical security at the level of the individual, the community and the State, but the Council must also facilitate the restoration, and rehabilitation, of a society, in economic and social terms and also in a manner that places the individual at its centre. The need to move beyond the *status quo* in case of potential threats to international stability, peace and security lies at the basis of

143 Optional Protocol ICESCR (n 139), Articles 9 and 12.
144 Breen (n 113), 81–82.

the expanding activity of International Organisations in post-conflict situations.[145] To such an understanding, it can be added that where the *status quo ante* was characterised by economic and social violence, there is a particular need to focus on positive peace and human security, a focus which should and, as Chapter 4 shows, can be imbued with protection of economic and social rights, rights which have equality and non-discrimination at their core. Imbuing post-conflict activity with economic and social rights on the part of the UN and contributing States can serve as a blueprint to avoid the damage caused to host States by ill-thought-out reconstruction activities and the consequent damage done to the credibility of peacekeepers and the UN. The question of accountability is a reminder that the Council operating as a UN entity must be mindful of its obligations stemming from the UN Charter's Purposes and Principles as well as those obligations stemming from its status as a collective of States bearing international legal obligations.

Peace and security, as reimagined in this chapter, provides the basis of a more nuanced approach on the part of the Security Council as it struggles to deal more effectively with the challenges to peace and security that are posed by post-conflict societies. For the Security Council, the ensuing proactive and holistic approach would indeed be challenging, as it would be expected that collective security responses would not only encompass more clear and specific obligations but would also be flexible enough to respond to different post-conflict situations. Nonetheless, the necessity for this kind of framework would appear to be all the more important given the suggestion that failed peacebuilding poses one of the worst risk factors for new wars, as between one-quarter and one-third of peace agreements ending civil wars collapse within five years, and that 'backlash violence' after a failed peace agreement is often worse than before an accord was reached.[146]

The Security Council's ability to respond dynamically to conflict and post-conflict situations must provide the room for an approach to peace and security that is informed by the needs of individuals and communities, as well as by the rights of individuals and the obligations of States and the international community. A more coherent approach drawing from *jus post bellum* theory, the Organisation's own policy documents, and the range of legal standards drawing from international, human rights law, and especially economic and social rights, would be beneficial because, despite its imperfections, the Council facilitates an insistence 'on collective oversight [which] reduces the likelihood of abuse and self-interested restructuring whilst increasing that likelihood that the "will of the people" and needs of international order will be taken into consideration'.[147] Imbuing the notion of peace and security with the notion of the creation and support of peace, so that it is more than the absence of conflict, and focusing on the individual as the major loser in conflict, allows for a more effective implementation of peace and security. In this regard, the Security Council has a responsibility to build positive peace, a peace that is inured with a life in larger freedom.

145 de Brabandere (n 4), 140.
146 Labonte (n 2), 215.
147 Bellamy (n 17), 623.

Conclusion

This work aims to refocus efforts to maintain international peace and security by emphasising the economic and social dimensions of conflict and peace. It advances the argument that economic and social progress and development is not solely a matter of charity, social welfare or development aid. Rather, such efforts should be underpinned by human rights, particularly economic and social rights, so as to legitimise the priority that must be given to ensuing improved economic and social conditions for all in post-conflict societies.

Economic and social rights have suffered from an unwarranted lack of credibility for much of their history to date. Some of this perceived lack of credibility has been driven by a lack of rigorous academic and legal analysis of the rights and obligations emanating from the ICESCR. Adherence to political values reflecting an unwillingness to embrace the economic and social policy implications, stemming from even the core minimum rights and obligations, has further compounded this perceived lack of credibility. However, the reality is that the failure to deliver the goods and services that advance economic and social rights can have economic, social, political and security consequences. Systematic social and economic exclusion, which also comprises violations of the fundamental principles of equality and non-discrimination that underpin human rights law, can lead to an increase in the likelihood of civil conflict, or that conflict will resume, particularly in fragile States and those which are transitioning from conflict. This increased recognition overlaps with the emergence of a detailed elaboration of the content of economic and social rights, and an equally detailed elaboration of the ensuing obligations for States.

The impact of the State's failure to deliver basic goods and services that satisfy immediate physical needs and which serve as a conduit for accessing the full spectrum of human rights is not always confined to its own borders. International law and policy on peacebuilding and peacekeeping recognise the need to combine peace and security and the promotion and protection of human rights in order to achieve a more sustainable peace. This broad approach to security and stability is increasingly permeating the relationship between the Security Council, the General Assembly and the ECOSOC as the Security Council discharges its responsibility to maintain international peace and security. The UN's peacebuilding and peacekeeping policies, as well as the Security Council's efforts in this regard, increasingly recognise that poor socio-economic conditions, where they reinforce economic, social and political marginalisation, have the potential to undermine the efforts of peacebuilders and peacekeepers. A further development is the recognition of the extraterritorial application of economic and social rights, which extends to States' contributions to peacekeeping operations. From this it can be concluded that contributing States' own behaviour must accord with these human rights standards. Consideration of the extraterritorial effect of contributing States' human rights obligations is one mechanism by which such behaviour can be measured. Together, both developments can inform States' efforts as they participate in peacekeeping operations and, to the extent that they are Member States of the UN, their efforts can inform that Organisation's efforts to maintain international peace and security. Going forward, this recalibrated view of peace and security can also serve to identify and inform legal obligations on the part of the UN as it deals increasingly with post-conflict societies wracked by internal conflict, conflicts that render questionable the narrow approaches to peace and security that have dominated that Organisation for most of its history.

Chapter 1 shows that the linking of socio-economic conditions to a peaceful order is not new, as theorists, and then States, through the adoption of law and policy, recognised the benefits of a healthy, educated and adequately remunerated workforce. Meeting such basic needs also served to defuse any threat to the social order posed by the disenfranchisement and economic exploitation of the poor. The benefits of international cooperation amongst States in technological, economic and social matters further encouraged States to improve the socio-economic conditions of their populations, improvements that were also driven by the impact of such measures upon efforts to maintain peace at the international level. The Covenant of the League of Nations was the first significant international effort to enshrine economic and social progress in international law. The UN Charter recognised social progress, international cooperation and the promotion and protection of human rights as its main tools to save succeeding generations from the scourge of war. The incorporation of these purposes and principles into the Charter was a first important step in establishing a very well-developed international legal framework for the realisation of economic and social rights since the middle of the 20th century. An introduction to some of the detailed content of economic and social rights and the concomitant obligations imposed upon ratifying States is important because it reveals what States must do and the type of behaviour that they must avoid. Not only that, the extent to which States are meeting their obligations is now measurable. These developments reaffirm that economic and social rights are real human rights that the Security Council, the General Assembly and the ECOSOC must promote and protect as part of the effort to advance economic and social progress and maintain international peace and security.

From the UN perspective, the triangular relationship between peace, social progress and development, and human rights demands that the Security Council, the General Assembly and the ECOSOC, as the Organisation's three pillars, work closely together. Such cooperation has a legal basis in the UN Charter, and Chapter 2 provides evidence of the extent to which such collaboration has taken place, as well as concern and resistance expressed by some members of the Security Council at the blurring of the roles of the three organs. Although such concerns should not be disregarded, sustainable peace requires coherence, sustained engagement, and coordination between the General Assembly, the Security Council and the ECOSOC. Moreover, the UN Charter allows the Security Council to draw from the expertise of these UN bodies charged with realising that Organisation's aim to promote economic and social progress, to give effective realisation to human rights and to save succeeding generations from the scourge of war. Increased and more effective usage of such mechanisms can only be to the advantage of the Security Council and the mechanisms themselves. The aim of Chapter 2 is to show that there is a legal basis for the adoption of a broader approach to the maintenance of international peace and security. Chapter 2 also shows that the statements of Security Council members, as well as decisions, presidential statements and resolutions of the Security Council as a UN body in its own right, recognise and even largely welcome this broader approach. This understanding of what comprises sustainable peace frames the role of the Council in peacebuilding and peacekeeping.

UN peacebuilding policy reflects the central role of economic and social progress and human rights to maintaining international peace and security. The Security Council's acceptance and elaboration of peacebuilding shows that the Security Council's approach to its own mandate to maintain international peace and security has evolved to include more proactive measures to advance economic and social development and human rights, not only as ends in themselves, but also as a means to prevent conflict. The shift towards peacebuilding and the logic of conflict prevention is significant because it shows that economic and social progress and development, with its overlap with human rights considerations, is being accorded a greater degree of significance by the Security Council. Because of their high visibility, peacekeeping operations are an important means by which the Security Council discharges its responsibility to maintain international peace and security. Peacekeeping mandates increasingly reveal requirements for peacekeepers to facilitate, or engage in, economic and social reconstruction and to prevent, monitor and report human rights abuses. If peacekeepers are the UN's most visible tool for conflict prevention, these developments are to be welcomed, but if peacekeepers are unable to adopt a broad view of peace and security, due to a lack of understanding and resourcing around the socio-economic dimensions of conflict and peace, their efforts will be, at best, less effective and, at worst, delegitimise the Security Council's most visible tool for conflict prevention. These types of concerns come at a time when peacebuilding and peacekeeping endeavours are subject to quite a degree of criticism because of their failure to prevent conflict and, on occasion, for reigniting a more bloody conflict. Chapter 3 points to the need to understand the particular role and contribution of economic and social rights to allow for a recalibration of peacebuilding and peacekeeping that more fully incorporates economic and social rights.

The integration of human rights into peacebuilding and peacekeeping can also be approached from a different perspective, which is the extraterritorial application of international human rights, including economic and social rights. Contributing States that have ratified the ICESCR incur a range of obligations to respect, to protect and to fulfil these rights. The use of economic and social rights indicators to measure the extent to which States are meeting their extraterritorial obligations in peacekeeping operations allows the identification of specific activities that may be undertaken by peacekeepers, which can then be viewed through the lens of specific rights. The outcome of this process permits an assessment of whether the activities of contributing States correlate with their obligations stemming from the extraterritorial application of economic and social rights. It also eases in recognition of the need to consider such rights as States plan their contribution to a peacekeeping operation, review that contribution and ultimately assess its success. The flexible, but still obligatory, language underpinning the protection and promotion of economic and social rights correlates with the need to recognise the different phases of a peace operation and the different requirements of each phase, particularly in complex peacekeeping operations. In this way, Chapter 4 makes two significant points. One, contributing States' efforts in peacekeeping operations may be circumscribed by their obligations stemming from economic and social rights, obligations that are measureable. Two, in terms of concerns at the current approach to peacebuilding and peacekeeping, which marginalises the impact of socio-economic conditions, giving effect to contributing States' obligations stemming from economic and social rights may help to recalibrate more broadly the understanding that is to be given to the peace that is to be built.

This work demonstrates the importance that is attached to meeting the challenges posed by post-conflict societies and that different approaches have been adopted to address the root causes of war and to build a sustainable peace. Many of these considerations have been considered by *jus post bellum* theory, which also addresses the various considerations that inform the immediate post-conflict environment and attempts to build a better state of peace. At the theoretical and policy level, attempts to reconfigure peace and security to include positive peace and human security are evident. A reimagined version of peace is one where peace is more than the absence of armed violence and is framed in terms of the absence of pervasive structural violence that facilitates economic and social insecurity amongst individuals. A reimagined security is one where security includes protection from hunger and disease, and takes account of the damage caused by sudden harmful disruptions to the patterns of everyday life. This type of insecurity is not to be ignored given that with the right set of circumstances, circumstances that are prevalent in a post-conflict society, such insecurity amongst individuals can lead to insecurity at the societal and State levels. This account of security as human security is also empowering for individuals and it allows them to make informed choices and to act on their own behalf. Decision-making that allows for informed participation by those affected by such decisions is likely to lead to a more enduring peace.

However, *jus post bellum* theory, like international human rights law, is State-centric and its development reflects the need to respond to international conflict. This leaves open the question of its relevance to an International Organisation, like the UN, which is increasingly responding to situations of internal conflict that threaten the peace. Chapter 5 provides a couple of responses to this question. One, *jus post bellum* theory is still important, especially for its account of the need to engage in post-conflict reconstruction and the setting of the parameters of such construction. Rehabilitation and reconstruction as an aspect of *jus post bellum* theory facilitates the significance to be attached to rebuild and improve socio-economic conditions. In this regard, the theory resonates with the approach of the UN and it could further inform the approach of the UN going towards building positive peace and ensuring human security. The Charter's provisions regarding the promotion and protection of human rights and the right to be free from non-discrimination, obligations that encompass the promotion and protection of economic and social rights, should bind the UN. Two, it is clear that the UN cannot act in an unfettered manner. As an International Organisation with international legal personality, the UN is subject to obligations (and rights), particularly those that identify the Organisation's Principles and Purposes, in accordance with the UN Charter. In addition, the UN is bound at a minimum by customary law and its prohibition of discrimination based on race. UN immunity from civil suit continues to be a matter of concern, which puts further focus on the accountability of contributing States for violations of human rights, and economic and social rights particularly. The international legal rules around State Responsibility and the complaints mechanism of the ICESCR are two means of examining States' behaviour. They are a tentative first start, perhaps held hostage by the need to maintain international good will amongst States. Imbuing the notion of peace and security with the notion of the creation and support of peace, so that it is more than the absence of conflict, and focusing on the individual as the major loser in conflict allows for a more effective implementation of peace and security. In this regard, the Security Council has a responsibility to build positive peace, a peace that is inured with the protection and promotion of economic and social rights and which facilitates a life in larger freedom.

Bibliography

Treaties and conventions

Charter of the United Nations (adopted 26 June 1945, entered into force 24 October 1945) 1 UNTS XVI.
Constitution of the International Labour Organisation (adopted 1 April 1919, entered into force 28 June 1919) 15 UNTS 40.
Convention on Privileges and Immunities of the United Nations (adopted 13 February 1946, entered into force 17 September 1946) 1 UNTS 15.
Convention on the Elimination of All Forms of Discrimination Against Women (adopted 18 December 1979, entered into force 3 September 1981) 1249 UNTS 13.
Convention on the Rights of Persons with Disabilities (adopted by UNGA Res 61/106 (24 January 2007) UN Doc A/RES/61/106, Annex 1, entered into force 3 May 2008).
Convention on the Rights of the Child (adopted 20 November 1989, entered into force 2 September 1990) 1577 UNTS 3.
Convention Relating to the Status of Refugees (adopted 28 July 1951, entered into force 22 April 1954) 189 UNTS 137.
Convention Relating to the Status of Stateless Persons (adopted 28 September 1954, entered into force 6 June 1960) 360 UNTS 117.
Convention Respecting the Laws and Customs of War on Land (Hague – IV) (signed 18 October 1907, entered into force 26 January 1910) (1907) 36 Stat. 2277.
Convention with Respect to the Laws and Customs of War on Land and its annex: Regulations Respecting the Laws and Customs of War on Land (Hague – II) (signed 29 July 1899, entered into force 4 September 1900) 32 Stat. 1803.
Covenant of the League of Nations (adopted 28 April 1919, entered into force 10 January 1920) 225 CTS 195.
Geneva Convention relative to the Protection of Civilian Persons in Time of War (signed 12 August 1949, entered into force 21 October 1950) 75 UNTS 287.
ILO No. 111 Convention Concerning Discrimination in Employment and Occupation (adopted 25 June 1958, entered into force 15 June 1960) 362 UNTS 31.
International Covenant on Civil and Political Rights (adopted 16 December 1966, entered into force 23 March 1976) 999 UNTS 171.
International Convention on the Elimination of All Forms of Racial Discrimination (adopted 7 March 1966, entered into force 4 January 1969) 660 UNTS 195.
International Convention on the Protection of the Rights of All Migrant Workers and Members of their Families (adopted 18 December 1990, entered into force 1 July 2003) 2220 UNTS 3.
International Covenant on Civil and Political Rights (adopted 16 December 1966, entered into force 23 March 1976) 999 UNTS 171.

International Covenant on Economic, Social and Cultural Rights (adopted 16 December 1966, entered into force 3 January 1976) 993 UNTS 3.

International Sanitary Convention (signed 3 December 1903, entered into force 6 April 1907) (1903) 35 Stat. 1770.

Minorities Treaty Between the Principal Allied and Associated Powers (The British Empire, France, Italy, Japan, and the United States) and Poland (signed 28 June 1919) 225 CTS 412.

Optional Protocol to the International Covenant on Economic, Social and Cultural Rights (adopted 10 December 2008, entered into force 5 May 2013) UNGA Res 117 (8 December 2008) UN Doc A/RES/63/117.

Protocol Additional to the Geneva Conventions of 12 August 1949, and relating to the Protection of Victims of Non-International Armed Conflicts (Protocol II) (adopted 8 June 1977, entered into force 7 December 1978) 1125 UNTS 609.

UNESCO Convention Against Discrimination in Education (adopted 14 December 1960, entered into force 22 May 1962) 1960 UNTS 429.

Vienna Convention on the Law of Treaties between States and International Organizations or between International Organizations (adopted 21 March 1986, not yet in force) 25 ILM 543.

International cases

Applicability of Article VI, Section 22, of the Convention on the Privileges and Immunities of the United Nations (Advisory Opinion) [1989] ICJ Rep 177.

Application of the Convention on the Prevention and Punishment of the Crime of Genocide (Bosnia and Herzegovina v Serbia and Montenegro) (Merits) [2007] ICJ Rep 43.

Armed Activities on the Territory of the Congo (DRC v Uganda) (Judgment) [2005] ICJ Rep 168.

Barcelona Traction, Light and Power Co Ltd (Belgium v Spain) (Second Phase) [1970] ICJ Rep 3.

Corfu Channel Case (Merits) (Judgment) [1949] ICJ Rep 4.

Difference Relating to Immunity from a Legal Process of a Special Rapporteur (Advisory Opinion) [1999] ICJ Rep 62.

Effect of Awards of Compensation Made by the United Nations Administrative Tribunal (Advisory Opinion) [1954] ICJ Rep 47.

Incident at Lockerbie (Libyan Arab Jamahiriya v United Kingdom) (Provisional Measures) [1992] ICJ Rep 3.

Interpretation of the Agreement of 25 March 1951 between the WHO and Egypt (Advisory Opinion) [1980] ICJ Rep 73.

Legal Consequences for States of the Continued Presence of South Africa in Namibia (South-West Africa) Notwithstanding Security Council Resolution 276 (1970) (Advisory Opinion) [1971] ICJ Rep 16.

Legal Consequences of the Construction of a Wall (Advisory Opinion) [2004] ICJ Rep 136.

Military and Paramilitary Activities in and against Nicaragua (Nicaragua v USA) (Merits) (Judgment) [1986] ICJ Rep 14.

Minority Schools in Albania (Advisory Opinion) PCIJ Rep Series A/B No. 64.

Questions of Interpretation and Application of the 1971 Montreal Convention arising from the Aerial Incident at Lockerbie (Libyan Arab Jamahiriya v United Kingdom) (Provisional Measures) [1992] ICJ Rep 3.

Rights of Minorities in Upper Silesia (Minority Schools) (1928) PCIJ Series A no 15.
Reparation for Injuries Suffered in the Service of the United Nations (Advisory Opinion) [1949] ICJ Rep 174.
South-West Africa Cases (Ethiopia v South Africa; Liberia v South Africa) (Second Phase) [1966] ICJ Rep 6.

United Nations General Assembly resolutions

UNGA Res 67/301 (16 September 2013) UN Doc A/RES/67/301.
UNGA Res 67/293 (24 July 2013) UN Doc A/RES/67/293.
UNGA Res 66/297 (17 September 2012) UN Doc A/RES/66/297.
UNGA Res 65/310 (19 July 2011) UN Doc A/RES/65/310.
UNGA Res 65/290 (30 June 2011) UN Doc A/RES/65/290.
UNGA Res 63/304 (23 July 2009) UN Doc A/RES/63/304.
UNGA Res 62/275 (11 September 2008) UN Doc A/RES/62/275.
UNGA Res 60/251 (15 March 2006) UN Doc A/RES/60/251.
UNGA Res 60/165 (2 March 2006) UN Doc A/RES/60/165.
UNGA Res 60/180 (30 December 2005) UN Doc A/RES/60/180.
UNGA Res 57/337 (3 July 2003) UN Doc A/RES/57/337.
UNGA Res 55/217 (21 December 2000) UN Doc A/RES/55/217.
UNGA Res 53/71 (4 December 1998) UN Doc A/RES/53/71.
UNGA Res 51/55 (10 December 1996) UN Doc A/RES/51/55.
UNGA Res 48/141 (20 December 1993) UN Doc A/RES/48/141.
UNGA Res 48/42 (10 December 1993) UN Doc A/RES/48/42.
UNGA Res 47/72 (14 December 1992) UN Doc A/RES/47/72.
UNGA Res 47/71 (14 December 1992) UN Doc A/RES/47/71.
UNGA Res 32/130 (16 December 1977) UN Doc A/RES/32/130.
UNGA Res 2200A (XXI) (16 December 1966) UN Doc A/RES/21/2200.
UNGA Res 1000 (5 November 1956) UN Doc 1000.
UNGA Res 998 (4 November 1956) UN Doc 998.
UNGA Res 997 (2 November 1956) UN Doc 997.

Other UNGA resolutions

UNGA, 'Resolution Adopted by the Human Rights Council: Special Rapporteur on the Promotion of Truth, Justice, Reparation and Guarantees of Non-Recurrence 18/7' (2011) UN Doc A/HRC/RES/18/7.
UNGA, '2005 World Summit Outcome 60/L.1' (2005) UN Doc A/60/L.1.
Universal Declaration of Human Rights (adopted 10 December 1948) UNGA Res 217 A(III).

Reports of the Secretary-General to the UNGA/UNSC

UNGA, 'Report of the Secretary-General 2015/682' (2015) UN Doc A/70/357-S/2015/682.
UNGA, 'Report of the Secretary-General 69/642' (2014) UN Doc A/69/642.
UNGA, 'Report of the Secretary-General 68/652' (2013) UN Doc A/68/652.
UNGA, 'Report of the Secretary-General 64/633' (2010) UN Doc A/64/633.

UNGA, 'Report of the Secretary-General 63/677' (2009) UN Doc A/63/677.
UNGA, 'Report of the Secretary-General 61/858' (2007) UN Doc A/61/858.
UNGA, 'Report of the Secretary-General 2006/145' (2006) UN Doc A/60/712-S/2006/145.
UNGA, 'Report of the Secretary-General 60/696' (2005) UN Doc A/60/696.
UNGA, 'Report of the Secretary-General 59/2005' (2005) UN Doc A/59/2005.
UNGA, 'Report of the Secretary-General 57/387' (2002) UN Doc A/57/387.
UNGA, 'Report of the Secretary-General 2002/278' (2002) UN Doc A/56/875-S/2002/278.
UNGA, 'Report of the Secretary-General 2001/574' (2001) UN Doc A/55/985-S/2001/574.
UNGA, 'Report of the Secretary-General 54/2000' (2000) UN Doc A/54/2000.
UNGA, 'Report of the Secretary-General 1998/318' (1998) UN Doc A/52/871-S/1998/318.
UNGA, 'Report of the Secretary-General 24111' (1995) UN Doc S/24111.
UNGA, 'Report of the Secretary-General 1995/1' (1995) UN Doc A/50/60-S/1995/1.
UNGA, 'Report of the Secretary-General 25944' (1993) UN Doc S/25944.
UNGA, 'Report of the Secretary-General 24111' (1992) UN Doc A/47/277-S/24111.

Other reports to the UNGA

UNGA, 'Final Draft of the Guiding Principles on Extreme Poverty and Human Rights, Submitted by the Special Rapporteur on Extreme Poverty and Human Rights, Magdalena Sepúlveda Carmona 21/39' (2012) UN Doc A/HRC/21/39.
UNGA, 'Interim Report of the Special Rapporteur on the Right to Food 68/288' (2013) UN Doc A/68/288.
UNGA, 'Report of the High-level Independent Panel on Peace Operations on Uniting Our Strengths for Peace: Politics, Partnership and People 2015/446' (2015) UN Doc A/70/95-S/2015/446.
UNGA, 'Report of the Human Rights Committee on Iraq' (1991) UN Docs A/46/40 and CCPR/C/SR.1080–1082.
UNGA, 'Report of the Panel on United Nations Peace Operations 2000/809' (2000) UN Doc A/55/305-S/2000/809.
UNGA, 'Report of the Special Rapporteur on Extreme Poverty and Human Rights, Philip Alston' (2016) Advance Unedited Version A/71/40823.
UNGA, 'Report of the Special Rapporteur on the Human Right to Safe Drinking Water and Sanitation, Catarina de Albuquerque 27/55' (2014) UN Doc A/HRC/27/55.
UNGA, 'Report of the Special Rapporteur on the Human Right to Safe Drinking Water and Sanitation 68/264' (2013) UN Doc A/68/264.
UNGA, 'Report of the Special Rapporteur on the Promotion of Truth, Justice, Reparation and Guarantees of Non-recurrence, Pablo de Greiff 21/46' (2012) UN Doc A/HRC/21/46.
UNGA, 'Report of the Special Rapporteur on the Promotion of Truth, Justice, Reparation and Guarantees of Non-Recurrence, Pablo de Greiff 30/42' (2015) UN Doc A/HRC/30/42.

UNGA, 'Report of the Special Rapporteur on the Right of Everyone to the Enjoyment of the Highest Attainable Standard of Physical and Mental Health, Paul Hunt, Addendum, Missions to the World Bank and the International Monetary Fund in Washington, D.C. (20 October 2006) and Uganda (4–7 February 2007) 7/11' (2008) UN Doc A/HRC/7/11/Add.2.

UNGA, 'Report of the Special Rapporteur on the Right to Education, Vernor Muñoz 8/10' (2008) UN Doc A/HRC/8/10.

UNGA, 'Report of the Special Rapporteur on the Right to Food, Jean Ziegler 7/5' (2008) UN Doc A/HRC/7/5.

United Nations Security Council Resolutions

UNSC Res 2282 (27 April 2016) UN Doc S/RES/2282.

UNSC Res 2272 (11 March 2016) UN Doc S/RES/2272.

UNSC Res 2267 (26 February 2016) UN Doc S/RES/2267.

UNSC Res 2248 (12 November 2015) UN Doc S/RES/2248.

UNSC Res 2243 (14 October 2015) UN Doc S/RES/2243.

UNSC Res 2233 (29 July 2015) UN Doc S/RES/2233.

UNSC Res 2226 (25 June 2015) UN Doc S/RES/2226.

UNSC Res 2223 (28 May 2015) UN Doc S/RES/2223.

UNSC Res 2217 (28 April 2015) UN Doc S/RES/2217.

UNSC Res 2213 (27 March 2015) UN Doc S/RES/2213.

UNSC Res 2210 (16 March 2015) UN Doc S/RES/2210.

UNSC Res 2203 (18 February 2015) UN Doc S/RES/2203.

UNSC Res 2190 (15 December 2014) UN Doc S/RES/2190.

UNSC Res 2189 (12 December 2014) UN Doc S/RES/2189.

UNSC Res 2180 (14 October 2014) UN Doc S/RES/2180.

UNSC Res 2173 (27 August 2014) UN Doc S/RES/2173.

UNSC Res 2171 (21 August 2014) UN Doc S/RES/2171.

UNSC Res 2169 (30 July 2014) UN Doc S/RES/2169.

UNSC Res 2164 (25 June 2014) UN Doc S/RES/2164.

UNSC Res 2157 (29 May 2014) UN Doc S/RES/2157.

UNSC Res 2158 (29 May 2014) UN Doc S/RES/2158.

UNSC Res 2149 (10 April 2014) UN Doc S/RES/2149.

UNSC Res 2147 (28 March 2014) UN Doc S/RES/2147.

UNSC Res 2144 (14 March 2014) UN Doc S/RES/2144.

UNSC Res 2137 (13 February 2014) UN Doc S/RES/2137.

UNSC Res 2121 (10 October 2013) UN Doc S/RES/2121.

UNSC Res 2119 (10 October 2013) UN Doc S/RES/2119.

UNSC Res 2116 (18 September 2013) UN Doc S/RES/2116.

UNSC Res 2112 (30 July 2013) UN Doc S/RES/2112.

UNSC Res 2110 (24 July 2013) UN Doc S/RES/2110.

UNSC Res 2103 (22 May 2013) UN Doc S/RES/2103.

UNSC Res 2102 (2 May 2013) UN Doc S/RES/2102.

UNSC Res 2100 (25 April 2013) UN Doc S/RES/2100.

UNSC Res 2099 (25 April 2013) UN Doc S/RES/2099.

UNSC Res 2097 (26 March 2013) UN Doc S/RES/2097.

UNSC Res 2086 (21 January 2013) UN Doc S/RES/2086.

UNSC Res 2090 (13 February 2013) UN Doc S/RES/2090.
UNSC Res 2088 (24 January 2013) UN Doc S/RES/2088.
UNSC Res 2085 (20 December 2012) UN Doc S/RES/2085.
UNSC Res 2070 (12 October 2012) UN Doc S/RES/2070.
UNSC Res 2066 (17 September 2012) UN Doc S/RES/2066.
UNSC Res 2065 (12 September 2012) UN Doc S/RES/2065.
UNSC Res 2063 (31 July 2012) UN Doc S/RES/2063.
UNSC Res 2061 (25 July 2012) UN Doc S/RES/2061.
UNSC Res 2037 (23 February 2012) UN Doc S/RES/2037.
UNSC Res 2030 (21 December 2011) UN Doc S/RES/2030.
UNSC Res 2014 (21 October 2011) UN Doc S/RES/2014.
UNSC Res 2012 (14 October 2011) UN Doc S/RES/2012.
UNSC Res 2008 (16 September 2011) UN Doc S/RES/2008.
UNSC Res 2003 (29 July 2011) UN Doc S/RES/2003.
UNSC Res 2001 (28 July 2011) UN Doc S/RES/2001.
UNSC Res 2000 (27 July 2011) UN Doc S/RES/2000.
UNSC Res 1998 (12 July 2011) UN Doc S/RES/1998.
UNSC Res 1996 (8 July 2011) UN Doc S/RES/1996.
UNSC Res 1983 (7 June 2011) UN Doc S/RES/1983.
UNSC Res 1979 (27 April 2011) UN Doc S/RES/1979.
UNSC Res 1974 (22 March 2011) UN Doc S/RES/1974.
UNSC Res 1973 (17 March 2011) UN Doc S/RES/1973.
UNSC Res 1969 (24 February 2011) UN Doc S/RES/1969.
UNSC Res 1959 (16 December 2010) UN Doc S/RES/1959.
UNSC Res 1949 (23 November 2010) UN Doc S/RES/1949.
UNSC Res 1947 (29 October 2010) UN Doc S/RES/1947.
UNSC Res 1944 (14 October 2010) UN Doc S/RES/1944.
UNSC Res 1941 (29 September 2010) UN Doc S/RES/1941.
UNSC Res 1938 (15 September 2010) UN Doc S/RES/1938.
UNSC Res 1936 (5 August 2010) UN Doc S/RES/1936.
UNSC Res 1927 (4 June 2010) UN Doc S/RES/1927.
UNSC Res 1917 (22 March 2010) UN Doc S/RES/1917.
UNSC Res 1908 (19 January 2010) UN Doc S/RES/1908.
UNSC Res 1902 (17 December 2009) UN Doc S/RES/1902.
UNSC Res 1894 (11 November 2009) UN Doc S/RES/1894.
UNSC Res 1892 (13 October 2009) UN Doc S/RES/1892.
UNSC Res 1885 (15 September 2009) UN Doc S/RES/1885.
UNSC Res 1883 (7 August 2009) UN Doc S/RES/1883.
UNSC Res 1876 (26 June 2009) UN Doc S/RES/1876.
UNSC Res 1868 (23 March 2009) UN Doc S/RES/1868.
UNSC Res 1867 (26 February 2009) UN Doc S/RES/1867.
UNSC Res 1840 (14 October 2008) UN Doc S/RES/1840.
UNSC Res 1836 (29 September 2008) UN Doc S/RES/1836.
UNSC Res 1830 (7 August 2008) UN Doc S/RES/1830.
UNSC Res 1806 (20 March 2008) UN Doc S/RES/1806.
UNSC Res 1802 (25 February 2008) UN Doc S/RES/1802.
UNSC Res 1798 (30 January 2008) UN Doc S/RES/1798.
UNSC Res 1791 (19 December 2007) UN Doc S/RES/1791.
UNSC Res 1780 (15 October 2007) UN Doc S/RES/1780.

UNSC Res 1770 (10 August 2007) UN Doc S/RES/1770.
UNSC Res 1769 (31 July 2007) UN Doc S/RES/1769.
UNSC Res 1746 (23 March 2007) UN Doc S/RES/1746.
UNSC Res 1745 (22 February 2007) UN Doc S/RES/1745.
UNSC Res 1743 (15 February 2007) UN Doc S/RES/1743.
UNSC Res 1707 (12 September 2006) UN Doc S/RES/1707.
UNSC Res 1702 (15 August 2006) UN Doc S/RES/1702.
UNSC Res 1674 (28 April 2006) UN Doc S/RES/1674.
UNSC Res 1662 (23 March 2006) UN Doc S/RES/1662.
UNSC Res 1659 (15 February 2006) UN Doc S/RES/1659.
UNSC Res 1658 (14 February 2006) UN Doc S/RES/1658.
UNSC Res 1645 (20 December 2005) UN Doc S/RES/1645.
UNSC Res 1646 (20 December 2005) UN Doc S/RES/1646.
UNSC Res 1640 (23 November 2005) UN Doc S/RES/1640.
UNSC Res 1625 (14 September 2005) UN Doc S/RES/1625.
UNSC Res 1608 (22 June 2005) UN Doc S/RES/1608.
UNSC Res 1599 (28 April 2005) UN Doc S/RES/15999.
UNSC Res 1580 (22 December 2004) UN Doc S/RES/1580.
UNSC Res 1576 (29 November 2004) UN Doc S/RES/1576.
UNSC Res 1543 (14 May 2004) UN Doc S/RES/1543.
UNSC Res 1542 (30 April 2004) UN Doc S/RES/1542.
UNSC Res 1528 (27 February 2004) UN Doc S/RES/1528.
UNSC Res 1511 (16 October 2003) UN Doc S/RES/1511.
UNSC Res 1509 (19 September 2003) UN Doc S/RES/1509.
UNSC Res 1500 (14 August 2003) UN Doc S/RES/1500.
UNSC Res 1483 (22 May 2003) UN Doc S/RES/1483.
UNSC Res 1419 (26 June 2002) UN Doc S/RES/1419.
UNSC Res 1401 (28 March 2002) UN Doc S/RES/1401.
UNSC Res 2041 (22 March 2002) UN Doc S/RES/2041.
UNSC Res 1378 (14 November 2001) UN Doc S/RES/1378.
UNSC Res 1366 (30 August 2001) UN Doc S/RES/1366.
UNSC Res 1346 (30 March 2001) UN Doc S/RES/1346.
UNSC Res 1320 (15 September 2000) UN Doc S/RES/1320.
UNSC Res 1312 (31 July 2000) UN Doc S/RES/1312.
UNSC Res 1279 (30 November 1999) S/RES/1279.
UNSC Res 1272 (25 October 1999) UN Doc S/RES/1272.
UNSC Res 1267 (15 October 1999) UN Doc S/RES/1267
UNSC Res 1244 (10 June 1999) UN Doc S/RES/1244.
UNSC Res 1233 (6 April 1999) UN Doc S/RES/1233.
UNSC Res 1230 (26 February 1999) UN Doc S/RES/1230.
UNSC Res 1212 (25 November 1998) UN Doc S/Res/1212.
UNSC Res 1170 (28 May 1998) UN Doc S/RES/1170.
UNSC Res 1127 (28 August 1997) UN Doc S/RES/1127
UNSC Res 1034 (21 December 1995) UN Doc S/RES/1034.
UNSC Res 955 (8 November 1994) UN Doc S/RES/955.
UNSC Res 935 (1 July 1994) UN Doc S/RES/935.
UNSC Res 925 (8 June 1994) UN Doc S/RES/925.
UNSC Res 917 (6 May 1994) UN Doc S S/RES/917.
UNSC Res 841 (16 June 1993) UN Doc S/RES/841.

UNSC Res 794 (3 December 1992) UN Doc S/RES/794.
UNSC Res 788 (19 November 1992) UN Doc S/RES/788.
UNSC Res 787 (16 November 1992) UN Doc S/RES/787.
UNSC Res 757 (30 May 1992) UN Doc S/RES/757.
UNSC Res 733 (23 January 1992) UN Doc S/RES/733.
UNSC Res 713 (25 September 1991) UN Doc S/RES/713.
UNSC Res 688 (5 April 1991) UN Doc S/RES/688.
UNSC Res 406 (25 May 1977) UN Doc S/Res/406.
UNSC Res 402 (22 December 1976) UN Doc S/Res/402.
UNSC Res 386 (17 March 1976) UN Doc S/Res/386.
UNSC Res 329 (10 March 1973) UN Doc S/Res/329.
UNSC Res 146 (9 August 1960) UN Doc S/4426.
UNSC Res 145 (22 July 1960) UN Doc S/4405.
UNSC Res 143 (14 July 1960) UN Doc S/4387.

United Nations Security Council Verbatim Records

UNSC Verbatim Record (22 December 2015) UN Doc S/PV.7596.
UNSC Verbatim Record (10 December 2015) UN Doc S/PV.7575.
UNSC Verbatim Record (20 October 2015) UN Doc S/PV.7539.
UNSC Verbatim Record (20 October 2015) UN Doc S/PV.7539 (Resumption 1).
UNSC Verbatim Record (6 March 2015) UN Doc S/PV.7400.
UNSC Verbatim Record (19 January 2015) UN Doc S/PV.7361.
UNSC Verbatim Record (22 December 2014) UN Doc S/PV.7352.
UNSC Verbatim Record (22 December 2014) UN Doc S/PV.7353.
UNSC Verbatim Record (23 October 2014) UN Doc S/PV.7285.
UNSC Verbatim Record (28 August 2014) UN Doc S/PV.7254.
UNSC Verbatim Record (21 August 2014) UN Doc S/PV.7247.
UNSC Verbatim Record (2 May 2014) UN Doc S/PV.7168.
UNSC Verbatim Record (16 April 2014) UN Doc S/PV.7157.
UNSC Verbatim Record (12 February 2014) UN Doc S/PV.7109.
UNSC Verbatim Record (29 October 2013) UN Doc S/PV.7052.
UNSC Verbatim Record (29 October 2013) UN Doc S/PV.7052 (Resumption 1).
UNSC Verbatim Record (19 August 2013) UN Doc S/PV.7019.
UNSC Verbatim Record (17 July 2013) UN Doc S/PV.7003.
UNSC Verbatim Record (17 July 2013) UN Doc S/PV.7003 (Resumption 1).
UNSC Verbatim Record (19 June 2013) UN Doc S/PV.6982.
UNSC Verbatim Record (19 June 2013) UN Doc S/PV.6982 (Resumption 1).
UNSC Verbatim Record (17 April 2013) UN Doc S/PV.6948.
UNSC Verbatim Record (12 February 2013) UN Doc S/PV.6917.
UNSC Verbatim Record (12 February 2013) UN Doc S/PV.6917 (Resumption 1).
UNSC Verbatim Record (26 November 2012) UN Doc S/PV.6870.
UNSC Verbatim Record (25 June 2012) UN Doc S/PV.6790.
UNSC Verbatim Record (25 June 2012) UN Doc S/PV.6790 (Resumption 1).
UNSC Verbatim Record (16 May 2012) UN Doc S/PV.6772.
UNSC Verbatim Record (25 January 2012) UN Doc S/PV.6707.
UNSC Verbatim Record (30 November 2011) UN Doc S/PV.6672.
UNSC Verbatim Record (30 November 2011) UN Doc S/PV.6672 (Resumption 1).

UNSC Verbatim Record (9 November 2011) UN Doc S/PV.6650.
UNSC Verbatim Record (9 November 2011) UN Doc S/PV.6650 (Resumption 1).
UNSC Verbatim Record (28 October 2011) UN Doc S/PV.6642.
UNSC Verbatim Record (7 June 2011) UN Doc S/PV.6547.
UNSC Verbatim Record (10 May 2011) UN Doc S/PV.6531.
UNSC Verbatim Record (10 May 2011) UN Doc S/PV.6531 (Resumption 1).
UNSC Verbatim Record (11 February 2011) UN Doc S/PV.6479.
UNSC Verbatim Record (11 February 2011) UN Doc S/PV.6479 (Resumption 1).
UNSC Verbatim Record (22 November 2010) UN Doc S/PV.6427.
UNSC Verbatim Record (22 November 2010) UN Doc S/PV.6427 (Resumption 1).
UNSC Verbatim Record (26 October 2010) UN Doc S/PV.6411.
UNSC Verbatim Record (23 September 2010) UN Doc S/PV.6389.
UNSC Verbatim Record (16 July 2010) UN Doc S/PV.6360 (Resumption 1).
UNSC Verbatim Record (7 July 2010) UN Doc S/PV.6354.
UNSC Verbatim Record (7 July 2010) UN Doc S/PV.6354 (Resumption 1).
UNSC Verbatim Record (22 April 2010) UN Doc S/PV.6300.
UNSC Verbatim Record (22 April 2010) UN Doc S/PV. 6300 (Resumption 1).
UNSC Verbatim Record (16 April 2010) UN Doc S/PV.6299.
UNSC Verbatim Record (16 April 2010) UN Doc S/PV.6299 (Resumption 1).
UNSC Verbatim Record (29 April 2009) UN Doc S/PV.6114.
UNSC Verbatim Record (29 April 2009) UN Doc S/PV.6114 (Resumption 1).
UNSC Verbatim Record (5 October 2009) UN Doc S/PV.6196 (Resumption 1).
UNSC Verbatim Record (21 April 2009) UN Doc S/PV.6108 (Resumption 1).
UNSC Verbatim Record (11 November 2009) UN Doc S/PV.6216.
UNSC Verbatim Record (11 November 2009) UN Doc S/PV.6216 (Resumption 1).
UNSC Verbatim Record (29 October 2008) UN Doc S/PV.6005.
UNSC Verbatim Record (21 October 2008) UN Doc S/PV.5997.
UNSC Verbatim Record (29 September 2008) UN Doc S/PV.5986.
UNSC Verbatim Record (27 August 2008) UN Doc S/PV.5968.
UNSC Verbatim Record (27 August 2008) UN Doc S/PV.5968 (Resumption 1).
UNSC Verbatim Record (17 July 2008) UN Doc S/PV.5936.
UNSC Verbatim Record (17 July 2008) UN Doc S/PV.5936 (Resumption 1).
UNSC Verbatim Record (19 June 2008) UN Doc S/PV.5916.
UNSC Verbatim Record (27 May 2008) UN Doc S/PV.5898.
UNSC Verbatim Record (27 May 2008) UN Doc S/PV.5898 (Resumption 1).
UNSC Verbatim Record (20 May 2008) UN Doc S/PV.5895.
UNSC Verbatim Record (12 February 2008) UN Doc S/PV.5834 (Resumption 1).
UNSC Verbatim Record (17 October 2007) UN Doc S/PV.5761.
UNSC Verbatim Record (28 August 2007) UN Doc S/PV.5735.
UNSC Verbatim Record (25 June 2007) UN Doc S/PV.5705.
UNSC Verbatim Record (25 June 2007) UN Doc S/PV.5705 (Resumption 1).
UNSC Verbatim Record (22 June 2007) UN Doc S/PV.5703.
UNSC Verbatim Record (20 February 2007) UN Doc S/PV.5632 (Resumption 1).
UNSC Verbatim Record (31 January 2007) UN Doc S/PV.5627.
UNSC Verbatim Record (4 December 2006) UN Doc S/PV.5577.
UNSC Verbatim Record (4 December 2006) UN Doc S/PV.5577 (Resumption 1).
UNSC Verbatim Record (22 June 2006) UN Doc S/PV.5474.
UNSC Verbatim Record (22 June 2006) UN Doc S/PV.5474 (Resumption 1).
UNSC Verbatim Record (9 December 2005) UN Doc S/PV.5319 (Resumption 1).

UNSC Verbatim Record (21 June 2005) UN Doc S/PV.5209.
UNSC Verbatim Record (13 May 2005) UN Doc S/PV.5178.
UNSC Verbatim Record (12 January 2005) UN Doc S/PV.5110.
UNSC Verbatim Record (12 January 2005) UN Doc S/PV.5110 (Resumption 1).
UNSC Verbatim Record (14 December 2004) UN Doc S/PV.5100.
UNSC Verbatim Record (22 September 2004) UN Doc S/PV.5041.
UNSC Verbatim Record (14 June 2004) UN Doc S/PV.4990.
UNSC Verbatim Record (14 June 2004) UN Doc S/PV.4990 (Resumption 1).
UNSC Verbatim Record (28 May 2004) UN Doc S/PV.4980.
UNSC Verbatim Record (15 April 2004) UN Doc S/PV.4943.
UNSC Verbatim Record (26 January 2004) UN Doc S/PV.4903.
UNSC Verbatim Record (7 July 2003) UN Doc S/PV.4784.
UNSC Verbatim Record (13 February 2003) UN Doc S/PV.4705.
UNSC Verbatim Record (22 May 2002) UN Doc S/PV.4538.
UNSC Verbatim Record (23 April 2001) UN Doc S/PV.4312.
UNSC Verbatim Record (15 December 1999) UN Doc S/PV.4081.
UNSC Verbatim Record (15 December 1999) UN Doc S/PV.4081 (Resumption 1) and Corr.1.
UNSC Verbatim Record (16 December 1998) UN Doc S/PV.3954.
UNSC Verbatim Record (25 November 1998) UN Doc S/PV.3949.
UNSC Verbatim Record (18 January 1995) UN Doc S/PV.3492.
UNSC Verbatim Record (18 January 1995) UN Doc S/PV.3492 (Resumption 1).
UNSC Verbatim Record (19 January 1995) UN Doc S/PV.3492 (Resumption 2).
UNSC Verbatim Record (1 July 1994) UN Doc S/PV.3400.
UNSC Verbatim Record (8 June 1994) UN Doc S/PV.3388.
UNSC Verbatim Record (23 November 1992) UN Doc S/PV.3139.
UNSC Verbatim Record (13 November 1992) UN Doc S/PV.3134.
UNSC Verbatim Record (6 October 1992) UN Doc S/PV.3119.
UNSC Verbatim Record (11 August 1992) UN Doc S/PV.3105.
UNSC Verbatim Record (11 March 1992) UN Doc S/PV.3059.

United Nations Security Council Presidential Statements

UNSC Presidential Statement UN Doc 19 (2015) S/PRST/2015/19.
UNSC Presidential Statement UN Doc 5 (2015) S/PRST/2015/5.
UNSC Presidential Statement UN Doc 3 (2015) S/PRST/2015/3.
UNSC Presidential Statement UN Doc 2 (2015) S/PRST/2015/2.
UNSC Presidential Statement UN Doc 15 (2014) S/PRST/2014/15.
UNSC Presidential Statement UN Doc 6 (2014) S/PRST/2014/6.
UNSC Presidential Statement UN Doc 3 (2014) S/PRST/2014/3.
UNSC Presidential Statement UN Doc 2 (2014) S/PRST/2014/2.
UNSC Presidential Statement UN Doc 8 (2013) S/PRST/2013/8.
UNSC Presidential Statement UN Doc 29 (2012) S/PRST/2012/29.
UNSC Presidential Statement UN Doc 18 (2011) S/PRST/2011/18.
UNSC Presidential Statement UN Doc 17 (2011) S/PRST/2011/17.
UNSC Presidential Statement UN Doc 4 (2011) S/PRST/2011/4.
UNSC Presidential Statement UN Doc 2 (2011) S/PRST/2011/2.
UNSC Presidential Statement UN Doc 26 (2010) S/PRST/2010/26.
UNSC Presidential Statement UN Doc 20 (2010) S/PRST/2010/20.

UNSC Presidential Statement UN Doc 18 (2010) S/PRST/2010/18.
UNSC Presidential Statement UN Doc 15 (2010) S/PRST/2010/15.
UNSC Presidential Statement UN Doc 7 (2010) S/PRST/2010/7.
UNSC Presidential Statement UN Doc 2 (2010) S/PRST/2010/2.
UNSC Presidential Statement UN Doc 4 (2009) S/PRST/2009/4.
UNSC Presidential Statement UN Doc 22 (2007) S/PRST/2007/22.
UNSC Presidential Statement UN Doc 16 (2007) S/PRST/2007/16.
UNSC Presidential Statement UN Doc 3 (2007) S/PRST/2007/3.
UNSC Presidential Statement UN Doc 1 (2007) S/PRST/2007/1.
UNSC Presidential Statement UN Doc 42 (2006) S/PRST/2006/42.
UNSC Presidential Statement UN Doc 28 (2006) S/PRST/2006/28.
UNSC Presidential Statement UN Doc 39 (2005) S/PRST/2005/39.
UNSC Presidential Statement UN Doc 20 (2005) S/PRST/2005/20.
UNSC Presidential Statement UN Doc 40 (2004) S/PRST/2004/40.
UNSC Presidential Statement UN Doc 20 (2004) S/PRST/2004/20.
UNSC Presidential Statement UN Doc 2 (2002) S/PRST/2002/2.
UNSC Presidential Statement UN Doc 5 (2001) S/PRST/2001/5.
UNSC Presidential Statement UN Doc 3 (2001) S/PRST/2001/3.
UNSC Presidential Statement UN Doc 25 (2000) S/PRST/2000/25.
UNSC Presidential Statement UN Doc 34 (1999) S/PRST/1999/34.
UNSC Presidential Statement UN Doc 38 (1998) S/PRST/1998/38.
UNSC Presidential Statement UN Doc 29 (1998) S/PRST/1998/29.
UNSC Presidential Statement UN Doc 46 (1997) S/PRST/1997/46.

Supplements to the repertoire of the practice of the Security Council

Eleventh Supplement to the Repertoire of the Practice of the Security Council (1989–1992), Chapter VI, Part II(A).
Fourteenth Supplement to the Repertoire of the Practice of the Security Council (2000–2003), Chapter VI, Part I(B).
Sixteenth Supplement to the Repertoire of the Practice of the Security Council (2008–2009), Vol 1, Part I(2).

Other UNSC materials

Security Council Report, Arria-Formula Meetings (19 August 2016) <http://www.securitycouncilreport.org/un-security-council-working-methods/arria-formula-meetings.php> accessed 28 September 2016.
UNSC, 'Letter Dated 23 December 2013 from the President of the Security Council Addressed to the Secretary-General 2013/759' (2013) UN Doc S/2013/759.
UNSC, 'Letter Dated 19 December 2013 from the Secretary-General Addressed to the President of the Security Council 2013/753' (2013) UN Doc S/2013/753.
UNSC, 'Letter Dated 14 December 2010 from the Secretary-General to the President of the Security Council 2010/660' (2010) UN Doc S/2010/660.
UNSC, 'Letter Dated 28 November 2007 from the Secretary-General Addressed to the President of the Security Council 2007/753' (2007) UN Doc S/2007/753.

UNSC, 'Letter Dated 8 May 2003 from the Permanent Representatives of the United Kingdom of Great Britain and Northern Ireland and the United States of America to the United Nations Addressed to the President of the Security Council 2003/538' (2003) UN Doc S/2003/538.

UNSC, 'Letter Dated 26 November 2001 from the Secretary-General Addressed to the President of the Security Council 2001/1128' (2001) UN Doc S/2001/1128.

UNSC, 'Letter Dated 7 April 1999 from the President of the Security Council to the President of the Economic and Social Council' (9 April 1999) UN Doc E/1999/12-S/1999/403.

UNSC, 'Note by the President of the Security Council 24836' (1992) UN Doc S/24836.

UNSC, Provisional Rules of Procedure of the Security Council, S/96/Rev.7 (1982).

UNSC, 'Report of the Secretary-General and the Chairperson of the African Union Commission on the Hybrid Operation in Darfur 2007/307' (2007) UN Doc S/2007/307/Rev.1.

UNSC, 'Report of the Secretary-General 2004/616' (2004) UN Doc S/2004/616.

UNSC, 'Report of the Secretary-General 2001/394' (2001) UN Doc S/2001/394.

UNSC, 'Report of the Independent Inquiry into the Actions of the United Nations during the 1994 Genocide in Rwanda 1999/1257' (1999) UN Doc S/1999/1257.

UNSC, 'Statement by the President of the Security Council Concerning General and Specific Obligations of Iraq under Various Security Council Resolutions Relating to the Situation between Iraq and Kuwait' (11 March 1992) UN Doc S/23699.

United Nations Secretary-General sources

UNSG, Ban Ki-moon, 'Renewing our Commitment to the Peoples and Purposes of the United Nations' (UN Headquarters, 22 November 2013) <http://www.un.org/apps/news/infocus/sgspeeches/statments_full.asp?statid=2068#.v53yu-jdrlg> accessed 29 July 2016.

UNSG, 'Note of Guidance on Integrated Missions' (2006) <https://www.regjeringen.no/globalassets/upload/UD/Vedlegg/missions/sgnote.pdf> accessed 28 July 2016.

UNSG, 'Report of the Secretary-General, Collective Economic Security' (1974) UN Doc E/5529.

UNSG, 'Secretary-General Outlines Key Lessons for Building Peace in War-Torn Societies, in Lecture at University of Ulster' (18 October 2004) Press Release UN doc SG/SM/9549 <http://www.un.org/press/en/2004/sgsm9549.doc.htm> accessed 21 July 2016.

UNSG, 'Summary of "Human Rights Up Front"' (undated) <http://www.un.org/News/dh/pdf/english/2016/Human-Rights-up-Front.pdf> accessed 1 February 2017.

United Nations publications

Cravioto Alejando and others, 'Final Report of the Independent Panel of Experts on the Cholera Outbreak in Haiti' <http://www.un.org/News/dh/infocus/haiti/UN-cholera-report-final.pdf> accessed 12 October 2016.

United Nations, Repertory of Practice of United Nations Organs, *Extracts relating to Article 65 of the Charter of the United Nations: Repertory of Practice (1945–1954)*, vol 3.

United Nations, 'A More Secure World: Our Shared Responsibility, Report of the Secretary-General's High-level Panel on Threats, Challenges and Change' (2004) <http://www.un.org/en/peacebuilding/pdf/historical/hlp_more_secure_world.pdf> accessed 15 July 2016.

United Nations, 'Decisions of the Secretary-General – Policy Committee Meeting of 26 October: Decision No. 2005/24 – Human Rights in Integrated Missions' (26 October 2005).

United Nations, 'Report of the Secretary-General's Internal Review Panel on United Nations Action in Sri Lanka' (November 2012) <http://www.un.org/News/dh/infocus/Sri_Lanka/The_Internal_Review_Panel_report_on_Sri_Lanka.pdf> accessed 29 July 2016.

United Nations, 'The Challenge of Sustaining Peace. Report of the Advisory Group of Experts for the 2015 Review of the United Nations Peacebuilding Architecture' (29 June 2015) <http://www.un.org/en/peacebuilding/pdf/150630%20Report%20of%20the%20AGE%20on%20the%202015%20Peacebuilding%20Review%20FINAL.pdf> accessed 15 July 2016.

United Nations materials on human rights

CEDAW, 'General Recommendation 18, Disabled Women' in 'Compilation of General Comments and General Recommendations Adopted by Human Rights Treaty Bodies' (2003) UN Doc HRI/GEN/1/Rev.6.

CESCR, 'General Comment 1, Reporting by States Parties' in 'Compilation of General Comments and General Recommendations Adopted by Human Rights Treaty Bodies' (2003) UN Doc HRI/GEN/1/Rev.6.

CESCR, 'General Comment 2, International Technical Assistance Measures' in 'Compilation of General Comments and General Recommendations Adopted by Human Rights Treaty Bodies' (2003) UN Doc HRI/GEN/1/Rev.6.

CESCR, 'General Comment 3, The Nature of States Parties' Obligations' in 'Compilation of General Comments and General Recommendations adopted by Human Rights Treaty Bodies' (2003) UN Doc HRI/GEN/1/Rev.6.

CESCR, 'General Comment 5, Persons with Disabilities' in 'Compilation of General Comments and General Recommendations Adopted by Human Rights Treaty Bodies' (2003) UN Doc HRI/GEN/1/Rev.6.

CESCR, 'General Comment 8, The Relationship between Economic Sanctions and Respect for Economic, Social and Cultural Rights' in 'Compilation of General Comments and General Recommendations Adopted by Human Rights Treaty Bodies' (2003) UN Doc HRI/GEN/1/Rev.6.

CESCR, 'General Comment 9, The Domestic Application of the Covenant' in 'Compilation of General Comments and General Recommendations Adopted by Human Rights Treaty Bodies' (2003) UN Doc HRI/GEN/1/Rev.6.

CESCR, 'General Comment 10, The Role of National Human Rights Institutions in the Protection of Economic, Social and Cultural Rights' in 'Compilation of General Comments and General Recommendations Adopted by Human Rights Treaty Bodies' (2003) UN Doc HRI/GEN/1/Rev.6.

CESCR, 'General Comment 12, Right to Adequate Food' in 'Compilation of General Comments and General Recommendations Adopted by Human Rights Treaty Bodies' (2003) UN Doc HRI/GEN/1/Rev.6.

CESCR, 'General Comment 13' in 'Compilation of General Comments and General Recommendations Adopted by Human Rights Treaty Bodies' (1999) UN Doc E/C.12/1999/10.

CESCR, 'General Comment 14, The Right to the Highest Attainable Standard of Health' in 'Compilation of General Comments and General Recommendations Adopted by Human Rights Treaty Bodies' (2003) UN Doc HRI/GEN/1/Rev.6.

CESCR, 'General Comment 15, The Right to Water' in 'Compilation of General Comments and General Recommendations Adopted by Human Rights Treaty Bodies' (2003) UN Doc HRI/GEN/1/Rev.6.

CESCR, 'General Comment 18, Article 6: The Equal Right of Men and Women to the Enjoyment of all Economic, Social and Cultural Rights' (2006) UN Doc E/C.12/GC/18.

CESCR, 'General Comment 20, Non-Discrimination in Economic, Social and Cultural Rights (art. 2, para. 2)' (2009) UN Doc E/C.12/GC/20.

Chinkin Christine, *The Protection of Economic, Social and Cultural Rights Post Conflict* (Paper series commissioned by OHCHR, 2009) <www2.ohchr.org/english/issues/women/docs/Paper_Protection_ESCR.pdf> accessed 5 August 2016.

ECOSOC, 'Consultation with the World Jewish Congress' Res 214B (VIII) (16 Feb 1949).

ECOSOC, 'Letter Dated 16 February 1999 from the President of the Economic and Social Council to the President of the Security Council' (18 February 1999) UN Doc E/1999/7-S/1999/170.

ECOSOC, 'Note by the High Commissioner for Human Rights Transmitting to the Commission the Report of the Twelfth Meeting of Special Rapporteurs/Representatives, Independent Experts and Chairpersons of Working Groups of the Special Procedures of the CHR' (2005) UN Doc E/CN.4/2006/4.

HRC, 'Consideration of Reports Submitted by States Parties under Article 40 of the Covenant: Concluding Observations of the Human Rights Committee on Belgium' (12 August 2004) UN Doc CCPR/CO/81/BEL.

HRC, 'Consideration of Reports Submitted by States Parties under Article 40 of the Covenant: Concluding Observations of the Human Rights Committee on Germany' (4 May 2004) UN Doc CCPR/CO/80/DEU.

HRC, 'Consideration of Reports Submitted by States Parties under Article 40 of the Covenant: Concluding Observations of the Human Rights Committee on Israel' (3 September 2010) UN Doc CCPR/C/ISR/CO/3.

HRC, 'Consideration of Reports Submitted by States Parties under Article 40 of the Covenant: Concluding Observations of the Human Rights Committee on Poland' (2 December 2004) UN Doc CCPR/CO/82/POL.

HRC, 'General Comment 6, Article 6' in 'Compilation of General Comments and General Recommendations Adopted by Human Rights Treaty Bodies' (1994) UN Doc HRI/GEN/1/Rev.1.

HRC, 'General Comment 18, Non-Discrimination' in 'Compilation of General Comments and General Recommendations Adopted by Human Rights Treaty Bodies' (1994) UN Doc HRI/GEN/1/Rev.1.

HRC, 'General Comment 31, Nature of the General Legal Obligation on States Parties to the Covenant' (2004) UN Doc CCPR/C/21/Rev.1/Add.13.

OCHCR, 'Enhancing and Strengthening the Effectiveness of the Special Procedures of the Commission on Human Rights: An Open-Ended Seminar in Consultation with the Expanded Bureau of the Commission, as Part of the Effort to Enhance and Strengthen the Effectiveness of the Special Procedures' (Background Paper) HCR December 2005/113.

OHCHR, 'Human Rights Fact Sheet N.27: Seventeen Frequently Asked Questions about United Nations Special Rapporteurs' <http://www.ohchr.org/Documents/Publications/FactSheet27en.pdf> accessed 8 July 2016.

OHCHR, 'Human Rights Indicators: A Guide to Measurement and Implementation' (2012) UN Doc HR/PUB/12/5 <http://www.ohchr.org/Documents/Publications/Human_rights_indicators_en.pdf> accessed 25 August 2016.

OHCHR, 'OHCHR Management Plan 2014–2017 – Working for Your Rights' (2014) <http://www2.ohchr.org/english/OHCHRreport2014_2017/OMP_Web_version/media/pdf/0_THE_WHOLE_REPORT.pdf> accessed 29 July 2016.

OHCHR, 'Statement of the High Commissioner for Human Rights' 26th Session of the Human Rights Council (10 June 2014) <http://www.ohchr.org/EN/NewsEvents/Pages/DisplayNews.aspx?NewsID=14674&LangID=E> accessed 15 July 2016.

OHCHR, 'Report on Indicators for Promoting and Monitoring the Implementation of International Human Rights Instruments 2008/3' (2008) UN Doc HRI/MC/2008/3.

OHCHR, 'The Right to Life and the Right to Housing, Presentation to the Human Rights Committee, Special Rapporteur on Adequate Housing as a Component of the Right to an Adequate Standard of Living and on the Right to Non-Discrimination in this regard, Ms Leilani Farha' (Geneva, 11 July 2016) <http://www.ohchr.org/Documents/Issues/Housing/11072016_SR_Housing_Presentation-HR_Committee.pdf> accessed 3 October 2016.

OHCHR, *Transitional Justice and Economic, Social and Cultural Rights* (HR/PUB/13/5, United Nations, New York, Geneva 2014).

UNCERD, 'Concluding Observations of the Committee on the Elimination of Racial Discrimination: Israel' (2012) UN Doc CERD/C/ISR/CO/14–16.

UNCERD, 'Concluding Observations of the Committee on the Elimination of Racial Discrimination: Israel' (1998) UN Doc CERD/C/304/Add.45.

UNCERD, 'Concluding Observations of the Committee on the Elimination of Racial Discrimination: Georgia' (2011) UN Doc CERD/C/GEO/CO/4–5.

UNCERD, 'Concluding Observations of the Committee on the Elimination of Racial Discrimination: Guatemala' (1997) UN Doc CERD/C/304/Add.21.

UNCERD, 'Concluding Observations of the Committee on the Elimination of Racial Discrimination: Kyrgyzstan' (2013) UN Doc CERD/C/KGZ/CO/5–7.

UNCHR Res 10 (2000) UN Doc E/CN.4/RES/2000/10.

UNCHR, 'Annual Report of the Special Rapporteur on the Right to Education, Katarina Tomasevski, Submitted Pursuant to Commission on Human Rights Resolution 2001/99' (2002) UN Doc E/CN.4/2002/60.

UNCHR, 'Effective Functioning of Human Rights Mechanisms: National Institutions and Regional Arrangements' (2000) UN Doc E/CN.4/2002/WP3.

UNCHR, 'Note Verbale Dated 86/12/05 from the Permanent Mission of the Netherlands to the United Nations Office at Geneva Addressed to the Centre for Human Rights' (8 January 1987) UN Doc E/CN.4/1987/17, Annex ('the Limburg Principles') reprinted in (1987) 9(2) *Human Rights Quarterly* 122.

UNCHR, (Sub-Commission), 'Report by Special Rapporteur Danilo Turk 1990/19' (1990) UN Doc E/CN.4/Sub.2/1990/19.

UNCRC, 'Concluding Observations of the Committee on the Rights of the Child: Burundi' (2000) UN Doc CRC/C/15/Add.133.

UNCRC, 'Concluding Observations of the Committee on the Rights of the Child: Guatemala' (2010) UN Doc CRC/C/GTM/CO/3–4.

UNCRC, 'Concluding Observations of the Committee on the Rights of the Child: Guatemala' (1996) UN Doc CRC/C/15/Add.58.

UNCRC, 'Concluding Observations of the Committee on the Rights of the Child: Sudan' (2010) UN Doc CRC/C/SDN/CO/3–4.

UNCRC, 'General Comment 5, General Measures of Implementation of the Convention on the Rights of the Child (arts. 4, 42 and 44, para. 6)' (2003) UN Doc CRC/GC/2003/5.

UNESC, 'Consideration of Reports Submitted by States Parties under Articles 16 and 17 of the Covenant: Concluding Observations of the Committee on Economic, Social and Cultural Rights on Israel' (16 December 2011) UN Doc E/C.12/ISR/CO/3.

UNESC, 'Report of the Special Rapporteur on the Right to Food, Jean Ziegler 2006/44' (2006) UN Doc E/CN.4/2006/44.

UNESC, 'Revised General Guidelines Regarding the Form and Contents of Reports to be Submitted by States Parties under Articles 16 and 17 of the International Covenant on Economic, Social and Cultural Rights 1991/1' (1991) UN Doc E/C.12/1991/1.

UNHRC, 'Manual of Operations of the Special Procedures of the Human Rights Council' (August 2008) <http://www.ohchr.org/Documents/HRBodies/SP/Manual_August_2008.doc> accessed 8 July 2016.

United Nations, 'Daily Press Briefing by the Office of the Spokesperson for the Secretary-General' (18 August 2016) <http://www.un.org/press/en/2016/db160818.doc.htm> accessed 12 October 2016.

United Nations Department of Public Information (New York), 'Haiti Cholera Victims' Compensation Claims "Not Receivable" under Immunities and Privileges Convention, United Nations Tells Their Representatives' (21 February 2013) UN Doc SG/SM/14828.

Other international materials

Closing Plenary Session. The United Nations Conference on International Organization. San Francisco, June 26, 1945 (Washington DC, 1946).

Department of Peacekeeping Operations and Department of Field Support, 'A New Partnership Agenda Charting a New Horizon for UN Peacekeeping' (A Non-Paper, 2009) <http://www.un.org/en/peacekeeping/documents/newhorizon.pdf> accessed 21 July 2016

Department of Peacekeeping Operations and Department of Field Support, 'The United Nations Peacekeeping Operations: Principles and Guidelines' (2008) <http://www.un.org/en/peacekeeping/documents/capstone_eng.pdf> accessed 21 July 2016.

ETO Consortium, 'Maastricht Principles on Extraterritorial Obligations of States in the Area of Economic, Social and Cultural Rights' (FIAN International, Heidelberg 2013) <http://www.etoconsortium.org/nc/en/main-navigation/library/maastricht-principles/?tx_drblob_pi1%5BdownloadUid%5D=23> accessed 1 October 2016.

Faite Alexandre and Jeremie Labbe Grenier, 'Expert Meeting on Multinational Peace Operations: Applicability of International Humanitarian Law and International Human Rights Law to UN Mandated Forces' (Geneva, 11–12 December 2003) 83.

Great Britain Prime Minister, *The Atlantic Charter: The Full Text of the Declaration* (Whitcombe & Tombs, Christchurch 1942).

International Commission of Jurists, *Courts and the Legal Enforcement of Economic, Social and Cultural Rights: Comparative Experiences of Justiciability* (International Commission of Jurists, Geneva 2008).

International Commission on Intervention and State Sovereignty, 'The Responsibility to Protect: Report of the International Commission on Intervention and State Sovereignty' (International Development Research Centre, Ottawa 2001).

International Conference on Human Rights, 'Proclamation of Teheran, Final Act of the International Conference on Human Rights Teheran 22 April–13 May 1968' (1968) UN Doc A/CONF.32/41.

International Law Commission, 'Draft Articles on Responsibility of States for Internationally Wrongful Acts', 53 UN GAOR Supp. (No. 10) at 43, U.N. Doc. A/56/10 (2001).

International Law Commission, 'Draft Articles on the Responsibility of International Organizations, with Commentaries' (2011) II *Yearbook of the International Law Commission*.

MINUSTAH, 'MINUSTAH Background' <http://www.un.org/en/peacekeeping/missions/minustah/background.shtml> accessed 1 September 2016.

S W M Broeks v The Netherlands (Communication No. 172/1984) (1990) UN Doc CCPR/C/OP/2.

The Atlantic Charter (signed 14 August 1941) reprinted in *United States President (1933–1945: Roosevelt)*.

The Maastricht Guidelines on Violations of Economic, Social and Cultural Rights, Maastricht, 22–26 January 1997 ('the Maastricht Guidelines') reprinted in (1998) 20(3) *Human Rights Quarterly* 691.

United Nations, 'Decision No. 2012/18 – Human Rights Screening of United Nations Personnel' (11 December 2012) <http://repository.un.org/handle/11176/387395> accessed 7 October 2016.

United Nations, 'Secretariat' <http://www.un.org/en/sections/about-un/secretariat/> accessed 30 September 2016.

United Nations, 'Statement Attributable to the Spokesman for the Secretary-General on Haiti' <https://www.un.org/sg/en/content/sg/statement/2016-08-19/statement-attributable-spokesman-secretary-general-haiti> accessed 1 February 2017.

UNMIT, 'UNMIT Background' <http://www.un.org/en/peacekeeping/missions/past/unmit/background.shtml> accessed 1 September 2016.

Unpublished letter of 3 February 2004 by the United Nations Legal Counsel to the Director of the Codification Division, cited in International Law Commission, Report of the ILC, GA Official Records, 56th session, Supplement No. 10, 111, UN Doc. A/59/10 (2004).

UN Secretariat, 'Secretary-General's Bulletin: Observance by United Nations Forces of International Humanitarian Law' (6 August 1999) UN Doc ST/SGB/1999/13.

UNTAEF, 'Regulation 2001/10 on the Establishment of a Commission for Reception, Truth and Reconciliation in East Timor' (2001) UN Doc UNTAET/REG/2001/10.

World Conference on Human Rights, 'Vienna Declaration and Programme of Action' (1993) UN Doc A/CONF.157/23.

Regional treaties and agreements

Additional Protocol to the American Convention on Human Rights in the Area of Economic, Social and Cultural Rights (entered into force 16 November 1999) OAS Treaty Series No. 69.

African Charter on Human and Peoples' Rights (adopted 27 June 1981, entered into force 21 October 1986) 2206 UNTS 230.

Association of Southeast Asian Nations, Human Rights Declaration (adopted 18 November 2012) <http://aichr.org/documents> accessed 3 October 2016.

Convention for the Protection of Human Rights and Fundamental Freedoms (adopted 4 November 1950, entered into force 3 September 1953) 213 UNTS 222.

Council of the League of Arab States, Arab Charter on Human Rights (adopted 15 September 1994) reprinted in (1997) 18 Human Rights Law Journal 151.

European Social Charter (Revised) (adopted 3 May 1996, entered into force 1 July 1999) 2151 UNTS 277.

Organization of American States, Inter-American Convention on the Elimination of All Forms of Discrimination against Persons with Disabilities (adopted 7 June 1999, entered into force 4 September 2001) OAS AG/Res 1608.

European cases on human rights

Airey v Ireland (App no. 6289/73) (1979) 2 EHRR 305.

Al-Jedda v The United Kingdom (App no. 27021/08) (2011) 53 EHRR 23.

Al-Skeini v The United Kingdom (App no. 55721/07) (2011) 53 EHRR 18.

Bankovic and Others v Belgium and Others (App no. 52207/99) (2007) 44 EHRR SE5.

Behrami and Behrami v France and *Saramati v France and Others* (App nos 71412/01 and 78166/01) (2007) 45 EHRR SE10.

Bosphorus Hava Yollari Turizm v Ireland (App no. 45036/98) (2006) 42 EHRR 1.

Hassan v The United Kingdom (App no. 29750/09) ECHR 16 September 2014.

Ilascu and Others v Moldova and Russia (App no. 48787/99) (2004) 40 EHRR 1030.

Issa v Turkey (App no. 31821/96) (2005) 41 EHRR 27.

Jaloud v The Netherlands (App no. 47708/08) ECHR 20 November 2014.

Joined Cases C-402 & 415/05 *Kadi v Council and Commission* [2008] ECR I-6351.

Loizidou v Turkey (App no. 15318/89) (1995) 20 EHRR 99.

Matthews v United Kingdom (App no. 24833/94) (1999) 28 EHRR 361.

T-306/01 *Yusuf and Al Barakaat International Foundation v Council and Commission* [2005] ECR II-3533.

T-315/01 *Kadi v Council and Commission* [2005] ECR II-3649.

Waite and Kennedy v Germany (App no 26083/94) (2000) 30 EHRR 261.

Inter-American Commission on Human Rights cases

Alejandre et al v Cuba (Case 11.589, Report No. 86/99) (1999) IACHR.

Coard et al v United States (Case 10.951, Report No. 109/99) (1999) IACHR.

Juridical Condition and Rights of the Undocumented Migrants, Advisory Opinion OC-18/03, IACHR Series A No. 18 (17 September 2003).

Other cases

Georges v United Nations 84 F Supp 3d 246, 2015 WL 129657.
M & Co v The Federal Republic of Germany (App no. 13258/87) (1999) DR 64.
Minister of Health v Treatment Action Campaign (2002) 10 BCLR 1033.
Prosecutor v Dusko Tadic (*Decision on the Defence motion for Interlocutory Appeal on Jurisdiction*) ICTY-94-1-AR72 (2 October 1995).
The Government of the Republic of South Africa v Grootboom (2000) 11 BCLR 1169 (CC).

Books

Bakker Karen, *Privatizing Water: Governance Failure and the World's Urban Water Crisis* (Cornell University Press, Ithaca 2010).
Chesterman Simon, *You the People: The United Nations, Traditional Administration and State-Building* (Oxford University Press, 2004).
Craven Matthew C R, *The International Covenant on Economic, Social, and Cultural Rights: A Perspective on Its Development* (Clarendon Press, Oxford 1998).
Da Costa Karen, *The Extraterritorial Application of Selected Human Rights Treaties* (11 Graduate Institute of International and Development Studies, Martinus Nijhoff Publishers, Leiden 2013).
de Gouges Olympe, *Declaration of the Rights of Woman* (Printed for the Author, Paris 1791).
Diehl Paul Francis and Daniel Druckman, *Evaluating Peace Operations* (Lynne Rienner Publishers, Boulder 2010).
Diehl Paul F and Alexandru Balas, *Peace Operations* (2nd edn, Polity Press, Cambridge 2014).
Frazer Trudy, *Maintaining Peace and Security?: The United Nations in a Changing World* (Palgrave, London 2015).
Fukuda-Parr Sakiko, Terra Lawson-Remer and Susan Randolph, *Fulfilling Social and Economic Rights* (Oxford University Press, New York 2015).
Gillespie Alexander, *A History of the Laws of War* (Hart, Oxford 2011).
Ginty Roger Mac, *International Peacebuilding and Local Resistance: Hybrid Forms of Peace* (Palgrave Macmillan, New York 2011).
Horne Thomas Allen, *Property Rights and Poverty: Political Argument in Britain, 1605–1834* (University of North Carolina Press, Chapel Hill 1990).
Hunt Lynn, *Inventing Human Rights: A History* (W W Norton, New York 2007).
Hunt Paul, *Reclaiming Economic, Social and Cultural Rights: International and Comparative Perspectives* (Dartmouth Publishing Company Ltd, Aldershot 1996).
Ishay Micheline R, *The History of Human Rights: From Ancient Times to the Globalisation Era* (University of California Press, Berkeley 2004).
Jenkins Robert, *Peacebuilding: From Concept to Commission* (Routledge, London 2008).
Korey William, *NGOs and the Universal Declaration of Human Rights: 'A Curious Grapevine'* (Palgrave, New York 2001).
Landman Todd and Edzia Carvalho, *Measuring Human Rights* (Routledge, Oxon 2010).
Larsen Kjetil Mujezinovic, *Human Rights Treaty Obligations of Peacekeepers* (Cambridge University Press, Cambridge 2012).

Lauren Paul G, *The Evolution of International Human Rights: Visions Seen* (3rd edn, University of Pennsylvania Press, Philadelphia 2011).

Liddell-Hart Basil Henry, *Sherman: Soldier, Realist, American* (Dodd, Mead and Company, Boston 1929).

Liddell-Hart Basil Henry, *Strategy* (Praeger Paperbacks, New York 1954).

MacFarlane Neil and Yuen Foong Khong, *Human Security and the UN: A Critical History* (University of Indiana Press, Bloomington 2006).

Macmillan Harold, *The Middle Way* (Macmillan & Co, London 1938).

Mani Rama, *Beyond Retribution: Seeking Justice in the Shadows of War* (Polity Press, Cambridge 2002).

Midgley James, *Social Welfare in Global Context* (Sage Publications, Thousand Oaks 1997).

Milanović Marko, *Extraterritorial Application of Human Rights Treaties: Law, Principles, and Policy* (Oxford University Press, Oxford 2011).

Morsink Johannes, *The Universal Declaration of Human Rights: Origins, Drafting and Intent* (University of Pennsylvania Press, Pennsylvania 1999).

Moyn Samuel, *The Last Utopia* (The Belknap Press of Harvard University Press, Cambridge 2010).

Orend Brian, *War and International Justice: A Kantian Perspective* (Wilfrid Laurier University Press, Waterloo, Ontario 2000).

Paris Roland, *At War's End: Building Peace after Civil Conflict* (Cambridge University Press, Cambridge 2004).

Rawls John, *The Law of Peoples* (Harvard University Press, Cambridge 1999).

Richmond Oliver, *A Post-Liberal Peace* (Routledge, London 2011).

Robertson Geoffrey, *Crimes against Humanity: The Struggle for Global Justice* (Penguin Books, London 2000).

Robinson Nehemiah, *The Universal Declaration of Human Rights: Its Origin, Significance, Application and Interpretation* (Institute of Jewish Affairs and World Jewish Congress, New York 1958).

Russell Ruth, *A History of the United Nations Charter: The Role of the United States 1940–1945* (Brookings Institution, Washington 1958).

Salomon Margot E, *Global Responsibility for Human Rights: World Poverty and the Development of International Law* (Oxford University Press, Oxford 2007).

Saul Ben, David Kinley and Jaqueline Mowbray, *The International Covenant on Economic, Social and Cultural Rights: Commentary, Cases, and Materials* (Oxford University Press, Oxford, 2014).

Shue Henry, *Basic Rights: Subsistence, Affluence and U.S. Foreign Policy* (2nd edn, Princeton University Press, Princeton 1996).

Sievers Loraine and Sam Daws, *The Procedure of the UN Security Council* (4th edn, Oxford University Press, Oxford 2014).

Spence Thomas, *The Rights of Infants, Or, the Imprescriptable Right of Mothers to Such a Share of the Elements As Is Sufficient to Enable Them to Suckle and Bring Up Their Young: In a Dialogue between the Aristocracy and a Mother of Children: To Which Are Added, by Way of Preface and Appendix, Strictures on Paine's Agrarian Justice* (Printed for the Author, London 1797).

Steiner Henry J, Philip Alston and Ryan Goodman, *International Human Rights in Context: Law, Politics, Morlas: Text and Materials* (3rd edn, Oxford University Press, Oxford 2008).

Stewart Frances and Graham Brown, *Fragile States* (CRISE, Oxford 2006).

Verhellen Eugeen, *The Convention on the Rights of the Child: Background, Motivation, Strategies, Main Themes* (3rd edn, Garant, Leuven 2000).
Walzer Michael, *Arguing about War* (Yale University Press, New Haven 2004).
Walzer Michael, *Just and Unjust Wars: A Moral Argument with Historical Illustrations* (3rd edn, Basic Books, New York 2000).
Wills Siobhan, *Protecting Civilians: The Obligations of Peacekeepers* (Oxford University Press, Oxford 2009).
Wollstonecraft Mary, *A Vindication of the Rights of Woman* (J Johnson, London 1792).

Edited books

Baderin Mashood A and Robert McCorquodale (eds), *Economic, Social and Cultural Rights in Action* (Oxford University Press, Oxford and Toronto 2007).
Benedek Wolfgang, Matthias C Kettemann and Markus Möst (eds), *Mainstreaming Human Security in Peace Operations and Crisis Management: Policies, Problems, Potential* (Routledge, London 2011).
Brownlie Ian and G S Goodwin-Gill (eds), *Basic Documents on Human Rights* (5th edn, Oxford University Press, Oxford and New York 2006).
Campbell Susanna, David Chandler and Meera Sabaratnam (eds), *A Liberal Peace? The Problems and Practices of Peacekeeping* (Zed Books, London 2011).
Coomans Fons and Menno T Kamminga (eds), *Extraterritorial Application of Human Rights Treaties* (Intersentia, Antwerp 2004).
Eibe Riedel, Gilles Giacca and Christophe Golay (eds), *Economic, Social, and Cultural Rights in International Law: Contemporary Issues and Challenges* (Oxford University Press, Oxford 2014).
Eide Asbjørn and others (eds), *The Universal Declaration of Human Rights: A Commentary* (Scandinavian University Press, Oslo 1993).
Gibney Mark and Sigrun Skogly (eds), *Universal Human Rights and Extraterritorial Obligations* (University of Pennsylvania Press, Philadelphia 2010).
Hunt Lynn (ed), *The French Revolution and Human Rights: A Brief Documentary History* (Bedford Books of St Martin's Press, Boston 1996).
Langford Malcolm (ed), *Social Rights Jurisprudence Emerging Trends in International and Comparative Law* (Cambridge University Press, Cambridge 2009).
Langford Malcolm and others (eds), *Global Justice, State Duties: The Extraterritorial Scope of Economic, Social and Cultural Rights in International Law* (Cambridge University Press, New York 2013).
Macpherson C B (ed), *John Locke: 1632–1704: Second Treatise of Government 1690* (Hackett Publishing, Indiana 1980).
Marshall Thomas H and T B Bottomore (eds), *Citizenship and Social Class* (Pluto Press, London 1992).
Morgan Peggy and Clive Lawton (eds), *Ethical Issues in Six Religious Traditions* (Edinburgh University Press, Edinburgh 1996).
Narayan Deepa (ed), *Empowerment and Poverty Reduction: A Sourcebook* (World Bank, Washington DC 2002).
Newman Edward, Roland Paris and Oliver P Richmond (eds), *New Perspectives on Liberal Peacebuilding* (United Nations University Press, Tokyo 2009).
Pagden Anthony and Jeremey Lawrence (eds), *Vitoria: Political Writings* (Cambridge Texts in the History of Political Thought, Cambridge University Press, Cambridge 1991).

Richmond Oliver (ed), *Advances in Peacebuilding: Critical Developments and Approaches* (Palgrave Macmillan, London 2010).

Richmond Oliver P and Audra Mitchell (eds), *Hybrid Forms of Peace: From Everyday Agency to Postliberalism* (Palgrave Macmillan, Basingstoke 2012).

Robinson Paul (ed), *Just War in Comparative Perspective* (Ashgate, Surrey 2003).

Simma Bruno and others (eds), *The Charter of the United Nations: A Commentary* (3rd edn, Oxford University Press, Oxford 2013).

Skogly Sigrun I, *Beyond National Borders: States' Human Rights Obligations in International Cooperation* (Intersentia, Antwerp and Oxford 2006).

Translated books

Bettenson Henry (tr), *St Augustine: Concerning the City of God Against Pagans* (2nd edn, Penguin Books, London 1984).

Douglas George and Howard Cole (trs), *The Social Contract: And, Discourses* (Dent Publishing, New York 1973).

Fenwick Charles Ghequiere (tr), *The Law of Nations, or, the Principles of Natural Law Applied to the Conduct and the Affairs of Nations and of Sovereigns* (vol III, Carnegie Institution of Washington, Washington DC 1916).

Griffin Miriam (tr), *Cicero: On Duties* (Cambridge Texts in the History of Political Thought, Cambridge University Press, Cambridge 1991).

Hastie William (tr), *The Philosophy of Law: An Exposition of the Fundamental Principles of Jurisprudence as the Science of Right* (Clark, Edinburgh 1887).

Kelsey Francis W (tr), 'Hugo Grotius on the Law of War and Peace' in James Brown Scott (ed), *The Classics of International Law* (Carnegie Institution of Washington, Washington DC 1925).

Lord Carnes (tr), *Aristotle's Politics* (2nd ed, Chicago University Press, Chicago 2013).

Williams Gwladys L (tr), 'The Three Theological Virtues' in James Brown Scott (ed), *The Classics of International Law* (Clarendon Press, Oxford 1944).

Book chapters

Alston Philip, 'Economic and Social Rights' in Louis Henkin and John Lawrence Hargrove (eds), *Human Rights: An Agenda for the Next Century* (American Society for International Law, Washington DC 1994).

Cahill-Ripley Amanda, 'Protecting Rights in the Face of Scarcity: The Right to Water' in Mark Gibney and Sigrun Skogly (eds), *Universal Human Rights and Extraterritorial Obligations* (University of Pennsylvania Press, Philadelphia 2010).

de Brabandere Eric, 'The Concept of Jus Post Bellum in International Law: A Normative Critique' in Carsten Stahn, Jennifer S Easterday and Jens Iverson (eds), *Jus Post Bellum: Mapping the Normative Foundations* (Oxford University Press, Oxford 2014).

De Mesquita Judith Bueno, Paul Hunt and Rajat Khosla, 'The Human Rights Responsibility of International Assistance and Cooperation in Health' in Mark Gibney and Sigrun Skogly (eds), *Universal Human Rights and Extraterritorial Obligations* (University of Pennsylvania Press, Philadelphia 2010).

Eide Asbjørn, 'Economic, Social and Cultural Rights as Human Rights' in Asbjørn Eide, Catarina Krause and Allan Rosas (eds), *Economic, Social and Cultural Rights: A Textbook* (2nd edn, Martinus Nijhoff, Dordrecht and London 2001).

Eide Asbjørn, 'Economic and Social Rights' in Januz Symonides, *Human Rights: Concepts and Standards* (UNESCO Publishing and Ashgate Publishing, Burlington 2000).

Haldemann Frank and Rachelle Kouassi, 'Transitional Justice Without Economic, Social, and Cultural Rights?' in Eibe Riedel, Gilles Giacca and Christophe Golay (eds), *Economic, Social, and Cultural Rights in International Law: Contemporary Issues and Challenges* (Oxford University Press, Oxford 2014).

Hertel Shareen and Lanse Minkler, 'Economic and Social Rights: The Terrain' in Shareen Hertel and Lanse Minkler (eds), *Economic Rights: Conceptual Measurement and Policy Issues* (Cambridge University Press, Cambridge 2007).

Jenks C W, 'Human Rights, Social Justice and Peace: The Broader Significance of the ILO Experience' in Asbjørn Eide and August Shou (eds), *International Protection of Human Rights: Proceedings* (Interscience Publishers, New York 1968).

Kunig Philip and Christian Tietje, 'Article 65' in Bruno Simma (ed), *The Charter of the United Nations: A Commentary. Volume II* (3rd edn, Oxford University Press, Oxford 2012).

Labonte Melissa, 'Jus Post Bellum, Peacebuilding, and Non-State Actors: Lessons from Afghanistan' in Eric A Heinze and Brent J Steele (eds), *Ethics, Authority, and War: Non-State Actors and the Just War Tradition* (Palgrave Macmillan, New York 2009).

Lagoni Rainier and Oliver Landwehr, 'Article 62', in Bruno Simma (ed), *The Charter of the United Nations: A Commentary. Volume II* (2nd edn, Oxford University Press, Oxford 2002).

Le Floch Guillaume, 'Responsibility for Human Rights Violations by International Organizations' in Roberto Virzo and Ivan Ingravallo (eds), *Evolutions in the Law of International Organizations* (Brill, Leiden 2015).

Leary Virginia, 'Lessons from the Experience of the International Labour Organisation' in Philip Alston (ed), *The United Nations and Human Rights: A Critical Appraisal* (Clarendon Press, Oxford 1992).

Lister Ruth, 'Unpacking Children's Citizenship' in Jane Williams and Antonella Invernizzi (eds), *Children and Citizenship* (Sage Publications, London 2008).

MacQueen Graeme, 'Setting the Role of the Health Sector in Context: Multi-track Peacework' in Neil Arya and Joanna Santa Barbara (eds), *Peace Through Health – How Health Professionals Can Work for a Less Violent World* (Kumarian Press, Sterling 2008).

McKeon Richard, 'Philosophy and History in the Development of Human Rights' in Howard Kiefer and Milton Karl Munitz (eds), *Ethics and Social Justice* (State University of New York Press, Albany 1968).

Meng Werner, 'Article 60' in Bruno Simma (ed), *The Charter of the United Nations: A Commentary. Volume II* (3rd edn, Oxford University Press, Oxford 2012).

Oberleitner Gerd, 'Humanitarian Law as a Source of Human Rights Law' in Dinah Shelton (ed), *The Oxford Handbook of International Human Rights Law* (Oxford University Press, Oxford 2013).

Paine Thomas, 'Agrarian Justice' in Bruce Kuklick (ed), *Paine: Political Writings* (Revised Student Edition, Cambridge University Press, Cambridge 2000).

Paris Roland, 'Post-Conflict Peacebuilding' in Thomas G Weiss and Sam Daws (eds), *The Oxford Companion on the United Nations* (Oxford University Press, Oxford 2009).

Roben Volker, 'Article 62', in Bruno Simma (ed), *The Charter of the United Nations: A Commentary. Volume II* (3rd edn, Oxford University Press, Oxford 2012).

Roben Volker, 'Article 62', in Bruno Simma and others (eds), *The Charter of the United Nations: A Commentary. Volume III* (3rd edn, Oxford University Press, Oxford 2012).

Rodin David, 'Two Emerging Issues of Jus Post Bellum: War Termination and the Liability of Soldiers for Crimes of Aggression' in Carsten Stahn and Jann K Kleffner (eds), *Jus Post Bellum: Towards a Law of Transition from Conflict to Peace* (T M C Asser Press, The Hague 2008).

Rosas Allan and Jan E Helgesen, 'Introduction' in Allan Rosas and Jan E Helgesen with the Collaboration of Donna Gomien (eds), *Human Rights in a Changing East-West Perspective* (Pinter Publishers, New York 1990).

Rosas Allan and Monika Sandvik-Nylund, 'Armed Conflicts' in Asbjørn Eide, Catarina Krause and Allan Rosas (eds), *Economic, Social and Cultural Rights: A Textbook* (2nd edn, Martinus Nijhoff, Dordrecht, London, 2001).

Scheinin Martin, 'Economic and Social Rights as Legal Rights' in Asbjørn Eide, Catarian Krause and Allan Rosas (eds), *Economic, Social and Cultural Rights: A Textbook* (2nd edn, Martinus Nijhoff, Dordrecht and London 2001).

Sharp Dustin N, 'Introduction: Addressing Economic Violence in Times of Transition' in Dustin N Sharp (ed), *Justice and Economic Violence in Transition* (Springer, New York 2014).

Sherman Jake, 'Measuring Effectiveness in Peace-Building and State-Building' in Sarah Jane Meharg (ed), *Measuring What Matters in Peace Operations and Crisis Management* (Queen's Policy Study Series, McGill-Queen's University Press, Montreal 2009).

Skogly Sigrun I, 'Causality and Extraterritorial Human Rights Obligations' in Malcolm Langford and others (eds), *Global Justice, State Duties: The Extraterritorial Scope of Economic, Social and Cultural Rights in International Law* (Cambridge University Press, New York 2013).

Skogly Sigrun I, 'The Obligation of International Assistance and Co-operation in the International Covenant on Economic, Social and Cultural Rights' in Morten Bergsmo and Asbjørn Eide (eds), *Human Rights and Criminal Justice for the Downtrodden: Essays in Honour of Asbjørn Eide* (Martinus Nijhoff Publishers, Leiden 2003).

Sriram Chandra Lekha, Olga Martin-Ortega and Johanna Herman, 'Beyond Justice Versus Peace: Transitional Justice and Peacebuilding Strategies' in Karin Aggestam and Annika Bjorkdahl (eds), *Rethinking Peacebuilding: The Quest for Just Peace in the Middle East and the Western Balkans* (Routledge, New York 2012).

Stephens Mamari, 'The Right to Social Security' in Margaret Bedggood and Kris Gledhill (eds), *Law into Action: Economic, Social and Cultural Rights in Aotearoa New Zealand* (Thomson Reuters, Wellington 2011).

van Zyl Paul, 'Promoting Transitional Justice in Post-conflict Societies' in Alan Bryden and Heiner Hanggi (eds), *Security Governance in Post-conflict Peacebuilding* (Centre for the Democratic Control of Armed Forces, Geneva 2005).

Vandenhole Wouter, 'EU and Development: Extraterritorial Obligations under the International Covenant on Economic, Social and Cultural Rights' in Wouter

Vandenhole, Arne Tostensen and Margot E Salomon (eds), *Casting the Net Wider: Human Rights, Development and New Duty-bearers* (Intersentia, Antwerp 2007).

White Nigel D, 'The Applicability of Economic and Social Rights to the UN Security Council' in Mashood A Baderin and Robert McCorquodale (eds), *Economic, Social and Cultural Rights in Action (*Oxford: University Press, Oxford 2007).

Journal articles

Agbakwa Shedrack C, 'A Path Least Taken: Economic and Social Rights and the Prospects of Conflict Prevention and Peacebuilding in Africa' (2003) 47(1) *Journal of African Law* 38.

Akande Dapo, 'The International Court of Justice and the Security Council: Is There Room for Judicial Control of Decisions of the Political Organs of the United Nations?' (1997) 46(2) *International and Comparative Law Quarterly* 309.

Allen Susan Hannah and Amy T Yuen, 'The Politics of Peacekeeping: UN Security Council Oversight Across Peacekeeping Missions' (2014) 58(3) *International Studies Quarterly* 621.

Alston Philip and Gerard Quinn, 'The Nature and Scope of States Parties' Obligations under the International Covenant on Economic, Social and Cultural Rights' (1987) 9(2) *Human Rights Quarterly* 156.

Alvarez Jose E, 'Judging the Security Council' (1996) 90(1) *American Journal of International Law* 1.

Andrieu Kora, 'Civilizing Peacebuilding: Transitional Justice, Civil Society and the Liberal Paradigm' (2010) 41(5) *Security Dialogue* 537.

Arbour Louise, 'Economic and Social Justice for Societies in Transition' (2007) 40(1) *Journal of International Law and Politics* 1.

Baker, Catherine and Jelena Obradovic-Wochnik, 'Mapping the Nexus of Transitional Justice and Peacebuilding' (2016) 10(3) *Journal of Intervention and Statebuilding* 281.

Baquero Oscar Flores, Alejandro Jiménez Fernandez de Palencia and Agusti Pérez Foguet, 'Reporting Progress on the Human Right to Water and Sanitation through JMP and GLAAS' (2015) 5(2) *Journal of Water Sanitation and Hygiene for Development* 310.

Barnett Michael, Songying Fang and Christoph Zurcher, 'Compromised Peacebuilding' (2014) 58(3) *International Studies Quarterly* 608.

Bass Gary, 'Jus Post Bellum' (2004) 32(4) *Philosophy and Public Affairs* 384.

Bellal Annyssa, 'Building Respect for the Rule of Law in Violent Contexts: The Office of the High Commissioner for Human Rights' Experience and Approach' (2014) 96(895–896) *International Review of the Red Cross* 881.

Bellamy Alex, 'The Responsibilities of Victory: Jus Post Bellum and the Just War' (2008) 34(4) *Review of International Studies* 601.

Besson Samantha, 'The Bearers of Human Rights' Duties and Responsibilities for Human Rights: A Quiet (R)Evolution?' (2015) 32(01) *Social Philosophy and Policy* 244.

Besson Samantha, 'The Extraterritoriality of the European Convention on Human Rights: Why Human Rights Depend on Jurisdiction and What Jurisdiction Amounts To' (2012) 25(4) *Leiden Journal of International Law* 872.

Biersteker Thomas J, 'Prospects for the UN Peacebuilding Commission' (2007) 2(2) *Disarmament Forum* 37.

Bode Thomas G, 'Cholera in Haiti: United Nations Immunity and Accountability' (2015) 47 *Georgetown Journal of International* Law 759.

Boon Kirsten, 'The Future of the Law of Occupation' (2008) 46 *Canadian Yearbook of International Law* 107.

Boon Kirsten, 'The United Nations as Good Samaritan: Immunity and Responsibility' (2016) 16(2) *Chicago Journal of International Law* 341.

Bosi Tanya Domenica, 'U.N. Report: Post-conflict Reconstruction: The United Nations' Involvement in Afghanistan' (2003) 19 *New York Law School Journal of Human Rights* 819.

Bratt Duane, 'Assessing the Success of UN Peacekeeping' (1996) 3(4) *International Peacekeeping* 64.

Breau Susan C, 'The Impact of the Responsibility to Protect on Peacekeeping' (2006) 11(3) *Journal of Conflict and Security Law* 429.

Breen Claire, 'Progressing Towards Peace? States' Extraterritorial Obligations in Peace Operations and the Added Value of Human Rights Indicators' (2015) 9 (2) *Human Rights and International Legal Discourse* 123.

Breen Claire, 'Rationalising the Work of UN Human Rights Bodies or Reducing the Input on NGOs? The Changing Role of Human Rights NGOs at the United Nations' (2005) 5(2) *Non-State Actors and International Law* 101.

Breen Claire, 'Revitalising the United Nations Human Rights Special Procedures Mechanisms as a Means of Achieving and Maintaining International Peace and Security' (2008) 12 *Max Planck Yearbook of United Nations Law* 177.

Breen Claire, 'The Edges of Extraterritorial Jurisdiction: The Integration of Economic, Social and Cultural Rights into Peace Support Operations' (2012) 16 *Journal of International Peacekeeping* 47.

Breen Claire, 'The Necessity of a Role for the ECOSOC in the Maintenance of International Peace and Security' (2007) 12(2) *Journal of Conflict and Security Law* 261.

Breen Claire, 'The Policy of Direct Provision in Ireland: A Violation of Asylum-seekers' Right to an Adequate Standard of Housing' (2008) 20(4) *International Journal of Refugee Law* 611.

Breen Claire, 'The Role of NGOs in the Formulation of and Compliance with the Optional Protocol to the Convention on the Rights of the Child on Involvement of Children in Armed Conflict' (2003) 25(2) *Human Rights Quarterly* 453.

Brett Roddy, 'Overcoming the Original Sin of the "Original Condition": How Reparations May Contribute to Emancipatory Peacebuilding' (2013) 14(3) *Human Rights Review* 257.

Buergenthal Thomas, 'The Normative and Institutional Evolution of International Human Rights' (1997) 19(4) *Human Rights Quarterly* 703.

Bulto Takele Soboka, 'Towards Rights-Duties Congruence: Extraterritorial Application of the Human Right to Water in the African Human Rights System' (2011) 29(4) *Netherlands Quarterly of Human Rights* 486.

Burgers Jan Herman, 'The Road to San Francisco: The Revival of the Human Rights Idea in the Twentieth Century' (1992) 14(4) *Human Rights Quarterly* 447.

Carmona M S, 'The Obligation of "International Assistance and Cooperation" under the International Covenant on Economic, Social and Cultural Rights: A Possible Entry Point to a Human Rights Based Approach to Millennium Development Goal 8' (2009) 13(1) *The International Journal of Human Rights* 86.

Cerone John, 'Human Dignity in the Line of Fire: The Application of International Human Rights Law During Armed Conflict, Occupation, and Peace Operations' (2006) 39 *Vanderbilt Journal of Transnational Law* 1447.

Cerone John, 'Minding the Gap: Outlining KFOR Accountability in Post-conflict Kosovo' (2001) 12(3) *European Journal of International Law* 469.

Chapman Audrey R, 'A "Violations Approach" for Monitoring the International Covenant on Economic, Social and Cultural Rights' (1996) 18(1) *Human Rights Quarterly* 24.

Chayes Antonia, 'Chapter VII½: Is Jus Post Bellum Possible?' (2013) 24(1) *European Journal of International Law* 291.

Coomans Fons, 'The Extraterritorial Scope of the International Covenant on Economic, Social and Cultural Rights in the Work of the United Nations Committee on Economic, Social and Cultural Rights' (2011) 11(1) *Human Rights Law Review* 1.

Corkery Allison and Sally-Anne Way, 'Integrating Quantitative and Qualitative Tools to Monitor the Obligation to Fulfil Economic, Social and Cultural Rights: The OPERA Framework' (2012) 8(3) *Nordic Journal of Human Rights* 324.

Courtis Christian and Magdalena Sepúlveda, 'Are Extra-Territorial Obligations Reviewable under the Optional Protocol to the ICESCR?' (2009) 27(1) *Nordic Journal on Human Rights* 54.

Cronin-Furman Kathleen Renée, 'The International Court of Justice and the United Nations Security Council: Rethinking a Complicated Relationship' (2006) 106(2) *Columbia Law Review* 435.

Dahl Marianne and Bjørn Høyland, 'Peace on Quicksand? Challenging the Conventional Wisdom about Economic Growth and Post-conflict Risks' (2012) 49(3) *Journal of Peace Research* 423.

Dankwa Victor, Cees Flinterman and Scott Leckie, 'Commentary to the Maastricht Guidelines on Violations of Economic, Social and Cultural Rights' (1998) 20(3) *Human Rights Quarterly* 705.

Dannenbaum Tom, 'Translating the Standard of Effective Control into a System of Effective Accountability: How Liability Should be Apportioned for Violations of Human Rights by Member State Troop Contingents Serving as United Nations Peacekeepers' (2010) 51(1) *Harvard International Law Journal* 113.

Davy Ulrike, 'Social Citizenship Going International: Changes in the Reading of UN-Sponsored Economic and Social Rights' 22(S1) *International Journal of Social Welfare* S15.

de Beco Gauthier, 'Human Rights Indicators: From Theoretical Debate to Practical Application' (2013) 5(2) *Journal of Human Rights Practice* 380.

de Beco Gauthier, 'Human Rights Indicators for Assessing State Compliance with International Human Rights' (2008) 77(1–2) *Nordic Journal of International Law* 23.

de Brabandere Eric, 'The Responsibility for Post-conflict Reforms: A Critical Assessment of Jus Post Bellum as a Legal Concept' (2010) 43(1) *Vanderbilt Journal of Transnational Law* 120.

De Schutter Olivier and others, 'Commentary to the Maastricht Principles on Extraterritorial Obligations of States in the area of Economic, Social and Cultural Rights' (2012) 34(4) *Human Rights Quarterly* 1084.

Di Meglio Anthony, 'Just War Tradition and Just Post Bellum' (2005) 186 *Military Law Review* 116.

Dorussen Han and Theodora-Ismene Gizelis, 'Into the Lion's Den: Local responses to UN Peacekeeping' (2013) 50(6) *Journal of Peace Research* 691.

Evans Derek, 'Human Rights and State Fragility: Conceptual Foundations and Strategic Foundations for State-Building' (2009) 1(2) *Journal of Human Rights Practice* 181.

Evans Matthew, 'Structural Violence, Socioeconomic Rights, and Transformative Justice' (2016) 15(1) *Journal of Human Rights* 1.

Faite Alexandre and Labbe Grenier Jeremie, 'Expert Meeting on Multinational Peace Operations: Applicability of International Humanitarian Law and International Human Rights Law to UN Mandated Forces' (Geneva, 11–12 December 2003) 83.

Fassbender Bardo, 'Uncertain Steps into a Post-Cold War World: The Role and Functioning of the UN Security Council after a Decade of Measures against Iraq' (2002) 13(1) *European Journal of International Law* 273.

Freedman Rosa 'UN Immunity or Impunity? A Human Rights Based Challenge' (2014) 25(1) *European Journal of International Law* 239.

Freedman Rosa and Nicolas Lemay-Hebert '"Jistis Ak Reparasyon Pou Tout Viktim Kolera MINUSTAH": The United Nations and the Right to Health in Haiti' (2015) 28(3) *Leiden Journal of International Law* 507.

Frerichs Ralph 'Nepalese Origin of Cholera Epidemic in Haiti' (2012) 18(6) *Clinical Microbiology and Infection* E158.

Fukuda-Parr Sakiko, 'Millennium Development Goal 8: Indicators for International Human Rights Obligations?' (2006) 28(4) *Human Rights Quarterly* 966.

Fukuda-Parr Sakiko, Terra Lawson-Remer and Susan Randolph, 'An Index of Economic and Social Rights Fulfillment: Concept and Methodology' (2009) 8(3) *Journal of Human Rights* 195.

Galtung Johan, 'Violence, Peace and Peace Research' (1969) 6(3) *Journal of Peace Research* 167.

Ginty Roger Mac, 'Where is the Local? Critical Localism and Peacebuilding' (2015) 36(5) *Third World Quarterly* 840.

Ginty Roger Mac and Oliver P Richmond, 'The Local Turn in Peace Building: A Critical Agenda for Peace' (2013) 34(5) *Third World Quarterly* 763.

Gillespie James A, 'International Organizations and the Problem of Child Health, 1945–1960' (2003) 23 *Dynamis* 115.

Goetze Catherine and Berit Bliesemann De Guevara, 'Cosmopolitanism and the Culture of Peacebuilding' (2014) 40(4) *Review of International Studies* 771.

Goldfinch Shaun and Karl Derouen Jr, 'In It for the Long Haul? Post-Conflict Statebuilding, Peacebuilding, and the Good Governance Agenda in Timor-Leste' (2014) 34(2) *Public Administration and Development* 96.

Green Maria, 'What We Talk About When We Talk About Indicators: Current Approaches to Human Rights Measurement' (2001) 23(4) *Human Rights Quarterly* 1065.

Gutter Jeroen, 'Special Procedures and the Human Rights Council: Achievements and Challenges Ahead' (2007) 7(1) *Human Rights Law Review* 93.

Hakimi Monica, 'State Bystander Responsibility' (2011) 21(2) *European Journal of International Law* 341.

Hameiri Shahar, 'The Crisis of Liberal Peacebuilding and the Future of Statebuilding' (2014) 51 *International Politics* 316.

Hampson Fen Osler and John Hay, 'Human Security: A Review of the Scholarly Literature' (2002) 1(2) *Human Security Bulletin* 4.

Hassmann Rhoda Howard, 'Human Security: Undermining Human Rights?' (2012) 34(1) *Human Rights Quarterly* 90.

Henkin Louis, 'Rights: American and Human' (1979) 79(3) *Columbia Law Review* 405.

Houle Christian, 'Why Class Inequality Breeds Coups but Not Civil Wars' (2016) 53(5) *Journal of Peace Research* 680.

Iasiello Louis V, 'Jus Post Bellum: The Moral Responsibilities of Victors in War' (2004) 57(3/4) *Naval War College Review* 33.

Jabri Vivienne, 'Peacebuilding, the Local and the International: A Colonial or a Post-colonial Rationality?' (2013) 1(1) *Peace-building* 3.

Jubilut Liliana Lyra, 'Towards a New Just Post Bellum: The United Nations Peace-building Commission and the Improvement of Post-conflict Efforts and Accountability' (2011) 20(1) *Minnesota Journal of International Law* 26.

Kalantry Sital, Jocelyn Getgen Kestenbaum and Stephen Arrigg Koh, 'Enhancing Enforcement of Economic, Social, and Cultural Rights Using Indicators: A Focus on the Right to Education in the ICESCR' (2010) 32(2) *Human Rights Quarterly* 253.

Katselli Elena, 'Holding the Security Council Accountable for Human Rights Violations' (2007) 1(2) *Human Rights and International Legal Discourse* 301.

Katselli Elena, 'International Peace and Security, Human Rights and the Courts: A Critical Re-Appraisal' (2012) 16(1) *The International Journal of Human Rights* 257.

Kertcher Chen, 'From Cold War to a System of Peacekeeping Operations: The Discussions on Peacekeeping Operations in the UN during the 1980s up to 1992' (2012) 47(3) *Journal of Contemporary History* 611.

Kirschner Adele J, 'The Human Right to Water and Sanitation' (2011) 15 *Max Plunk Yearbook of United Nations Law* 445.

Koch Ida Elisabeth, 'The Justiciability of Indivisible Rights' (2003) 72(1) *Nordic Journal of International Law* 3.

Kreilkamp Jacob S, 'U.N. Postconflict Reconstruction' (2003) 35(3) *New York University Journal of International Law and Politics* 619.

Lambourne Wendy, 'Transitional Justice and Peacebuilding after Mass Violence' (2009) 3(1) *International Law Journal of Transitional Justice* 28.

Landman Todd, 'Measuring Human Rights: Principles, Practice, Policy' (2004) 26(4) *Human Rights Quarterly* 906.

Laplante Lisa J, 'Transitional Justice and Peace Building: Diagnosing and Addressing the Socioeconomic Roots of Violence through a Human Rights Framework' (2008) 2(3) *International Journal of Transitional Justice* 331.

Luquero Francisco J and others, 'Mortality Rates during Cholera Epidemic, Haiti, 2010–2011' (2016) 2(3) *Emerging Infectious Diseases* 410.

Mamiya Ralph and Haidi Willmot, 'Early Warning, the Protection of Civilians and United Nations Peacekeeping Operations' (2013) 22(2) *African Security Review* 68.

Marks Stephen P, 'From the "Single Confused Page" to the "Decalogue for Five Billion Persons": The Roots of the Universal Declaration of Human Rights in the French Revolution' (1998) 20(3) *Human Rights Quarterly* 459.

Martenczuk Bernd, 'The Security Council, the International Court and Judicial Review: What Lessons from Lockerbie' (1999) 10(3) *European Journal of International Law* 545.

Maus Sylvia, 'Jus Post Bellum a la United Nations: Human Rights, UN Peace Operations, and the Creation of International Law' (2014) 32 *Wisconsin International Law Journal* 675.

Mayeda Graham, 'Legal Aspects of the Security-Development Nexus: International Administrative Law as a Check on the Use of Development Assistance in the War on Terror' (2012) 13(1) *Chicago Journal of International Law* 71.

McCready Doug, 'Ending the War Right: Jus Post Bellum and the Just War Tradition' (2009) 8(1) *Journal of Military Ethics* 66.

McEvoy Kieran, 'Beyond Legalism: Towards a Thicker Understanding of Transitional Justice' (2007) 34(4) *Journal of Law and Society* 411.

McInerney-Lankford Siobhán, 'Human Rights and Development: A Comment on Challenges and Opportunities from a Legal Perspective' (2009) 1(1) *Journal of Human Rights Practice* 52.

Mégret Frédéric, 'Between R2P and the ICC: "Robust Peacekeeping" and the Quest for Civilian Protection' (2015) 26(1) *Criminal Law Forum* 101.

Mégret Frédéric and Florian Hoffmann, 'The UN as a Human Rights Violator?: Some Reflections on the United Nations Changing Human Rights Responsibilities' (2003) 25(2) *Human Rights Quarterly* 314.

Meier Benjamin Mason and others, 'Examining the Practice of Developing Human Rights Indicators to Facilitate Accountability for the Human Right to Water and Sanitation' (2014) 6(1) *Journal of Human Rights Practice* 159.

Meier Benjamin Mason and Yuna Kim, 'Human Rights Accountability Through Treaty Bodies: Examining Human Rights Treaty Monitoring for Water And Sanitation' (2015) 26 *Duke Journal Of Comparative and International Law* 141.

Melander Erik, Therése Pettersson and Lotta Themnér, 'Organized Violence, 1989–2015' (2016) 53(5) *Journal of Peace Research* 727.

Melandri Manuela, 'The State, Human Rights and the Ethics of War Termination: What Should a Just Peace Look Like? A Critical Appraisal' (2011) 7(3) *Journal of Global Ethics* 241.

Milanović Marko, 'From Compromise to Principle: Clarifying the Concept of State Jurisdiction in Human Rights Treaties' (2008) 8(3) *Human Rights Law Review* 411.

Millar Gearoid and Jesse Lecy, 'Disciplinary Divides in Post-conflict Justice and Peace: Tracking If and How We Share Ideas' (2016) 10(3) *Journal of Intervention and Statebuilding* 302.

Mollendorf Darrell, 'Jus ex Bello' (2008) 16(2) *Journal of Political Philosophy* 123.

Moody Zoe, 'The United Nations Declaration of the Rights of the Child (1959): Genesis, Transformation and Dissemination of a Treaty (re)constituting a Transnational Cause' (2015) 45 *Prospects*, 15, 16–17.

Moore Jennifer, 'Collective Security with a Human Face: An International Legal Framework for Coordinated Action to Alleviate Violence and Poverty' (2004) 33(1) *Denver Journal of International Law and Policy* 43.

Muller Amrei, 'Limitations to and Derogations from Economic, Social and Cultural Rights' (2009) 9(4) *Human Rights Law Review* 557.

Muller Amrei, 'The Right To Health and International Humanitarian Law: Parallel Application for Building Peaceful Societies and the Prevention of Armed Conflict' (2014) 32(3) *Wisconsin International Law Journal* 415.

Murthy Sharmila L, 'The Human Right(s) to Water and Sanitation: History, Meaning and the Controversy over Privatization' (2013) 31(1) *Berkeley Journal of International Law* 89.

Naples-Mitchell Joanna, 'Perspectives of UN Special Rapporteurs on Their Role: Inherent Tensions and Unique Contributions to Human Rights' (2011) 15(2) *International Journal of Human Rights* 232.

Nayar M G Kaladharan, 'Human Rights and Economic Development: The Legal Foundations' (1980) 2(3) *Universal Human Rights* 81.

Newbrander William, Ronald Waldman and Megan Shepherd-Banigan, 'Rebuilding and Strengthening Health Systems and Providing Basic Health Services in Fragile States' (2011) 35(4) *Disasters* 639.

Nolan Aoife, 'Addressing Economic and Social Rights Violations by Non-State Actors through the Role of the State: A Comparison of Regional Approaches to the "Obligation to Protect"' (2009) 9(2) *Human Rights Law Review* 225.

Oaks Dumbarton, 'Washington Conversations on International Peace and Security Organisation, October 7, 1944 Proposals' (1945) 39 (Supplement) *American Journal of International Law* 42.

O'Flaherty Michael, 'Future Protection of Human Rights in Post-conflict Societies: The Role of the United Nations' (2003) 3(1) *Human Rights Law Review* 53.

Oberleitner Gerard, 'Human Security: A Challenge to International Law' (2005) 11(2) *Global Governance* 187.

Ogata Sadako and Johann Cels, 'Human Security: Protecting and Empowering the People' (2003) 9(3) *Global Governance* 274.

Orakhelashvili Alexander, 'The Impact of Peremptory Norms on the Interpretation and Application of United Nations Security Council Resolutions' (2005) 16(1) *European Journal of International Law* 59.

Orend Brian, 'Jus Post Bellum' (2000) 33(1) *Journal of Social Philosophy* 117.

Orend Brian, 'Jus Post Bellum: The Perspective of a Just-War Theorist' (2007) 20(3) *Leiden Journal of International Law* 573.

Orend Brian, 'Justice after War' (2002) 16(1) *Ethics and International Affairs* 43.

Orentlicher Diane F, 'Addressing Gross Human Rights Abuses: Punishment and Victim Compensation' (1994) 26 *Studies in Transnational Legal Policy* 425.

Orentlicher Diane F, 'Settling Accounts: The Duty to Prosecute Human Rights Violations of a Prior Regime' (1991) 100(8) *The Yale Law Journal* 2537.

Osterdahl Inger, 'The Exception as the Rule: Lawmaking on Force and Human Rights by the UN Security Council' (2005) 10(1) *Journal of Conflict and Security Law* 13.

Osterdahl Inger and Esther van Zadel, 'What Will Jus Post Bellum Mean? Of New Wine and Old Bottles' (2009) 14(2) *Journal of Conflict and Security Law* 191.

Paris Roland, 'Human Security: Paradigm Shift or Hot Air' (2001) 26(2) *International Security* 87.

Paris Roland, 'Saving Liberal Peacebuilding' (2010) 36(2) *Review of International Studies* 337.

Pattison James, 'Jus Post Bellum and the Responsibility to Rebuild' (2015) 45(3) *British Journal of Political Science* 635.

Payandeh Mehrdad, 'With Great Power Comes Great Responsibility? The Concept of the Responsibility to Protect Within the Process of International Lawmaking' (2010) 35(2) *Yale Journal of International Law* 471.

Peou Sorpong, 'The Limits and Potential of Liberal Peacebuilding for Human Security' (2014) 2(1) *Asian Journal of Peacebuilding* 37.

Perry Donna J, Christian Guillermet Fernández and David Fernández Puyana, 'The Right to Life in Peace: An Essential Condition for Realizing the Right to Health' (2015) 17(1) *Health and Human Rights* 148.

Peter Mateja, 'Between Doctrine and Practice: The UN Peacekeeping Dilemma' (2015) 21(3) *Global Governance: A Review of Multilateralism and International Organizations* 351.

Pillay Navanethem, 'Establishing Effective Accountability Mechanisms for Human Rights Violations' (2013) 49(4) *UN Chronicle* 8.

Quénivet Noëlle, 'You Are the Weakest Link and We Will Help You! The Comprehensive Strategy of the United Nations to Fight Terrorism' (2006) 11(3) *Journal of Conflict and Security Law* 386.

Quinivet Noëlle, 'Binding the United Nations to Human Rights Norms by Way of the Laws of Treaties' (2010) 42(3) *George Washington International Law Review* 587.

Randazzo Elisa, 'The Paradoxes of the "Everyday": Scrutinising the Local Turn in Peace Building' (2016) 37(8) *Third World Quarterly* 1351.

Reinisch August, 'Developing Human Rights and Humanitarian Law Accountability of the Security Council for the Imposition of Economic Sanctions' (2001) 95(4) *American Journal of International Law* 851.

Renn Duu (Jason) and Paul F Diehl, 'Déjà vu All Over Again and Peacekeeping Reform?: The HIPPO Report and Barriers to Implementation' (2015) 19(3–4) *Journal of International Peacekeeping* 211.

Richmond Oliver P, 'Emancipatory Forms of Human Security and Liberal Peace-building' (2007) 62(3) *International Journal* 458.

Richmond Oliver P, 'Resistance and the Post-liberal Peace' (2010) 38(3) *Millenium* 665.

Richmond Oliver P, 'The Impact of Socio-Economic Inequality on Peacebuilding and Statebuilding' (2014) 16(4) *Civil Wars* 449.

Richmond Oliver P and Jason Franks, 'Liberal Peacebuilding in Timor Leste: the Emperor's New Clothes?' (2008) 15(2) *International Peacekeeping* 185.

Richmond Oliver P and Roger Mac Ginty, 'Where Now for the Critique of the Liberal Peace?' (2015) 50(2) *Cooperation and Conflict* 171.

Roberts David, 'Post-Conflict Peacebuilding, Liberal Irrelevance and the Locus of Legitimacy' (2011) 18(4) *International Peacekeeping* 410.

Rodin David, 'First View: Ending War' (2011) 25(3) *Ethics & International* Affairs 59.

Rosga Ann Janette and Margaret L Satterthwaite, 'The Trust in Indicators: Measuring Human Rights' (2009) 27(2) *Berkeley Journal of International Law* 253.

Roznai Yaniv, 'The Insecurity of Human Security' (2014) 32(1) *Wisconsin International Law Journal* 95.

Rudderham M A, 'Canada and United Nations Peace Operations: Challenges, Opportunities, and Canada's Response' (2008) 63(2) *International Journal* 359.

Russell Anna F S, 'International Organizations and Human Rights: Realizing, Resisting or Repackaging the Right to Water?' (2010) 9(1) *Journal of Human Rights* 1.

Sandoval Clara Transitional Justice and Social Change, (2014) 20(11) *Sur International Journal On Human Rights* 181.

Sari Aurel, 'Jurisdiction and International Responsibility in Peace Operations: The Behrami and Saramati Cases' (2008) 8(1) *Human Rights Law Review* 151.

Sari Aurel, 'UN Peacekeeping Operations and Article 7 ARIO: The Missing Link' (2012) 9(1) *International Organizations Law Review* 77.

Sari Aurel, 'Untangling Extra-territorial Jurisdiction from International Responsibility in Jaloud v. Netherlands: Old Problem, New Solutions' (2014) 53 *Military Law and Law of War Review* 287.

Schmid Evelyne and Aoife Nolan, '"Do No Harm"? Exploring the Scope of Economic and Social Rights in Transitional Justice' (2014) 8(3) *International Journal of Transitional Justice* 362.

Schoiswohl Michael, 'Linking the International Legal Framework to Building the Formal Foundations of a "State at Risk": Constitution-making and International Law in Post-conflict Afghanistan' (2006) 39(3) *Vanderbilt Journal of Transnational Law* 819.

Schuck Michael J, 'When the Shooting Stops: Missing Elements in Just War Theory' (1994) 111(30) *Christian Century* 982.

Sharp Dustin N, 'Beyond the Post-conflict Checklist: Linking Peacebuilding and Transitional Justice Through the Lens of Critique' (2013) 14(1) *Chicago Journal of International Law* 165.

Simma Bruno and Philip Alston, 'The Sources of Human Rights Law: Custom, Jus Cogens, and General Principles' (1988–1989) 12 *Australian Year Book of International Law* 82.

Slaughter Anne-Marie, 'The Value of Spirited Debate' (2004) *Newsletter of the American Society of International Law* 8.

Skogly Sigrun I, 'The Right to Adequate Food: National Implementation and Extraterritorial Obligations' (2007) 11 *Max Planck Yearbook of the United Nations* 339.

Smith Rhona, '"To see Themselves as Others see Them": The Five Permanent Members of the Security Council and the Human Rights Council's Universal Periodic Review' (2013) 35(1) *Human Rights Quarterly* 1.

Stahn Carsten, '"Jus Ad Bellum", "Jus in Bello" . . . "Jus Post Bellum"? – Rethinking the Conception of the Law of Armed Force' (2006) 17(5) *European Journal of International Law* 929.

Stewart Frances, 'Horizontal Inequalities in Kenya and the Political Disturbances of 2008: Some Implications for Aid Policy' (2010) 10(1) *Conflict, Security & Development* 133.

Talmon Stefan, 'The Security Council as World Legislature' (2005) 99 *American Journal of International Law* 182.

Thoms Oskar N T and James Ron, 'Do Human Rights Violations Cause Internal Conflict?' (2007) 29(3) *Human Rights Quarterly* 674.

Vandenbogaerde Arne and Wouter Vandenhole, 'The Optional Protocol to the International Covenant on Economic, Social and Cultural Rights: An *Ex Ante* Assessment of its Effectiveness in Light of the Drafting Process' (2010) 10 *Human Rights Law Review* 207.

Vandenhole Wouter, 'Beyond Territoriality: The Maastricht Principles on Extra-territorial Obligations in the Area of Economic, Social and Cultural Rights' (2011) 29(4) *Netherlands Quarterly of Human Rights* 429.

Vandenhole Wouter, 'Economic, Social and Cultural Rights in the CRC: Is There a Legal Obligation to Cooperate for Development?' (2009) 17 *International Journal of Children's Rights* 23.

Verdirame Guglielmo, 'What to Make of Jus Post Bellum: A Response to Antonia Chayes' (2013) 24(1) *European Journal of International Law* 307.

Vierdag Egbert W, 'The Legal Nature of the Rights Granted by the International Covenant on Economic, Social and Cultural Rights' (1978) 9 *Netherlands Yearbook of International Law* 69.

Visoka Gëzim and John Doyle, 'Peacebuilding and International Responsibility, International Peacekeeping' (2014) 21(5) *International Peacekeeping* 673.

Vite Sylvain, 'The Interrelation of the Law of Occupation and Economic, Social and Cultural Rights: The Examples of Food, Health and Property' (2004) 90(871) *International Review of the Red Cross* 629.

Vizard Polly, Sakiko Fukuda-Parr and Diane Elson, 'Introduction: The Capability Approach and Human Rights' (2011) 12(1) *Journal of Human Development and Capabilities* 1.

Waldorf Lars, 'Anticipating the Past: Transitional Justice and Socio-Economic Wrongs' (2012) 21(2) *Social and Legal Studies* 171.

Welling Paul E, 'Human Rights: The Measure of Success in Nontraditional War' (2014) 32 *Wisconsin International Law Journal* 267.

Whittle Devon, 'Peacekeeping in Conflict: The Intervention Brigade, MONUSCO, and the Application of International Humanitarian Law to United Nations Forces' (2014) 46 *Georgetown Journal of International Law* 837.

Williams Robert E and Dan Caldwell, 'Just War Theory and the Principles of Just Peace' (2006) 7(4) *International Studies Perspectives* 309.

Willmot Haidi and Scott Sheeran, 'The Protection of Civilians Mandate in UN Peacekeeping Operations: Reconciling Protection Concepts and Practices' (2013) 95(891–892) *International Review of the Red Cross* 517.

Winkler Inga T, Margaret L Satterthwaite and Catarina De Albuquerque, 'Treasuring What We Measure and Measuring What We Treasure: Post-2015 Monitoring for the Promotion of Equality in the Water, Sanitation, and Hygiene Sector' (2014) 32(3) *Wisconsin International Law Journal* 547.

Zenko Micah and Rebecca R Friedman, 'UN Early Warning for Preventing Conflict' (2011) 18(1) *International Peacekeeping* 21.

Documents, papers and reports

Army Information School, *Pamphlet No. 4, Pillars of Peace – Documents Pertaining to American Interest in Establishing a Lasting World Peace: January 1941–February 1946* (Book Department, AIS, Carlisle Barracks 1946).

Commission on Global Governance, *Our Global Neighbourhood: Report of the Commission on Global Governance* (Oxford University Press, Oxford 1995).

Commission on Human Security, *Human Security Now: Protecting and Empowering the People* (CHS, New York 2003).

Coomans Fons, 'Situating the Maastricht Principles on Extraterritorial Obligations of States in the Area of Economic, Social and Cultural Rights' (Maastricht Faculty of Law Working Paper, 2013) <http://ssrn.com/abstract=2256836> accessed 13 August 2016.

de Beco Gauthier, 'Right to Education Indicator Based on the 4 A Framework: Concept Paper for The Right to Education Project' (May 2009) <http://www.right-to-education.org/sites/right-to-education.org/files/resource-attachments/RTE_RTE_indicators_Concept_Paper_De%20Beco_2010.pdf> accessed 12 September 2016.

Esping-Andersen Gøsta, 'After the Golden Age: The Future of the Welfare State in the New Global Order' (1994) United Nations Research Institute for Social Development Occasional Paper No. 7, World Summit for Social Development <http://www.unrisd.org/80256B3C005BCCF9/(httpAuxPages)/D93F019CFA85A04280256B650041F3F5/$file/OPWSSD7.pdf> accessed 2 October 2016.

Flynn Patrice, Jon Lickerman and Hazel Henderson, *Calvert-Henderson Quality of Life Indicators* (Calvert Group, Maryland 2000).

Inter-American Commission on Human Rights, 'Fifth Report on the Situation of Human Rights in Guatemala' (6 April 2001) OEA/Ser.L/V/II.111 doc. 21 rev.

Inter-American Commission on Human Rights, 'Guidelines for Preparation of Progress Indicators in the Area of Economic, Social and Cultural Rights' (5 October 2007) OEA/Ser/ L/V/II. 129.

International Council on Human Rights Policy, *Negotiating Justice?: Human Rights and Peace Agreements* (International Council on Human Rights Policy, Versoix 2006).

Jensen Mads Holst, Marie Villumsen and Thomas Døcker Petersen, *The AAAQ Framework and the Right to Water: International Indicators for Availability, Accessibility,*

Acceptability and Quality (The Danish Institute for Human Rights, Copenhagen 2014).

Krause Keith, 'Towards a Practical Human Security Agenda' (Policy Paper 26, Geneva Centre for the Democratic Control of Armed Forces 2007) <www.dcaf.ch/content/download/35420/526057/file/PP26.pdf> accessed 26 September 2016.

Narayan Deepa and others, 'Can Anyone Hear Us? Voices from 47 Countries' (Voices of the Poor, Volume 1, Poverty Group, PREM World Bank, December 1999) <http://siteresources.worldbank.org/INTPOVERTY/Resources/335642-1124115102975/1555199-1124115187705/vol1.pdf> accessed 31 January 2017.

Nolan Aoife, Bruce Porter and Malcolm Langford, 'The Justiciability of Social and Economic Rights: An Updated Appraisal' (CHRGJ Working Paper No. 15, 2009) <http://socialrightscura.ca/documents/publications/BP-justiciability-belfast.pdf> accessed 12 August 2016.

Organisation for Economic Co-operation and Development, *Evaluating Peacebuilding Activities in Settings of Conflict and Fragility: Improving Learning for Results* (OECD, Paris 2012).

Organisation for Economic Co-operation and Development, *Principles for Good Engagement in Fragile States* (OECD, Paris 2007).

Riedel Eibe, 'The IBSA Procedure as a Tool of Human Rights Monitoring' (2009) <http://riedel.uni-mannheim.de/inhalt/unterdokumente/downloads/ibsa/ibsa2/2_the_ibsa_procedure_as_a_tool_of_human_rights_monitoring_1_1.pdf> accessed 3 October 2016.

Right to Education Project, 'The Right to Education: Indicators' (May 2013) <http://www.right-to-education.org/sites/right-to-education.org/files/resource-attachments/RTE_List_Right_to_Education_Indicators_May_2013.pdf> accessed 9 September 2016.

Salomon Margot E, 'Legal Cosmopolitanism and the Normative Contribution of the Right to Development' (LSE Legal Studies Working Paper 16/2008, 2008) <http://papers.ssrn.com/sol3/papers.cfm?abstract_id=1272582> accessed 22 August 2016.

Stockholm International Peace Research Institute, 'Data and Trends for Multilateral Peace Operations' (Number of Peace Operations, 2006–2015, undated) <https://www.sipri.org/research/conflict-and-peace/peace-operations-and-conflict-management/data-and-trends-multilateral-peace-operations> accessed 17 September 2016.

Stewart Frances, 'Development and Security' (CRISE Working Paper 3, 2004) <http://www3.qeh.ox.ac.uk/pdf/crisewps/workingpaper3.pdf> accessed 25 August 2016.

Stewart Frances, 'Policies towards Horizontal Inequalities in Post-conflict Reconstruction' (2005) CRISE Working Paper No. 7 <http://www3.qeh.ox.ac.uk/pdf/crisewps/workingpaper7.pdf> accessed 27 September 2016.

Timor-Leste Commission for Reception, Truth and Reconciliation, 'Chega! The Report of the Commission for Reception, Truth and Reconciliation' (CAVR, 2005).

United Nations Development Programme, *Human Development Report 9* (UNDP, New York 2000).

United Nations Development Programme, *Human Development Report 1994* (UNDP, New York 1994).

World Bank, *World Development Report 2011: Conflict, Security, and Development* (World Bank, Washington DC 2011).

Newspaper articles and speeches

Boutros-Ghali Boutros, 'Beleaguered Are the Peacekeepers' *New York Times* (New York 30 October 1994) <http://www.nytimes.com/1994/10/30/opinion/beleaguered-are-the-peacekeepers.html> accessed 8 July 2016.

Roosevelt Franklin D, 'Annual Message to Congress on the State of the Union' (Speech to the Congress on 6 January 1941) <http://www.presidency.ucsb.edu/ws/?pid=16092> accessed 26 September 2016.

Roosevelt Franklin D, 'Second Inaugural Address' (Inaugural Address on Wednesday 20 January 1937) <http://www.bartleby.com/124/pres50.html> accessed 1 October 2016.

Roosevelt Franklin D, 'State of the Union Message to Congress' (Speech to the Congress on 11 January 1944) <http://www.presidency.ucsb.edu/ws/?pid=16518> accessed on 2 October 2016.

Index

For Product Safety Concerns and Information please contact our EU representative GPSR@taylorandfrancis.com
Taylor & Francis Verlag GmbH, Kaufingerstraße 24, 80331 München, Germany

www.ingramcontent.com/pod-product-compliance
Ingram Content Group UK Ltd.
Pitfield, Milton Keynes, MK11 3LW, UK
UKHW021303190926
475701UK00009B/629
9780367266448